contested closets

contested closets

THE
POLITICS
AND ETHICS
OF OUTING

Larry Gross

UNIVERSITY OF MINNESOTA PRESS
Minneapolis
London

The author gratefully acknowledges permission to reprint the following articles (complete publication information appears with individual articles): Larry Bush, "Naming Gay Names," reprinted by permission of the author and the *Village Voice*; Edwin Diamond, "Celebrity AIDS: Decoding the News," © 1992 by K-III Magazine Corporation, all rights reserved, reprinted with the permission of *New York* magazine; Steve Warren, "Telling 'Tales' about Celebrity Closets"; William A. Henry III, "Forcing Gays out of the Closet," © 1990 by Time Inc. Magazine Company, reprinted by permission; David Tuller, "Uproar over Gays Booting Others out the Closet," © *San Francisco Chronicle*, reprinted by permission; Dirk Johnson, "Privacy vs. the Pursuit of Gay Rights," © 1990 by the New York Times Company, reprinted by permission; Mike Royko, "Antsy Closet Crowd Should Think Twice," Tribune Media Services, reprinted by permission; Randy Shilts, "Is 'Outing' Gays Ethical?" © 1990 by the New York Times Company, reprinted by permission; Michael Bronski, "Outing: The Power of the Closet"; C.Carr, "Why Outing Must Stop," reprinted by permission of the author and the *Village Voice*; Richard Goldstein, "The Outer Limits"; Richard Rouilard, editorials from the *Advocate*.

Every effort has been made to obtain permission to reproduce copyright material in this book. The publisher asks copyright holders to contact them if permission has inadvertently not been sought or if proper acknowledgment has not been made.

Published by the University of Minnesota Press
2037 University Avenue Southeast, Minneapolis, MN 55455-3092
Printed in the United States of America on acid-free paper

Gross, Larry P., 1942–
    Contested closets : the politics and ethics of outing / Larry Gross.
        p. cm.
    Includes bibliographical references and index.
    ISBN 0-8166-2178-0 (acid-free).—ISBN 0-8166-2179-9 (pbk. : acid-free)
    1. Gay liberation movement—United States. 2. Homosexuality—Moral and ethical aspects. 3. Coming out (Sexual orientation)—United States. I. Title.
HQ76.8.U5G76   1993
305.9'0664—dc20   93-394
                                                                   CIP

The University of Minnesota is an
equal-opportunity educator and employer.

To Vito Russo (1946–90), in gratitude for much good
conversation and great gossip,
and to Scott Tucker, for more than even he knows

Contents

Preface

This is a book about secrets and the telling of secrets, it is about lies and the telling of lies. It is about codes that bind some people to keep others' secrets, and conventions that require some people to tell lies about others. And it is about the breaking of these codes and the violation of these conventions. It is about the deliberate revelation by lesbian and gay people of the hidden homosexuality of prominent people. It is also about the conflicting loyalties of journalists—mainstream and alternative, straight and gay—caught between the obligation to tell the truth as they know it (even if not the whole truth) and the rules of the game that protect the sexual secrets of celebrities and public officials. It is about the shifting boundaries between the public and private realms, and the dangers of building a political strategy on the narrow platform of the right to privacy. It is a book about outing.

Outing has a long past, if only a short history. The issue, although not the term, arose at the end of the nineteenth century, the dawn of modern gay consciousness. The idea that homosexuals constitute a "people" set apart from the society they live among, however invisibly, led inevitably to the question of what obligations they have to this community. This question has remained at or near the surface of gay awareness, just as the steady exchange of celebrity gossip served as a tributary stream swelling a rising tide of lesbian and gay consciousness. Yet, while adhering to the code of silence, many have also resented those who benefit from its protection in order to have it both ways: to take advantage of the opportunities for gay existence created by those who have been open enough to fight for them, yet simultaneously enjoying the privileges bestowed by their ostensible heterosexuality. This resentment has been particularly acute, and the temptation to break the code especially compelling, in the case of politicians and celebrities whose public lives and actions fan the fires of heterosexism and homophobia.

But until very recently the rules were respected even by those who had never volunteered to play by them. As I argue, there is no single cause for the breakdown of respect for the sanctity of the closet, but chief among the causes are the experience of fighting a deadly epidemic made worse by government, media, and public indifference and the resurgence of naked bigotry expressed verbally by "respectable" public figures and physically by anonymous gay bashers. For those who experienced the 1980s as wartime, prominent lesbian and gay people hiding in their closets became silent collaborators at best and active traitors at worst.

This is also a book about journalism and the rules journalists follow or circumvent. Outing presents a challenge to journalists because it tries to hold them to their most fundamental principles: telling the truth and not knowingly telling lies. In the case of closeted lesbian and gay public figures, the press is faced with a dilemma, and it responds by applying various criteria to determine whether the "private truth" is newsworthy. Newsworthiness being one of the more intangible qualities possessed by information, it is hardly surprising that journalists and editors make inconsistent and often indefensible decisions. Gossip writers who happily prattle about the private lives of straight celebrities are struck dumb (or blind) when it comes to lesbian and gay public figures. Reporters who assume the public has a right to know about the personal lives of politicians draw the line at the privacy of lesbian and gay officials.

Journalists do not merely avoid the topic of gay subjects' private lives, however; they also collude in disinformation by printing gossip items and personal profiles that are positively misleading or outright lies, and most of the time they know what they're doing. So, when gay journalists began to take them to task for playing the game by the usual rules, gossip writers and other journalists were taken aback and responded angrily. But, for a brief period at least, one New York City gay publication took full advantage of its weekly appearance on newsstands to start a new game and announce new rules. Michelangelo Signorile's "Gossip Watch" column in *OutWeek* became the playing field for this new game, and Signorile was both batter and sportscaster, blasting celebrities out of the closet and simultaneously commenting on the action. Although he was not the first to play the outing game in public—that honor probably goes to writer Armistead Maupin—Signorile unquestionably was, and remains, the game's first champion.

Like many academic projects, this book began with a collection of clippings and scribbled notes about a change in the cultural climate. I was researching and writing about the struggles I have come to think of as the battlefields of the sexual counterrevolution, and I saw the emergence of outing as an interesting sideline to the main action (which, at the time, seemed to be the controversies concerning the National Endowment for the Arts and funding for political and sexually explicit art), another front in the fight to maintain and extend lesbian and gay visibility in the public world. But, as often happens, the peripheral topic kept stealing more and more of my attention, and I decided to write an article about outing. The article soon outgrew the bounds of a standard academic journal, although a portion of this book appeared under the same title in *Critical Studies in Mass Communication* (Gross 1991), and it seemed best to write a book.

An additional motive for writing a book was the opportunity to include a sampling of the original press articles that constitute the "texts" of outing and the debates it has evoked in the mainstream, alternative, and lesbian/gay press. As a professor of communication who has both conducted and supervised studies of the mass media, I am very sensitive to the fact that the availability of source material can either facilitate or, all too often, hinder research and analysis. In the case of outing, it was obvious that the long-term picture available to future scholars and students would be mostly one-sided, because few libraries receive and archive the lesbian/gay publications in which so much of outing and its controversies took place. Thus, for all of the heat—and light—generated by outing, the most important original documents at the heart of the debate, as well as many of the most interesting arguments presented in defense of this controversial tactic, are largely unavailable at present and will be still less available in the future. *OutWeek* magazine, the primary forum for outing and its proponents, no longer exists, and it is held by very few libraries. Some of the most important writings about outing—both pro and con— likewise appear in publications that are not widely available: *Gay Community News* (on "hiatus" as of fall 1992), the *Advocate*, and even the *Village Voice*.

The collection of original press articles included in this book is intended to present a comprehensive picture of the outing story that will both augment and illustrate my analytic narrative. In addition to the lesbian/gay and alternative press articles, there are also representative selections from *Time*, the *New York Times*, the *San Francisco Chronicle*, and the *Chicago Tribune*. Scores more that might have been included are cited in the references and are readily available in most research libraries.

Two of the articles were written before the official "outing" season began, dramatizing the conflicts experienced by gay people and by journalists over whether and how to keep closeted public figures' secrets. The second section includes articles in which Michelangelo

Signorile and Armistead Maupin began to challenge and violate the sanctity of the closet, followed by the two articles that probably did the most to catapult outing onto the public agenda: William Henry's "Ethics" essay in *Time* magazine, which used the term *outing* for the first time in print, and Signorile's *OutWeek* cover story posthumously outing Malcolm Forbes. The two following sections give a very limited sampling of the firestorm of writing about outing, uniformly hostile in the mainstream press and more balanced (and thoughtful) in the alternative and lesbian/gay press. The next section includes five of Michelangelo Signorile's "Gossip Watch" columns from 1990 and 1991. Considerations of space prevented me from including more of my favorites, but I hope that these will give you a sense of this innovative journalistic show that played on Broadway for only two years but still managed to make history. The final section includes an article and two editorials about Signorile's exposé of Pete Williams, assistant secretary of defense in the Bush administration. The article itself, which appeared in the *Advocate* in August 1991, was without doubt the single most influential example of outing. It is also the most notable omission from the selection of articles included here—a result of copyright stipulations by the publisher who will print Signorile's own book, *Queer in America*, in 1993. My regret is tempered by the availability of Signorile's account in bookstores today and libraries in the future. As soon as you have bought and read this book, rush out and buy *Queer in America*.

One of the rewards of finishing a book is the opportunity to acknowledge debts and express thanks to many of those who have inspired, commented on, and in other ways assisted in the research and writing. In this case there is a particularly critical contribution that must be acknowledged, and that is to Michelangelo Signorile. In an obvious sense, already noted, this book wouldn't have been written without him because he played such a central role in the events I describe. But beyond that he has also contributed to my thinking and writing about outing by generously sharing documents and clippings, by reading and commenting and discussing, by filling me in on past events and alerting me to future ones. One of the nicer by-products of working on this book was making a friend.

Others played important roles by reading early drafts (and sometimes rereading successive ones), commenting, criticizing, and questioning as well as suggesting angles and interpretations I had missed or failed to explore adequately. Allan Berube gave one of the earliest and closest readings. The three readers for the University of Minnesota Press, Larry Grossberg, Andrew Ross, and Kath Weston, gave encouragement and insightful suggestions; Kath Weston's review, in particular, is a model of the genre and I hope I have done justice to her suggestions and criticisms.

I benefited greatly from the published writings of (and in many cases conversations with) Michael Bronski, Victoria Brownworth, Douglas Crimp, Richard Goldstein, Richard Mohr, and Ed Stein. Other especially helpful readers were Carolyn Marvin, Sari Thomas, Tom Wilson Weinberg, John Whyte, and Barbie Zelizer. I appreciated comments, encouragement, and clippings from many friends and colleagues, among them Rita Addessa, Howard Becker, Steve Beery, Michael Botkin, Gus Brannigan, John DeCecco, Martin Duberman, Ann Linda Furstenberg, Frank Furstenberg, George Gerbner, Bert Gross, Sammy Gross, Teddy Gross, Kathleen Hall Jamieson, Michael Morgan, Peter Nardi, Jay Ruby, Eve Sedgwick, Barbara Herrnstein Smith, and Kate Stimpson. I learned a lot from discussion conducted on the computer "Gaynet" and particularly enjoyed contributions by Ron Buckmire and Chris Bartlett.

A good deal of technical assistance goes into most scholarly writing projects, and a project that depends on tracking down and copying hundreds of often obscure items is especially dependent on others' efforts. I am grateful for the help provided by Jay Blotcher, Janice Fisher, Lorrie Kim, Eric Krody, Deb Porter, and Susan Williamson. Tim Blake, Henry Colough, David Graper, and Mike Lakis provided essential and often lifesaving computer support. Special thanks for assistance above and beyond to Steve Browne and Geoff Falen. Much of the research and writing represented here was carried out during a sabbatical year in San Francisco, for which I am grateful to Dean Kathleen Hall Jamieson of the Annenberg School for Communication, and the University of Pennsylvania.

Janaki Bakhle at the University of Minnesota Press responded with interest and enthusiasm to my unorthodox concept for a book that combines an essay with an extensive set of original press articles, and her encouragement helped me get on with, and through, the project. Lynn Marasco was a careful and helpful copy editor, who may finally have taught me when to use *that* instead of *which*.

Teaching has many rewards, and possibly chief among them is having one's students become both colleagues and friends. I have been fortunate to have many such present and former students and two in particular, Lisa Henderson and James Woods, played central roles in shaping this book.

Working in lesbian and gay studies gives the advantage of being in a relatively new and small field, and thus one can know—intellectually and often personally—many of those who are creating and shaping a scholarly enterprise. I have been fortunate to know, as friends and as models, two of the pioneers in the domain of lesbian/gay media studies, Richard Dyer and Vito Russo. They set a high standard for me, as for many others, in the clarity and the precision of their writing, but mostly in demonstrating that not only are the political and personal realms intertwined, they are also inseparable from the intellectual. Those familiar with their work will readily see echoes and influences in this book.

It is traditional to leave the most important acknowledgments for last, and I have followed this convention. There are more ways than I can summarize here in which my life has been changed by sharing it for the past seventeen years with my lover, Scott Tucker. This book would never have been written without the benefit of his companionship and love, but the debt goes much further. Scott Tucker is one of the most intelligent and insightful people I have known, as well as the best writer I have observed at close quarters, and I have learned a great deal from this observation. More than anything else, however, Scott is the most deeply honest and morally sensitive intellectual and political thinker I have encountered, and his example and encouragement have held me to a higher standard than I might otherwise have settled for. I am lucky and grateful.

Finally, a caution. Among the pitfalls of writing about current events is the fact that history refuses to stop during the frustratingly long period between writing a book and its appearance in print. Outing is a story that has not ended simply because I have finished this book, and it is more than likely that between the time I hand the manuscript over to the publisher and the time you hold this book in your hands some new and dramatic chapters will unfold. Indeed, I hope this does happen, because I believe that outing represents a necessary development in sexual politics and a challenge to all journalists to, in Gabriel Rotello's words, "treat homosexuality as equal to heterosexuality." This book will not be the final word on outing: once truth telling has begun, it can be delayed but it will not be stopped.

Philadelphia
December 1992

Contested Closets

The Unwritten Rule

The late Terry Dolan headed the National Conservative Political Action Committee and routinely solicited funds for viciously antigay candidates and causes;[1] he was also a homosexual man who died of AIDS. Was it a violation of journalistic norms and common decency to expose his sexual orientation and thus his hypocrisy? Although after his death his brother Tony, then President Ronald Reagan's chief speechwriter, took out an ad in the Washington press to make this claim (Hitchens 1987), most journalists—both in the mainstream and the gay press—had little ambivalence about this example of "outing." For this is a clear-cut case: a dead hypocrite who had been accused by gay writer and activist Larry Kramer (in a famous cocktail party confrontation) of "fucking us by night and fucking with us by day."

Malcolm Forbes, one of the most public and visible capitalists in the world, died shortly after his lavish and very well reported seventieth birthday party in Morocco, a party featuring as guest of honor Forbes's frequent companion and oft-rumored lover, Elizabeth Taylor, possibly the world's most famous heterosexual. Shortly after Forbes's death, *OutWeek*, a New York lesbian/gay weekly magazine, published a cover story entitled "The Secret Gay Life of Malcolm Forbes" (Signorile 1990a), and a major journalistic controversy erupted.

Although the topic had already begun to emerge in the gay and the mainstream press as a result of the "outing" by AIDS activists of politicians whose (in)actions they opposed (e.g., Oregon Senator Mark Hatfield, Illinois Governor James Thompson, New York City Mayor

---

1. "Before the 1980 elections, the National Conservative Political Action Committee (NCPAC) and allied groups targeted House and Senate liberals for defeat partly because of their tolerance of homosexuality" (Branch 1982: 46). NCPAC fund-raising letters claimed that "our nation's moral fiber is being weakened by the growing homosexual movement" (Hitchens 1987: 72).

Ed Koch),[2] it was the Forbes story that raised the level of attention above the fold. Accounts of the Forbes story in the mainstream and gay press featured a range of responses. Mainstream columnists and editorial writers opposed the outing. Although the New York Times pretended that it was not playing the game, refraining from identifying the "famous businessman who recently died," it did produce a quote from someone who considered this the "sleaziest piece of tabloid trash disguised as journalism" and went on to say, "Who are you to humiliate his family and destroy the memories that they might have had of him?" (Johnson 1990). Gay journalists and activists ranged from those who denounced outing as a violation of the right to privacy to those who defended outing as a political tactic, with others coming down firmly in the middle. The supermarket tabloids, never averse to exposing celebrities' (real or imagined) secrets, took off in a feeding frenzy of outing, closely followed by the television talk show circuit.

In 1975 Oliver Sipple, a bystander in a crowd watching President Gerald Ford in San Francisco, deflected Sara Jane Moore's gun hand and possibly saved Ford's life. In the ensuing publicity, gay activists made known that the ex-marine was gay, a fact that some newspapers then printed and that his family hadn't known. Sipple's life after that has been described as unhappy. Most who have written about Sipple's outing have agreed with Fred Friendly (1990), who wrote that the "press had a legal license, but no ethical justification, to rip away the harmless mask that protected his sexual orientation." At the time, however, San Francisco gay activists insisted that the White House failed to honor Sipple because of his homosexuality.

Finally, imagine a small-town high school gym teacher who is a closeted lesbian living quietly with her lover and her children by a former marriage until a local newspaper decides to write a feature article about lesbian mothers and identifies her by name, thus leading to her being fired and threatening to cost her the custody of her children. This is a hypothetical case and, fortunately, an extremely unlikely one. Neither the mainstream press nor the militant gay activists who promote outing would endorse exposing nonpublic lesbian and gay people, even when the consequences would not be so dreadful. Simply

---

2. Time magazine publicized outing in an article that appeared several months earlier. Although the Time article by William Henry III is often credited with inventing the term "outing," the article refers to "a phenomenon known as 'outing,' the intentional exposure of secret gays by other gays" (Henry 1990: 67), a phrasing that does not present itself as the coining of a new term.

put, the story isn't "news" by current journalistic standards,[3] and the proponents of outing make no case for exposing people whose closets are truly necessary camouflage.

So, we can hypothesize a continuum stretching from Terry Dolan, or right-wing lawyer and one-time McCarthy aide Roy Cohn, or former Republican Congressman Robert Bauman—all known to be homosexuals who supported antigay causes (this group *might*, then, include Senator Hatfield, Governor Thompson, Mayor Koch)—all the way to our lesbian gym teacher. At the first extreme there are hardly any voices raised to condemn the outing of homosexual political hypocrites. As openly gay Congressman Barney Frank said in an often-quoted remark, "There's a right to privacy but not to hypocrisy" (Gup 1988: 31). At the other extreme there are *no* advocates of the indiscriminate outing of individuals who are not public figures. In short, the real issue is not to decide *whether* outing is, by one view, always a violation of journalistic and human ethics or, by the opposing view, a necessary political weapon of an oppressed minority whose pervasive invisibility fuels their oppression. For both sides would largely agree at the extremes of my imaginary continuum. The real question, therefore, is *where* in the middle one draws the line, and *who* has the right to decide on which side of the line any particular instance falls.

Most accounts of outing have noted that disclosing someone's homosexuality is not currently a respectable journalistic practice,[4] although the motives given for this discretion vary depending on who is writing. Editorial writers in the mainstream press climb to moral high ground, from which they state that "sex is a private matter unless it affects the performance of public duties or has adverse effects on the lives of others" (*San Francisco Chronicle* 1990). From another perspec-

---

3. Of course, in some parts of the country homophobic crusaders might argue that a homosexual gym teacher *is* news and that a lesbian mother raising children with her lover is also newsworthy. In the many mainstream media articles about outing, however, no such examples of forced exposure have been cited. There have been numerous articles and television features about lesbian mothers in recent years (e.g., Kolata 1989; Bauers 1991), but the writers have carefully recruited women who are willing to be identified by the media, or have refrained from naming the people described.

4. Which is not to say that it doesn't happen. Despite assurances by journalists that "a person's sexual orientation is generally off-limits to the press" (Gup 1988), an unfortunate practice of printing the names of people arrested for homosexual acts still survives. In a recent example, the Adrian, Michigan, *Daily Telegraph* printed the names and addresses of sixteen men arrested for homosexual activity after months of covert surveillance and videotaping in a public park. Several of the accused men lost their jobs (Hentoff 1991).

tive, Randy Shilts, the openly gay national correspondent for the *Chronicle*, wrote on the *New York Times* op-ed page that "the refusal of newspapers to reveal a person's homosexuality has less to do with ethical considerations of privacy than with an editor's homophobia. In my experience, many editors really believe that being gay is so distasteful that talk of it should be avoided unless absolutely necessary" (1990a).[5]

What is new about outing is not only that the *San Francisco Chronicle* and the *New York Times* and the *Washington Post* are writing about it or even doing it, but also that they are following the lead of self-identified gay journalists. What is new about outing is not that the code of silence is being broken, but that it is being broken by gays themselves.

Nearly all accounts of outing begin with an assertion that it represents the abandonment of a long-standing agreement among gay people that they kept each others' secrets. When the *Philadelphia Inquirer* ran a lengthy feature on the subject, gay author Neil Miller was quoted saying, "There was an unwritten rule among gay people that you didn't 'out' someone" (Matza 1990). Of course, private gossip was another matter (few of the names published in the recent outing season would have surprised those plugged into extensive gossip networks), and there were occasional lists of famous closet cases in gay publications. But on the whole the gay press abided by the unwritten rules: "Since the birth of the gay-liberation movement 20 years ago, we gay journalists have adhered to a fairly rigid code of conduct on the matter of bringing people unwillingly out of the closet. With the possible exception of closeted political figures who were actively working against the movement (such as the late Terry Dolan and Roy Cohn), it was strictly verboten, an absolute no-no" (Byron 1990).

The news media proclaim their devotion to truth and objectivity, yet they devote substantial (and increasing) amounts of attention to "infotainment" gossip, much of which is simply untrue, and they know it. The gossip arm of journalism is really a branch of public rela-

---

5. When eight men died in a fire at a homosexual club in Washington, D.C., in 1977, the *Washington Post* did not publish the names of all those who were killed, prompting the paper's ombudsman to note in an editorial, "I can recall no tragedy of [this magnitude] in which a local newspaper did not publish the names of all the identified dead. . . . In effect, *Post* editors said that homosexuality is so shameful that extraordinary steps had to be taken to protect the families of the victims. . . . Does this have the effect of underscoring the stigma of homosexuality, of shoving it back into the closet at a time when efforts are being made to bring it out and address it as a social fact?" (Seib 1977).

tions, a colonizing of the news media by the entertainment industry (they are often owned by the same corporations), and one of the most frequent services performed by gossip writers is the construction and maintenance of celebrity closets.

The devotion of mainstream media to discretion and privacy in the case of gays (even after they are dead) suggests a heterosexist double standard on the part of the folks who made household names out of Jessica Hahn, Donna Rice, Marla Maples, and Gennifer Flowers, who told all about Franklin Roosevelt's and JFK's affairs but steadfastly deny the evidence of Eleanor Roosevelt's longtime lesbian relationship with Lorena Hickok (Cook 1992), and who made sure only the most isolated hermit was unaware of Nancy Reagan's premarital sex, shotgun wedding, and alleged adultery with Frank Sinatra (Dowd 1991).

The lesbian and gay movement is also divided, with prominent figures quoted on both sides. Armistead Maupin, who helped inaugurate the outing hunting season, said, "What it boils down to is, the message that is being communicated is that there is something wrong with us. . . . If you are being secretive about the people you love, you are conveying the impression that you are ashamed of who and what you are" (Warren 1989). On the other side, Debra Chasnoff, then editor of the lesbian/gay quarterly *Out/Look*, was quoted in the *San Francisco Chronicle* as saying that "forcing someone out of the closet publicly is feeding into the public perception that there's something wrong with homosexuality by suggesting that it's hidden and shameful" (Tuller, 1990: A9).

Analyzing the arguments underlying the outing strategy is critical to an understanding of the political struggle that is going on within the gay community. The proponents of outing embrace a minority group politics that sees all homosexuals as members of a group to which they owe loyalty. As one pro-outing writer stated, "When we talk about outing, what are we really talking about? We're talking about exposing the collaborators, we're talking about exposing those who think they'll never get marched to the gas chambers because 'nobody knows' " (Brownworth 1990).

In this book I place the current debates over outing in the context of the evolving struggles of gay people during the past hundred years, as well as in the context of changing journalistic norms and practices, and I will attempt to illuminate the underlying ethical and normative assumptions made by opponents and proponents of outing in both the mainstream and the gay press, and the tensions and contradictions revealed on all sides.

Outing has a long past, if only a short history. The issue of outing, although not the term, arises at the very dawn of modern gay consciousness. The idea that homosexuals—lesbian women and gay men—constitute a "people" set apart from the society they live within, however invisibly, leads inevitably to the question of what obligations they have to this "community." Indeed, the historical thread that I will trace through the unfolding fabric of lesbian and gay existence for the past century reveals that the temptation to proclaim publicly the secret of prominent persons' homosexuality has frequently been felt though rarely yielded to. On the contrary, until recently the only exposure gay people feared came through inadvertence, or the prying and publicity of public authorities and media sensationalism.

The narrative I will unfold here is part of the story of the emergence and evolution of the lesbian and gay community in this country, and of its usually adversarial relationship with the institutions that define and control the public agenda of issues and images. It is also part of the story of the changing role and norms of journalism and other mass media. The exposure of closeted homosexuals was long a favored tactic of social control threatened and employed by our enemies. The adoption of outing as a political tactic has challenged their ability to determine the meaning of gay identity and the consequences of its visibility.

The Path over Corpses

The political tactic of exposing closeted homosexuals had been used by homosexuals themselves in at least one instance long before the emergence of the contemporary gay liberation movement. To understand the context of the first outings, we have to briefly set the stage for this fin-de-siècle drama.

The nineteenth century saw the emergence of distinctive homosexual subcultures in Western Europe and the United States, made possible by the industrialization and urbanization that transformed these societies. This was not a development welcomed by the guardians of public morality. While the Napoleonic Code had decriminalized homosexual acts in France and the Netherlands,[6] in Great Britain and Germany the legal plight of homosexual acts between men worsened

---

6. Despite the absence of criminal sanctions, the Parisian police "began to keep tabs on the growing homosexual community" of the 1880s, eventually holding records on "7242 homosexuals . . . who had come to the attention of the police—3049 native Parisians, 3709 provincials, and 484 foreigners" (Bullough 1979: 5-6).

during the latter part of the nineteenth century. The Abominable Vice of Buggery had been a capital crime in Britain since 1533, but there was a decline in the number of convictions in the late eighteenth and early nineteenth centuries (Weeks 1977: 12). In the early nineteenth century, a series of criminal reforms were enacted as part of

> the process whereby the local, semi-amateur system of law-enforcement of the eighteenth century was replaced . . . by a network of professional police forces, responsible for the prevention of crime, the detection of offenders and, above all, the maintenance of order. This was an essential ruling-class response to the problems created by the spread of industrial capitalism and urbanization and the growth of a mass working class. (ibid.: 13)

Although the death penalty for buggery was abolished in England in 1862, the Criminal Law Amendment Act of 1885 included the famous Labouchère Amendment, which made "acts of gross indecency" between men punishable by up to two years at hard labor (the sentence meted out ten years later to Oscar Wilde), and "in effect brought within the scope of the law all forms of male homosexual activity" (Weeks 1981: 102).[7] The unification of the German Empire under Prussian leadership after the Franco-Prussian War of 1870 led to the adoption of the Prussian penal code by the entire Second Reich, including Paragraph 175, the section of the German penal code that punished "unnatural vice" between men with imprisonment for up to five years (Steakley 1975: 21).

Thus, the growth of a self-conscious homosexual subculture was intertwined with a counterforce of moral outrage and legal persecution. The criminal status of those engaging in homosexual acts ensured that few would publicly announce themselves as homosexuals and that their secret lives would render them vulnerable to blackmail and intimidation. But, despite these forces of repression, homosexual emancipation crusaders and even movements began to emerge in England and Germany (Weeks 1977; Steakley 1975). These emancipationists in nineteenth-century Germany and England were among the first to articulate theories of homosexuals as a type of person for whom homosexual behavior was as "natural" as heterosexual behavior was for het-

---

7. British law ignored lesbians in 1885, and when an unsuccessful attempt was made in 1921 to extend the Labouchère Amendment to women, it was opposed on the grounds that "you are going to tell the whole world that there is such an offence, to bring it to the notice of women who have never heard of it, never thought of it, never dreamt of it" (Weeks 1981: 105).

erosexuals. The term "homosexual" was proposed in 1869 by the Hungarian writer Karoly Benkert (or Kertbeny), who at the same time coined the term "heterosexual" as its opposite (Herzer 1990). By openly naming an identity defined by deviant sexual and affectional desires, these leaders articulated a sense of being that had been tacitly expressed by the words and actions of thousands of men and women. This may have been the true crime against which the forces of order were mobilized: being visible.[8]

The anonymity of urban life permitted contacts and consummations (and commercial transactions) across class lines, and it created the conditions in which a sexual iceberg could coalesce below the surface of public consciousness. But, in a series of scandals well covered by the growing popular press, the tip of the iceberg was repeatedly exposed to a horrified public (Weeks 1977, 1981). In England these included the trial of two transvestites, Ernest Boulton and Frederick Park, in 1870; a scandal involving high officials in Dublin Castle in 1884; the Cleveland Street homosexual brothel scandal of 1889–90, hushed up because of the involvement of prominent aristocrats; and, most sensational and influential of all, the three trials of Oscar Wilde in 1895:

> The Wilde trials were not only the most dramatic, but also the most significant events, for they created a public image for the homosexual, and a terrifying moral tale of the dangers that trailed closely behind deviant behavior. They were labelling processes of the most explicit kind, drawing an impassable border between acceptable and abhorrent behavior. (Weeks 1977: 21)

The prosecution of Oscar Wilde taught a lesson that was widely understood by homosexuals who sought secrecy, by blackmailers who made them pay dearly for it (the Labouchère Amendment was often referred to as "Blackmailer's Charter"), and by those who wished to use sexual secrets for political purposes.

In the early years of the century, Imperial Germany was rocked by

---

8. In his remarkable book on Oscar Wilde and the gay world of nineteenth-century London, Neil Bartlett assembles a collage of "fragments from twenty years in the life of London, the twenty years to 1895. Studies, translations, histories, case histories, poems, novels, foreign novels, children's books, classics, newspapers from the *Star* to the *Times*, police reports, playscripts, reviews, magazines, porn magazines, official proclamations, militant declarations, obscure suggestions, but all in print. . . . In each item, sometimes obviously, sometimes discreetly, homosexuality is spoken of and discussed in public" (Bartlett 1988: 95).

scandals focusing on accusations that many of the kaiser's closest associates were homosexual (Steakley 1975, 1989). In 1902 German "munitions king" Friederich Krupp was expelled from Italy by the authorities when his homosexual activities on Capri came to the attention of the police. The story was widely publicized by the Italian socialist press and subsequently picked up by the German press. The antigovernment Social Democratic newspaper *Vorwärts* ran the story under the headline "Krupp on Capri" (the German Catholic paper had reported the story without naming Krupp) and suggested that the authorities invoke Paragraph 175 against the powerful ally of the kaiser. Although Krupp began to bring legal action against the paper, he died of an apparent suicide a week after the article appeared (Manchester 1968).

The Krupp scandal occurred at the moment when the newly emerging German homosexual emancipation movement was working for abolition of the laws against homosexual acts. In 1897 Magnus Hirschfeld founded the first homosexual emancipation organization, the Scientific Humanitarian Committee, and in the preface to its first *Jahrbuch*, in 1899, he wrote that he hoped Paragraph 175, "whose existence besmirches the escutcheon of German justice, will not be carried into the new century" (Steakley 1975: 24).[9] When Krupp was exposed by a socialist press that also called for the repeal of Paragraph 175, the Scientific Humanitarian Committee was caught in a tactical and ethical dilemma. The decision of the committee was that exposure of prominent homosexuals would not be an effective or moral strategy, and the *Jahrbuch* for 1903 promised that "the frequently suggested 'path over corpses' will not be taken by us under any circumstances" (ibid.: 33).

In 1905 the German Reichstag defeated a motion by the Social Democrats to reform Paragraph 175, and the Scientific Humanitarian Committee began to discuss the tactic of *self*-denunciation. What if a thousand homosexuals were to turn themselves in to the police and demand to be prosecuted? Not surprisingly, this strategy did not get very far. But now another wing of the movement took the initiative.

Adolf Brand was the founder of *Der Eigene*, the first homosexual periodical in the world. Like Hirschfeld, Brand was a crusader for the abolition of Paragraph 175, but unlike Hirschfeld, Brand was an anti-Catholic anarchist who favored the exposure of homosexual hypo-

---

9. Paragraph 175, which survived in German law through the Third Reich, was abolished by the East Germans in 1988, but was repealed by the West German government only after the 1990 reunification of Germany (Wockner 1991).

crites. Brand published a pamphlet that revealed that Chaplain Das-bach, a leader of the antireform Center Party, had been the blackmail victim of a male prostitute. Under threat of libel action, Brand printed a retraction, yet many viewed the incident as a success for the homo-sexual movement (Steakley 1975; Gray 1991).

The most serious round of scandals began when a socialist jour-nalist, Maximilian Harden, exposed the homosexuality of Prince Philipp zu Eulenburg, known as the kaiser's closest friend, in an at-tempt to undermine his political influence. The result was a series of civil and criminal trials in which figures on both sides were charged—with libel or with violations of the law prohibiting homosexual be-havior. In some of these trials, two of the pioneers of the early homo-sexual emancipation movement played major roles. When the mayor of Berlin, General Kuno Count von Moltke, sued Harden for implying that he and Eulenburg were lovers, Hirschfeld testified that Moltke's " 'unconscious orientation' could 'objectively' be labelled 'homosex-ual,' even if he had never committed sodomy" (Steakley 1989: 242).

The next major trial pitted the imperial chancellor, Prince von Bülow, against Brand, who was charged with writing a new pamphlet that claimed that Bülow had been blackmailed because of homosexual-ity, that he had participated in all-male gatherings hosted by Eulen-burg at which homosexual activities occurred, and that he was "morally obligated as a homosexual to use his influence for the repeal of Paragraph 175" (ibid.). Brand's defense of his exposure of Bülow is little different from many present-day defenses of outing public figures:

> On the stand, Brand maintained the truth of the leaflet and stated that he had by no means intended to insult Bülow by calling him a homosexual, since he had a positive view of those who shared his own sexual orientation.[10] He had exposed Bülow with the political goal of hastening the repeal of Paragraph 175, for he had come to be-lieve that this could only be achieved by creating martyrs—the strategy of "the path over corpses." (ibid.)

The fallout from the series of scandals and trials was devastating to the fledgling German homosexual movement. Steakley notes that

---

10. Similarly, Armistead Maupin dismisses the danger of being sued for libel. "Mal-ice is usually required to prove libel. I would challenge anyone to find malice in my ac-tions, because I'm happy about being gay and I celebrate the other people that are gay" (quoted in Warren 1989: 20).

the wave of antihomosexual sentiment stirred up by the scandals along with reaction against the women's emancipation movement led in late 1909 to the introduction of a draft penal code which ignored previous reform efforts and even extended Paragraph 175 to homosexual acts between women. It was scornfully noted by anti-feminists that this measure would advance equality of the sexes. (1975: 40)

Hirschfeld's decision to testify as an expert witness for Harden seemed a betrayal of the Scientific Humanitarian Committee's stand against the "path over corpses," and it "outraged and terrified many of the financial sponsors of the Committee, who were (perhaps justifiably) afraid that he might someday give testimony against them. Instead of pulling together when confronted with a crisis, the membership of the Committee began to melt away" (Steakley 1975: 38).

After the judge prevented Brand from presenting his evidence, Brand's trial ended in a conviction for libeling Bülow, and he served an eighteen-month prison term. Eventually Brand, too, renounced the tactic of exposing highly placed homosexuals, because "decent society can not stand the truth" (Gray 1991: 49).

The rise of the Nazis revived the debate about the tactic of outing because of the prominence of Ernst Röhm, the chief of staff of Hitler's *Sturmabteilung* (SA) paramilitary organization and a known homosexual. In the early 1930s, in a political move reminiscent of the Krupp and Eulenberg scandals, "Röhm and other SA leaders were attacked for their homosexuality in the left-wing media. Social Democrats and Communists suggested that nepotism and abuse of power in the SA and the Hitler Youth had contributed to making homosexuality an essential characteristic of the fascist system" (Oosterhuis 1991: 251).

Writing about "the Röhm case" in *Der Eigene*, Adolph Brand once again stated the argument for outing. Declaring that "every sexual contact is a private matter," he went on to note that

in the moment, however, when someone—as teacher, priest, representative, or statesman . . . would like to set in the most damaging way the intimate love contact of others under degrading control—in that moment has his own love-life also ceased to be a private matter and forfeits every claim to remain protected henceforward from public scrutiny and suspicious oversight.

Rather, from that moment on the public has the undoubted right to be occupied also with his own love-life, to hold up to him the mirror of his strict party morality and—if only the least trace of erotic inclinations and sexual acts are established, which his party morality publicly condemns—to relentlessly accuse him personally, as the representative of that party morality, of political hypocrisy and to ex-

pose him as an insolent swindler of the people! For he is then enjoying the joys of life that he wants to withhold from the people."
(Brand 1991: 235–36)

Possibly daunted by the memory of the earlier outing scandals,
Brand limited himself to naming Röhm, who had already been exposed by the left press, noting somewhat surprisingly that "I will not
name names here, although many deserve nothing else. For the
deserters from our ranks really should be mercilessly pilloried in public" (ibid.).

At the time, despite the Nazi's official position condemning homosexuality and supporting Paragraph 175, Hitler defended Röhm and
declared that he "preferred in principle not to interfere with the private life of SA members"—the SA was, after all, "a gathering of men
with a political aim, an association of raucous warriors," not a "moral
institution for the education of the daughters from the better classes"
(Oosterhuis 1991: 251). In 1934, after the Nazis had come to power and
internal power struggles led to the elimination of Röhm and his fellow
SA leaders in the famous "night of the long knives," Hitler declared
that homosexuals represented a poison that needed to be eradicated.

The German homosexual movement slowly regained its momen-
tum during the Weimar years, spurred by the encouraging example of
the abolition of all antihomosexual laws by the new Soviet government. On October 16, 1929, as part of the consideration of a penal code
reform bill, legalization of homosexual acts between consenting adults
was approved by a committee of the Reichstag. The bill was ready for
action by the Reichstag when the American stock market crash
sparked a crisis that diverted parliamentary attention, and the bill was
tabled. Before it could be revived, the Nazis had gained sufficient
strength in the Reichstag to prevent consideration of it, and shortly
thereafter they came to power, thus ringing down the curtain on the
world's first homosexual emancipation movement (Steakley 1975: 84).

The first stirrings of the postwar homosexual rights movement in
the United States came about during a period of political and sexual
repression. From the late 1940s through the 1950s, actual and suspected homosexuals were the targets of witch-hunts, just as real and
suspected communists were; in fact, the categories were often col-
lapsed into the commie-queer bogeyman. As historian John D'Emilio
points out, it took little effort to incorporate lesbian women and gay
men into the demonology of the period:

According to extreme anticommunist ideologues, left-wing teachers
poisoned the minds of their students; lesbians and homosexuals cor-

rupted their bodies. Communists bore no identifying physical charac-
teristics. . . . Homosexuals too could escape detection. Coming
from all walks of life, they insinuated themselves everywhere in society, including the highest reaches of government. . . . Communists
taught children to betray their parents; mannish women mocked the
ideals of marriage and motherhood. (1983: 48–49)

Because most people confronted with accusations of homosexuality
during these witch-hunts quietly resigned, it is impossible to determine the number of careers and lives that were destroyed. In 1949,
during the early stages of McCarthyism, ninety-six "perverts" were
fired by the State Department; by 1953 the Los Angeles Hearst newspaper could run the headline: "State Department Fires 531 Perverts,
Security Risks" (Bullough 1979: 71). A Senate committee reported
4,954 cases between 1947 and 1950 (Van Dyne 1980: 99).

In this environment, it is probably more surprising that gay people
began to organize than that the organizations they created emphasized secrecy and discretion. The earliest important organization, the
Mattachine Society, took its name from "mysterious mediaeval figures
in masks . . . [who] might have been homosexuals" (D'Emilio 1983:
67),[11] and its form "was modeled on the Communist party, in which
secrecy, hierarchical structures, and centralized leadership predomi-
nated" (ibid.: 64). As D'Emilio shows, however, a combination of
homophobia on the part of the Communist party and a desire to avoid
tarring either group with the other's stigma led the primary founder
of the Mattachine Society, Harry Hay, to leave the party. Within a few
years of its founding, as the Mattachine Society began to attract attention and increased membership, the original leftist leadership was
purged and the centralized structure relaxed. After 1953 the Mattachine Society was much more assimilationist than radical, as "accommodation to social norms replaced the affirmation of a distinctive
gay identity" (ibid.: 81).

While the gay community was beginning to form a distinct identity,
America was shocked by the 1948 publication of Alfred Kinsey's *Sexual Behavior in the Human Male*. Kinsey gave empirical evidence that
homosexuality was pervasive in all strata of American society and

---

11. Other homosexual organizations formed around that time had similarly discreet
names, drawn from similarly obscure sources: One, Inc., which chose its name from a
quotation from Thomas Carlyle ("A mystic bond of brotherhood makes all men one");
and the first lesbian organization, the Daughters of Bilitis, named after French poet
Pierre Louys's prose poems, *Songs of Bilitis* (Bullough 1979: 72).

that homosexuals could not be identified by stereotypes. The *Kinsey Report* told homosexuals what they already knew: they were everywhere. Kinsey also reinforced many heterosexuals' most basic fear: the invisible, undetectable enemy *was* everywhere. (Bronski 1984: 77)[12]

Throughout the 1950s and into the 1960s, the homophile movement, as it was then generally called, slowly expanded and deepened the self-awareness of lesbian and gay people as a distinct, self-conscious, and embattled minority. Central to this awareness was the process known as "coming out"—the individual realization that one was homosexual, and the acknowledgment of this sexual identity to other gay people. It was nearly universally taken for granted that this knowledge was to be kept within the group, which did not exclude sharing it with other gay people as long as outsiders were not told. The process of selective sharing often resorted to code phrases that could be exchanged even in mixed company: someone might be described as "family," "a club member," "a friend of Dorothy's," "a friend of Mrs. King." While less necessary today for people living in major urban centers, the practice of using code phrases to signal a lesbian or gay identity is alive and well in many parts of the country and in many occupational and social contexts (cf. Woods 1992). The term "gay" was probably the most widely used code phrase for homosexuals until the word itself was outed when it was adopted by the political movement that came into being in 1969. While it is impossible to say that non-voluntary exposure was never used as a political tactic during this period, it is certainly true that the "path over corpses" was not the road taken by the movement.

---

12. The Kinsey report gave birth to one of the most resilient pseudostatistics in the history of social science: the standard estimate that 10 percent of the population is homosexual. In fact, Kinsey and his colleagues give a number of different figures in the 1948 volume, ranging from a low of 4 percent (males who are exclusively homosexual) to a high of 37 percent (males who reported at least one same-sex orgasm), with a final estimate that "only fifty percent of the [white male] population is exclusively heterosexual throughout its adult life" (Kinsey et al. 1948: 656). The equivalent figures for women were lower in all categories, and "the accumulative incidences of homosexual responses had ultimately reached 28 percent. . . . This means that homosexual responses had occurred in half as many females as males" (Kinsey et al. 1953: 474–75). However, in the absence of a true probability sample survey—difficult to conduct with an invisible population that has reason to fear exposure—it is impossible to obtain an accurate estimate of the lesbian and gay population.

A Tale of Two Leaders

The 1950s can well be described as a period of wintry despair for homosexuals in the United States, a time when the culture seemed determined to impose a coercive conformity in personal as well as political life. Yet it was also a period in which homosexual self-consciousness began to germinate and political activism began to push shoots above the surface; it was also a spring of hope. Part of the flavor of this era can be captured in reflecting on the contrasting styles and directions represented by two key figures, Donald Webster Cory and Franklin Kameny.

In 1951 the American homosexual movement received a significant boost with the publication of the first full-scale analysis and polemic for equality, Donald Webster Cory's *The Homosexual in America: A Subjective Approach*. Writing as a gay man, but under a pseudonym that might have subtly referred to André Gide's homosexual apologia, *Corydon*, Cory presented a forceful argument for the view that homosexuals constitute a minority within American society: "Our minority status is similar, in a variety of respects, to that of national, religious and other ethnic groups: in the denial of civil liberties; in the legal, extra-legal and quasi-legal discrimination; in the assignment of an inferior social position; in the exclusion from the mainstream of life and culture" (1951: 13–14).

Cory's powerfully written, openly subjective description and analysis of the conditions of gay male life in mid-century America served as a stimulus to the emerging homosexual self-consciousness, and Cory was viewed as an inspirational leader of the nascent homophile movement.[13] In the next fifteen years Cory published a book on homosexuality in other cultures (1956), *The Lesbian in America* (1964), and, with John LeRoy, a follow-up book, *The Homosexual and His Society: A View from Within* (1963).

In the 1963 book, Cory and LeRoy restate the thesis of Cory's first book that "the invert is a member of a minority group, differing from ethnic and other minorities essentially in that his status as a minority group is unrecognized," and they celebrate the "feeling of group recognition [that] has grown among these people," leading to the launching "of a struggle for the rights guaranteed to all citizens of a

---

13. I can readily recall the powerful impact the book had on me, as a sixteen-year-old in the late 1950s, when I found it on the shelves of a university library and devoured it in one sitting, literally, on the floor between the library stacks where I would not be seen by anyone.

free democratic society" (Cory and LeRoy 1963: 240). Describing the beginnings of that movement in "small secret underground groups," Cory and LeRoy note that "with diminishing secrecy, several distinct groups and societies have found their way on the American scene, fighting a legal, social and political battle in order to help win public acceptance for the invert and his way of life" (ibid.).

By the mid-1960s, however, something was happening to Donald Webster Cory, and his days as a leader of the homosexual liberation movement were numbered. Cory had asked Alfred Kinsey to write an introduction to *The Homosexual in America*, and Kinsey, refusing because of "the special position he was in" (Cory 1965: 8), referred Cory to psychotherapist Albert Ellis, describing him as "just about the most consistent liberal on sex of anyone in America" (ibid.). Ellis wrote the introduction to Cory's book, and the two remained associated afterwards. Although Cory later wrote (ibid.: 8–9) that each influenced the other, it is Ellis's growing influence on Cory that is most remarkable.

In the 1963 book with John LeRoy, Cory argued against the prevailing psychoanalytic view that homosexuality is a curable sickness and that "those who remain homosexual are trapped by their own perversity, since it is a matter of choice, after all. Nothing could be farther from the truth" (235). Yet, despite this apparent resistance to the claims of psychiatry, Cory was already shifting toward a medical, even cure-oriented perspective. In 1965 Cory returned Ellis's favor by writing the introduction to Ellis's *Homosexuality: Its Causes and Cure*. In his introduction, Cory defended Ellis against criticisms from the homophile movement, criticisms that Cory saw as directed against two of Ellis's major points: First, "that homosexuals . . . are disturbed individuals, and the state of being a confirmed homosexual is hence a disturbance. . . . They are compulsive, neurotic, . . . and, in fact, they are frequently borderline psychotics." Second, that "homosexuality, as learned condition, can be unlearned . . . homosexuality is curable" (1965: 9–10). Cory was now promoting the key positions he had opposed in his earlier writings.

Cory's conversion to a psychiatric perspective and his abandonment of the minority analysis he had pioneered led to a struggle within the homophile movement and the rejection of Cory's position by the New York Mattachine Society in a 1965 election (D'Emilio, 1983: 167–68). At this point there occurred a strange and possibly unique example of a *reverse coming out*: the pseudonymous Donald Webster Cory suddenly disappeared from sight, and the space previously occupied by his body was taken by an apparently heterosexual sociologist named Edward Sagarin, now writing about the homophile movement under his real name, as an "objective" social scientist. In 1966 Sagarin submitted a doctoral dissertation to New York University titled "Structure and Ideology in an Association of Deviants." The dissertation consisted of an analysis of the Mattachine Society but did not mention the fact that its author, the sociologist of deviance Edward Sagarin, was also the homophile leader Donald Webster Cory (ibid.).

By the early 1970s Sagarin was well known within sociology as a fierce opponent of gay liberation. In a 1973 essay surveying a spate of recent books on homosexuality, many of them works of the early gay liberation movement, Sagarin defines gay identity as false consciousness, criticizing the minority model he had promulgated in his earlier (and now unacknowledged) existence as Donald Webster Cory. Sagarin ends his essay on a truly bizarre note, defending the continued hiding by "secret deviants" and warning that those who "call on gay people to accept and assert themselves, blatantly to proclaim themselves, . . . may be proceeding on the road to their own undoing." The undoing he is warning against is that, once unmasked, gay people "could . . . [no longer] be quoted and cited as scholars in whatever their area of specialization, protected by the mantle of objectivity, for their vested interest would place their work under a shadow" (1973: 11–12).

Sagarin's fears of unmasking were not unfounded. Sociologist Laud Humphreys described a debate he held with Sagarin at the 1974 meetings of the American Sociological Association in Montreal in which Sagarin accused Kinsey, Evelyn Hooker, Humphreys, and other researchers of falsifying data:

> I blew his cover, "accidentally" addressing him as Professor Cory. I said, before that audience of my peers, "I want to be honest with you and I want you to know that I am gay. I have done my research and written my book [*Tearoom Trade*] as a gay person, closeted, trying to come out of that closet, dealing with my own personal pain. Now I want to ask Professor Cory—I mean Sagarin—to be honest with us. Never has he said who he studied, never has he identified his research population—he's always just said that we are lying. I want to know who he has studied." When I finished the whole audience rose in a standing ovation. I was crying. Then Sagarin got up to give his rebuttal. He burst into tears and all he could say between sobs was, "I am my data." They called it "Monday, Bloody Monday." (Lazere 1987)

If Donald Webster Cory's early writing provided one kind of inspiration for the nascent homosexual movement, Franklin Kameny was an important pioneer of another kind of militancy. In 1957, as a thirty-two-year-old astronomer recently hired by the Army Map Service, Kameny was confronted by civil service investigators with a charge of homosexuality and fired a few months later. Unlike most of those dismissed during the witch-hunts of the period, Kameny refused to leave quietly and fought back through the federal courts, taking his case all the way to the U.S. Supreme Court, which refused to hear his appeal. Kameny did not take even this defeat as final, and in 1961 he joined with others to form the Mattachine Society of Washington, D.C. (Van Dyne 1980).

As a vocal leader of the growing homosexual rights movement, Kameny approached the issue in a way that "differed markedly from the neutrality espoused by the homophile movement of the 1950s" (D'Emilio 1983: 152). Stepping out from behind the masked modesty of the Mattachine's dependence on liberal professional authorities, Kameny modeled his strategies on the civil rights movement, arguing for unapologetic public actions. A key ingredient of Kameny's militant strategy was the rejection of the homophile movement's concern with medical theories of the causes of homosexuality and its possible cure – precisely the concerns increasingly embraced by Cory/Sagarin. Articulating a minority civil rights analysis clearly paralleling other groups' struggles, Kameny noted that we do not see "the NAACP and CORE worrying about which chromosome and gene produced a black skin, or about the possibility of bleaching the Negro" (ibid.: 153):

> "I remember sitting here one day watching Stokely Carmichael on television talking about how 'Black is Beautiful,' and that started me thinking we needed some sort of slogan," [Kameny] says. "I fooled around awhile with 'Gay is Great,' but finally settled on 'Gay is Good.' " (Van Dyne 1980: 100)

The cornerstones of Kameny's political position were the cultivation of gay pride and the conviction that "we must instill in the homosexual community a sense of worth of the individual homosexual." This could only be done by a movement openly led by homosexuals themselves, because "the *only* people in the world who are doing this are the pitifully small handful of us in the homophile movement" (quoted in Marotta 1981: 62–63).

Adopting a strategy of visible, civil rights-oriented actions led Kameny and the Mattachine Society of Washington to initiate meetings with government officials, to challenge the government's discriminatory policies in court, and to go public: picketing the White House, the State Department, the Pentagon, and the Civil Service

Commission. In 1964 their efforts led to the American Civil Liberties Union's reversal of its 1957 policy statement supporting the constitutionality of antigay discrimination, and in 1965 the first court victory was won when the U.S Court of Appeals ruled that the dismissal of a gay job applicant rested on overly vague charges of unfitness (D'Emilio 1983: 155–56).[14]

Although few in number, the newly militant homosexual activists allied with Kameny were marking significant new territory, and, while they were still overshadowed by the much larger civil rights and antiwar movements of the 1960s, they represented a significant change in the rules of the game:

> On the same day [in the spring of 1965] that Students for a Democratic Society attracted 20,000 to an antiwar demonstration at the Washington Monument, seven men and three women paraded at the White House for gay rights; at a repeat performance in October, the numbers had only risen to forty-five. Picketing implicitly involved an open avowal of one's homosexuality, and although many might applaud it, few were prepared to risk the possible consequences of a public stand. That some did, however, signaled a change and provided a model for others to emulate. (ibid.: 165)

Treason or the Better Part of Valor?

In June 1969 the riots that erupted during a routine police raid on the Stonewall Inn, a gay bar in Greenwich Village, served as the spark that ignited a new gay liberation movement. The homophile movement of the early 1950s was founded by men "who were either members of the Communist party or traveled in left-wing circles. Standing outside the political mainstream, they also broke with accepted notions of homoerotic behavior and pioneered in conceiving homosexuals as an oppressed minority" (D'Emilio 1983: 58). A few years later Frank Kameny and his allies in Washington and New York crafted a public

---

14. The unprecedented success of the ACLU in pursuing the case of a gay man fired from his government job prompted a major *Life* magazine exposé of "Homosexuality in America," which informed its readers that "homosexuals are discarding their furtive ways and openly admitting, even flaunting, their deviation. . . . The myth and misconception with which homosexuality has been clothed must be cleared away, not to condone it but to cope with it." The article concluded that, no matter what the outcome of the legal challenges, "no legal procedures are likely to change society's basic repugnance to homosexuality as an immoral and disruptive force that should somehow be removed" (Welch 1964: 75).

strategy modeled on the civil rights movement of the late 1950s and early 1960s, using court challenges and small-scale symbolic public actions. The movement that spread like wildfire across the country after Stonewall was inspired by the New Left, and its leaders were veterans of the civil rights and antiwar movements of the 1960s.[15]

This new generation of gay leaders was faced with the problem of creating a 1960s-style mass movement out of a group that had long learned to hide its identity from public view. The influence of the "Black Is Beautiful" rhetoric of the civil rights movement—translated by Frank Kameny into "Gay Is Good"—can be seen in the central emphasis gay liberationists placed on the affirmation of gay pride, but for this to be a political as well as a personal achievement gay identity needed to be publicly affirmed. The new movement was founded on the importance of coming out as a *public* as well as an individual act:

> Gay liberationists . . . recast coming out as a profoundly political act that could offer enormous personal benefits to an individual. The open avowal of one's sexual identity, whether at work, at school, at home, or before television cameras, symbolized the shedding of the self-hatred that gay men and women internalized, and consequently it promised an immediate improvement in one's life. To come out of the "closet" quintessentially expressed the fusion of the personal and the political that the radicalism of the late 1960s exalted.
>
> Coming out also posed as the key strategy for building a movement. . . . Visible lesbians and gay men also served as magnets that drew others in. Furthermore, once out of the closet, they could not easily fade back in. Coming out provided gay liberation with an army of permanent enlistees. (ibid.: 235–36)

On the first anniversary of Stonewall, the first gay pride march was held in New York City—it is now an annual event in cities across the country—and even the *New York Times*, which had buried the Stonewall riots on its inside pages, took notice. The "quote of the day" was a statement by one of the organizers that summarized the core belief of gay liberation: "We're probably the most harassed, persecuted minority group in history, but we'll never have the freedom and civil

---

15. In 1972 Karla Jay and Allen Young published *Out of the Closets*, a 400-page collection of the "voices of gay liberation," which included a listing of lesbian and gay organizations in thirty-six states, the District of Columbia, and ten other countries. California alone was represented by seventy-four organizations, sixteen of them called Gay Liberation Front.

rights we deserve as human beings unless we stop hiding in closets and in the shelter of anonymity" (Marotta 1981: 170).

The gay liberation movement that placed coming out at the top of its agenda was largely a young person's movement, made up at least initially of New Left activists or counterculturalists who "had already decided that American society was corrupt and oppressive" (D'Emilio 1983: 246). They had relatively little to lose by coming out publicly. But most older lesbian and gay people had reason to feel more cautious about adopting the slogan of the gay liberation movement and coming "out of the closets and into the streets!" Writing at the dawn of the new era, Dennis Altman noted that most older homosexuals had "already established an identity and a way of coping with the world. Indeed to such persons, gay liberation is as much a threat as it is to straight society, for it undermines the whole complex set of roles and social relationships they have built up" (1971: 121).

One of the earliest sociological studies of a gay male community, conducted in a Canadian city in the mid-1950s, described two distinct subgroups: the overt and the secret homosexuals (Leznoff and Westley 1956). Those defined as overt were not political activists; indeed, there was no political movement for them to join. They were, rather, the ones who could not or would not hide their sexuality, "persons of low socioeconomic status who [had] jobs where concealment [was] not a prerequisite" (262). The secret homosexuals, not surprisingly, were drawn from occupations of relatively high status, in which known homosexuals were not tolerated. As might have been expected, "the distinctions between these groups [were] maintained by the secret homosexuals who [feared] identification and [refused] to associate with overt homosexuals" (260).

Twenty years later, a few years into the era of gay liberation, an openly gay sociologist wrote about the more complex homosexual community in Toronto (Lee 1977). Assuming a total population of around 150,000 male homosexuals in metropolitan Toronto, Lee estimated that perhaps 5,000 were "out" at work, between 500 and 1,000 belonged to a gay liberation group, and possibly 50 were publicly identified in the media.

Lee's analysis postulates a multistep process that is vastly oversimplified by the term "coming out," and we will return to this complex question later on, but for the moment it is important to note that the theory and strategy of the post-Stonewall movement was centered on the ideology of public self-disclosure as the key to psychological health for individual gay people and to liberation from oppression for the gay community. Thus, from the start there was a rift between the openly lesbian and gay activists of the movement and the majority of homo-sexuals who remained, and remain today, in the closet. While under-standing and sympathizing with those who would be truly vulnerable to discrimination and reprisals if they were to come out, gay activists have long expressed impatience and anger with those whose wealth and position would protect them from such dangers. Of course, these are the very people who are less likely to feel pinched by the con-straints of disguise and evasion. After all, "they can make their closets as commodious as castles" (Tucker 1982: 31).

Lesbian and gay organizers quickly learned the frustrations of try-ing to garner support from the older generation—the ones most likely to have money. As Martin Duberman noted in speaking to the second annual conference of the Gay Academic Union in 1974:

> Anyone who has worked with any gay organization . . . will tell you that even when total anonymity is guaranteed . . . it's been possible to raise only pitiful sums from those gay men who have the most to give—doctors, lawyers, professional chiefs. Even anony-mously, even indirectly, even marginally, these men have refused any identification with or any contribution to the gay movement. (Duberman 1974/1986)[16]

Despite his bitterness, Duberman hastened to add that he didn't "mean we should harass or 'expose' " these people. After all, in his keynote address to the founding conference of the group a year earlier, he had affirmed the basic credo that coming out was a personal matter: "I realize, of course, that everyone has to decide this matter in terms of his or her own timetable and circumstances—and absolutely free from external coercion" (1973/1986).[17]

The tension that can be felt in Duberman's speeches—between the affirmation of an individual right to free choice and the realization that most gay people do not choose to come out—has remained a discor-

---

16. I can testify from much bitter personal experience that this situation still obtains today. The one exception to this rule is AIDS, and even then many affluent gay men will only give money to such certifiably "mainstream" organizations as the American Foundation for AIDS Research (AmFAR), headed by Elizabeth Taylor. AmFAR was the recipient of Malcolm Forbes's only known contributions to any gay-related cause.

17. Duberman's memoir, Cures, published in 1991, reveals his own ambivalence at this time as a recently public gay man. Writing of the difficulties he encountered in rais-ing funds for gay publications, and the similar experiences of Dr. Howard Brown (who had come out when he resigned as New York City's health commissioner) trying to raise funds for the campaign to get the American Psychiatric Association to drop homosexu-ality from its list of diseases, Duberman noted that "Howard could never get over the

dant theme in the rhetoric of gay leaders. In a 1987 article in *The Chronicle of Higher Education* titled "Homosexual Professors Owe It to Their Students to 'Come Out,' " John D'Emilio contradicts his own title somewhat by also asserting that "the decision to do so must, of course, be an individual one, made after careful thought and with a strong support network to count on" (1987: A52).[18]

The resentment against those who choose to stay in well-appointed closets rests on more than the understandable anger at their refusal to join or assist the gay liberation movement. The argument that is made most often is that by staying in the closet, successful, prominent homosexuals in all walks of life help perpetuate the invisibility that fuels antigay stereotypes. On the one hand, their secrecy reinforces the belief that homosexuality is shameful, and on the other, it reduces the possibility of disconfirming this belief by providing positive examples of gay people. In particular, it has long been argued, this secrecy deprives others, especially young people, of role models.

One of the strongest polemics of the early years of gay liberation is a British pamphlet called *With Downcast Gays: Aspects of Homosexual Self Oppression*, which asserted that the new and important contribution of the movement was the realization that "by oppressing *ourselves*, we allow homosexual oppression to maintain its overwhelming success" (Hodges and Hutter 1974: 3). Hodges and Hutter single out the writer E. M. Forster as a particular example of a "privileged closet [gay who is a] traitor to the gay cause" (ibid.: 16). Noting that Forster was known as a moralist and social commentator who stressed the value of personal honesty, they point out that his own honesty never extended to a public acknowledgment of his homosexuality:

> Perhaps Forster's most famous remark was that if he were forced to choose between betraying his country and betraying his friends, he hoped he would have the courage to betray his country. Since the choice was unlikely ever to be presented, this was an easy, if star-

---

insularity and indifference of closeted gay eminences, whether in the arts or medicine, and no amount of reminding ourselves that we, too, had once (and recently) been locked away in fearful silence, could quite dull our sense of indignation" (1991: 291).

18. In his current role as co-chair of the National Gay and Lesbian Task Force, D'Emilio was queried by the media for a response to the recent outings, and he took the same position: "A very sharp line needs to be drawn that one person does not bring out another. It has to be a personal decision" (Longcope 1990). The article suggests that D'Emilio was referring to the outing of "closeted gays [who harm] others by political pronouncements." In the case of Malcolm Forbes, however, who was outed posthumously, it's hard to see why a historian would object to the disclosure.

tling, claim to make. The real choice for Forster lay between damaging his reputation and betraying his fellow homosexuals. Alas, it was
his reputation that he guarded and gay people whom he betrayed.
(ibid.: 20)[19]

Forster wrote a novel in 1914 that had a homosexual theme and,
even more unusual, a happy ending. But *Maurice* was not published
until after his death in 1970, and by this time it was neither innovative
nor significant to gay people except as a historical curiosity. Hodges
and Hutter quote a "friend in his sixties . . . [who said] 'What a
difference it would have made to my life if I had been able to read it
[*Maurice*] when I was twenty.' "

Besides depriving others of role models, the continued secrecy of
most gay people keeps alive the belief that gay people are much fewer
than they really are, and that they are confined to inner city "gay
ghettos" and to stereotypically gay professions. Thus, in a true classic
of bigotry, Midge Decter wrote in *Commentary* that "I do not suppose,
but would not be certain, that homosexuals have established much of
a presence in basic industry or government service or in such classic
professions as doctoring or lawyering, but then for anyone acquainted
with them as a group the thought suggests itself that few of them have
ever made much effort in these directions" (1980: 40).[20]

When such hateful drivel can be printed in respectable publications
it is easy to understand why gay activists have insisted on the importance of gay visibility across the social and professional spectrum.
After Harvey Milk was elected as the first openly gay supervisor in San
Francisco, aware of the possibility that he would be assassinated, he
recorded a political will in which he said, "If a bullet should enter

---

19. In 1971 Merle Miller wrote an unprecedented *New York Times Magazine* article on
"What It Means to Be a Homosexual." He began the article by citing Forster's remark
as an example of courage. Although he also notes that Forster was not open about being
homosexual, he continues, "it is one thing to confess to political unorthodoxy but quite
another to admit to sexual unorthodoxy." Miller was more forgiving than Hodges and
Hutter. But, then, he was also closer to Forster's age, and not exactly militant. Although
he was coming out in the pages of the *New York Times*, he expressed the sort of ambivalence that might be termed self-oppression: "Gay is good. Gay is proud. Well, yes, I
suppose. If I had been given a choice (but who is), I would prefer to have been straight."

20. Realizing that the phrase "acquainted with them as a group" might raise hackles,
she later goes on, "No doubt this will in itself seem to many of the uninitiated a bigoted
formulation. Yet one cannot even begin to get at the truth about homosexuals without
this kind of generalization. They are a group so readily distinguishable that . . . they
can in a single sweeping glance around a crowded room and with unerring accuracy
recognize one another." I wish.

my brain, let that bullet destroy every closet door. . . . I would like to see every gay lawyer, every gay architect come out, stand up and let the world know. That would do more to end prejudice overnight than anybody could imagine. I urge them to do that, urge them to come out. Only that way will we start to achieve our rights" (Shilts 1982: 373–74).

Yet, despite all the passionate rhetoric and all the dispassionate analysis of gay liberationists, there was no rush to force open the closets of the rich and famous. The unwritten rules were respected, though not because the idea hadn't occurred to anyone. As Michael Bronski reminded us:

> As early as 1972, writer and gay liberationist John Paul Hudson predicted/speculated . . . that in the future a group of radical gays . . . would launch a campaign to bring famous people out of the closet, either by persuasion or force. And although Hudson's nearly 20-year-old fantasy was not the blueprint for '90s outing, it speaks to the tension that has *always* existed between those who live openly lesbian and gay lives and those who remain closeted. There is no doubt that the emotional pain of the closet is also accompanied by considerable social privilege, and that this is going to engender anger and resentment. (1990: 6)

An Uneasy Truce

For most of the period from the late 1950s through the 1980s there was rarely any concerted effort made to expose the sexual identities of prominent closeted gays. After the fires of McCarthyism died down, the government winked at the presence of discreet lesbian women and gay men, while officially continuing to prohibit known homosexuals from government service and covertly gathering information about suspect individuals.

The FBI, it was revealed in the early 1980s, had long been conducting Operation HOMEX (Homosexual Extortion) to identify prominent homosexuals in Washington, "ostensibly to prevent their being compromised by the Russians" (Branch 1982: 46). Presumably their lists didn't include J. Edgar Hoover, now widely considered to have been homosexual (by inclination, if not by action). It is important to know that

> there is no evidence to suggest that individuals have been induced to compromise the country's security under threat of being exposed as homosexual. In August 1987, a federal court in San Francisco . . .

cited a 1985 Senate hearing on espionage in which not one of the more than 40 major espionage cases prosecuted since World War II was found to involve the blackmail of a homosexual. (Gup 1988: 32)

The power of exposure as a political and personal threat can perhaps best be seen in its appearance in two fictional accounts of national politics. In Allen Drury's 1961 novel, *Advise and Consent*, a U.S. senator commits suicide after political enemies threaten to expose a homosexual episode in his past. At about the same time, in Gore Vidal's successful Broadway play *The Best Man*, a leading contender for the Democratic presidential nomination is forced out of the race by a similar threat.[21] Such backstage threats may well have been used, and may have worked, but public exposures remained few and were usually the result of the victim's carelessness.

Occasionally a scandal would break through the veil of secrecy, as when President Johnson's closest aide, Walter Jenkins, was arrested in 1965 for sexual solicitation in a Washington YMCA rest room, just two blocks from the White House (Van Dyne 1980: 100).

Few are likely to be surprised to learn that Richard Nixon was interested in the possibility of using sexual secrets against his enemies in the press. A 1970 memorandum written by J. Edgar Hoover reveals that "H. R. Haldeman . . . stated the President wanted . . . a rundown on the homosexuals known and suspected in the Washington press corps. . . . We ought to be able to send it over certainly not later than Friday" (quoted in Harwood 1991b). And some members of the press were apparently willing to use similar tactics, even against innocent bystanders. In September 1970 syndicated columnist Jack Anderson revealed, in what was billed as an "unusual exclusive," that "Vice President Spiro Agnew is deeply troubled about his son Randy, who has broken up with his wife and has been living for the past month with a male hairdresser in Baltimore" (1970). The details of the story were more ambiguous than suggested by the lead sentence and the description of the "townhouse apartment in the fashionable Bolton Hill section of Baltimore. The decor was elegant, with wall-to-wall carpeting, arty paintings on the walls and an ornate table dominating the front room." Despite the unmistakable implications of Anderson's

---

21. Readers of Allan Berube's *Coming Out under Fire* (1990), which describes the central role of wartime experiences in creating post-World War II gay culture, will not be surprised that both of these fictional gay episodes were set during the war while the protagonists were in the military.

coded language, the media furor was brief and Randy Agnew soon reverted to the anonymity he clearly sought.

By the late 1970s and the early 1980s, the police had forced a series of political figures out of the closet by arresting them for homosexual solicitation. In 1978 and 1979 two Democratic congressmen, Frederick Richmond and Joseph Wyatt, made the papers in this ignominious fashion. More startling, however, were the arrests in 1980 of two right-wing Republican congressmen, Jon Hinson and Robert Bauman. Hinson, from Mississippi, was arrested (rumor had it) in a Capitol washroom in flagrante delicto with a male federal employee; he subsequently was defeated for reelection. Robert Bauman was a much more significant figure, and his arrest for soliciting sex with a male minor sent shock waves throughout much of Washington.[22] Bauman, a married Roman Catholic with four children, was a founder and former head of the Young Americans for Freedom and national chairman of the American Conservative Union. "In the House, he was widely considered the most intelligent, promising leader of the New Right—a crusader against busing, abortion, deficit spending, communism, and homosexuality" (Branch 1982: 45).

The election of Ronald Reagan as president brought a distinct chill to the Washington atmosphere for the lesbian and gay rights movement, and a growing sense that the hard-won gains of the 1970s were about to be reversed. The Carter White House staff, which had included at least one highly placed partly out lesbian, Midge Constanza, was replaced by a staff that included more than a few gay men, but they were deeply closeted men who were publicly allied with the "moral majority." The arrest of Robert Bauman focused a question frequently raised in gay circles: "should gays protect gays, as they had [protected] Bauman, no matter how antigay their politics?" (Bush 1982: 22). Virginia Apuzzo, New York Democratic activist and director of the Fund for Human Dignity, a leading gay educational nonprofit organization, spoke to gay journalist Larry Bush:

> I think the gay community has been extremely patient, and behaved with responsibility. I know gay men who have stood in bars with Congressman Bauman, when that man contributed to a kind of atmosphere that has resulted in the kind of violence that we see in the

---

22. After their arrests for homosexual activity, both Hinson and Bauman responded by invoking what might be labeled the "liquid fifth"—they insisted that they were alcoholic, not homosexual. This is a version of what gay people call the "Boy, was I drunk last night!" defense.

gay community today. They rely on our silence, and respond by abandoning all reasonable responsibility to protect our basic civil rights. My feeling is that there is a tacit contract among gays, where we do respect the right to privacy that so many of us need to survive. However, when a public official who is closeted uses his or her power in a way that hurts gay people, I feel that tacit contract has been broken. (Bush 1982: 24)

But, while many activists would have agreed with Apuzzo that Bauman broke his part of the tacit agreement that cemented the code of silence, the gay community did not expose him; the Washington, D.C., police did. Similarly, gay activist and Democratic party official Jim Foster told Bush of a public debate he held in Miami against one of Anita Bryant's aides in her successful campaign to repeal Dade County's gay rights ordinance. Shortly before the debate Foster learned that his opponent was a closeted gay man, but neither Foster nor anyone else exposed this person. Bush recounts several other political situations that highlight these issues even more starkly. The mayor of a mid-Atlantic city "urged his police department to begin cracking down on gays" despite the fact that "the mayor was homosexual and was known personally by gay activists in another city he visited for private encounters with other gays."[23] A candidate for governor in a southern state was a closeted homosexual who "has previously used his public position to ridicule gay rights claims as 'bizarre,' and refuses as a candidate to meet with gay groups. Members of these same groups find him at parties, where he smiles indulgently and pleads that his position is 'just politics' "(Bush 1982: 22). Anger was beginning to undermine the foundations of the code of silence. As Larry Bush suggested, many gays felt as Adlai Stevenson had during the 1952 presidential campaign when he said, "If our enemies don't stop telling lies about us, we're going to start telling the truth about them." But, of course, they kept silent.

It was in this atmosphere that Terry Dolan was exposed as a gay hypocrite when Perry Deane Young published God's Bullies (1982), focusing on the New Right Christian fundamentalists who had emerged as a political force in the late 1970s; the book includes an account of Dolan's secret gay life and refers to other unnamed closeted right wingers. Dolan denied the allegations to the New York Times

---

23. Many saw this as a reference to former mayor William Schaefer of Baltimore, who later went on to be elected governor of Maryland.

(Gailey 1982b), and on the whole the mainstream media paid little attention to this revelation.[24] In March 1982 Democratic lawyer Dan Bradley, about to be ousted by the Reagan administration as president of the federally funded Legal Services Corporation, submitted his resignation and simultaneously came out in the pages of the *New York Times* (Gailey 1982a), thus becoming the highest government official ever to declare publicly that he was a homosexual. Taylor Branch's article on Bradley in *Harper's Magazine* in October 1982 was the most detailed account to that date of the secret world of Washington's closeted gays and one of very few mentions of Terry Dolan's homosexuality in the mainstream press:

> Closeted homosexuals have been lining up on both sides of an impending war. Right-wing activists, including many closeted homosexuals, have sought to drive homosexuals from public life. . . . Editors from the *Spotlight*, journal of the far-Right Liberty Lobby, began publishing a scandal sheet called *Deep Backgrounder* naming more than a dozen allegedly homosexual members of Congress in the first issue. . . . [Some homosexual] militants want to fight fire with fire by exposing the closeted homosexual leaders of the Republican Party and the New Right. They propose to deprive the homosexual question of its political slant by giving unfriendly politicians a shove towards the closet door. This tactic of enforced honesty is called "outage." (Branch 1982: 46–47)

Despite the exposure of Terry Dolan, the outage war never happened; both sides drew back from the brink. Then the "page scandals" broke. On the evening of June 20, 1982, Dan Rather informed his national audience that "CBS News has learned that federal law enforcement officials have a wide-ranging investigation under way into allegations of illicit sex and drug use on Capitol Hill. The allegations include congressmen engaging in sex with underage employees, often

---

24. It doesn't seem that it would have been a journalistic feat to detect Dolan's sexuality. Christopher Hitchens talked about this to the editor of the *Advocate*: "I don't think it would've been possible for *anyone* to have met Terry Dolan and not realize within 10 seconds that he was gay. . . . There's a hilarious description of Dolan hosting the NCPAC [National Conservative Political Action Committee] barbecue in Dallas during the 1984 Republican convention. Here were all these huge heterosexual men in ten-gallon hats—sitting astride steers and waving branding irons—and their wives. Jerry Falwell was there as a guest of honor. And there was Terry Dolan with his silk shirt split down to the navel, and the gold chain and the mustache. But he was the host, so there was nothing they could do about it" (Giteck 1987).

members of the same sex" (quoted in Klaidman and Beauchamp 1987: 114).

Although the investigations conducted by the Justice Department, the House Ethics Committee, and a special counsel appointed by Congress eventually exposed one heterosexual and one homosexual congressman for engaging in sexual relations with congressional pages, CBS News's reporting was more narrowly focused on the allegations of homosexuality. The follow-up stories broadcast by CBS centered on accusations by two congressional pages, appearing on-camera but masked by shadows, who claimed to have engaged in homosexual relations with three members of Congress and one staff employee, and to have procured a male prostitute for a senator. These charges were later determined to be lies or misleading exaggerations. The special counsel's report strongly suggested that John Ferrugia, the CBS correspondent covering the story, had encouraged the former pages to make their sensational statements. "If Ferrugia had not pushed them much of the harm done [to the pages and to Congress] would have been avoided, as would whatever harm was done to Ferrugia's reputation as a result of broadcasting a story based on unfounded rumors" (Klaidman and Beauchamp 1987: 116).

As a result of the investigation, Congressman Gerry Studds of Massachusetts became the first member of Congress to respond to being outed by acknowledging his homosexuality, and, while he admitted his error in having a relationship with a seventeen-year-old page, he affirmed his gay identity. In a subsequent interview with the gay press, Studds described his emotional state in much more positive terms than most anti-outing rhetoric would predict:

> [I feel] better than I've ever felt in my life. I suspect that's something that would be easy for your audience of gay people to understand. But I've found that in giving that response to the media in general, to folks who have had this experience themselves, that it requires a great deal of explanation as to how in the midst of what for a lot of reasons appears to be a disastrous situation, one can candidly say, "I've never felt better in my life." Any person who has ever gone through the experience of coming out will understand that. I feel as if the remaining seven cylinders had just kicked in for the first time in 46 years. And that's a powerful feeling. (Bush 1983: 15)

The response of Studds's constituents was overwhelmingly supportive (he has been reelected ever since), and this episode might have dampened the outing spirit in Washington. Within a few years, in May 1987, Barney Frank, another liberal Democratic Massachusetts congressman, revealed one of the worst-kept secrets in Washington by becoming the first member of Congress to come out voluntarily.[25]

For much of the 1980s the question of whether a public figure's secret homosexuality should ever be exposed was the topic of much backstage discussion among the press as well as nongay and gay political activists. A former *Washington Post* reporter cites high-level consideration of the conflicts between "what is in the public interest and what the public may merely have an interest in" (Gup 1988: 30).

After prominent liberal Democratic organizer Allard Lowenstein was assassinated by a mentally disturbed former protégé in March 1980, an account by Teresa Carpenter published in the *Village Voice* and abridged in the *Washington Post* noted stories about Lowenstein having made sexual overtures to many young men who worked with him in antiwar and other organizing efforts; his killer had been one such target of his sexual advances. The counterattack from the political and media establishment was fierce. Fifteen members of Congress wrote to the *Post*, charging the newspaper with deeply offensive "unsubstantiated assertions and gratuitous inuendo." *New York Post* editor James Wechsler wrote that Carpenter "was guilty of irresponsible defamation of a dead man . . . of unattributed gossip-mongering and political malice that could shadow the lives of Lowenstein's family."[26] Despite these attacks, the *New York Native*, a gay paper, carried a documented story that included accounts of Lowenstein's conversations with a gay leader about his bisexuality (Harris 1982: 328–34).

Sometimes the press's reluctance to report allegations of homosexuality may be justified on more appropriate grounds. Just before the 1983 Mississippi gubernatorial election, the Jackson *Clarion-Ledger* decided not to print a story, supported by affidavits from male prostitutes, alleging that the front-running Democratic nominee was homosexual (Wilkie 1984). The editor refused to base a story on private, anonymous allegations, but the story continued to circulate and was capitalized on by the Republican candidate, whose wife declared, "I'm running for first lady and I'm unopposed." As the rumors percolated

---

25. Ever vindictive, Robert Bauman, in his autobiography, *The Gentleman from Maryland* (1987), had identified Frank as a gay man, later claiming disingenuously that he thought this was already public knowledge.

26. Ironically, Wechsler's attack was occasioned by the award of the Pulitzer Prize to Carpenter for several stories, the Lowenstein story among them, after the prize was withdrawn from its first recipient, Janet Cooke, a *Washington Post* reporter who was discovered to have fabricated her award-winning series about an eight-year-old heroin addict.

just under the surface, press and broadcast editors agonized and conferred among themselves. The story broke through their reluctance when the Republican political operative spearheading the story held a press conference. The impact of the story is not clear since the accused candidate won handily and, on the day he was inaugurated, "the *Clarion-Ledger* reported that three of the male prostitutes had retracted their story, saying they had been paid to make their statements" (ibid.: 58).

Despite cases such as this one, in which editorial caution can be attributed to journalistic responsibility, it is often difficult to determine whether media discretion results from a respect for the individual's privacy or from the fact that "many in the newsroom are still ill at ease with the topic of homosexuality" (ibid.). In other circumstances the media have been at least implicitly engaged in outing.

When Linda Chavez ran for the Senate from Maryland she characterized her opponent, Congresswoman Barbara Mikulski, as a "San Francisco-style Democrat." Although she was criticized for this transparent ploy, when Chavez found herself behind in the polls she returned to this tactic. In a story headlined "Chavez's 'Tough' Strategy Hits at Mikulski's View of Men," *New York Times* reporter Maureen Dowd filled in for her readers some details behind Chavez's attacks on the unmarried Mikulski: "It was widely reported that [radical Australian feminist Teresa] Brennan had lived at Ms. Mikulski's modest Fells Point house for two months" (1986).[27]

In May 1988 Tom Pappas, an aide to Maryland Congressman Roy Dyson, committed suicide after the *Washington Post* printed a front-page story on his unorthodox administrative practices that suggested he had sexually harassed male staff members. Although the paper did not say Pappas was gay, the implication was clear, and subsequent coverage focused on the question of Pappas's and Dyson's sexuality (Gup 1988).

At the same time, the mainstream media failed to cover stories concerning homosexuality that presented no danger of violating anyone's privacy. For example, media coverage of the Mariel "exodus" of 116,000 Cubans generally failed to report on the thousands of homo-

---

27. Four years later, when the right-wing *Washington Times* ran a cover story on outing that included an editor's note citing its belief that "to repeat a name, particularly if the person denies being gay, is to repeat a grave wrong," the paper nonetheless cited Chavez's "San Francisco Democrat" line and noted that "many voters thought it was a catty reference to lesbianism" (Allen 1990: 9).

sexuals escaping persecution under Castro: "The story of the gay refugees was a good one. Why didn't anyone want to tell it? . . . The timidity and awkwardness of the American press in handling stories involving gays" (Massing 1980: 49).

Thus, it is not surprising that in 1987 it "was a gay reporter at National Public Radio—Frank Browning—who . . . revealed that the contra fund-raising network was largely gay and that [contra fundraiser Carl "Spitz"] Channel's male lover was on the tax-exempt foundation's payroll as a consultant" (Gup 1988: 32). As Browning pointed out to those who objected to his exposure of Channel, there would have been no such hesitation had the money gone to a spouse. Besides, here was a classic example of hypocrisy from an administration known for hostility toward gays. In a less visible forum, an article in the national gay magazine the *Advocate* about the 1988 Republican convention in New Orleans identified two gay Republicans by name, noting that they were not publicly known to be gay. The reporter later said that he had permission to use their names, although those identified denied this. Writing about this incident in the *Village Voice*, press critic Geoffrey Stokes noted a growing disenchantment in the gay press with the practice of protecting the security of prominent closets, concluding that, "since it is to the *practice* and not the politics of the gay press that the straight press has generally deferred in the matter of closets, we could have some ugly times indeed ahead" (Stokes 1988). The ugliness Stokes foresaw wasn't long in coming.

AIDS Raises the Stakes

The willingness of the gay movement to respect the privacy of political closets was increasingly strained in the late 1980s as the reactionary backlash against the gains of the 1970s was fueled by the AIDS-induced association of gay sexuality and deadly disease. We will unfortunately never know how gay identity and the gay movement *might* have developed after the emergence of a visible lesbian and gay subculture in the 1970s. Just as the Third Reich forever changed the history of European Jews, revealing the fragility of the ground on which Jewish assimilation was built, the AIDS epidemic fundamentally affected the fate of gay people and dramatically reminded us of the deep-seated homophobia of American culture.

The gay movement of the early 1980s, when AIDS first began to appear, had placed the right to privacy at the center of its agenda. Flying the same banner liberalizing movements had used to secure the right to contraception and abortion and to force back the forces of sexual censorship, the reformist wing of the gay movement used the rhetoric of privacy rather than the more subversive language of sexual liberation. But by the mid-1980s this strategy was neither sufficient nor viable in itself. The resurgent right wing, triumphantly occupying the White House in 1981, undertook a concerted campaign to deny gay people whatever degree of social legitimacy had been gained in several decades of struggle. In all of this the issue of lesbian and gay visibility played a central role, a role that revealed the double edge of the sword of privacy.

The invisibility of closeted gay people, particularly those who are prominent members of society, played into the hands of the antigay reactionaries, making it easy for them to deny the extent of lesbian and gay people's dispersion throughout diverse social strata, and thus reinforcing our marginalization. In the early days of the AIDS epidemic (at a point when widespread educational efforts might have saved thousands of lives since lost), Congressman Henry Waxman of California made this point in April 1982 by contrasting public response to AIDS and to Legionnaire's disease:

> Legionnaire's disease hit a group of predominantly white, heterosexual, middle-aged members of the American Legion. The respectability of the victims brought them a degree of attention and funding for research and treatment far greater than that made available so far to the victims of Kaposi's sarcoma. . . . I want to emphasize that contrast, because the more popular Legionnaire's disease affected fewer people and proved to be less fatal. What society judged was not the severity of the disease but the social acceptability of the individuals affected with it. (quoted in Shilts 1987: 143)

AIDS thus taught two lessons. First, a disease that strikes gay people (and people of color, and drug users, and poor people) will not receive adequate attention.[28] Second, people will begin to pay attention when famous and important people are involved—even if they are revealed to be gay—or when "innocent" victims untainted by minority stigma are featured. Ronald Milavsky, then vice president of NBC, described the coverage of AIDS:

---

28. In the case of AIDS, of course, there is the further obstacle of our unwillingness to deal honestly with sex in any form. As Dennis Altman noted long before AIDS, "Western societies rely on very considerable hypocrisy about sexual behavior, preferring epidemics of venereal disease and crippling back-yard abortions to any honest acceptance of the realities of sexual life" (1971: 182).

The most striking thing . . . is the low level of reporting until Rock Hudson's illness and the rather continuous high level after that. AIDS did, after all, have a focal event, like the Tylenol poisonings, the death, after thousands of others, of a famous person who most people did not think of as being homosexual. Rock Hudson's illness, death, and his admission that he was indeed dying of AIDS was a very unusual combination *that was big news and stimulated the public's interest.* From July to December 1985, NBC broadcast over 200 stories on AIDS—three times as many as during the entire 1980 to 1984 period. The other news media reacted similarly. (Milavsky 1988; emphasis added)[29]

This double realization of the reality of homophobia is the prime spark that lit the outing bonfire: "How many lives might have been saved had there been many more truly important uncloseted stars and athletes testifying before congressional committees and leading AIDS marches?" (Byron 1990).

The passion of outing is fueled by the anger of those working furiously to counter the ravages of AIDS against those who seem to be more concerned about retaining their membership on society's A list. The language of outing is the language of community and accountability, of the condemnation of passing and the demand for public affirmations of gay identity by the legions of closeted stars and athletes, fashion designers and fashion plates, politicians and tycoons.

Thinking the Unthinkable

In June 1986 the U.S. Supreme Court dealt a devastating blow to lesbian and gay hopes for constitutional redress through the federal courts. The Court explained, in *Bowers v. Hardwick,* that gay people simply did not enjoy the right to privacy taken for granted as a constitutional guarantee by Americans. On October 14, 1987, two days after the National March on Washington for Lesbian and Gay Rights had assembled one of the largest demonstrations in the capital's history, and one day after 600 civilly disobedient demonstrators had been arrested on the steps of the Supreme Court, Jesse Helms rose on the floor of the U.S. Senate to introduce an amendment to a health care funding bill. The amendment states that "none of the funds made available . . . shall be used to provide AIDS education, information,

---

29. Note the implication that it was the low level of *public* interest that was responsible for the lesser amount of coverage before Rock Hudson.

or prevention materials and activities that promote, encourage, or condone homosexual activities." In fact, the amendment forbids funding anything that might "promote, condone or encourage sexual activity outside a sexually monogamous marriage" (S 14204).

In introducing his amendment, Senator Helms illustrated the evils he was legislating against by referring to materials produced by the Gay Mens Health Crisis (GMHC) in New York City and a safe-sex education program they had received federal funding to support. In particular his ire was focused on a comic book that introduces and demonstrates the use of condoms for anal intercourse. As Helms noted on the floor of the Senate, "Obviously, I cannot describe the book in any detail." He did, however, note that he had sent copies of it to fifteen or twenty senators, in brown envelopes marked "confidential" and that the senators were duly revolted. Encouraged by their response, Senator Helms took the comic book over to the White House and showed it to President Reagan, whose reaction was to shake his head and "hit his desk with his fist."

Senator Helms allowed that he was not a "goody-goody two-shoes," having lived a long time and served four years in the Navy. And yet, he said, "the subject matter is so obscene, so revolting, that I am embarrassed to try to discuss it in sufficient detail to understand that we have a problem here." The senator managed to overcome his embarrassment sufficiently to describe in detail the elements of the GMHC proposal, concluding, "Good Lord, Mr. President, I may throw up" (*Congressional Record*, October 14, 1987; S 14203).

The delicately stomached senator was not concerned only with the repugnant details of safe-sex education. He was clearly focused on a larger picture of which this was a small but significant detail. His move against AIDS education was not made without awareness of the political context. He noted in passing the enormous demonstration that had just occurred—"Now we had all this mob here over the weekend which itself was a disheartening spectacle"—and went on to his central concern about "moral priorities": "We have got to call a spade a spade and a perverted human being a perverted human being, not in anger, but in realism." The action he was demanding of the Senate would, he claimed, take courage, but "it will force this country to slam the door on the wayward, warped sexual revolution which has ravaged this nation for the past quarter of a century."

This was the true agenda behind Helms's amendment, as was clear to everyone, and apparently it didn't take all that much courage after all, since only Lowell Weicker, then senator from Connecticut, spoke against the proposal. The amendment was passed (ninety-six to four) and turned out to be only the first of what has become a steady stream of similar amendments introduced by Jesse Helms and his friends. New Hampshire Senator Gordon Humphrey had a resounding success with an amendment similar to the infamous Clause 28 passed by Margaret Thatcher's conservatives in Britain, banning the use of federal education funds for anything that "promotes homosexuality."

In this atmosphere of relentless attack from the right, with supposed friends caving in to Helms's blackmail, and despite the unparalleled size of the October 1987 march, the movement began to question its strategies. In February 1988 the National Gay and Lesbian Task Force organized a "war conference" to consider and debate options for the political struggles of the late 1980s. At this conference, the option of exposing closeted politicians was once more put on the table and debated. Some advocated "bringing out" those who were proving to be unreliable allies in the fight against antigay politicians; several of the senators who voted for the Helms amendment on AIDS funding, and many in both houses who caved in on restrictions on the National Endowment for the Arts, were potential targets for such action. As one activist put it, "We're going to have to change the rules of the game, . . . to take away the protection of the code, the code of silence" from closeted politicians who do not support gay interests (Weiser 1989). At one point during the conference discussion focused on

> a liberal senator who was believed to be gay and had generally supported gay causes until joining the majority in the Helms vote. "The anger was tremendous," recalled Andy Humm, a New York activist and journalist. If another unfriendly vote occurred, the activists decided, they would "bring out" the politician by affixing a pink triangle—a symbol of homosexuality—to the senator's office door. (ibid.)

Despite the new willingness to think the previously unthinkable, the war conferees did not decide to break the uneasy truce that protected Washington's closets of power. But not everyone was willing to respect the code of silence unconditionally. Although Urvashi Vaid, then executive director of the National Gay and Lesbian Task Force, maintained that "our movement should [not] be about the business of dragging other people out of the closet," Vic Basile, then head of the Human Rights Campaign Fund, the leading gay political action committee, was quoted as saying that "those who participate in the gay community and then vote against it are guilty of hypocrisy—hypocrisy that causes harm to a whole class of people. They are like Jews who put other Jews into the ovens. . . . Their duplicitous, devious, harmful behavior ought to be exposed" (ibid.).

It wasn't long before members of the AIDS Coalition to Unleash Power (ACT UP) acted on that belief, organizing a demonstration against Oregon Senator Mark Hatfield after he cast a vote they considered antigay. Robert Bray, then a Human Rights Campaign Fund staff member, argued that Hatfield "was a moderate with a mixed record on gay issues, but not someone whom the gay community should alienate, because he can 'be worked with' " (ibid.: A4). But several months later, Bray himself named another senator—a conservative known for antigay views—in a speech to a gay group, asserting that his voting record was unconscionable (ibid.: A5).

As a tactic, however, outing depended on media cooperation. Like the proverbial noise made by a tree falling in a forest, outing a politician required an audience, and this proved to be an obstacle to those who were willing to break the code of silence. In reporting on these incidents, neither the *Washington Post* (Weiser 1989) nor the *Washington Times*, which ran a story (Richardson 1989) obviously based on the *Post* account, named any of the politicians who had been outed.[30]

When Chicago ACT UP members decided to expose Governor James Thompson after he supported legislation allowing hospitals to test patients for HIV without their consent, they marched outside his home carrying signs naming him as a homosexual, but "the mainstream press ignored their claims, reporting only that a protest had taken place" (Richardson 1989).[31] New York activist Andy Humm, one of those who favored outing in the war conference discussions, agreed that "as a tactic, it isn't going to work until we start getting some atten-

---

30. The discretion of the Washington press was demonstrated when the *Washington Times* broke a story "exposing" a "Homosexual Prostitution Inquiry [Ensnaring] VIPs with Reagan, Bush," according to the headline. Although the *Times* and the *Washington Post* were competing for circulation, neither followed up on the sensational story: the *Times* promised names of key officials but only delivered two low-level figures; the *Post* delayed so long in covering the story that its own ombudsman criticized the paper for delays in checking out the facts, which included such juicy details as an alleged midnight tour of the White House given to a Republican lobbyist and a group of his friends that included two male prostitutes (Perry 1989).

31. Rumors concerning Governor Thompson's sexual orientation were well known to Chicago political and media insiders, and his marriage shortly before running for office had been seen by many as motivated by politics rather than romance. According to Chicago gay insiders, Thompson was familiar with certain leather bars, where he might have been known as Big Jim.

tion from the mainstream press. If it never gets picked up, it doesn't make any difference" (ibid.).

Gay activists did not expect the mainstream press to assist them by reporting their charges, but they may have been more disappointed that the gay press was not willing to join in outing politicians. The *Washington Blade*, the capital's gay newspaper, refused to carry outing stories. According to *Blade* editor Lisa Keen, "The allegation of hypocrisy was not enough. . . . Privacy is supreme" (Weiser 1989: A5). The code of silence may have been weakened, but as long as the mainstream and the gay media refused to play the game, outing remained an ineffective weapon.

The next threat to the code came from the other side. Early in the era of George Bush's "kinder, gentler" politics, the Republican National Committee circulated a memo "saying that soon-to-be-elected House Speaker Tom Foley was 'out of the liberal closet' " (Matza 1990), thus falsely implying that Foley is homosexual. In response, Barney Frank threatened to expose the names of closeted Republican officeholders; the memo was withdrawn, its author was sacrificially fired, and the rumors ceased. "Frank did not carry out his threat, and he was at pains to underscore the limited circumstances in which he would apply it: 'I referred only to those gay people who shamefully use the fact or accusation of homosexuality as a weapon against others.' " (Henry 1990).

But the genie was out of the bottle again, and this time it wouldn't get back in. The political landscape in 1989 was very different from earlier years, and the "path over corpses" had a very different meaning after more than 100,000 AIDS-related deaths. The Republican smear and Frank's counterthreat had ignited a spark in the gay press:

> "That got us thinking," said Gabriel Rotello, editor-in-chief of the New York magazine *OutWeek*, which has led the way with outing. . . . The billionaire Malcolm Forbes was the first target. After [Forbes's] death, *OutWeek* revealed that he was gay in anger at the fiction of his glamorous heterosexual activities. It was a story that worked globally. Show business was next. (Appleyard 1990)

Glitter and Be Discreet

In a society increasingly inclined to choose entertainment figures as its cultural heroes, it is hardly surprising that the stars of stage and screen have been as devoted to the sanctity of the closet as any Washington politician. Despite, or perhaps because of, the stereotypical assumption that Broadway and Hollywood are havens for homosexuals, there has never been a major star of stage, screen, or television who has voluntarily come out.[32] This is not exactly a matter of personal choice. The entire industry operates on the principle that the American public is suffused with prejudices that must be catered to. In earlier decades, the same logic required Jewish actors to submerge and hide their ethnicity:

> In Hollywood, stars assumed neutral names like Fairbanks, or Howard, or Shaw; actresses underwent plastic surgery; some made a point of going to Christian churches or donating money to Christian charities. This was not so much a denial of Jewishness—though it was that—as an effort to make Jewishness appear insignificant. (Friedrich 1986: 48)

New York actor Jules Garfinkle changed his name to Jules Garfield for the Broadway stage, but when he arrived in Hollywood Jack Warner told him that Garfield didn't sound like an American name. When he was told that Garfield had been the name of an American president, Warner relented, but "Jules" had to go. As one of Warner's executives put it, "We wouldn't want people to get the wrong idea." "But I *am* Jewish," said the future John Garfield. "Of course you are," said the Warners executive. "So are *we* . . . most of us. But a lot of people who buy tickets think they don't like Jews. . . . And Jules is a Jew's name" (ibid.: 355).

With only minor changes, the same discussion could have occurred in connection with homosexuality. But while there may now be less pressure on Jewish actors to change their names or, *pace* Barbra Streisand, their noses, lesbian and gay performers are still expected to stay quietly in the closet:

---

32. This is less true in England, where the prominent stage actor Ian McKellen came out in 1988 as part of the campaign against the antigay Clause 28. McKellen was knighted in 1991. When he was criticized for accepting a knighthood from the antigay Thatcher government, a letter from eighteen gay theater professionals (among them director John Schlesinger, producer Cameron Mackintosh, and actors Simon Callow and Alec McCowen) defending his decision was also published: "never again will public figures be able to claim that they have to keep secret their homosexuality in fear of it damaging their careers" (*Guardian* letters column, January 9, 1991). Still, while British cultural traditions have tended to be hospitable to semiopen gay figures, Sir Ian's fellow gay knights John Gielgud and Noel Coward never came out publicly, and we only learned in 1992 that, in addition to his three marriages, Laurence Olivier conducted a lengthy affair with American comedian Danny Kaye (Spoto 1992a).

"Hollywood creates its own myths about what is and is not acceptable and it does not believe the public will accept an actor kissing a
woman on screen if he goes home at night with a guy," said Kim
Fellner, information director for the Screen Actors Guild. "It's not
morals, it's just a dollar-and-cents decision. That's what runs this
town," said (publicity agent Alan) Eichler. (Dubin 1985)

The studios went beyond changing names when it came to lesbian
and gay actors. Scandal magazines of the 1950s and 1960s such as *Confidential, Exposé,* and *Vice Squad*—the precursors of today's supermarket
tabloids—frequently exposed the sexual secrets of the stars, and the
studios were constantly engaged in evasive actions. Publications occasionally had to defend themselves in court for claiming that a celebrity
was homosexual. Liberace sued the London *Daily Mirror* in the 1950s
for hinting that he was gay—and he won! (French 1989).

The July 1955 issue of *Confidential* offered readers "the untold story
of Marlene Dietrich—Dietrich Going for Dolls," listing several of her
female lovers, characterizing them variously as a "blonde Amazon,"
a "mannish maiden," and a "baritone babe" (quoted in Weiss 1991:
283). However, as Andrea Weiss points out, "by the time her 'unspeakable' sexuality was spoken in *Confidential* . . . Marlene Dietrich
was no longer a major star. She had not yet stopped making movies,
but she was not a major box-office draw in the United States, and
would soon return to the European cabaret stage on which she began. . . . Had the article been published in the 1930s, when Dietrich
was at her peak, it may well have cut her career short" (ibid.: 286).[33]
Similarly, when Johnny Mathis came out voluntarily in a 1982 interview with *US* magazine, the story did not cause a sensation or end his
career as a singer; but it is also true that by then he was past his peak,
with a faithful coterie of fans who identified the singer and his music
with their youth. Others who came out after their media peaks include
poet Rod McKuen, religious writer Malcolm Boyd, and, more recently,
actors Dick Sargent (Pela 1991) and Dack Rambo (Walters 1991).

Rock Hudson (formerly Roy Fitzgerald) was hastily married off to

---

33. When Marlene Dietrich died in 1992, aged somewhere around 90, obituary articles used familiar coded language to maintain her heterosexual image for readers who
had long forgotten or never knew about her bisexuality: "This was a woman with a
strong mind of her own . . . who, though she had a husband, apparently didn't hesitate to have affairs with whomever she wanted at her own convenience" (Canby 1992).
(Similar discretion was exercised in the case of Greta Garbo, Janet Gaynor, Jean Arthur,
and Mary Martin.) A posthumous biographer was more direct, stating that Dietrich was
"bisexual, with a very definite preference for women over men" (Spoto 1992b).

his agent's secretary after *Confidential* threatened to expose his homosexuality.[34] Similar pressures and motives are widely rumored to lie behind many of Hollywood's most prominent and apparently romantic couplings, prompting movie star Nelson Eddy to joke to Noel Coward that "marriage is the tax on stardom" (Hadleigh 1991: 72). Nowadays, at least, actors aren't necessarily required to get married or engage in other charades, such as the hunting trip arranged by the studio "for MGM actor Carleton Carpenter in the early 1950s. 'I hated guns,' said Carpenter, now 58 and openly gay, in an interview, 'but it was very macho' " (Dubin 1985). What *is* required, of course, is that they steadfastly present themselves as heterosexual. Gay actor Michael Kearn speaks of "a gay agent who makes it a habit to tell 'fag' jokes at the close of interviews with new actors. If an actor laughs, he's signed up; if he doesn't, he isn't (Hachem 1987: 48)."

We are frequently treated to showbiz gossip intended to convey the heterosexual bona fides of any actor cast in a gay role. The *New York Times* ran a lengthy feature article, "How Stars of *La Cage* Grew into Their Roles," the week *La Cage aux Folles*, a musical comedy about a gay couple, opened on Broadway. One of the stars of the show was Gene Barry, "best known to millions of television viewers as the debonair star of 'Bat Masterson,' 'Burke's Law,' and 'The Name of the Game.' " As the *Times* put it, he "did have a public image." Barry was concerned about "the possibility of being stigmatized," and he had conferred with his wife and three children before he accepted the role (Bennetts 1983).[35]

It isn't only studios and actors who are frightened of the stigma associated with homosexuality. When the popular television series "thirtysomething" ran an episode that included a scene depicting a gay male couple—seen in bed together after lovemaking, but not shown touching—"several advertisers . . . pulled advertising from [the]

---

34. According to some accounts, as part of a deal to save their box-office star, studio executives traded the gossip magazine the story that another young actor—Rory Calhoun—had been arrested once for auto theft. In the made-for-television movie "biography" of Rock Hudson, his short-lived marriage to Phyllis Gates was portrayed as the only truly romantic love in his life. Right.

35. This habit dies hard. In a 1992 article reporting a pioneering effort by a television soap opera to "examine where homophobic fears come from," we read about Ryan Phillippe, the actor cast as a gay teen on 'One Life to Live': "Phillippe, 17 and straight, was hesitant about accepting the role at first. 'I wasn't sure how my friends and family would handle it. I worried about telling my parents, about hate mail, you know. . . . A lot of people can't separate reality and fantasy" (Gable 1992).

episode, costing the network about $1.5 million in lost sales" (Fabrikant 1989). Although the producer said that "advertiser cancellations won't deter him from continuing [the] story line about homosexual lovers" (Ross 1989), the network deleted the episode from the rerun schedule. The gay characters made brief appearances in the following season: in one episode they kissed on the cheek, and in one episode one of them announces (to his straight boss) that he is HIV positive (Gross 1993). Shortly afterward, "thirtysomething" was canceled.[36]

In the period between the late 1940s and the mid-1960s that is often dubbed the golden age of postwar American drama, it was well known —within theater circles, at least—that some of the most acclaimed playwrights were gay. But although the plays of Tennessee Williams and William Inge often allowed homosexuality and homosexual characters to be visible just at the threshold of undeniability, for the most part these writers abided by the rules of the game and created closet drama. "The closet was an agreement between playwright and audience and between playwright and critical establishment" (Clum 1992: 174). And the critics patrolled the perimeter of that closet, ever vigilant lest the playwrights venture out of the darkness. In 1963, Howard Taubman, then the *New York Times* reviewer, wrote a "primer," as a "public service": "Helpful Hints on How to Scan the Intimations of Symbols of Homosexuality in Our Theater" (ibid.: 175).

By the early 1960s, Williams and Inge had been joined on Broadway by Edward Albee, and the critics, who had applauded Albee while he

---

36. About 18 months after the "thirtysomething" episode, the first lesbian kiss on a network television series occurred on "L.A. Law" when unorthodox C. J. Lamb kissed her divorced colleague Abby Perkins and the gesture was reciprocated. "According to NBC, some advertisers yanked their ads . . . and at least half of viewer calls to the station were negative" (Carlson 1991). Of course, this suggests that the other half were positive. After protests from the Reverend Donald Wildmon's American Family Association, an NBC spokeswoman told the press that "we were not attempting to create a lesbian character. . . . It was much more of an attempt to add texture to C. J.'s character" (Enrico 1991). At the end of the 1991 season the status of the two women's possible relationship remained in the cliffhanger category, but the actress playing Abby left the show over the summer and C. J. was left on her own. The producers continued to toy with her bisexuality and in fall 1991 introduced a former woman lover on one episode. As the spring 1992 season ended, Lamb was beginning a relationship with a man, and in June 1992 the press reported that the actress was leaving the program. Whatever concerns the producers felt were apparently shared by the actors: neither Peter Frechette of "thirtysomething" nor Amanda Donohoe of "L.A. Law" would agree to be interviewed for an article on "the needless fear of playing queer" (Steele 1991: 39).

was off-Broadway, were vicious in defense of the Great White (Heterosexual) Way. Albee's smash hit *Who's Afraid of Virginia Woolf?* provoked a storm of critical outing of the playwright and—despite his denials, to this day—of the fictional characters. On the artistic left, Richard Schechner screeched, "I'm tired of morbidity and sexual perversity which are only there to titillate an impotent and homosexual theater and audience. I'm tired of Albee" (quoted in Clum 1992: 178). Writing in the then new organ of the cultural elite, the *New York Review of Books*, "Philip Roth, the bard of masturbation and Jewish sexual neurosis . . . [cited Albee's] ghastly pansy rhetoric and repartee" (ibid.). The next year, Stanley Kauffmann, newly enshrined as the *New York Times*'s chief drama critic, returned to the topic in a front-page article in the Sunday Arts and Leisure section: "Homosexual Drama and Its Disguises." Kauffmann alerted his readers to the need for discussion of the topic since "three of the most successful American playwrights of the past twenty years are (reputed) homosexuals and because their plays often treat of women and marriage" (Kauffmann 1966). "Kauffmann's column is a classic example of the mixed signals that entrapped American playwrights: a few liberal posturings about society's responsibility for the closet, followed by gross oversimplifications that dismiss the work of the dramatists in question" (Clum 1992: 181).[37]

Things have changed in the years since Taubman, Schechner, Roth, and Kauffmann stood guard outside the theatrical closet, and there is now a flourishing gay theater that makes an occasional successful foray onto Broadway and even wins awards. But the closet police still patrol the nationally televised Tony award ceremonies. The producer of *Torch Song Trilogy*, John Glines, was criticized for thanking his (male) lover in his 1980 acceptance speech, and the composer of the gay-themed musical *Falsettos* agreed to modify the lyrics in two numbers performed on the 1992 awards program, replacing "homosexuals" with "screwy families" and "spikey lesbians" with "spikey families" (Jacobs 1992b).

There is an unshakable conviction on the part of most people in positions of power in the entertainment industry that the American public will not accept openly lesbian and gay performers, and the industry

---

37. Ironically, according to some accounts, the column upset the matriarch of the *New York Times* clan, Iphigene Sulzberger, who was opposed to any mention of homosexuality in the paper, even, apparently, when it was hostile. In any event, "Kauffmann was fired soon thereafter" (Byron 1972: 62).

isn't too crazy about them in backstage roles, either. The consequence of all this is a continuing devotion to the sanctity of the closet that pervades show business in the United States. As Ian McKellen remarked to a gay American journalist, "There's not one [homosexual leading actor] in your country. Not one. It's odd, isn't it? It's the one area of American life where there are no openly gay people" (Stuart 1992: 34). Lesbian and gay actors and others who begin to achieve success and celebrity are quickly taught the rules of the game, if they haven't already demonstrated their discretion.[38]

" 'One of the unwritten laws of gay life,' [writer Armistead] Maupin sighs, 'is where you reach a certain level of fame, you shut up about your homosexuality. You're not told this by straight people, you're told it by other famous homosexuals who are ushering you into the pantheon of the right' " (Warren 1989).

A Bodyguard of Lies

If, as Winston Churchill said, in wartime truth has a bodyguard of lies, then Hollywood's image factory is always at war. Its defensive strategy relies heavily on a fifth column within the ranks of the press: gossip writers. The progeny of Louella Parsons and heirs of Hedda Hopper follow in the footsteps of their infamous ancestors, "two vain and ignorant [columnists who] tyrannized Hollywood" in the 1940s (Friedrich 1986: 92). Long before the 1980s, the component parts of the image-manufacturing complex were firmly in place: on the one side studio publicists, publicity agents, and public relations flacks, and on the other side an array of media writers ranging from free-lance stringers to staffers working for supermarket tabloids, mainstream personality gossip magazines like *People* and *US*, and television programs like "Entertainment Tonight," to syndicated gossip columnists who reach millions of readers through their local newspapers. But despite the occasional adversarial pretense, these two groups really collude in providing the sort of gossip they believe the public is interested in. Gossip may not have the journalistic respectability of "hard" news, but it is an increasingly visible feature of the media landscape. "Even

---

38. Those who merely aspire to media fame often start playing the game even earlier. Gay porn star Rex Chandler, "attempting to 'cross-over' from adult entertainment to a career in mainstream television and movies," told an interviewer for the gay press that "his natural sexual orientation is heterosexual" (Ocamb 1991a), which, if true, is the best testimonial to his acting skills one could ask for.

the venerable *New York Times* has succumbed to the trend and now runs a daily 'Chronicle' column, which rounds up personality news that doesn't fit elsewhere in the paper" (McHugh 1990: 100).

It may be a commonplace of journalism courses that the ultimate standard for news media is honesty—never knowingly to report something that is untrue, even if the "whole" truth may not be reportable for a variety of reasons (such as protecting one's sources)—but when it comes to celebrity gossip, "the standards are different, [said] Jerry Nachman, [then] editor of the *New York Post*, 'that's why I always say gossip pages should come with little warning labels: The rules of regular journalism were not followed in reporting these stories' " (ibid.).

In the case of homosexuality, we begin with a topic that already puts a strain on the rules of journalism. Former *New York Times* columnist Roger Wilkins, the first black writer appointed to the paper's editorial board, said that during his two years as the urban affairs columnist "only three of his columns were killed—and two of them were on gay topics" (Pierson 1982: 28). So it should surprise no one that one of the most common departures from the rules of regular journalism is the collusion of gossip writers and other, more "respectable," journalists in maintaining the security of celebrity closets:

> Hundreds of publicity agents in Hollywood and New York make their living by planting items in entertainment columns about whom celebrities are dating. Many of these items are patently false and intended only to cover up the celebrity's homosexuality. Many newspaper writers and editors know this and cheerfully participate in the deception because the bits help fill their columns. Editors who would never reveal that a public figure was gay have no problem with routinely saying that same person is straight. (Shilts 1990b: 165)

"Celebrity publications are lied to up, down, and sideways," said a longtime editor at *Ladies' Home Journal* and *US* who now works at the tabloid the *Star* (Broeske and Wilson 1990), but this is highly disingenuous and ignores the fact that celebrity writers and publications are willing participants in a process that might be called *inning*.[39] The gossip writers, many of them lesbian or gay, who speculated about

---

39. Inning is not, of course, the sole prerogative of the mass media; we all encounter it first in school, where teachers and textbooks assiduously refrain from revealing the homosexuality of such standard curricular figures as Walt Whitman and Willa Cather, among many, many others.

when Malcolm Forbes would marry Elizabeth Taylor, or when Merv Griffin would marry Eva Gabor, knew what they were doing.[40]

Richard Goldstein has noted that in the 1960s the *New York Times* did not hesitate to reveal that the head of the New York Ku Klux Klan was Jewish (he killed himself after the story was published), but felt no parallel urge to expose the hypocrisy of closeted homosexuals pursuing antigay politics, such as Roy Cohn or Terry Dolan.[41]

Inning also serves to keep openly "gay people in the closet even when they have no desire to be there" (Van Gelder 1990: 53). Armistead Maupin once talked about how the *New York Times* held an op-ed piece he wrote about gay pride month (Maupin 1981) until they could "clear" his reference to fellow gay activist Vito Russo—to protect themselves from a possible libel action for mentioning Russo by name.

Media inning isn't confined to public figures; even anonymous gay people can be denied a significant measure of humanity in the name of discretion. "When a murdered lesbian was found . . . with a picture of her lover and a letter of devotion in her pocket" and "the *Times* reported that the person in the picture was her boyfriend" (Goldstein 1990), they knew what they were doing.

"How often have you seen this photograph: two men, holding hands, shot from behind so their blue-jeaned butts show instead of their faces? This is the 'acceptable' public image of homosexuals. It's easier to hate a cipher" (Beery 1990: 46).[42]

---

40. After Merv Griffin's closet door was blasted open by a highly publicized "palimony" suit filed by an alleged former lover, a group of gossip columnists appearing on "The Joan Rivers Show" in April 1991 all cited this as an example of a "story" they had known but not revealed in their columns. When they were asked what they thought the outcome of the palimony suit would be, one promptly replied, "Eva Gabor will probably finally get an engagement ring."

41. By the time Roy Cohn was dying of an AIDS-related illness in 1986 he had lost most of his political clout after being disbarred and condemned by the appellate court in New York State, and the media were less considerate of his privacy. On CBS's "60 Minutes" Mike Wallace accused him of lying about his illness, and after his death the *New York Times* ran a front-page obituary that reported both the cause of his death and his attempt to conceal it. The lengthy obituary made Cohn's homosexuality clear, although mostly by quoting "snickering suggestions" by his political enemies and pointing out that the lifelong bachelor probably had face lifts and owned an "extensive collection of stuffed animals" (Krebs 1986: 33).

42. At a conference on "Sexuality and Disease: Metaphors, Perceptions and Behavior in the AIDS Era" at the Kinsey Institute (December 1988), openly gay ABC News producer Joseph Lovett described such a "standard" shot kept by his organization for use in stories about gay men.

A Book ahead of Its Time

In 1983 the first full-length critical biography of pianist Vladimir Horowitz was published, setting off a stir in the press "by casually mentioning that the maestro had been actively gay for most of his life" (Bronski 1983). The author of the biography, Glenn Plaskin, was himself an openly gay man who had been determined not to allow this facet of his subject's life to be kept out of the book. "If they try to take out any of the gay stuff," he told the editor of the gay magazine *Christopher Street*, "I'll withdraw the book" (Steele 1983: 37).

Reviewing Plaskin's book in the *Gay Community News*, critic Michael Bronski distinguished between the biography of Horowitz and a recent "spate of biographies that sensationalize, or at any rate use as a selling point, their subject's homosexuality: Charles Laughton, Errol Flynn, Tyrone Power," noting that Plaskin discussed his subject's "personal and sexual habits only in terms of how they relate to his larger life and the career" (Bronski 1983). Most reviewers were not so understanding. The *New York Times* assigned the review to a close friend of Horowitz's who was predictably hostile to the book. The Metropolitan Opera House bookstore refused to carry the work.

The author soon learned that the revelations dominated his book-tour interviews, forcing him to defend his decision to include this material. His responses wavered between noting that the discussion of Horowitz's sexuality "would not fill more than 2 out of over 600 pages"[43] (ibid.) and claiming that the book "is the first one about an artist—a veritable superstar—to address the issue of his homosexuality while he's still living" (Grzesiak 1983). Plaskin said of Horowitz that

> his musicianship was never in question when I was writing the book. But when you're doing a biography, you're dealing with the man himself. I'm constantly asked by prudish interviewers, "Why did you have to talk about his personality?" My answer is that in order to understand someone's career, particularly Horowitz's, you have to understand his life. How else can you explain a great artist's absence from the stage for 22 years? (quoted in Grzesiak 1983)

To the critics who argued that he should not have delved into the personal life of a great artist, Plaskin responded by noting the fre-

---

43. When Plaskin made this point in a radio interview in Boston, the interviewer quickly pointed out that the book was well indexed and any reader could easily find these passages. Michael Bronski noted that this might be "the first time in the history of criticism that a book has been faulted for being indexed too *well!*" (1983).

quency with which heterosexual aspects of artists' lives are discussed by biographers: "Would people have us pretend that Clara and Robert Schumann never met, never affected each other's work? That Alma Mahler had no impact on Gustav Mahler? With Horowitz, I think the better we understand his inner feelings, his torment, the more we can appreciate his approach to music." Horowitz's sexuality is relevant "as another factor that led into his general feelings of depression and anguish" (Steele 1983: 38–39).

In interviews with the gay press, Plaskin went beyond the question of Horowitz's artistry and its possible relationship to his sexuality. "I was thinking this morning about how much people who are in the closet actually promote homophobia," he said to *Christopher Street* editor Tom Steele. " Horowitz feels that if people would just accept his homosexuality, he wouldn't have to hide it, but he doesn't understand that he wouldn't have to hide if he came out. No one really cares anyway" (ibid.: 39).

Going even farther in an interview with the *New York Native*, Plaskin claimed that his outing of Horowitz had a wider significance because "through the book I have been coming out of the closet. Middle America needs to know about us. In every interview I've granted I refer to my gayness so they can print my picture, see that I'm attractive, successful, and proud" (Grzesiak 1983).

The response from the lesbian and gay press was not uniformly positive. Writing in *Gay Community News* in reaction to Michael Bronski's favorable review, Nancy Walker attacked Plaskin for "yanking out" Horowitz and Bronski for praising the book. In a preview of the debate over outing that would appear in the gay press seven years later, Walker articulated many arguments that are still being made:

> Though I have often wished that all gay people would turn blue at the same moment and thereby put an end to our oppression (naive assumption, of course) I do not, never have, and never will believe that it is permissible to force anyone out of a closet—any type of closet. People's secrets are theirs, and the fact that someone is a "public figure" does not make him/her less a human being, nor does it give "private" figures[,] like most of us, the right to probe into their most sensitive areas. . . .
>
> I understand the yearning for an honor roll composed of gays who were, or are, famous. It makes us feel better and maybe it is a selling point we could use in our campaign to win gay rights. But if in the course of our battle for freedom we injure our fellows, we degrade the very cause we claim to espouse. I have put a great deal of my life into the fight for justice for gay people, but if that is not also

a fight for justice and kindness to be meted out *by* gays, what is the
battle for? (Walker 1983)

Despite Plaskin's claim to be pioneering new territory for openly
gay writers and a new honesty in artistic biographies, there is little reason to believe that his book on Horowitz did very much to change the
rules of the publishing game. In praising the book, Michael Bronski
called it

> a wonderfully written, fascinating biography that in attempting a
> simple honesty has managed to ruffle many feathers. It's been more
> than 10 years since Stonewall and more open and honest discussion
> of sexuality . . . but much of the criticism that Plaskin and the book
> received comes from the most regressive thinking and homophobia
> of past decades. . . . *Horowitz*, without doing anything extraordi-
> nary, may be a book ahead of its time. (Bronski 1983)

Confirmed, Eligible, and Lifelong Bachelors

When composer Aaron Copland died in December 1990, at the age of
ninety, the *New York Times* devoted almost a full page to his obituary.
It is standard practice in such lengthy treatments to include extensive
details about the person's private life. But "this country's official
'newspaper of record' disposed of the great man's private life by toss-
ing in, between commas, only three words: 'a lifelong bachelor' "
(Moor 1991: 54).

The obituary was written by senior *Times* critic John Rockwell, who
also wrote a lengthy article on Copland that described him as "the central figure in . . . American composition." Writing in the elaborate
code that is part of the etiquette of inning, Rockwell ventured to suggest that Copland's choice "to veil his private life in discretion" might
have had consequences for his music as well. "One can regret that the
decorous inhibition of his private life infused his public creativity"
(Rockwell 1990).

The press was only slightly more honest in discussing the life of
Leonard Bernstein, who died just a few months before Copland, but
then Bernstein's homosexuality had been written about in at least one
"unauthorized" (and homophobic) biography (Peyser 1987).[44] Similar

---

44. The story that has never been told, or even broached, in the media (or, for that
matter, in more scholarly publications) is the astounding preponderance of gay men
among twentieth-century American composers. Without revealing any secrets, it is possible to assemble a list that includes Samuel Barber, Leonard Bernstein, Marc Blitzstein,

"discretion" was exercised by the press in writing obituaries for long-time civil rights leader Bayard Rustin (whose homosexuality had been used, behind the scenes, in an attempt to derail the 1963 march on Washington, which he coordinated; see Chauncey and Kennedy 1987), writer James Baldwin, and many other prominent figures who died outside the closet. For those who die in the closet even stronger measures may be employed:

> In 1984, after prominent Catholic laymen protested to *Times* corporation Vice Chairman Sidney Gruson, author John Cooney was forced to delete materials about the homosexuality of Francis Cardinal Spellman from *The American Pope*, his biography of the powerful prelate, which was to be published by Times Books. . . . What had been four pages of reporting about Spellman's affairs with priests, altar boys and laymen was reduced to an innocuous paragraph that mentioned "rumors" of the cardinal's sexual exploits. (DeStefano 1986: 46)

Lifelong and confirmed bachelorhood[45] tends to be conferred on gay men after they die; living gay male celebrities are more likely to be described as eligible. Unmarried women are less likely to be described as eligible bachelorettes (except on television's "Dating Game"), although gossip columnists are always willing to ascribe heterosexual romantic involvements to female stars who are fixtures of gay gossip constellations.[46]

A familiar genre of magazine feature writing is the roundup of eligible bachelors. In the mid-1970s, then-closeted lawyer Dan Bradley, while serving as Florida racing commissioner, found himself "featured in a series on Miami's most eligible bachelors" based on an interview in which he was quizzed "on his ideal woman, his marriage and family plans, his romantic history," and so forth. As he later told Taylor Branch, "That was the most difficult interview I ever had; I had to

---

Paul Bowles, John Cage, Aaron Copland, Henry Cowell, David Diamond, Gian Carlo Menotti, Ned Rorem, Stephen Sondheim, and Virgil Thomson (see Moor 1990: 66).

45. Appropriately, the first homosexual organization proposed by Mattachine Society founder Harry Hay was to be called Bachelors for Wallace, and was intended to gather support among gay men in return for "a sexual privacy plank in the [Henry] Wallace platform" during the 1948 presidential campaign (D'Emilio 1983: 60).

46. When Whitney Houston's first prime-time television special, "Whitney Houston: My Life," was aired in May 1992, the star was shown in a "candid interview" format, talking at length about her love for her fiancé, singer Bobby Brown, and singing "He fills me up." The program did nothing to remove her name from the gay gossip lists, but it did suggest to many that perhaps his should be added.

make up the whole thing" (Branch 1982: 43). In February 1991, *Los Angeles* magazine ran one such piece, "Why L.A. Men Don't Commit," profiling ten "eminently eligible bachelors" and asking "just what is holding men back these days?" A reader responded to this question in a letter to the magazine, pointing out that he "recognized one of the eligible bachelors from a gay country-and-western bar" (cited in *San Francisco* magazine, July 1991, 16).

Fashion magazines like *Vogue, Vanity Fair,* and *GQ* have long operated on a double standard in writing celebrity stories. Kevin Sessums, a gay writer-editor for *Vanity Fair,* says a heterosexual star's boyfriend/girlfriend, husband/wife, and affairs are all appropriate subjects for the magazine's profiles. "But, if someone is gay or has had gay affairs, then that's something I'm supposed to remove from the fabric of the story. This has become a personal problem for me and one that I'm currently giving a lot of thought" (Yarbrough 1992a: 35). The fashion magazines' "shelter" counterparts *House and Garden* (now *HG*) and *Architectural Digest* "have for years written stories about gay decorators and gay architects, about houses and apartments inhabited by gays or lesbians alone or in couples, and about the interior design community as a whole—all the while omitting any references to homosexuality" (ibid: 37).

For some prominent bachelors, a brief but highly visible relationship with a showbiz celebrity can attach to their name a media "tag" that is forever associated with them. The 1992 presidential campaign was notable in its early stages for the presence of two unmarried candidates—former California governor Jerry Brown and Nebraska Senator Bob Kerrey—but neither man seemed hampered by the lack of a potential first lady. As it happens, Jerry Brown had been "involved" many years earlier in a well-publicized relationship with popular singer Linda Ronstadt (herself never married), and when the press wrote about him they would often reinstate the heterosexual image of the governor who vacationed in Africa with a rock star.[47] Much the same service was provided by Bob Kerrey's brief relationship with movie star Debra Winger, whom he met when he was governor of

---

47. A lengthy article in the *Washington Post* during the 1992 primary season focused on Brown's social life. Although the article noted his famous "linkage" with Linda Ronstadt, it mostly dwelt on his elusiveness and on his current mysterious relationship with an equally elusive woman, San Francisco lawyer Ann Gust. The article also quoted San Francisco Supervisor Angela Alioto: "Jerry and I go to dinner all the time. . . . I don't think of Jerry as dating one specific person. He's so driven and everything—politically speaking—it's not been apparent to anyone that he's dating one person" (Hall 1992: D4).

Nebraska and she was filming in the state. Reporters seemed never to tire of reminding us that the movie star stayed in the governor's mansion. An article in *USA Today* in September 1991 remarking on the presence of so many unmarried presidential hopefuls (at that time the list included divorced Virginia Governor Douglas Wilder) ran a photograph of Kerrey holding hands with Winger in 1984 and captioned a picture of Brown "Ex-Governor Dated Singer Linda Ronstadt" (L. Phillips 1991).

With the advent of AIDS it became more difficult to maintain the practice of inning, as more and more prominent men fell ill and died, but the media cooperated in turning celebrity coffins into permanent closets. Despite the unprecedented publicity surrounding Rock Hudson's involuntary coming out as the world's most famous person with AIDS, other famous bachelors preferred to die of other causes. Liberace, fashion designers Perry Ellis and Halston, Roy Cohn and Terry Dolan—these men are only the tip of an iceberg safely submerged by obituary policies. Analysis of obituaries in *Variety* for the years 1980 (pre-AIDS), 1984, and 1986 revealed a pattern of coding "to conceal the actual stigmatizing cause of death and stigmatizing life style" (Nardi 1990: 167).

> Furthermore, it is customary for many newspapers (and a policy of *Variety*), not to report any male lovers as survivors. When they are mentioned, they are typically referred to in the concealing language of "long-time companion." *Variety* does not even use this language; not a single case was found of any hint of a surviving male lover. Not only, then, is the stigma removed from the cause of death, but so is the stigma of an alternative gay life-style. (Nardi 1990)

In 1986, when AIDS had claimed the lives of more than eleven thousand Americans, the *Columbia Journalism Review* noted that the *New York Times* had cited AIDS as a cause of death in only a handful of obits; similar patterns were found in the *Miami Herald*, the *Los Angeles Times*, and most other large and small newspapers (Jetter 1986). The lone exception at that time was the *San Francisco Chronicle*, whose openly gay reporter Randy Shilts noted, "We had been running all these stories trying to remove the stigma from AIDS, and I think we all saw that not printing it in obituaries would utterly contradict our policy as a news organization" (ibid.: 15).

As with the familiar profiles of "eligible bachelors," gay readers have become astute decoders of obituaries. They look for the causes of young, unmarried men's deaths—pneumonia, lymphoma, and other opportunistic diseases associated with AIDS. "For the cognoscenti, there are other tip-offs. Certain funeral homes, for example, are known for accepting AIDS victims" (ibid.: 16). Sometimes the attributed cause of death is bizarre, as when the noted travel writer Bruce Chatwin told the press he was suffering from an obscure Chinese bone disease presumably acquired in a remote part of the globe. After his death at age forty-eight it was revealed that he had had AIDS (French 1989).

Part of the reason for this posthumous euphemizing lies in the routines of newspaper obituary preparation. Most often it is the families of AIDS victims who try to hide the true cause of death. In writing an obituary, "reporters must call the deceased person's family to verify the cause of the death. Often forced to confront grieving parents, reporters say they usually take explanations at face value, even if their instincts tell them they are not getting the truth" (Jetter 1986: 15). When Tommy Lasorda, Jr., a thirty-three-year-old gay artist who was the son of Los Angeles Dodgers manager Tommy Lasorda, died of an AIDS-related illness in 1991, the media reported that he died of pneumonia and severe dehydration, and the sports section of the *Los Angeles Times* noted that "the family asked that in lieu of flowers donations be sent to the National Baseball Players Association" (Ocamb 1991c). When the Reverend David McGowan, age forty, "familiar to TV viewers as the former host of the weekly Roman Catholic television show 'Reel to Reel,' " died at his family's home in suburban Philadelphia, family members said "his heart gave out after a long illness" (Cipriano 1991). AIDS-astute readers probably had other ideas.

Republican Congressman Stewart McKinney died of AIDS complications in 1987 at age fifty-six, leaving a widow as well as a gay lover with whom he shared a Washington house. The lover, Arnold Denson, was "asked to keep his relationship with the congressman secret, [and] in exchange for his silence, [the family] would not contest McKinney's bequest to him" (Harding 1989: 13). McKinney's Washington office issued a statement claiming the congressman had contracted HIV from a blood transfusion, and, despite McKinney's record of outspoken support for AIDS and gay rights issues, his staff and family denied that he had been gay. Despite their promise, McKinney's family challenged the late congressman's bequest to his lover, and the dispute became public when it ended up in a Connecticut probate court.

The 1988 death of Max Robinson, who in 1978 became the first black news anchor on network television, occasioned a flurry of defensive maneuvering. Robinson himself had kept his AIDS-related illness a secret, but he was later reported to have wanted his death to "emphasize the need for AIDS awareness among black people." However, as Phillip Harper shows, the palpable desire on the part of Robinson's friends to distance their late friend from any suspicion of homosexuality "work[ed] to the detriment of [their] attempts to make factual statements about the nature of HIV transmission" (Harper 1991: 80). A similar pattern of homophobic distancing was readily discernible in the furor following Magic Johnson's disclosure that he was HIV positive in fall 1991.

When television actor Robert Reed died in May 1992, his family was unable to keep the secret for long that AIDS contributed to the death of the dad of the Brady Bunch, or to suppress the related fact of his homosexuality. The changes that had begun to take place in media practice over the decade of the AIDS epidemic can best be seen in the response of a senior—and openly gay!—*New York Times* editor:

> "It's important that people know that someone like this died of AIDS," said Jeffrey Schmaltz, assistant national editor at the *New York Times*, who himself has AIDS. Schmaltz, who suspected Reed had died of AIDS, said he was angry when he saw that his own newspaper's obituary writer had accepted the family's story apparently without question. "An obituary is a news article; it's not an article written to please the survivors; it's not written for any other reason than to tell the truth." (Broder 1992)

It is not only famous people and AIDS victims who are buried in the closet, even against their wishes. Lindsay Van Gelder reports an instance of inning after the 1989 Bay Area earthquake when photos of a grieving

> survivor pounding the earth were so riveting . . . that they were sent around the world . . . but nowhere was there a mention that the body under the building was anyone more intimate than a "friend." I later learned that the woman, a long-time lesbian activist, had been widely interviewed and completely open about the nature of their relationship; indeed, she had insisted that it should be acknowledged. Most reporters refused. (1990: 53)

When Rock Hudson died, many gay activists thought that the seriousness of the AIDS crisis might shock show business gays into coming out and joining in efforts to force the government to pursue prevention and cure of the disease. But although Hudson inadvertently succeeded in changing the pattern of media inattention to AIDS, his tumble from the closet did not precipitate a mass exodus. Quite the contrary, as Armistead Maupin noted: "there seems to have been a rash of Hollywood marriages. That's what 'having to get married' means today. Tom Selleck, Jamie Lee Curtis, and other stars got married around that time, just as Rock Hudson got married in the 1950s and Cary Grant got married in the '30s, '40s, '60s, and '80s" (Warren 1989).

The gossip writers have happily joined in, turning out reams of copy about the celebrities' newfound joys in marriage and parenthood. Suddenly, it turns out, some lifelong bachelors may no longer be quite so confirmed, or so eligible. Designer Calvin Klein's marriage occasioned many articles, including one by Glenn Plaskin in the *New York Daily News* that outer-in-chief Michelangelo Signorile wrote about in *OutWeek*. Plaskin's piece "is all about *transformations*," which is what supposedly happened to Klein since marrying. But we're never told "what Klein was supposedly transformed *from*":

> "The 47-year-old designer used to like modern furniture, bachelorhood, vodka, late nights and sexually provocative jeans, and perfume ads. No longer," writes Plaskin, going on to give us this very coded line: "Commitment, Klein has learned, is the cure-all for a formerly party-prone bachelor." (Signorile 1990d)

Later in the column, Signorile quotes Plaskin as saying to him, "I don't think [a person's sex life] is anyone's business. I don't think we should be discussing sex," and responds, "We shouldn't be discussing sex? But you just wrote an entire column about Calvin Klein's *relationship* with this woman and how wonderful it is. Why, Glenn, does a discussion of someone's heterosexual involvement—and marriage—not constitute 'talking about sex' but discussion of a homosexual relationship does?"[48]

Young, Queer, and Loud

The AIDS Coalition to Unleash Power—ACT UP—came into being in March 1987 and quickly injected a new burst of militant energy into the AIDS and gay movements. ACT UP combined streetwise activists and newly radicalized middle-class professionals whose complacency had

---

48. Yes, dear reader, this is the very same Glenn Plaskin whose 1983 biography of Vladimir Horowitz caused such a stir. In 1990 Plaskin, now a columnist for the *New York Daily News*, seemed to take a rather different position on the relevance of sexuality to an understanding of a person's life. In contrast to his self-presentation as an openly gay writer in 1983, he responded thus to a query from Signorile: "Oh, I'm such a nonperson, so who cares?"

been destroyed by the realization that when they fell ill with AIDS-related diseases, they were no longer "us" but had joined the ranks of the marginalized "them." It was a group of men and women, largely lesbian and gay, who believed in doing their homework and in using outrageous media-attracting tactics that dramatized the issues of AIDS research, treatment, and health care.

The journalists who broke the code and changed the rules are members of the ACT UP generation, a generation that has lived its entire life in the age of mass media gossip and infotainment. From *People* magazine to Liz Smith, from Johnny and Jay and Arsenio to Phil and Oprah and Joan and Sally Jessy and Geraldo and Larry, from Robin Leach to Kitty Kelley, from the *National Enquirer* and the *Globe* to the *Philadelphia Inquirer* and the *Boston Globe*, we have become a society drenched in gossip and "news" about celebrities of all sorts. Whether it's the fifteen minutes of fame haphazardly awarded to random individuals (remember Jessica McClure?) or the perennial allure of Liz Taylor or Jackie O on the cover of a magazine, when the media spotlight hits someone, we expect to know the details of his or her private life. We now take for granted that, in prescient words written a century ago, "what is whispered in the closet shall be proclaimed from the housetops" (Warren and Brandeis 1890).

In such a climate, it should not surprise us that some gay journalists became increasingly impatient with the code of *omerta* that bound the media in a conspiracy of silence and deception about the real lives of lesbian and gay celebrities. As we have seen, the media not only draw the line of discretion much farther from home when they are dealing with gay people; they actively engage in obfuscation and collude in outright lies. Outing was adopted as a tactic in opposition to the tacit agreement by which gay private lives were granted an exemption from the public's "right to know," thus protecting the closets of the rich and famous and leaving unchallenged the distaste of the media—and the public—for facing the reality of lesbian and gay existence.

Michelangelo Signorile is a member of this generation who came of age after the explosion of gay liberation—he was born in 1960—but who scarcely knew the gay world in its brief "golden age" between Stonewall and AIDS. Signorile graduated from the Newhouse School of Public Communication at Syracuse University, where he studied journalism, and returned to New York City, where he landed a job with a Broadway press agent and quickly learned the difference between the "rules" of journalism and the practice of gossip writing, which he describes thus:

"I was a column planter. How it works is you'd give gossip columnists a list of items several times a week. You give them items about
your client and items that are called frees, juicy gossip items. They
would use the juicy items and they'd have to pay us off with the
planted items. Some of my anger about the media came from seeing
these people. To me it was so corrupted." (Kasindorf 1990: 88)

After two years as a "planter" Signorile became a free-lance writer
and gossip columnist for *Nightlife* magazine. Around this time he became involved with ACT UP and quickly became politically engaged
in AIDS activism. In June 1989, when phone-sex entrepreneur Kendall
Morrison and musician Gabriel Rotello began *OutWeek*, a lesbian and
gay weekly news magazine, they signed Signorile as features editor
and columnist. His disillusionment with the ethics of gossip journalists, fueled by his newly militant gay politics and AIDS activism,
turned to anger, which he unleashed in his "Gossip Watch" column.
The rest is gossip history:

"I have extremely mixed feelings about what Michael's doing," says
Harvey Fierstein, the actor and playwright, "but I love his anger.
There are very few writers who can make you enjoy their anger the
way he can. When *OutWeek* arrives in the mailbox, my lover and I
tear the magazine open to that page before we get to the house and
skim it to see what names are in there." (ibid.: 86)[49]

The names that appeared in Signorile's columns were likely to be
those of the targets of his ire; for this was not the usual gossipy listing
of who had been seen where and with whom. This was a weekly dis-
section of New York's and Hollywood's celebrity and gossip elite, with
a particular focus on the media, who were attacked for failing to pay
enough attention to AIDS, for pretending that lesbian and gay celebrities are heterosexual, and for flattering politicians such as Presidents
Reagan and Bush and New York City Mayor Ed Koch, "who are keeping us down at best, murdering us at worst" (ibid.).

All of these enemies came together in the context of New York society's ritual of the charity ball, where celebrities would be seen—and

---

49. The following year, Fierstein's feelings seemed less mixed when he spoke to *People* magazine: "Outing is something I would never do. There is no situation that I have
ever been in where it was necessary. I have a problem with the outing of [certain celebri-
ties]. I think it would be wonderful if [they] came out and admitted it—*if* they were
gay—because it would help so many kids feel that they weren't bizarre. But what good
does it do *anyone* to watch someone kicking and screaming that they're straight?" (Castro 1991).

their presence duly reported in the gossip columns—partying amid fashionable luxury while raising money for various groups of unfortunates. The grass-roots organizations that sprang up within the gay community in response to the AIDS crisis soon found themselves overwhelmed by the demand for their services, and in the absence of adequate public funding were forced to turn to the private charity circuit and cultivate the generosity of the rich and famous. Signorile aimed some of his nastiest barbs at socialite Pat Buckley, a charity-ball fixture whose husband, William F. Buckley, Jr., is a notorious homophobe who suggested in a famous column that men who test HIV positive should be tattooed on the buttocks. But Signorile's most frequent targets were the gossip writers who reported on the doings of the elite, flattering their egos and, in many cases, reporting on their nonexistent heterosexual romances. From the beginning, Signorile attacked gossip columnists—James Revson of *Newsday*, Billy Norwich of the *Daily News*, and especially the widely syndicated Liz Smith—for playing this game.

This wasn't the first time Liz Smith had tangled with the gay press over her penchant for inning, for "keeping the lid on, covering for her friends, conveniently reporting heterosexual 'dates' to help mask the truth" (Beery 1990). She was taken to task by *Advocate* film columnist Steve Beery in 1984 after she "expressed disgust at Harvey Fierstein for thanking his lover on the Tony Awards, all the while continuing to report such unlikely romantic pairings as Tommy Tune and Twiggy, and Richard Chamberlain and Linda Evans." Smith wrote:

> Richard Chamberlain and Linda Evans *do* go out together. I have no idea what they do or don't do in their private moments. I don't believe I ever said they were madly physically in love because I don't know. Do you? . . . Don't these people (even or especially the gay ones) have the right to change their minds, experiment, practice bisexuality or fake it? . . . I like to let my intelligent readers draw their own conclusions about the depth, sincerity and veracity of public liaisons. (ibid.)

While this would be a somewhat astonishing statement for a journalist to make, it is not so surprising coming from a gossip columnist, especially one who wrote that she had "once dreamily doodled 'Mrs. Rock Hudson' in the margins of her notepad" and who took offense when this was described as high camp. Smith's insistence that she hadn't known that Rock Hudson was gay—"he never said anything about it to me or to anyone else I knew" (ibid.)—shows that her penchant for claiming to be blind rather than dishonest did not begin with her later statement that she never "saw any evidence" of Malcolm Forbes's homosexuality and that "in fact, it never occurred to me." Liz Smith obviously preferred to impugn her own journalistic skills rather than admit to having engaged in one of the most common forms of journalistic deception.

But the ire directed at Liz Smith by Beery and Signorile was fueled as well by the simple fact that they were well aware that Liz Smith's inning began at home. Liz Smith, along with other gossip writers like Rex Reed, Billy Norwich, and *Newsday* columnist James Revson, as well as being purveyors of misleading and dishonest gossip, were themselves appropriate targets for outing (Revson died of an AIDS-related illness in July 1991). Steve Beery recalled an earlier occasion, in 1981, when he transcribed a taped interview with Liz Smith for *Interview* magazine, and her roommate, archaeologist Iris Love, could be heard making comments in the background: Smith "trusted us to play by the same rules she applies to her own reporting" and discreetly edit Love out, "to make it appear as though Liz lived there alone. She was right," Beery wrote (ibid.).

When Revson wrote in his column that outing was "truly frightening and offensive," Signorile replied, "You see, homosexuality seems to be the only area in which journalism in New York is mandated to pursue lies and cover-ups rather than the truth. If you write about a closeted gay man's woman friend as his 'lover,' that is applauded. If you print the truth you are deemed 'frightening and offensive' " (1990b).

The Code Cracks

The Berlin Wall wasn't the only barrier that fell in 1989. In the August 7 issue of *OutWeek*, on the page facing Signorile's "Gossip Watch" column, there appeared in a box entitled "Peek-A-Boo" sixty-six names listed without comment, but none was necessary for readers to get the point, since many of the people named were already familiar fixtures of gay gossip. A follow-up list of thirty-two names appeared a few weeks later. Signorile acknowledges that the "Peek-A-Boo" list included many names whose presence resulted more from wishful thinking than from evidence. Once outing began to be taken seriously it was necessary to develop more rigorous criteria: "We realized that now that it was something that had become a political tool, that this wasn't the way to do it. . . . So we stopped doing it. Now, if I put people in a box again, I'd make sure I was 100 percent sure," Signorile said (Kasindorf 1990: 92).

Around the same time, Armistead Maupin began spicing up book-tour interviews with the gay press by naming names and challenging the reporters and editors to print them:

"If the gay press has any function at all," Maupin believes, "it's to tweak the conscience of famous people who are in the closet; and certainly we shouldn't continue to lionize those among us who are making a success of themselves in the mainstream while remaining so determinedly in the closet . . . even if they are doing all the benefits and everything. . . . I'm taking the hard line on it and saying homophobia is homophobia." (Warren 1989)

Maupin's disclosures were printed in many gay papers and magazines, but the mainstream press ignored this novelty, just as it had earlier declined to specify precisely what ACT UP demonstrators were saying about Illinois Governor James Thompson (Wockner 1990). Within a few months, however, the mainstream media had joined the gay press in playing the game while simultaneously debating the rules. An Ethics section article in *Time* by media critic William Henry described the new developments without naming any names (Governor Thompson became "an outing victim [who] had endorsed legislation allowing hospitals to test patients for AIDS without their consent") and posed the ethical conflict between the right to privacy and the importance of coming out. Henry came down against outing: "it claims an unjustifiable right to sacrifice the lives of others" (Henry 1990).

In February 1990 Malcolm Forbes died, and the outing season was soon to be in full swing. After what an editor described as "much agonizing," *USA Today* published an article about an upcoming biography by Chris Winans (1990) that would reveal Forbes's secret:

"This was a book by a reputable journalist, and we found out that new chapters were hastily being added that would allegedly discuss Forbes' homosexual life," [the editor] says. "We felt that Forbes was a public figure whose private life in many ways was part of his persona—which he flaunted—and we sort of went down a whole list of why we felt this had news value." (Mills 1990)

USA Today's decision may also have been influenced by knowledge that *OutWeek* was about to break the story. In fact, it was Winans's questioning of Signorile about Forbes's gay life that planted the seed for the *OutWeek* story, a seed that germinated rapidly once Forbes died. The March 18, 1990, cover of *OutWeek* showed a photo of Malcolm Forbes on his motorcycle, with the bold headline "The Secret

Gay Life of Malcolm Forbes." The article begins with Forbes's funeral, noting the presence among the mourners of many prominent homophobes—Richard Nixon, William F. Buckley, Al Neuharth—and asks whether they knew that they "were coming to pay homage to someone who embodied what they ultimately detested" (Signorile 1990a). Signorile reported a pattern of sexual behavior that was attested to by many young men, described here by a man Signorile called Dan:

> "He really went after the waiters. I mean he did it a lot—as much as he possibly could. If he liked them he'd ask them to show up the next time early—at the townhouse. He'd ask them to go in the Jacuzzi with him. Then, of course, they'd have sex. He'd give them a 100-dollar bill when he finished—they used to love to talk about it. They got the money even if they refused the sex." (ibid.)

This isn't the sort of story that people keep to themselves, and Signorile makes clear that "people talked and, in quite a few segments of the gay male community at least, it seemed that *everyone* knew *someone* who'd done it with Malcolm Forbes. He was also quite showy, liking to ride around with his 'dates' on his motorcycle" (ibid.). Among those who were aware of these stories were New York's gossip columnists, the very writers who were "major perpetrators of the false Forbes/Taylor romance, . . . trying to convince readers that they were a hot item" (ibid.).[50] As Signorile prepared his story, he found these "columnists, writers and editors . . . quite upset" and hostile to the possibility of disclosure: " 'Why dig up all this stuff?' angrily asked a one-time columnist who'd enjoyed a friendship with Forbes over the years. 'I mean, what does it matter now?' "

Signorile concluded his article with a defense of outing Forbes. First, he noted that "all too often history is distorted" and said the fact that one of the most influential men in America was gay should be recorded. Second, "it sends a clear message to the public at large that we are everywhere." The third reason Signorile gave was that this story illuminated a choice made by many gay people. In researching the story, Signorile tried to interview a gay man who had been close to Forbes and his family, someone who could have shed light on "the real inner workings of Forbes' mind"

---

50. Signorile had implicitly outed Forbes several times in columns that referred to his penchant for riding his motorcycle with "young, hot, hunky cyclemate(s)" and to his "dating" Elizabeth Taylor (August 21, 1989).

but, after considerable thought, he decided not to speak to me. Currently living a closeted existence with regard to his own family and business, he said, "My choice in speaking to you is between myself and the greater gay community. And—at this moment—I have to go with myself." (ibid.)[51]

Although several papers outside New York picked up the Forbes story, the New York press avoided it until reports from other places made it difficult to ignore (Signorile added to the discomfort of the New York press by writing an article for the *Village Voice* on "Gaystyles of the Rich and Famous: How I Brought Out Malcolm Forbes and the Media Flinched"). The stories that began to appear all carried headlines that focused on the issue of conflict between privacy and the tactics of outing: "Uproar over Gays Booting Others Out of the Closet" (Tuller, *San Francisco Chronicle*, March 12), "Whose Sex Secret Is It?" (Krier, *Los Angeles Times*, March 22), "Privacy vs. the Pursuit of Gay Rights" (Johnson, *New York Times*, March 27), " 'Outing': An Unexpected Assault on Sexual Privacy" (Gelman, *Newsweek*, April 30), "Gays Divided on Tactic of Forcing Others Out of the Closet" (Longcope, *Boston Globe*, May 3), and even the London *Sunday Times*: "Closet Gays Fear Terrorism by a Militant Tendency" (Appleyard, May 6).[52]

The next round of mainstream newspaper analyses also focused on the dilemma outing posed for the media. The *Sunday Oregonian* accompanied its thoughtful article on outing, "Controversial Tactic to Expose Alleged Closet Homosexuals Just One Example of New Militancy Splitting AIDS Lobby," with a sidebar, "Practice Puts Press on Spot" (Ota 1990), quoting the editor's determination to make decisions about whether to publish allegations of homosexuality on a case-by-case basis. The *Washington Post* devoted a lengthy feature in July almost en-

---

51. Note that Signorile did not out this person, which can be taken as evidence of the restraint used by outers. It can also be seen as the necessary journalistic rule of protecting one's sources; Signorile's armory is stocked with weapons provided by gay people who inhabit many backstage areas (see his column of December 17, 1989).

52. In their eagerness to defend the privacy of those named by outers, some mainstream writers exposed their own bias and confusion, as when *Boston Globe* columnist Mike Barnicle, after naming Richard Chamberlin, Malcolm Forbes, John Travolta, David Bowie, and Mick Jagger as targets of outing while criticizing the tactic, goes on to say, "If you're a guy who wants to dress like Kate Smith or Crocodile Dundee and you hop into bed with another available and willing man, well, good luck to you and the Red Sox. That's your business. *Just don't invade my privacy* by marching down Boylston Street or appearing on one of those dreadful TV talk shows to discuss what goes on within the walls of your own home" (Barnicle 1990, emphasis added).

tirely to the debate within the mainstream media, although it quoted gay editor Don Michaels and National Gay and Lesbian Task Force director Urvashi Vaid, both of whom opposed outing, and Michelangelo Signorile and Gabriel Rotello, who favored it. The *Washington Post*, while noting that names had been named "in a number of West Coast newspapers and several Knight-Ridder newspapers, including the *Miami Herald* and the *Philadelphia Inquirer*, and aired on National Public Radio," cited antidisclosure policies of the *San Francisco Chronicle*, the *New York Times*, and the *Post* itself (Randolph 1990).

But the papers were not always consistent in their unwillingness to name any names. The *San Francisco Chronicle*, which editorialized against outing the day after running an article on the subject, cited not only Forbes and deceased California publisher C. K. McClatchy as outing victims (it was a newspaper, not gay activists, that revealed that McClatchy had had AIDS, after he died of a heart attack), but also named living outing targets Ed Koch, Calvin Klein, and Cher's daughter, Chastity Bono (who had been the subject of front-page stories in the tabloids). *Chronicle* city editor Dan Rosenheim did not see a contradiction between the paper's policy not to out people and the printing of these names: "It was our feeling that the information had been distributed sufficiently widely that it had become part of the general public awareness" (quoted in Randolph 1990: C4). The *Los Angeles Times*, which also editorialized against outing, named only dead people: Forbes, Rock Hudson, Liberace, Roy Cohn, Terry Dolan, Perry Ellis, and Oliver Sipple. *Newsweek* limited itself to Forbes (reproducing the *OutWeek* cover photo and headline) and Liz Smith, a "favorite target" of the outers, who is quoted as saying, "I may be a gossip columnist, but I do respect the right of people not to tell me 'everything,' and I reserve the same right for myself." The *New York Times* would refer only to "an Illinois politician" and "a famous businessman who had recently died." *Times* spokesman William Adler took a hard line, saying that the paper would not print "hearsay" even if the subject was no longer living: "The thinking at the *Times* is that in most cases an individual's private sex life should not be the subject of coverage by the newspaper unless the person wishes it to be so. That perspective extends through their lifetime and even after their death" (quoted in Randolph 1990: C4).[53]

---

53. While the *New York Times* may have been far-reaching in its respect for posthumous privacy (although the later comments of assistant senior editor Jeffrey Schmaltz suggest an evolution in their policy), *US* magazine revealed startling ignorance of

The *New York Times*'s reluctance to name gay names even when the person in question is dead was tellingly contrasted with their front-page article detailing many of Kitty Kelley's juiciest claims about Nancy Reagan, even while noting that these claims might "prove devastating for the former president and his wife" (Dowd 1991). Not surprisingly, while the article mentions stories of premarital promiscuity and pregnancy, adultery and drug use, the allegation of a possibly lesbian relationship in college is discreetly omitted. Equally revealing of a double standard was the *Times*'s printing of the name and many personal details about the woman who accused a Kennedy of rape; this "outing" of a private person caused an intense debate within the *Times* itself (Carmody 1991).

The *Philadelphia Inquirer* ran its feature entry on the topic in late June, discussing in detail the outing of Forbes and Senator Mark Hatfield and mentioning John Travolta and Richard Chamberlain as targets of tabloid outing. Mark Matza wrote that:

> In the past three months alone, the targets have included: two governors, one lieutenant governor, seven members of Congress, a recording industry mega-mogul, a renowned athlete, a school superintendent from a West Coast city, a married American fashion designer, two male actors who play "straight" love interests on television and in the movies, the female co-star of a network series, the daughter of a female pop singer, and four Philadelphia TV-news personalities. (Matza 1990)

When Washington activists Michael Petrelis and Carl Goodman held a press conference in May on the Capitol steps and read the names of "twelve men and women in politics and music who . . . are secretly gay," the press showed up but "the people . . . named denied through a spokesman being homosexual, declined comment or could not be reached because an aide refused to ask. No major news organization published or broadcast their names" (Matza 1990). Writing about the press conference, the Capitol Hill newspaper *Roll Call* noted that the list included "three Senators, five House members, two governors, one official of a Northeastern city, and, inexplicably, one leading figure in the entertainment industry." *Roll Call*'s "Press Gallery" columnists posed the hypothetical question of whether the press should report that a member of Congress with an *antigay* voting record

---

elementary libel law by noting that, "surprisingly, the Forbes story ran without legal clearance" (Lazar 1990: 42). Someone should tell them that you cannot libel the dead.

was gay if evidence for this claim was provided. Their answer, citing a spokesman for the gay lobby Human Rights Campaign Fund and the publisher of Washington's gay paper, the *Blade*, was "a resounding no," although they might report the fact that someone else had accused such a person of "being a homosexual hypocrite" (Simpson and Winneker 1990).

The closest I have come to finding a defense of outing in the mainstream press is a 1990 column in the *Chicago Tribune* by Clarence Page, who conceded that "on matters of great concern to the public, 'outing' may have its place. Everyone is entitled to privacy in those matters that do not affect anyone else. But powerful moral arbiters like Terry Dolan who preach one thing by day and practice another by night deserve to be exposed." Clearly, however, this defense is limited to the least controversial cases of hypocritical public figures and politicians.

The mass media's other leading forums for social issues didn't take long in fastening onto the topic of outing. In May 1990, "L.A. Law" (NBC) ran an episode featuring the outing of a heroic policeman (clearly modeled on Oliver Sipple) by a gay activist editor; the policeman sues but loses in court on First Amendment grounds. In January 1991, "Gabriel's Fire" (ABC) ran a story that was both unconvincing and homophobic: a divorced pro football quarterback is falsely outed by a gay man who is a member of (the fictional) Outers of America. While the football player, who professes to "have nothing against homosexuals," wins a lawsuit against the outer, the program shows his son choosing to live with his mother, his hopes for endorsements dashed, and his camp for underprivileged children destroyed.

Also quick to condemn outing while milking it for all it was worth were the national and local television talk shows. Many ran programs on which "outers" were invited to "perform" while being criticized for doing it (some of these shows added new names to the list of outed celebrities; the tabloids followed up with details). Gay journalist Michael Bronski watched

> an episode of Joan Rivers' morning talk show that focussed on gossip columnists: all of the dirt was being dragged out—the Trumps, the Helmsleys, Bess Meyerson and most everyone in Hollywood. Suddenly Joan got very angry and said, "But sometimes people go too far. That New York paper is saying those terrible things about a certain man who just died, I won't even say his name, and it just makes me sick." This from a woman who built her stand-up comedy and talk show career recycling gossip and quizzing people about their personal lives. Of course, Joan's message is clear and familiar:

being gay is bad, it is a dirty secret, and it should be kept quiet. (Bronski 1990)[54]

The alternative and gay press joined the debate over outing, but in these cases the articles were written by openly gay people who presented the issues in a longer historical context and with a more complex awareness of the arguments on both sides.[55] In addition to articles, these papers carried letters to the editor that contributed to the ongoing debate. In the letters column of the *Village Voice*, two leading gay writers responded to some of the central arguments of the outing controversy. Lesbian novelist Sarah Schulman, while admitting her ambivalence over the morality of outing, objected to the characterization of the tactic as an invasion of privacy: "Most gay people stay in the closet—i.e., dishonor their relationships—because to do so is a prerequisite for employment. Having to hide the way you live because of fear of punishment isn't a 'right,' nor is it 'privacy.' Being in the closet is not an objective, neutral, or value-free condition. It is maintained by force, not choice" (Schulman 1990).

In the same issue, longtime gay activist and writer Vito Russo noted that to say someone is gay is to talk "about *sexual orientation*, not their sexual activity." But, most critically, he pointed out that "what Signorile is saying that if being gay is *not* disgusting, is *not* awful, then why can't we talk about it? After all, it's not an insult to call someone gay. Is it?" (Russo 1990).

On June 4, Boston gay activist Warren Blumenfeld, speaking on a local television talk show, said, "There is someone running for governor right here in Massachusetts—[Lieutenant Governor] Evelyn Murphy—who the entire gay community knows is gay [and who] will not come out" (Bull 1990). There was an immediate furor when this was picked up by the *Boston Herald*, and Blumenfeld came under attack from local gay activists who supported Murphy as someone who "has an excellent record on gay and lesbian issues." On the other side were those, like Blumenfeld, who cited her opposition to condom distribution in schools and to needle-exchange programs, both important measures to prevent HIV infection. Shortly afterward Blumenfeld apologized for the outing, but this didn't settle the matter. As one per-

---

54. Joan Rivers seems to have recovered from her *OutWeek*-induced illness; when I tuned in to her show in February 1991 I heard her throw in several Richard Chamberlain "jokes" along with several other instances of what might be called outing humor.

55. For example, Stuart Byron in the *Advocate*, Richard Goldstein in the *Village Voice*, Michael Bronski in *Gay Community News*, and seven writers in a forum in *OutWeek*.

son put it, he "managed to alienate half of the community by outing [Murphy] and the other half by apologizing for it." Blumenfeld's public statement referred to poor judgment and a loss of compassion. "Evelyn Murphy has integrity and dignity and is a friend to the lesbian and gay community," he concluded. "I am deeply sorry for hurting a friend." But his fellow outer, Derek Link, was unrepentant, insisting that sexual identity is a relevant political issue and saying:

> "The important thing is not whether Murphy is a dyke but that she be open about her identity. When she . . . says that sexuality is a private issue, she undercuts the entire basis of the gay move-ment. . . . Gays say, 'Why Murphy?' because she is not a pig. But if the gay community is going to be supporting candidates, we have to demand that they acknowledge their sexuality. . . . I'm tired of the 'nudge, nudge, wink, wink' thing of the back rooms." (ibid.)

The Murphy episode highlights the central issue of the debate over outing as it occurred in the various press venues: what does the right to privacy mean, and is it the bedrock upon which the lesbian and gay movement is, or should be, built? When the mainstream media attended to lesbian and gay responses to outing, they presented the views of leaders of national lesbian and gay organizations, who criticized outing as a violation of privacy rights, although acknowledging its appropriateness in the extreme case, "where a gay politician is openly pursuing an anti-gay agenda and building a career on that kind of dishonesty," as Nan Hunter, then director of the Lesbian and Gay Rights Project of the American Civil Liberties Union, put it in talking to the *New York Times* (Johnson 1990).

Despite the mainstream editorial condemnation of outing and the negative tenor of the news and feature articles occasioned by the Forbes story, in August 1990 Signorile reported a barrage of "queries from leading newspapers and television news divisions wanting to know if it were true that *OutWeek* was planning to out U.S. Supreme Court nominee David Souter" (Signorile 1990f). These news organizations, which included the *New York Times*, the *Washington Post*, and "NBC Nightly News," had been engaging in familiar indirection when writing about Souter: "If there are any qualms about [Souter], it is the quiet concern over his circumscribed way of life. As a young man, he was briefly engaged to the daughter of a State Superior Court justice, but he never married, and even his admirers wonder whether his solitary style has limited his empathy or level of human understanding" (Margolick 1990: A12).

Responding to such coded expressions of concern, William F. Buckley, Jr., in a *Daily News* column quoted by Signorile, offered a calming reassurance that might otherwise have surprised readers familiar with Buckley's fervent Catholicism: "On Sundays, [Souter] serves as a vestryman in the Episcopal church. He is unmarried, but while in law school, the papers report, he cohabited with a female law student."[56]

Despite the inquiries at *OutWeek*, David Souter was safely confirmed without any sensational revelations, and, in fact, after the Murphy episode the outing spotlight shifted away from politics and turned on Hollywood. After the initial round of news stories, editorials, and feature articles, the outing story receded from mainstream media attention, and pending the exposure of another political or public figure it remained confined to media and gossip columns. But in the realm of the entertainment industry the hunting season was in full swing, and neither the accusations and counteraccusations nor the fear and trembling abated.

Frying the Big Media Fish

By the end of 1990 outing was largely back where it began, in Michelangelo Signorile's "Gossip Watch" column in *OutWeek*; but it had not lost its power to raise hackles as well as issues, and to inject fear into the rarefied air of many elite closets. Signorile was well supplied with information in the form of backstage gossip, leaks, and personal testimony, and he was spearheading a campaign that had narrowed its targets. Whereas traditional gay gossip, as well as tabloid exposures, had concentrated on the sexual secrets of the stars, Signorile was more interested in those who controlled the stars' destinies and made, or broke, their careers: media executives and gossip columnists. In a column that began by reassuring the legions of queer performers in Hollywood who are reportedly "petrified" of his column that "the constant worrying about being 'decloseted' by [him] is vastly exaggerated," he went on to make his priorities clear:

> Though I see nothing wrong in openly writing about ANY AND EVERY
> lesbian or gay man as such, this column does have certain
> parameters. As a media column of sorts, it is mandated to speak
> specifically about people who control, participate in and actively

---

56. Readers who remain worried about Souter's "circumscribed way of life" and "solitary style" may be relieved to know that my Washington and Boston sources suggest the possibility of a less solitary existence than that reported in the press, although not one likely to gladden William Buckley's heart.

shape the popular media. What that means is that I'm much more inclined to write about, and to expose the hypocrisies of, the powerful columnists, producers, recording company honchos, editors, publishers and everyone else behind the scenes – the power people. Of course, if you're a secretly queer performer actively and publicly engaged in homophobia and/or ardently trying to pass yourself off as heterosexual by having your publicist match you up with faux het lovers, you will, without question, wind up here at some point. . . . But for the most part, just because of the way the chips fall, it's the big media fish who are fried up here. (Signorile 1990e)

One performer who did attract considerable attention was Sandra Bernhard, who moved into the center ring of the gossip circus when she appeared on the David Letterman television show with her buddy, Madonna. The pair, who were dressed identically, clearly managed to unsettle their host by implying that they were more than just good friends. Letterman no doubt recovered from the shock, but the reverberations echoed throughout the gossip big top. Eventually Ms. Bernhard felt compelled to tell *People* magazine, "I am not a lesbian, and I'm sick of being called one. I'm not, and I want to set the record straight" (quoted in Signorile 1990g). Signorile countered with a blast:

Well, Sandy, let's suppose, for a moment, that you aren't a dyke. Isn't it still quite homophobic to say, "I'm sick of being called one," in a national magazine? And the only response I have to that statement anyway is: "But ya are, Blanche! Ya are!" . . . So says that flashy, arty editor girlfriend of yours. So say lots of other close friends of yours. So says your cute but faux ex-boyfriend who you used simply for press "bearding" purposes (and who I know isn't straight also because, well . . . I've slept with him myself! . . . And he's now explained everything about you to us). (ibid.)[57]

Such cases of defensive homophobia by performers aside, most of the outing darts were aimed at Signorile's longtime foes, the New York gossip columnists, and at Hollywood show business moguls. The

---

57. After this exchange Bernhard became more open about her sexuality, and in June 1992 she told an interviewer for the gay paper *QW*, "Well, sure . . . I'm GAY!!! I'm happy, I'm fabulous, I'm whatever I want to be. At the end of the fucking world, what difference does it make if you're a Jew, if you're gay or if you're black, if you're a fucking cock-sucker or a pussy-eater, who gives a fuck about that?" (Wayne 1992: 47). In fall 1992 the character played by Bernhard on the hit TV show "Roseanne" came out as a lesbian when she introduced her lover, played by Morgan Fairchild.

New York gossip elite had responded to the Forbes exposé with immediate attacks on outing and on outers like Signorile. And no wonder, since they were quite clearly implicated as accomplices in the construction of Forbes's very visible if misleading heterosexual persona. In particular, Liz Smith had been fingered as "one of the major perpetrators of the false Forbes/Taylor romance . . . trying to convince readers that they were a hot item" (Signorile 1990a).

The angriest attacks of that period were directed at several of Hollywood's most powerful executives, in particular Barry Diller, formerly head of Paramount and then head of Twentieth Century-Fox, and record and film producer David Geffen.[58] Diller was criticized repeatedly for promoting performers who had consistently engaged in antigay "humor" while doing little to further lesbian and gay interests. Film writer Steve Beery summed up the feelings expressed by those who were outing executives: "As long as Eddie Murphy can insult 'faggots' in front of an audience of millions, I don't feel timid about questioning the sexuality of Barry Diller, the man who greased the skids at Paramount for Murphy's rise to the top" (1990: 46).

Having moved to Fox, Diller found himself under fire for the offensive comedy routines of Andrew Dice Clay, who had signed a three-picture deal with the company. Signorile and his colleagues may have been right in claiming partial credit for Fox's decision not to release one of the films, a live concert that was "apparently so offensive that Diller felt Fox couldn't handle it" (Signorile 1990e). The decision might have been influenced by graffiti sprayed on Dice Clay billboards in Los Angeles: "Brought to You by a Closet Case, Barry Diller."

David Geffen is among the most successful of the younger generation of Hollywood tycoons—when Matsushita bought Hollywood giant MCA in 1990 Geffen's shares brought him $710 million—and his was one of the most frequent names to crop up in *OutWeek*'s gossip column. Geffen Records produced the recordings of the extremely

---

58. Diller surprised Hollywood when he suddenly resigned as head of Fox in February 1992 (Weinraub 1992), and Liz Smith may have surprised those who know Diller when she gushed in her column of March 6, 1992, about "the countless occasions I've run into Diller at home and abroad in the company of a woman who intrigues him, his lifelong friend, Diane von Furstenberg. He is forever being reported as giving expensive gifts to her—a car, jewelry, you name it." On the other hand, perhaps Hollywood insiders wouldn't have been surprised, given Sandra Bernhard's answer to a question about "the hardest thing about being a homosexual in Hollywood": "probably Barry Diller's cock. . . . When me and Diane von Furstenberg are over . . . both sucking his cock . . . now that's a *real* homosexual act" (Wayne 1992: 47).

popular heavy metal band Guns n' Roses that became known for its antigay lyrics, and Geffen was attacked for keeping the group on his label. When Geffen, who has given large sums to AIDS organizations,[59] tried unsuccessfully to have Guns N' Roses perform at an AIDS benefit, he was quoted as saying that "if you need a blood donor, and the only person who can give you a transfusion is Hitler, you take the blood." Eventually Geffen showed signs of responding to the pressure from gay activists. In June 1990 he removed the Geffen Records name from an Andrew Dice Clay record that his company was distributing, and later the same year the company dropped the rap group the Geto Boys altogether after complaints about their sexist and antigay songs.

After letting up in October ("David Geffen Should Be Commended —At Least a Little Bit") and November ("David Geffen Seems to Be Heeding Warnings and Bowing to Pressure"), however, Signorile headed his December 26 column "ZAP GEFFEN AGAIN!" and supplied Geffen's phone number. His sin? The publicity surrounding the sale of his company included an article in *Newsweek* "depicting Geffen much like Malcolm Forbes—a jet-setting, rich, hetero bachelor who'd dated a movie actress," and a cover story in *Forbes* magazine that states in the first paragraph that "Geffen is well on his way to achieving his well-known ambition of becoming Hollywood's first billionaire. And he's a bachelor to boot."

An illuminating contrast to the articles on Geffen is an article on Cameron Mackintosh, "the most successful, influential and powerful theatrical producer in the world," that appeared in the *New York Times Magazine* and elsewhere. The profile of Mackintosh, producer of *Cats, Les Misérables, Phantom of the Opera,* and *Miss Saigon,* says "Mackintosh claims that the circumstances of his public life have not changed his private ways. He has had, he says, a long-term relationship—nine years—with one man, a London photographer. Mackintosh is not a jet-setter who runs from party to party trying to get his name and photograph into the gossip and society pages" (Rothstein 1990). Signorile cited this profile as a refreshing demonstration of

"the distinction between 'private life' and being gay. . . . Here Mackintosh is, in essence, pointing out that the reality of his own homosexuality is not a *private* issue (it's simply a fact of life), even

---

59. In the Spring 1991 *Lambda Update* (the newsletter of the Lambda Legal Defense Fund) both Diller and Geffen are listed as benefactors who gave $10,000 or more; Geffen has also donated to the Gay and Lesbian Alliance against Defamation (GLAAD), an organization that has protested Andrew Dice Clay and Guns N' Roses.

though he leads a quiet life and is very much a *private* person. Yes, gay public figures *can* have private lives and still be *openly* gay (just as straight public figures can retain private lives and still be openly straight)." (1990i)

Very likely as a result of Signorile's relentless prodding, and the increasingly hostile tactics of groups like Queer Nation (who held up posters outside a star-spangled Hollywood AIDS benefit denouncing "Miss Geffen" and "La Diller"), David Geffen opened his closet door at least halfway. In an interview for a *Vanity Fair* article, Geffen described himself as having gone from being "in love with Cher to being in love with Marlo Thomas to being in love with a guy at Studio 54. . . . I date men and I date women" (Rosenfield 1991). While this is reminiscent of the bisexual halfway house many gay people have occupied on their journey out of the closet, it was also part of Geffen's strategy for defusing the outers' charges. Geffen's response to questions about outing was to deny that he'd ever been anything but open while remaining a private person:[60]

> The private life he does have he feels should be just that. Geffen is not like some married producers in Hollywood who lead double lives, pretending to be straight; he shows up at dinner parties with whomever he's seeing at the time, whether a man or a woman. "I have not kept any secrets," Geffen says. "There's not a person who doesn't know my story." Referring to threats from certain quarters of the gay press that they would "out" Geffen, he says, "No one can threaten me with exposure of something I'm not hiding." The fact is, sex is a non-issue and a non-problem. And nobody's business. (ibid.)

Signorile was quick to claim at least partial credit for Geffen's response to his "incessant and (admittedly) insidious prodding" and passes up the question of his purported bisexuality to emphasize "the

---

60. Apparently irked at Geffen's decision to give an interview to *Vanity Fair*, rival magazine *GQ* proceeded to run a story on him that dwelt on his deadliness to his enemies, including an industry figure who "made a crack to the effect that he'd like his girlfriend to get lessons from Geffen in 'sucking cock.' . . . 'David goes out to kill people who hurt him,' explains one movie executive. 'The cocksucker line was it. He went after [the figure], and he got him. David is not in the closet or anything' " (Connant 1991). As Signorile was quick to point out, *GQ* was engaging in precisely the kind of outing for which he had been pilloried: "According to everyone who attacked us, it is the person himself—not some unnamed source—who has to tell you directly that he is not 'in the closet,' " and he speculated whether *GQ* would now revert to discretion when "next month they have some closet case on the cover, and I ask them why they don't mention his or her homosexuality" (1991c).

point . . . that Geffen has finally let America know that queers are everywhere, including in Hollywood and the upper-upper-upper crust of this society" (1991b).[61]

Beyond the basic issue of openness about their sexual orientation, the anger directed at Geffen and at Barry Diller, Merv Griffin, and other allegedly closeted tycoons focuses on their failure to use their power to change the ways gay people and gay issues are treated in Hollywood. Simply put, they do not exercise influence to prevent anti-gay attacks in the media they run and to promote better treatment of lesbian and gay people:

> We're not asking for censorship. We're merely asking for treatment equal to that of other groups Fox is mindful of and tries not to offend. . . . What we want is for Fox to develop, back, distribute and release films about us—about the lesbian and gay community and about this horrific crisis we've suffered through for ten years. . . . Why don't they simply say that they won't stand for homophobia and won't back homophobes? None of these people is going to lose anything. (Signorile 1990e)

In fact, as we might expect, closeted gays are unwilling to be identified with gay stories or characters. A cover story in the *Advocate* on "Homophobia in Hollywood" quoted numerous "key gay and lesbian players," most of whom would not permit their names to be used, and the consensus view was that

> high ranking gays in positions to make a difference, with few exceptions, don't back gay material and don't speak out against negative stereotyping. "People at the studios are so far in the closet, they're getting splinters," says a studio publicist, who asked not to be named. "People in the industry feel they have to cover themselves.

---

61. It may take more than coming out, however, to stop Liz Smith. In November 1991 she brought her readers exciting news: "David Geffen and Madonna! From Los Angeles to New York City, the rumor mill is grinding itself down to powder over stories of a romance between the mogul and the mega-star. Some even claim that Geffen had proposed to Madonna! Those putting this forth point out that Geffen adores powerful, glamorous women, recalling his friendship with Cher years back. I spoke with David Geffen, and here is what he had to say: 'I like Madonna a lot. We are intimate friends, and we've kidded around about getting married. Maybe that's how the story began. I should only be so lucky, but we're not getting married.' " Perhaps Liz was confused by Madonna's May 1991 interview with the *Advocate*, in which she noted Geffen's coming out, saying she thought "it'll help. Maybe when people realize that he's not going to be assassinated in the town square, other people will do the same." She also recalled Geffen once saying, "Madonna, I was going to go straight for you" (Shewey 1991: 50).

They are nervous at times to challenge something or push a gay or lesbian theme, thinking that they would be identified as gay or lesbian because of it," says a television writer. . . . One lesbian agent at a major talent agency says that a gay male colleague of hers has stated flatly that he would never allow one of his straight clients to play a gay role, "because it will be the death of his career." (Ryan and Whitington 1991)

It remains to be seen whether Geffen's semivoluntary coming out makes a difference by encouraging others to follow his example, or at least be less concerned about guilt by association. Geffen himself, though cited by the *Advocate* as "a hero to many gays and lesbians in Hollywood" because of his *Vanity Fair* interview, doesn't seem ready to lead a crusade. While telling the *Advocate* interviewers that "there are heads of studios who are gay" (presumably this included his close friend Barry Diller, then head of Fox), he shrugged off the problem of industry homophobia with a mixture of cynicism and possibly disingenuous ignorance:

"There are stereotypical portrayals of all minorities: black people, Jews," Geffen says. "This happens in life. Movies have always done this. So does theater. So do songs. I don't think gays are particularly disadvantaged in this matter. Hollywood makes movies that will make money. That is their only motive for making movies. There isn't as big an audience for [gay stories]." (ibid.)

The Silence of the Star

Pioneering gay film historian and critic Vito Russo died of AIDS-related complications in November 1990. At a Manhattan memorial service for Russo in December, Larry Kramer, the Jeremiah of the AIDS movement, lived up to his self-appointed role by castigating those present for having "killed Vito" by not doing enough to stop AIDS. Even many accustomed to Kramer's often excessive rhetoric were taken aback by his self-indulgent tantrum; but it was another part of Kramer's speech that sparked the most long-lasting flames: he attacked Oscar-winning actress Jodie Foster for her role in the still-unreleased movie *The Silence of the Lambs*. According to Kramer, the film, which was set as the centerpiece of a major fund-raising benefit for AmFAR (the American Foundation for AIDS Research), depicted "Buffalo Bill," the serial killer who preys on young women and is hunted by Jodie Foster's character, as another in the long series of Hollywood's gay psychokillers described in Vito Russo's *The Celluloid Closet* (1987).

Kramer's speech set off a flurry of controversy—AmFAR quickly scuttled the benefit, and other AIDS organizations declined similar offers from the producers—that escalated into a full-scale frenzy once the film opened in February 1991. Having been warned by Kramer's attack of the impending debate, director Jonathan Demme attempted to foreclose the issue in prerelease interviews. *New York Times* film critic Janet Maslin was an easy sell: one subhead in her highly sympathetic interview with Demme read "Not a 'Gay Psycho Killer' " (Maslin 1991: B3).

Some of Demme's most empathetic interviewers turned out to be gay writers, among them several *Village Voice* regulars. In the January 1991 *Interview* magazine, *Voice* critic Gary Indiana set up the question of the killer's identity by referring to experiences of hearing movie audiences applaud the killing of gay characters and asked Demme his thoughts about such an "unlooked-for response" to Buffalo Bill.[62] Demme replied that the filmmakers were indeed concerned about the possibility of such a "misinterpretation": "We were terrified that Gumb could be a subject for homophobia. . . . If *Silence of the Lambs* is found—eventually, through debate on the subject—to be guilty to some extent, however unwittingly, of functioning as a tool of homophobia, then I will learn a lot from it" (Indiana 1991).

Readers who might have been less interested in Demme's education than in other potential consequences of the film's arguably homophobic depiction were not likely to have been satisfied by Amy Taubin's interview with Demme in the *Village Voice* (Taubin 1991: 77). Responding to Taubin's faux naïf question, "Are you aware of the reaction of some gay critics . . . that this is just one more gay psycho?" Demme responded with matching disingenuousness:

> "I don't think it's there. I don't feel defensive about this. We went into the movie knowing we had to protect gay people from negative interpretations. . . . If you don't understand that this guy isn't gay, you don't understand the story. It's about a man who doesn't want to be a man, he wants to become as different from himself as he can. He wants to become a woman." (ibid.)

Taubin took him up on this: "But the criticism is that a mass audience already steeped in negative gay stereotypes won't understand the subtle distinctions between a psychopath who's totally confused

---

62. In fact, many accounts of audiences for *The Silence of the Lambs* reported shouts of "Kill the fucking faggot!" during the climactic scene.

about sexual identity and a gay man." To which Demme replied, "Then perhaps the movie will provide a forum for this. Hopefully there will be a dialogue."

Demme's hope was certainly fulfilled, although the passions aroused by *The Silence of the Lambs* cannot be characterized as a polite dialogue or a tutorial for a director obviously in need of education on the subject of homophobia. Fueling the fire was the unavoidable truth that the characterization of the killer was precisely as Larry Kramer had promised. Although the novel by Thomas Harris and, apparently, the early film scripts, make clear that the killer is a self-hating hetero-sexual male—the novel emphasizes this by matching the violence against women with episodes of fag-bashing—in the film

> Demme has elicited . . . a performance so fruity, so filled with the accoutrement of gay male stereotypes that it is almost *impossible* not to see Buffalo Bill as a woman-hating queer intent on mutilating women to re-create himself as his own mother. Not only does [he] scamper about in chi-chi kimonos, don cheap jewelry, apply tacky makeup, even sport a nipple-ring, but most damning of all, dotes on a white poodle named Precious. (Bronski 1991: 81–82)

For all the heat created by the debate over the sexuality of the film's fictional killer, the most long-lasting fallout came from the explosions set off by the sexuality of the film's star, Jodie Foster. Although she had long been known in the lesbian and gay community as a lesbian—as an undergraduate at Yale in the early 1980s she had frequently been seen at parties with girlfriends—when she returned to Hollywood in 1985 she followed the rules and reentered the closet. Her film career only simmered until she landed the role of the rape victim in *The Accused*, for which she won the best actress Oscar in 1989. Now she was truly in the spotlight, but she had a unique shield against media intrusiveness: John Hinckley. In 1981, when she was a first-year student at Yale, a deranged fan of her early film role as a child prostitute in *Taxi Driver* shot President Reagan—in order, as Hinckley put it, to impress Jodie Foster. The ensuing publicity left her with what is probably a sincere as well as a convenient reason to protect her privacy. In the same year that *The Silence of the Lambs* opened she also directed her first film, *Little Man Tate*, and when she received cover-story celebrity treatment from the *New York Times Magazine* (Van Meter 1991) and *Time*, they tactfully respected her reticence. After reminding its readers about the Hinckley episode, *Time* continued, "Understandably, she does not speak on the subject . . . or on other aspects of her personal life. . . . Foster is determined to separate public persona from private person" (Smilgis and Williams 1991: 71).

But Foster's determination was not sufficient to protect her from the fury aroused by *The Silence of the Lambs*. In the February 20, 1991, column in which he began the attack on the film, Signorile addressed Jodie Foster: "TIME'S UP! If lesbianism is too sacred, too private, too infringing of your damned rights to discuss publicly, then the least you could fucking do is refrain from making movies that insult this community! Is that too much to ask of you? Jesus, you want to have your queer, little cake and eat it too, right? No WAY, SISTER!" The column then went on to berate gay writers who had recently published interviews with Foster for avoiding the topic of her participation in the film.

The attack on Foster for her participation in *The Silence of the Lambs* opened a new front in the outing wars as feminist critics lined up in defense of the film and in opposition to outing. Writing in a *Village Voice* symposium on the film, lesbian critic B. Ruby Rich was not concerned with the sexual identity of the killer: "I'm not willing to give up the immense satisfaction of a heroine with whom women can identify. Not willing to reduce all the intricate components of this movie down to the pass/fail score of one character. Please excuse me if my attention is focussed not on the killer, but on the women he kills" (Rich 1991a).

Similar sentiments were expressed by Amy Taubin and Cindy Carr, though their contributions to the symposium were mostly attacks on the male critics who focused on the killer rather than the heroine; more balanced views were presented by Martha Gever and Jewelle Gomez, who acknowledged both the pleasure provided by the heroism of Foster's character and the problems presented by the film's sexual politics. At a panel on film held at the San Francisco Lesbian and Gay Writer's Conference, filmmaker and critic Maria Magenti, faced with three gay male critics who condemned the film for its homophobia, seemed to draw upon current theories of gender-based interpretation: "You boys just don't get it. There is more than one way to look at a movie and women see something entirely different here than you do" (quoted in Bronski 1991: 83).

The counterattack on the critics of *The Silence of the Lambs* and of Jodie Foster for her participation in it soon spilled over into an attack on outing as a male tactic. In a letter to the *Village Voice* published in April 1991, Leslie Larson claimed that "it's no coincidence that Jodie Foster is being singled out as the target of a uniquely vicious outing campaign, being waged largely by gay men." Why?

You don't have to look far to find a reason why a culture with screen idols such as Marilyn Monroe and Judy Garland would object so vociferously to an actress like Jodie Foster. Like their straight brothers, the gay men who condemn Jodie Foster and *Lambs* are out to destroy a woman who doesn't put male interests first and doesn't conform to their ideas of what a woman should be. Under the guise of promoting gay consciousness, they're falling back on the same reliable weapon that men have used against women who claim a little too much for themselves—they're calling her a dyke. (Larson 1991)

Despite the attempts to characterize outing as a manifestation of gay male sexism—B. Ruby Rich sent a letter to the *Voice* shortly after Larson's, in which she called it "fraternity fascism under a different name" (Rich 1991b)[63]—the proponents and opponents of outing cannot be simply divided along gender lines. Letters to the editors of *OutWeek*, *Gay Community News*, and the *Village Voice*, among other lesbian/gay and alternative papers, included attacks on and praises of outing by both men and women writers. In the symposium on the pros and cons of outing published in *OutWeek* in May 1990, one of the harshest critics of outing is a man, Hunter Madsen (who is, incidentally, far from being a feminist), and one of the most unambiguous defenses is by lesbian feminist writer Victoria Brownworth. When the New York lesbian monthly paper *Sappho's Isle* included a question about outing in a readership survey, the anti-outing editor was somewhat disconcerted to discover that "on outing we seem to be truly divided. While more oppose outing than support it, there is a large margin of unsure or depends on circumstances. So perhaps this controversial tactic is actually one considered by many as justified and we will continue to see it used" (Sidebottom 1991).

In fact, some of the anger directed at Jodie Foster came from lesbians who were less than persuaded that she was advancing the cause of feminism. For example, Heidi Dorow, a lesbian activist who was

---

63. What are we, then, to call the following passage from an article Rich wrote about lesbian country and western music fans?: "Jean Carlomusto has immortalized one aspect of the new lesbian lovelorn fan club in her recent videotape, *L is for the way you look*, 1991, in which half a dozen dykes recall the thrill of sighting Dolly Parton at a Reno [a well-known lesbian comedienne] performance in New York's P.S. 122. They go on and on, remembering her hair, her clothes, her breastly 'endowment'—and their own relentless pursuit of her in the name of dyke history. Put *that* in the Lesbian Herstory Archives and smoke it. Or, at least, play 'Jolene' " (Rich 1992). Sorority solidarity?

beaten by a gang of teenagers in Manhattan one afternoon as she embraced another woman, had this to say to Michelanglo Signorile:

> Every time Jodie Foster fucks her girlfriend, I feel like she's bashing me over the head. She's locked away in her big California home, while I get beaten up on the streets. She gets all the benefits of this straight culture because she passes, because she has the looks, because she has money. . . . Jodie Foster gets away with murder. . . . It's our own internalized homophobia that makes us want to love her. . . . We even go so far as to put Jodie Foster on a pedestal as a feminist. Where does that come from? When was the last time you saw her at an abortion-rights rally or standing up for women or for other movements, like the lesbian and gay movement? She's no feminist. A feminist puts women first and stands up for women—*all* women. And that includes lesbians. (Signorile 1991b)

One of the criticisms leveled by lesbian critic C.Carr in a scathing column, "Why Outing Must Stop" (1991), written during the middle of the *Lambs* controversy, was that outers are oblivious to the damage they do to their targets' livelihoods: "Signorile has insisted that he doesn't ruin careers; homophobia does and straight people do that. In other words, 'I just push 'em in front of the truck. The *truck* hits them.' " But, in the relevant cases in point, the evidence hardly supports the conclusion that outing has hurt anyone's career. David Geffen is still a Hollywood megamogul, and Barry Diller, despite his decision to leave Fox, is still a major player. Of course, as a producer quoted by Carr put it, "I don't think anyone cares if a writer or director or studio executive is gay, because it doesn't affect viewing the movie. There *would* be consequences for actors. They're supposed to embody our fantasies." So what happened to Jodie Foster after she was outed by *OutWeek*, followed shortly in supermarkets around the country by the *Star? Time* did a cover story on her, and her performance in *The Silence of the Lambs* won her a second Oscar. This is the sort of truck many actors would love to be hit by. The truly cynical might wonder how many votes for Foster were motivated by sympathy for her ordeal—although the movie's sweep of the top honors makes this less persuasive—but even they could be forgiven for smiling when she thanked "all the people in this industry who have respected my choices and have not been afraid of the power and the dignity that entitled me to" (Ehrenstein 1992).

We're Here, We're Queer, Get Used to It!

At the New York Gay and Lesbian Pride parade in June 1990, fifteen thousand copies of an anonymous broadside were distributed bearing the simple but arresting title *Queers Read This: I Hate Straights*. The essay, which quickly spread around the city and was reprinted in *Out-Week*, articulated a sense of gay rage that was widely felt, and it struck a responsive chord in communities around the country. The essay began with the writer's feelings of being marginalized in a straight world: "I have friends. Some of them are straight. . . . Year after year I continue to realize that I am only half listened to, that I am an appendage to the doings of a greater world, a world of power and privilege, of the laws of installation, a world of exclusion." The essay went on to focus on the mounting rage of those caught up in the fight against AIDS and for equal treatment of lesbians and gay men, the rage of those for whom marginality is a constant experience:

> I hate having to convince straight people that lesbians and gays live in a war zone, that we're surrounded by bomb blasts only we seem to hear, that our bodies are heaped high, dead from fright or bashed or raped, dying of grief or disease, stripped of our personhood.
>
> I hate straight people who can't listen to queer anger without saying, "Hey, all straight people aren't like that. I'm straight, too, you know," as if their egos don't get enough stroking or protection in this arrogant, heterosexist world. . . . They've taught us that good queers don't get mad. They've taught us so well that we not only hide our anger from them, we hide from each other. WE EVEN HIDE IT FROM OURSELVES. . . . They bash us and stab us and shoot us and bomb us in ever increasing numbers and still we freak when angry queers carry banners or signs that say BASH BACK . . . LET YOURSELF BE ANGRY. Let yourself be angry that the price of our visibility is the constant threat of violence, anti-queer violence to which practically every segment of this society contributes. Let yourself feel angry that THERE IS NO PLACE IN THIS COUNTRY WHERE WE ARE SAFE, no place where we are not targeted for hatred and attack, the self-hatred, the suicide—of the closet. The next time some straight person comes down on you for being angry, tell them that until things change, you don't need any more evidence that the world turns at your expense. . . . Tell them "GO AWAY FROM ME, until YOU can change." . . . Go tell them go away until they have spent a month walking hand in hand with someone of the same sex. After

they survive that, then you'll hear what they have to say about queer anger. Otherwise, tell them to shut up and listen.

Although written and distributed by a group largely made up of ACT UP members, the essay was widely considered to be the work of Queer Nation,[64] an organization that had recently spun off from ACT UP in order to organize direct action focusing on lesbian/gay issues. ACT UP's focus was AIDS and related health issues, not the wider range of problems confronting lesbian and gay people (nor is the membership of ACT UP exclusively lesbian and gay). Most immediately, the alarming rise in antilesbian and antigay violence—reported incidents rose by over 100 percent in the first quarter of 1990—motivated four activists, among them Michelangelo Signorile, to call a meeting at the Lesbian and Gay Community Center in Manhattan. Sixty people showed up, which far exceeded the organizers' expectations, and by the second meeting the number had swelled to over a hundred. In early June, Queer Nation held a march in Greenwich Village that drew more than a thousand demonstrators and attracted media attention—"Gay Rage" was the headline on the front page of the *New York Post*—further swelling the attendance at meetings that already drew more than 350 people each week (Trebay 1990: 35).

It was clear that Queer Nation was a movement whose time had come, and the *Queers Read This: I Hate Straights* broadside captured the imagination of the moment. Much as the Stonewall riots had in 1969, this essay served as a spark on a pile of kindling, and within days it seemed that groups calling themselves Queer Nation were springing up around the country. Some of the earliest actions of the Queer Nation groups—in New York City, San Francisco, and Philadelphia, among others—were marches against antilesbian and antigay street attacks: "Queers Bash Back!" read the banners in a Brooklyn march. But

---

64. The adoption of the term "queer" was among the group's more controversial moves, and sparked a controversy that eventually drew the attention of the *New York Times* (Stanley 1991). Just as "gay" was adopted in the late 1960s by radicals who wanted to distinguish themselves from the earlier reformers of the homosexual and homophile movements, now "queer" "underscores a growing generation gap within the gay community. It divides youthful, self-described 'separatists,' roused to a new militant rage by the AIDS epidemic, from those who came of political age in the 60s, and for whom political struggle has long focused on issues like privacy and tolerance" (ibid.). In addition, using the term "queer" effectively combines references to gay men and lesbian women, along with bisexuals, transsexual, and transgendered people—in fact, as people often pointed out at Queer Nation meetings, *queer* meant anyone who didn't fit into society's confining sexual roles or play by society's restrictive sexual rules.

the focus of Queer Nation was broader than countering physical attacks, and their tactics were consciously provocative.

Queer Nationals saw themselves as militantly visible—wearing T-shirts and stickers with blatant slogans in unavoidable Day-Glo colors: PROMOTE HOMOSEXUALITY. GENERIC QUEER. FAGGOT. MILITANT DYKE. The tactics adopted by Queer Nation can best be characterized by a phrase that has since become a colloquial cliché—in your face—and they took their tactics on the road. Queer Nation groups in New York and San Francisco organized "Nights Out," forays into heterosexual bars wearing their striking T-shirts and staging "kiss-ins." "Queer Shopping Networks" visited suburban shopping malls outside New York City and San Francisco, where they chanted, "We're here, we're queer, we're fabulous—and we're not going shopping!"

Not surprisingly, the activists of Queer Nation were in favor of visibility for lesbian and gay celebrities as well. Among their first actions was an outing that consisted of altering bus kiosk ads for the Gap clothing chain featuring photos of country singer k. d. lang by changing the p to a y.[65] Queer Nationals showed up at a promotional appearance by Olympic diving champion Greg Louganis and told him "[they] were just there as members of the lesbian and gay community to say [they] would love to have [him] as an out member" (Trebay 1990: 35).

Absolutely Queer

In the spring of 1991 another front in the outing wars was opened with the birth of OutPost, a spiritual lovechild of *OutWeek* and Queer Nation, which began to put up posters around Manhattan with large photographs of celebrities over large type reading ABSOLUTELY QUEER.[66] The first group of anonymous posters—they were "signed"

---

65. k. d. lang, a longtime favorite of lesbian audiences, was at that time "semi-closeted" and has since come out in an interview with the *Advocate*. She attributed her discretion to her mother's concerns about the reactions of the small town of Consort, Alberta, where she was born: "I want to be out. I want to be out! Man, if I didn't worry about my mother, I'd be the biggest parader in the whole world" (Lemon 1992: 44). As it turned out, her mother's fears may have been exaggerated; when asked about lang's announcement, the mayor of Consort replied, "She's done more to put us on the map than anybody and we are extremely pleased with her. She's still personable and very approachable, and her preferred lifestyle is insignificant to me" (Broderick 1992).

66. The words were an obvious reference to the ads featuring artwork with the tag "Absolut [artist's name], "familiar to gay people because Absolut vodka has long been one of the few mainstream products to advertise regularly in the gay press.

with the words "OutPost—Cleaner Closets Today Mean a Better Tomorrow"—featured rich and famous folks already familiar to gossip and outing circles: Jodie Foster and Merv Griffin.[67]

The text under Jodie Foster's photograph read "Oscar Winner. Yale Graduate. Ex-Disney Moppet. Dyke." *Village Voice* columnist Guy Trebay, who had written dispassionately about Queer Nation's outing of k. d. lang and Greg Louganis (1990), wrote a hostile account of the OutPost campaign, in which he repeated the text but wouldn't cite the actress by name: "well, let's just call her a famous young actress who's much in the news" (1991). He was equally discreet about the posters of Merv Griffin, referring only to "a former daytime perennial" and quoting the photo caption: "Casino magnate. 'Jeopardy' creator. Ex talk-show host. Fag."

A third OutPost production took a different tack, depicting late-night talk show host Arsenio Hall under the headline "When Arsenio Gets Busy, Queers Get Bashed." Below the picture, the text said, "If you watch the Arsenio Hall show, you'll think dykes and fags are just there for your entertainment and ridicule and you'll think that queers don't live or hurt or deserve respect like any other minority."

Although the posters were widely assumed to be a product of Queer Nationals, Jay Blotcher, a spokesperson for Queer Nation and an *OutWeek* staffer, was quoted as saying he did not know who was behind them, and Michelangelo Signorile said (in a personal communication) that he never knew the OutPosters. According to Trebay's account in the *Voice*, OutPost was the work of Ken K., an editor, and his lover, Brendan W., a graphic artist, and their anonymity was used as an argument against their outing tactics. When Michael Musto devoted his *Village Voice* column of April 16, 1991, to OutPost, reproducing the Foster and Griffin posters (Trebay had already run the Hall poster), several letters to the editor took the opportunity to attack outing in general (one of these was the letter by B. Ruby Rich mentioned earlier) and OutPost in particular. In addition to familiar arguments about the invasion of privacy, these writers deplored the use of the terms "dyke," "fag," and "queer" and questioned the factual basis of

---

67. Griffin had been outed by a lawsuit filed by an alleged former lover, but this was not news to gay gossip circles, despite his well-publicized "romance" with Eva Gabor. Nor was his plight likely to elicit much sympathy from gay people, whatever their position on outing. "Unlike many other closeted Hollywood power brokers, Griffin is not known to have made major contributions to gay or lesbian causes, nor was he often seen at events or locales that attract celebrities who are sympathetic to gay rights" (Gallagher 1991a).

the outings: "Do they have *documented evidence* that a certain actress is a lesbian?" (M. Harwood 1991). They also questioned the chosen anonymity of those who presume to expose others' sexual secrets: "The OUTPOST cowards see fit to reserve exclusively to themselves the right to anonymity" (Loder 1991). Given their anonymity, Musto's replies can stand as the response to OutPost's critics as well as a general defense of outing:

> OUTPOST remains anonymous not for fear of libel, but because the outed celebrities (or anyone) could use their influence to have them punished for vandalism and/or using unauthorized photos. Their source material is every bit as good as that of the scores of reporters who've ever told us some star or other is straight—*better*, in many cases. These celebrities proposition us, sleep with our friends, steal our lovers, and reveal themselves to our mutual business contacts. There's documentation on all of them, and it's homophobic to call this information shoddy and vicious. (Musto 1991c)

> Since tabloid journalism does happen to dominate the media, celebs are regularly dissected for things they may not want in print; funny, it's only called fascistic or McCarthyistic when it involves gayness. If anti-outers want a social upheaval, to protect famous people from all kinds of intrusion, they should appoint themselves the heads of *that* movement, and get to work. In the meantime, to leave homosexuality the last unspoken taboo seems very hypocritical. (Musto 1991a)

The OutPosters' fear of legal action proved not completely unfounded, although they were not the targets. After the first few posters attracted a great deal of attention, they increased the pace of their efforts and eventually covered much vacant Manhattan wall space with an array of posters depicting actors, writers, athletes, and media figures variously labeled Absolutely Queer and Absolutely Het (this category included actor Mel Gibson, who is known for antigay statements).[68] In July 1991, the *Globe*, a supermarket tabloid with a circulation of over a million, reprinted sixteen of the posters in an article titled " 'Gay' Stars Stop Traffic." One of the sixteen was television actor Tom Selleck, who had previously complained about allegations printed in the *Globe* that he is gay. When the paper refused to print a retraction—

---

68. An independent spin-off of the Absolutely Queer posters opened yet another outing frontier, showing selected celebrities (Charles Bronson, Ted Danson, Larry Hagman, and Joe Namath) minus their hairpieces and labeled Absolutely Bald (Musto 1991d).

an understandable response under the circumstances, as they had printed the photograph in a news story but not made any claim about Selleck—he sued the company for $20 million, saying he is "singularly heterosexual." A few weeks later it was widely reported that the suit had been settled and that Selleck would receive an apology, printed in the *Globe*, and an undisclosed financial settlement (Gallagher 1991b). It didn't take long, however, for word to leak out—via very reliable sources—that the undisclosed amount of the settlement was five dollars. Thus was honor satisfied.

Outing Goes on the Road

Outing arose as a political tactic within the context of national politics and the fight against repressive measures occasioned by AIDS and HIV testing. Despite the outing of Senator Hatfield in Oregon, Governor Thompson in Illinois, and Lieutenant Governor Murphy in Massachusetts, most of the outing action and controversy was concentrated in Washington, D.C., and in the cultural capitals of New York and Hollywood. Observers of, participants in, and opponents of outing wondered whether the drama that had opened on Broadway would play on the road. For the most part, activists and journalists around the country did not join in the fray, and there was no nationwide firestorm of outing. But there were some exceptions.

When Philadelphia's gay weekly, *Au Courant*, ran a feature on outing in March 1990, the cover listed thirty-nine names without comment. The names included such nationally known targets of outing as Calvin Klein, Whitney Houston, John Travolta, and Debbie Reynolds, along with many other familiar targets of gossip, such as Tracy Chapman, George Michael, J. Edgar Hoover, and Pope Paul VI. The list also included the names of four well-known local television news, sports, and weather announcers, whose presence reflected their status in local gossip. This implied outing was not amplified by any other medium (although it did occasion much private discussion) and had no noticeable effect on their careers. But not all outing targets were so lucky. The revelation by a married Minneapolis rabbi that he had "twice pleaded guilty to charges of sexual misconduct and had an extramarital affair with another man" led to his being suspended from his congregation (Bull 1991). The rabbi apparently gave the story to the Minneapolis *Star Tribune* because he had been questioned by a local gay paper, the *GLC Voice*, about an anonymous letter that described his sexual history. Although the rabbi himself gave the story to the press,

Tim Campbell, editor of the *Voice*, said, "In the long run, I did out him, because he thought we were going to [publish the allegations]." Campbell, who had advocated outing before, said, "People trying to reap the benefits of the gay rights movement while holding on to heterosexual privilege had better watch out. The hypocrites have to go."

A clear-cut example of political outing took place in April 1991 in connection with the increasingly notorious Los Angeles Police Department and its infamous chief, Daryl Gates. The L.A.P.D. had been sued by a former officer, Mitch Grobeson, who charged antigay discrimination and demanded recruitment, hiring, and protection of openly lesbian and gay police officers (Ocamb 1991). The suit was bottled up in the City Council, which has the power to settle such disputes, when the Rodney King beating became America's most famous home video. The furor surrounding the beating put the spotlight again on the council and its failure to act against Chief Gates. At this point, openly gay attorney Thomas Coleman made public a letter he sent to councilmember Joel Wachs. The letter read, in part:

> As one gay man to another, three questions: 1. Why bother sponsoring and passing laws prohibiting discrimination and then fail to enforce them? 2. When a well known and documented bigot like Chief Gates is placed on paid leave, why do you jump through hoops of fire to put him back on the job to continue his policies of discrimination, but when one of L.A.P.D.'s finest officers, Sgt. Mitch Grobeson, asks to meet with you to discuss homophobic bigotry on the force, you refuse to do so? 3. Given your refusal to deal with homophobia at L.A.P.D., as well as your shrill defense of Gates, the chief enforcer of homophobic bigotry in the Police Department, haven't you disgraced yourself, as well as all other gays and lesbians in Los Angeles upon whom the department's abuse has been inflicted? (quoted in Dwyer 1991)

The report of Coleman's letter in the local newsletter *Vanguard News & Views* noted that Wachs had, "rightly or wrongly, been assumed to be a closeted gay man" who had never "included himself when talking about issues facing the gay and lesbian community, but has always used the third person" (ibid.). Coleman distanced himself from the suggestion that he intended to out Wachs, saying "outing would be a consequence, but outing is not the primary purpose" of his letter: "The primary purpose is to make him accountable. . . . Unless we can make our own public officials accountable, we are not going to make any significant changes in this community." Other members of Coleman's law firm defended his action; as one of them put it, "I think this is almost a textbook type situation for outing, because Joel is a political figure who has taken a significant act against the gay community" (ibid.). Senior partner Leroy Walker went even further in defending outing in this, and possibly other, cases:

> "Let's say [Wachs] is secretly working behind the scenes . . . to stop discrimination in the police department or help Mitch Grobeson. Wouldn't it be much better if he got on television and said this behavior is intolerable, this behavior is illegal? Let alone add, 'and as a gay man, I will not tolerate it, and I will lead a constituency to stop it?' He can't even be a leader because of his closet. . . . And if there are people in the community who say they don't approve of outing, well, I guess then we're all paralyzed. We'll have to live with people who are self-hating and maybe even doing destructive things to us, because otherwise then, we've invaded their privacy, right? Even when they're public officials." (ibid.)[69]

Distant Outposts

The gay movement that spread across the United States after the 1969 Stonewall riots did not stop at the country's borders. The explosion set off in Greenwich Village had aftershocks that revived or instigated lesbian and gay militance in many parts of the world.[70] The lesbian and gay movement in the United States has remained a trendsetter and an inspiration for its counterparts in other countries, carried in large part on the wave of American popular and consumer culture that has

---

69. Not every incident in which a public official is exposed as a secret homosexual can be defended as a move intended to further the cause of gay liberation. Sometimes it is just old-fashioned homophobia in the service of political combat. For example, after Calvin Hinshaw, a Republican county commissioner in Guilford, North Carolina, resigned for "reasons of health," a political opponent, Democratic commissioner Jim Kirkpatrick, revealed that Hinshaw "had been involved in a sexual relationship with his 24-year-old son" that had "apparently gone on for about six years." Hinshaw's family issued a statement attacking Kirkpatrick's motives in "spreading gossip and rumors of sexual misconduct," but the son later issued a statement confirming that the relationship had occurred, characterizing it as sexual abuse and not something he sought (Gant 1991).

70. The political upheavals of May 1968 had prepared the ground for the rapid growth of a post-Stonewall gay liberation movement in Europe. When Rosa von Praunheim's film *It Is Not the Homosexual Who Is Perverse, but the Society in Which He Finds Himself* premiered in Berlin in 1970, it "stimulated the formation of gay activist groups in Frankfurt, Cologne, Munich and other German cities" (Dyer 1990: 216). Militant liberation groups espousing both revolutionary and reformist politics were formed around the same time in Britain, France, and Italy.

swept across the world in recent decades. Styles set on Christopher and Castro streets have come to define and mark gay male identity in Amsterdam, Hamburg, Liverpool, and Melbourne, and political tactics have often followed in the wake of clothing styles and disco lyrics. The pattern was repeated as the AIDS epidemic first appeared in gay male circles in the United States before its effects were felt among gay men in other countries; AIDS activists around the world have often adopted tactics first deployed in America.

In January 1989 a British ACT UP was founded, joining the many other organizations and support services built by British AIDS activists. The following year the news of Queer Nation's founding in New York spread rapidly across the ocean in the form of OutRage, started in London in May 1990 and soon engaged in "kiss-ins," mock weddings, and other public tactics intended to draw attention to antigay discrimination and violence.

The British gay movement in the late 1980s was seething with anger and frustration. In addition to the political and public hostility stirred up by AIDS, Margaret Thatcher's government had made a point of using antigay sentiment as a convenient political weapon. The Conservatives were also retaliating against the growing visibility of lesbian and gay people, culminating in 1987 in the introduction of legislation prohibiting local authorities from "promoting homosexuality." This was the notorious Clause 28, which set off a wave of gay counterorganizing, including the coming out of Ian McKellen and other previously closeted public figures.

The passage of Clause 28 sharpened the tactical debate within the British gay movement because it was voted upon by a Parliament in which "dozens of MPs [members of Parliament], perhaps as many as 60 or 70, are known by their colleagues to be gay" (Appleyard 1990) but only one, Labour MP Chris Smith, is openly gay. When outing began in the United States it was only to be expected that questions would be raised about the continued safety of parliamentary closets. In May 1990, when the London *Sunday Times* reported on the new development in militant tactics in the United States, the article was clearly focused on

> the fact that more mainstream gay activists [in Britain] are seeing the appeal of the idea as a means of explosively recreating the gay consciousness momentum of the 1960s and 1970s. "I personally don't feel there is any justification in this country . . . yet," said Michael Mason, editor of the magazine *Capital Gay*, "but one gets bloody angry. If you look at the parliamentary voting list on Clause 28, there

are at least three gay Tory MPs who voted in favour. I wouldn't shed any tears if somebody outed them." (ibid.)[71]

A year later, on July 28, 1991, the *Sunday Times*'s front-page lead headline read "Gays Threaten to 'Out' MPs in Poster Campaign" (Gerard and Rayment 1991). The article reported on the activities and plans of a group that called itself FROCS, although the *Times* declined to translate the name for its readers (other British papers were willing to decode the acronym: Faggots Rooting Out Closeted Sexuality). The anonymous group (its members all identified themselves as Mikey Angelo in homage to the American pioneer of outing, Michelangelo Signorile) had first attracted attention by putting up posters claiming that British pop star Jason Donovan is gay. They now promised a further series of posters, beginning with three MPs—presumably the three cited the previous year, but not named, who voted for Clause 28. The *Times* article went on:

> The MPs are on a list of 200 targets, said to include 52 MPs, eight judges and 12 senior church figures, together with musicians, film and television stars and a member of the royal family. It has been drawn up by a group supported and endorsed by Peter Tatchell, the former Labour parliamentary candidate who is now a leading homosexual rights campaigner. Last week he defended their aims and said: "Gay public figures who support decisions against homosexual people are the worst hypocrites. They deserve to be exposed. We are targeting police and judges because we feel victims. Some of the police and judges are themselves gay." Other people . . . will also be named . . . to show that homosexuality is widespread and to provide "role models" for people coming to terms with their sexuality. (ibid.)

The British tabloid press was unanimous in expressing outrage at the tactics proposed by FROCS. A *Daily Express* columnist referred to "mincing militants . . . ferocious faggots . . . a limp-wristed army of insecure Wicked Fairies" (Cockburn 1991: 221). The *Daily Mail* took a more dignified tone, proclaiming that "the decision about whether

---

71. Alan Amos, a Conservative Party MP who voted for Clause 28, resigned his seat in March 1992 three days after his arrest for having sex with another man in a London park and less than 24 hours after Britain's largest tabloid, the *Sun*, reported the arrest on the front page as "MP's Gay Sex Shame." The following day, the Liberal Democrat candidate in Amos's district came out as gay, reportedly in order to preempt a front-page story outing him in the conservative *News of the World* ("News in Brief," the *Advocate*, April 21, 1992: 31).

a homosexual wishes to go public should be private" (Gordon 1991), perhaps forgetting that the *Daily Mail* itself had outed Labour MP Maureen Colquhoun in 1976, and she subsequently lost her seat in Parliament (Cockburn 1991: 221). The elite papers approached the story in a less sensational but equally enthusiastic fashion, as in the aforementioned front-page story in the *Sunday Times*. Matthew Parris, a former Conservative MP who came out after leaving Parliament in 1986 and who opposed outing on tactical rather than moral grounds, noted that he had turned down many requests to give newspaper interviews or appear on radio and television to discuss outing (Parris 1991).

FROCS announced a press conference for Thursday, August 1, at which they promised to reveal their list of 200 prominent closeted gays. The press conference was packed with journalists (who had to pay 20 pence at the entrance), but they were to be disappointed. The press was met by FROCS members who claimed that the entire affair had been a hoax meant to expose the hypocrisy of the media. "We have never outed anyone, or even intended to, however much the press begged us to. The whole purpose of this hoax is to expose the double standards, hypocrisy and homophobia in the media." They then read a list of celebrities who had been outed by the media in recent years and asked why the same papers had not reported the violence and police harassment against homosexuals with the same vigor. One tabloid reporter complained, "We've been shafted by the buggers" (Renton 1991).

Opinions and accounts varied on the question of whether FROCS had intended all along to proclaim a hoax or had changed their minds at the last moment out of fear of libel suits, as *Capital Gay* reported (Baxter 1991). Given that British libel law is far more expansive in its coverage than U.S. law (since the 1964 *Sullivan v. New York Times* ruling limiting the privacy rights of public figures), the latter explanation is reasonably persuasive. The legal peril that may have dissuaded the FROCS group soon befell the magazine the *Face*. In the August 1991 issue of the trendy British monthly, the topic of outing was featured in a story illustrated with a full-page reproduction of the poster claiming that pop star Jason Donovan was "queer as fuck" (the words were superimposed on the singer's T-shirt in the poster photograph). Despite the magazine's more or less anti-outing take—"We don't know if the celebrities featured in this campaign *are* gay or not, and, since it's no one's business except their own, we don't really care"—and the inclusion of Donovan's denial that he is gay, it lost a libel suit brought by the singer. The jury seemed persuaded that the article had supported the outing charge by noting that "speculation has surfaced time and again about the private preferences of the boy with the bleached hair" (Summerskill 1991) and awarded the plaintiff £200,000 in damages. The singer offered to lower the damages to £95,000 (about $173,000) if the magazine didn't appeal the judgment, but the *Face* still found itself in drastic financial straits as a result of the case (Aaron 1992).

"Few people ever thought that outing . . . would ever reach Australia," noted an article in the *Sydney Morning Herald* the week after the FROCS episode in London, "but come to Australia, outing has"—when the local ACT UP group distributed leaflets denouncing MP "Franca Arena: Homophobe" for her stance on AIDS funding (Stapleton and McCarthy 1991). The Sydney paper went beyond reporting on the leaflets, running a front-page story saying that "a *Herald* journalist . . . had learnt that Queer Nation . . . was planning to plaster the city with posters alleging that [Arena's] sons are homosexual." The leaflets denouncing Arena had not mentioned her sons, yet she held a press conference, "denying the allegations that her sons are homosexual. . . . 'We're a decent and loving family' " (Larriera 1991). ACT UP issued a statement distancing itself from the outing, which had never actually taken place, as did the single openly gay member of the Australian Parliament, Paul O'Grady.

The *Herald*'s analysis of outing presented the arguments made by outing proponents and opponents. Tony Westmore, identified as one of the most prominent members of both ACT UP and Queer Nation in Sydney, was quoted as saying that the voices of closeted conservative politicians are fired by the fear of exposure and "these fires might be damped by the cleansing waters of truth." The authors reported the emergence of militant tactics in the wake of AIDS and antigay violence in the United States, and went on to acknowledge that "violence against gays in central Sydney has escalated to the point where a gay man is now estimated to be killed every six weeks. . . . Hundreds of people have been bashed in the past few years" (Stapleton and McCarthy 1991).

The article, which noted that "outing poses a moral and ethical dilemma for the media . . . [since] its proponents need the media in order to effectively 'out' their subjects," nevertheless included the names of many outing targets in the United States (Barry Diller, Richard Chamberlain, Mark Hatfield, Ed Koch, Calvin Klein, Billie Jean King, Chastity Bono, John Travolta, David Geffen, Merv Griffin, Malcolm Forbes, Pete Williams, Tom Selleck, Jodie Foster, and Whitney Houston). The article cited the recent "self-outing" by Sydney

Symphony conductor Stuart Challender (after a threat of exposure from a Melbourne tabloid) and MP Paul O'Grady. Both Challender and O'Grady are quoted as saying they felt empowered by their openness – Challender said he "never felt freer" and O'Grady said he felt safe from embarrassment or blackmail – but the article maintained that the gay community, like the community at large, condemns outing.

When a forty-seven-year-old Queensland judge committed suicide around this time, the *Melbourne Age* claimed that the motive was fear that he was going to be outed by gay activists threatening a campaign that would name prominent judges, clerics, sports figures, and media personalities. As far as I have been able to discover, however, no such widespread outing campaign has taken place in Australia, nor, for that matter, anywhere else.

"I Am Out! I'm in This Bar, Aren't I?"

When the outing stories burst on the American political scene, one gay leader who was often quoted by the mainstream press is Robert Bray, then communications director of the Human Rights Campaign Fund, the major gay political action committee (he now holds a similar position with the National Gay and Lesbian Task Force). Bray told the *Washington Post* that

> he recognized a conservative Republican congressman on the dance floor of a gay nightclub in Southeast Washington. Bray was surprised because he had not known that the congressman was gay and he was not a supporter of gay issues on Capitol Hill. Seeing the congressman as a potential convert to the cause, Bray quickly decided that this was not a politician who should be exposed. Amid the loud music, he approached the congressman, introduced himself and explained that the gay community needed his support. Startled at being recognized, Bray said, the congressman stopped dancing and, with his boyfriend in tow, hurriedly left the nightclub. (Weiser 1989: A5)

In other versions of this story, Bray went on to report that the congressman "got the message. He started voting progay and has been ever since. Outing would have been inappropriate in his case" (Krier 1990).

Bray may not have known that the congressman was gay before the nightclub encounter, but others seem to have been in on the secret. In May 1990, "Inside the Beltway," the political gossip column of the right-wing *Washington Times*, ran the following short item: "Cryptic remark: Rep. Steven Gunderson was taking Rep. Fred Grandy to task for his position on parental leave. 'Well, at least I don't wear panty-hose,' Mr. Grandy fired back."

It seems likely that Gunderson, Republican of Wisconsin, was the congressman Bray approached at the Washington nightclub. It also appears that others disagreed about Bray's success in converting Gunderson. At the very least, they wondered why Gunderson refused to cosponsor the federal gay rights bill.

On the night of June 30, 1991, D.C. AIDS activist and Queer National Michael Petrelis received word that Gunderson was in a gay bar in Alexandria, Virginia, and hurried over to confront him in a somewhat different style than that used by Bray. Finding Gunderson at the bar, Petrelis began to demand that the congressman come out and that he support the gay rights bill. Gunderson responded by saying, "I am out. I'm in this bar, aren't I?" to which Petrelis replied, "That's not enough!" and, chanting "Come out, Gunderson, come out!" threw a Coke in Gunderson's face. The bar manager ejected Petrelis and someone called the police (according to some reports it was Petrelis who did this, in order to attract press attention to the incident), but no arrest or police report was made.

Petrelis sent out a press release recounting the event, and the *Washington Times*'s "Inside the Beltway" column "became the first newspaper in the nation's capital to print the name" whereas the *Washington Post*, which "reported on the incident two days later, [mentioned] the *Times* column, but only [referred] to Gunderson as a 'Wisconsin congressman' " (O'Neill 1991b). The story also made it home to Wisconsin, where it was reported in the *Milwaukee Journal* on July 3. The story gave a slightly different account of the confrontation, claiming that a "gay activist threw a drink at [Gunderson] after shouting at him for not supporting financing for AIDS research more strongly." The story identified the bar-restaurant and quoted an Alexandria, Virginia, police officer as saying that "it's considered a gay bar" and the owner as noting that "about 50 percent of our clients at dinner are straight."

The day after this article appeared, Gunderson was the featured honoree at the La Crosse, Wisconsin, Fourth of July celebration. Queer National Tim Campbell of Minneapolis prepared two thousand hot-pink flyers that called on Gunderson to "Come out now for gay rights. . . . Join the sponsors of the gay and lesbian rights bill in Congress." Campbell was distributing the flyers along the parade route when he was arrested and charged with littering. "Campbell said he was told by the officer an ordinance prohibits the distribution of flyers during a parade" (Hardie 1991). Campbell was released from jail after about an hour and returned to the parade route just in time to hand one of the flyers to Gunderson. " 'He read it and did not make any comment,' Campbell said" (ibid.).

Gunderson was not able to avoid comment entirely, however, as the drink throwing incident and the arrest of Tim Campbell had drawn media attention. On July 21 the *La Crosse Tribune* published an interview with Gunderson that was subsequently reported by the *St. Paul Pioneer Press*. In the interview Gunderson was asked how he felt about someone coming into his district and passing out a leaflet "claiming you were in gay bars on two occasions and are not supporting the gay rights bill." Gunderson replied,

> It is one of many of Tim Campbell's pathological lies. Yes, I was in a gay-owned restaurant to get dinner. There are lots of gay-owned restaurants in Washington. I would take my parents there; there was nothing wrong with being there. . . . I have gay friends, black friends, women friends, Jews; anyone who knows me knows I am a strong advocate of civil rights for everybody. (quoted in Kraemer 1991)

In Tim Campbell's letter to the editor replying to the interview, he asked why Gunderson failed to support gay rights and why he voted "against the 1991 Civil Rights Act just a few weeks ago? These are not the signs of 'strong advocates' of civil rights" (Campbell 1991a).

The interviewer had also asked Gunderson about his stand on the federal gay rights legislation, to which the congressman replied, "To be honest, I have not studied the issue. I have been consumed with the dairy and higher education bills." This might have been a calculated answer coming from a representative of a dairy state, but Gunderson had been in Congress for nearly twelve years, during which time, as Campbell pointed out, he had managed to vote repeatedly with Jesse Helms and antigay Congressman William Dannemeyer on amendments attached to various bills to hinder education, art, and legal services related to gay issues and AIDS prevention. His claim not to have paid attention to the issue of gay rights strained the credulity of anyone who believed the allegation that he is gay.[72] The *La Crosse*

---

72. The news attention generated by the outing also resulted in the resurfacing of an earlier outing that had not received much media attention. In July 1980, shortly before Gunderson was first elected to Congress, "a Madison attorney filed a lawsuit against Gunderson in which he claims that the Congressman gave him anal warts through sexual intercourse . . . [and] the case was dismissed by mutual consent of both parties" (Campbell 1991b: 13).

Tribune interviewer pressed Gunderson to talk about the issue of out-ing and the right of the public to know about politicians' sexual orien-tation. Gunderson responded that outing was despicable, and that his personal life is no one's business:

> "The key here is, I'm married to my job. I don't really have a per-sonal life, that's it. I'm here at 7 o'clock and here late at night. For better or worse, I've committed my life to public office. The rest is pretty boring. Nothing in my personal life is legitimate discussion unless I am breaking the law or using my position for it. I have been accused of all of these things, but I can't prove it to you."
>
> " . . . Are you gay?"
>
> "I can't answer that, because I can't prove it to you." (Kraemer 1991)

The congressional closet door was opened again a few months later, but this time the deed was done by a nongay journalist. During a live television discussion of Oliver North's memoirs, journalist Christopher Hitchens challenged Representative Dana Rohrabacher's support of North and commented, "Look, Congressman Rohrabacher is known around the Hill as a person who's very easily excited by young men in uniform."[73] Rohrabacher gasped, while Hitchens continued, "That's fine in itself, but it's warping his political judgment in this case." Rohrabacher exploded, "I don't have to take this. This is a terri-ble thing to say on the air. What kind of a scum bag are you?" Hitchens later claimed "it was not his intention to out Rohrabacher, but to 'plant the idea that he has internal conflicts about his sexual orientation.' " The executive director of the Human Rights Campaign Fund said that Rohrabacher, a Republican from conservative Orange County in Southern California, was "almost always on the other side of our is-sues. He's no friend of the gay community, but I know nothing about his sexual orientation" (Zeh 1991). Six months later, when the District of Columbia passed legislation mandating domestic partnership be-nefits for lesbian and gay employees, Washington liberals prepared for the usual move by the House Home Rule Committee to overturn the

---

73. Hitchens, who had outed Terry Dolan in a 1987 *Harper's* article, has a history of outing closeted gays that seems tainted with a strain of bigotry. The *Harper's* article, sub-titled "Fear and Self-loathing on the Gay Right," refers to "a long and not so surprising connection between homosexuality and the right," citing Yukio Mishima and, of course, Nazi Germany (1987: 72). Hitchens's counterparts on the right prefer to spice their ex-posés with commie-queer red-baiting, typically citing Soviet spies Guy Burgess and Donald Maclean.

law, and they were pleased that this time Congressman Rohrabacher seemed less interested in leading the fight against a piece of progay legislation.

The Pentagon Provides a Poster Boy

Connoisseurs of closet coverage will have enjoyed a half-page *New York Times* profile of Pete Williams, assistant secretary of defense for public affairs and the "voice of the Pentagon" during the Gulf War, that concluded with five paragraphs about his bachelorhood, attributed primarily to his workaholic schedule. Friends and relatives are quoted to make the point that "he always put his energy into his job, and in Washington all he does is work. Frankly, I've never seen him make room in his life for a woman" (Sciolino 1991). This article, written in February 1991, took on an ironic twist six months later when the story of Pete Williams became a milestone in the unfolding saga of outing.

Michelangelo Signorile had long been receiving tips about Pete Williams from people angry over the Department of Defense's policy of excluding lesbian and gay people from the military. With Williams's sudden media visibility during the Gulf War he "got a tidal wave of information about the topic once again as well as a lot of pressure from colleagues urging [him] to expose the truth" (Signorile 1991e: 34). Signorile was well aware of the severity and the cost—in dollars and in human suffering—of the military's discriminatory policies. In fact, despite the gay movement's dramatic gains in securing protection against discrimination in cities and states around the country, under the Reagan and Bush administrations the Pentagon's antigay efforts had intensified:

> The Pentagon relentlessly conducts witchhunts year after year and has netted almost 13,000 queers since 1982, all of whom have been discharged because they're "incompatible" with military service. People are interrogated and tormented after their homosexuality is revealed, their superiors demanding to know who else in the service may be gay. They're threatened with their children being taken away, their families being informed of their sexuality, and their lives being ruined. Whether they cooperate or not, the queers are kicked out of the military and branded with a mark on their discharge papers that stigmatizes them forever. Some are so demoralized by their treatment and shaken by the disclosure of their homosexuality that they are driven to murder and suicide. While a handful of lesbians and gay men have fought back and gone public with their stories, most slink into obscurity, humiliated and afraid. (ibid.)

One of those who refused to slink into obscurity was Air Force Captain Greg Greeley, who marched in the Washington, D.C., gay pride parade on June 23, 1991, the day before he was due to be discharged. He was interviewed by a reporter at the march, and the next morning he was quoted on the front page of the *Washington Post* (Bruni 1991b). Rather than getting the honorable discharge he was expecting, Greeley was ordered to appear for questioning by the Office for Special Investigations, where he was threatened with a full-scale investigation if he refused to name other gays in the Air Force. Faced with a lengthy delay that would cost him the civilian job he was due to begin, but unwilling to give in to the pressure, Greeley went to veteran Washington activist Frank Kameny, who helped bring the case to the attention of the media and sympathetic members of Congress, who "put pressure on Air Force officials to stop the investigation of Greeley. On June 25 Greeley was granted his honorable discharge" (O'Neill 1991c).

The Air Force acted quickly once the harassment of Greeley became public—the *Washington Post* had put the story on the front page—but this incident proved to be the spark that exploded Pete Williams's closet door. When Michael Petrelis read the *Post* account, he promptly called a press conference for June 28 at which he announced that "Pete Williams, an openly closeted gay man, hypocritically remains silent in his job as Pentagon spokesman while the Department of Defense continues its irrational policy of ejecting thousands of gays and lesbians from the armed services" (quoted in Signorile 1991e: 35).

The press conference was attended by reporters from the *Washington Post*, the Associated Press, and other print and electronic media outlets, but no one ran the story. Petrelis and his associates in Washington's Queer Nation chapter also put up posters around town, showing Pete Williams surrounded by large print: "ABSOLUTELY QUEER. PETE WILLIAMS. PENTAGON SPOKESMAN, TAP DANCER. CONSUMMATE QUEER." In somewhat smaller print it read, "Gay Bush appointee sits by while gay servicemen and women are burned." The posters were quickly torn down, but the town was buzzing with the news, which "had become the chatter of Washington dinner parties, the buzz in gay and right-wing circles, and, according to insiders, the hottest gossip in every boardroom at the Pentagon itself," according to Michelangelo Signorile. Signorile's phone

rang endlessly as network correspondents, major daily reporters, producers, and editors inquired as to what I was doing, looking for information. They saw a scandal, not unlike any other involving hypocrisy within the government hierarchy, and they were eager to do the story themselves. Indeed, many of them tried. But it seemed that when the decision went to the very top of their news organizations, their pieces were always nixed. (ibid.)

Signorile was indeed working on a Williams article and had completed the bulk of the research by the time the Greeley incident turned Pete Williams into the latest Queer Nation poster boy. But before it could be published, Signorile's story hit a snag of a totally different kind. On the same day that Michael Petrelis held his press conference and unveiled the Pete Williams poster, *OutWeek*, the magazine that launched outing and gave Signorile a platform, was closed down by a fight among its owners. Contrary to the assumptions trumpeted by media accounts of the magazine's demise, it wasn't its outrageous politics that killed *OutWeek*:

> Big business killed *OutWeek*, not the street action of political struggle but the universal arena of human greed. . . . The magazine [became] little more than a footnote in a symphony of million-dollar lawsuits and countersuits . . . [pitting] *OutWeek*'s ex-publisher Morrison against his former friends and business partners, Steven Polakoff, Lawrence Basile and Michael Carver, in a battle for control of DIAL Information Services, three multimillion-dollar phone-sex companies Morrison virtually invented." (Kaiser 1992b: 28)

As Larry Kramer bitterly remarked, "*OutWeek* didn't have to die. It was killed by those assholes who thought more of their own greedy needs than of this precious child they'd brought into the world" (ibid.: 31).

Signorile's story about Pete Williams, scheduled as the cover story for the next issue of *OutWeek*, was now orphaned and up for adoption. The first taker was the *Village Voice*, where "it was accepted by executive editor Richard Goldstein, bought by editor-in-chief Jonathan Larsen, and set to run" (Signorile 1991d). But the story's troubles were not yet over. Attentive readers are probably aware by now that the *Village Voice* staff included several vociferous critics of outing who had previously tangled in print with Signorile; they loudly protested the piece on Williams. In an atmosphere of tension heightened by the recent condemnations of the *New York Times*'s decision to report the identity of the accuser in the William Kennedy Smith rape trial—the uproar at the *Times* led to an "emotional meeting [at which] 300 staffers hissed, booed and hooted their displeasure before some of the *Times*'s top brass" (Lacayo 1991)—the *Voice* editors held an unprecedented open staff meeting on July 3 to discuss the story. According to Richard Goldstein's account of the meeting (1991), "a cross-section of writers and editors—male and female, gay and straight—agreed that it would be inappropriate" to out Williams. Goldstein was the only openly gay staff member to speak in favor of the story, and he presented arguments based on the military's active discrimination and the "hypocrisy of an institution that applies one standard to recruits and another to a man close to the seat of power." His words unavailing, Goldstein "was left with an ominous sense that, for many in that meeting, there are no grounds for disclosing someone's homosexuality without consent" (ibid.).

After the turnaround at the *Voice*, Signorile's article finally found a home at the *Advocate*, which set it as the cover story for the August 27 issue. Aware that mainstream media had ducked the story when Queer Nation outed Williams in Washington, the *Advocate* decided to build an irresistible ground swell by distributing advance copies of the article and by linking the outing of Williams to "the military's increasingly violent exclusion of gays and lesbians from the armed forces" (Rouilard 1991b).

Because the *Advocate* had previously maintained an anti-outing stance (despite various occasions on which it had revealed someone's hidden homosexuality), the editors apparently felt obliged to defend this highly visible outing by demonizing Pete Williams sufficiently to make his crime fit the punishment. The cover showed Williams's familiar face juxtaposed with a large headline: "Did This Man Ruin 2,000 Lives, Know About the Suicides, Waste Taxpayers' Millions on Military Witch-hunts?" The issue opened with a two-page editorial comment introduced by this statement: "We commit ourselves to this singular instance of outing in the name of the 12,966 soldiers who have been outed by the military since 1982" (Rouilard 1991a), which recounted some of the details of the military's antigay policies and put Williams on the spot:

> We have been reporting military horror story after horror story since the beginning of this newsmagazine. Williams clearly is intimately involved in policy-making on the highest levels. His silent complicity in this noxious conspiracy allows his superiors to continue the blanket exclusion, the hateful investigations, the dishonorable discharges, the ruination of lives. . . . All reports confirm that Williams has never once interceded on behalf of gay and lesbian soldiers. He remains silent. We choose not to be, and we have that right. We censure. (ibid.)

In addition to establishing that Williams is, indeed, a gay man who has regularly moved in Washington's gay circles and reviewing the shameful details and consequences of the military's antigay policies, Signorile's lengthy article focused attention on the particularly embarrassing case of the Gulf War veterans. The military conflict that put Pete Williams on the nation's TV screens had also put the army's discriminatory policies under a spotlight when the *Wall Street Journal* reported

> that those lesbians and gay men who served in the Persian Gulf with their superiors' full knowledge of their homosexuality and without any actions being brought against them at the time would now be discharged, having been useful to the U.S. government, it seems, only during wartime. In late July, the *Journal* reported that discharge proceedings had begun on at least seven veterans of Operation Desert Storm. (Signorile 1991e: 36)

The blatant contrast between military policy and Williams's sexuality led a vociferous opponent of outing to reconsider. Speaking to Signorile, Sandra Lowe, an attorney with the Lambda Legal Defense and Education Fund who has defended gay servicemen, supported the outing:

> "There are rare times in history when I think extraordinary steps must be taken. . . . Pete Williams's silence, in the last couple of years, has hurt us. And I think his silence right now is hurting us. If his homosexuality being known becomes a major issue, it can make a difference in the policy. We all have an obligation, when we see injustice, not to hide behind privilege when our brothers and sisters are being hung out to dry. It almost seems like being a Jew in the SS and relying on everybody's silence and complicity." (ibid.: 44)

The *Advocate*'s strategy paid off, because this time the story broke through the resistance of the media gatekeepers who had squelched the June outing. On July 31, a local New York television station, Channel 11 (WPIX), "broadcast a segment using Williams' name and reporting that the *Advocate* was outing him, airing footage from a Queer Nation press conference back in June" (Ledbetter 1991), but no one else picked up the story. Then, on August 3, Jack Anderson's syndicated column was headlined "Gay Group Tries to 'Out' Pentagon Spokesman" (Anderson and Van Atta 1991a).[74] The Anderson column de-

---

74. The column's lead sentence added a new and, as it turned out, fictitious twist to the story: "Pete Williams, the lanky, bespectacled Pentagon spokesman who became a household face during the Persian Gulf War, is considering resigning because of accusations that he is a homosexual." Questioned by *Time*, Anderson's associate Dale Van

scribed the outing of Williams by Queer Nation and made clear its connection with the military's "dubious policy against gay soldiers." In a later letter to *Time* magazine, Anderson and his associate, Dale Van Atta, claimed that "it was not our intention to out [Williams]. The gay media and others had already done that. Our purpose was to out the Pentagon policy from the closet of bigotry and paranoia" (1991b).

Anderson's column is syndicated in approximately 800 newspapers around the country, but some of the largest, such as the *Washington Post* and the *San Francisco Chronicle*, declined to run this installment. Still, the story did run in hundreds of papers, and many more picked up the lead and ran their own stories. The majority of the articles, whether they included Pete Williams's name (e.g., *Detroit News, Detroit Free Press, New York Daily News, Oakland Tribune, Philadelphia Inquirer*, and Williams's home-state *Saturday Wyoming Tribune-Eagle*)[75] or declined to print the name (e.g., *New York Newsday, New York Post, New York Times, Los Angeles Times*), clearly framed the issue in terms of hypocrisy and discrimination, as when *New York Newsday* coyly referred to "a prominent, high-ranking civilian official of the Department of Defense, an agency that routinely discharges members of the armed forces for being gay or lesbian" (Firestone 1991).

The exposure of Pete Williams's homosexuality at the same time that the Pentagon was booting out lesbian and gay Gulf War veterans put the military on the defensive. Defense Secretary Dick Cheney was squarely on the hot seat because Pete Williams was his protégé, a Wyoming journalist who had joined Cheney's staff when Cheney was a congressman and had moved with him to the Defense Department. Two days after Anderson's column appeared, Cheney was a guest on a Sunday-morning television program, ABC News's "This Week with David Brinkley," where he was asked about the *Advocate* story. The *New York Times*, which ran an unsigned three-paragraph article on the bottom of page ten, reported that Cheney "defended the right of homosexuals to hold civilian jobs at the Pentagon, saying that as long

---

Atta admitted that Williams "directly said . . . he had no plans to quit. . . . 'I said he was considering resigning, and that's a far cry from saying he was seriously considering it' " (Henry 1991).

75. It is interesting to note that both Detroit newspapers ran articles on Pete Williams written by openly gay reporters; in the case of the *Detroit News* the writer of the front-page story was media critic Michael McWilliams. Detroit's history of pioneering openly gay mainstream journalism was furthered in May 1992 when Deb Price initiated the first regular column on lesbian and gay issues in a daily newspaper, the *Daily News*, also syndicated in other Gannett papers including *USA Today* (Clark 1992).

as they fulfilled their professional responsibilities their private lives were their own business" (August 5: A10). In other interviews he distanced himself from a policy he said he had "inherited" and discounted the security risk argument against gays as "a bit of an old chestnut," although he stood by the basic military policy of exclusion, repeating the military code mantra that "homosexuality is incompatible with military service."[76] But the magical powers of this phrase had been seriously weakened by the exposure of the hypocrisy embodied by Pete Williams. Within weeks of the *Advocate* article both the *New York Times* and the *Washington Post* ran editorials attacking the military's antigay policy, and *Time* magazine published a lengthy account of the controversy surrounding the issue that was clearly sympathetic to the gay cause (Gibbs 1991). The fissure created by the Williams case continues to undermine the Pentagon's position.

In a 1992 presidential campaign speech to a lesbian and gay organization in Los Angeles, Bill Clinton, then governor of Arkansas, referred to a study commissioned and then suppressed by the Pentagon that found no evidence to support the exclusion of homosexuals: "As soon as the Pentagon issued a study, ironically by a spokesperson who himself is said to be gay, which said there was no basis in national security [for the discriminatory policy], I said I would act on the study." When the *Dallas Morning News* broke the story in May 1992 that the Federal Emergency Management Agency (FEMA) had coerced a gay employee to name other closeted lesbian and gay employees "because gays might be security risks and thus susceptible to blackmail" (Signorile 1992b), the story became a national scandal, with numerous newspaper editorials condeming FEMA. A *New York Times* May 15 editorial, "Witch Hunt at FEMA," made a thinly veiled reference to Pete Williams by noting that, "at the Pentagon, where comparable concerns might have more validity, top officials say they're not concerned that gays, even closet gays, are security risks."

The outing of Pete Williams is a prime exhibit for the defense of outing as a political strategy: it placed the issue of military antigay discrimination squarely on the public agenda and helped keep it there (partly as a result of Williams's continued visibility as Pentagon

---

76. Williams himself, when asked at his regular Pentagon press briefings if he would confirm or deny the allegations, replied, "As a government spokesman, I stand here and I talk about government policy. I am not paid to discuss my personal opinions about that policy or talk about my personal life, and I don't intend to" (Federal News Service, August 6, 1991).

spokesperson). At the same time, this case reopened the debate about outing in both gay and mainstream circles.

Thomas Stoddard, then executive director of the Lambda Legal Defense and Education Fund, who had previously criticized outing in newspaper interviews and on TV talk shows, said that the Pete Williams story was "the *only* example in which outing has advanced the interests of gay people" (quoted in Kaiser 1992a: 77). Some mainstream media writers agreed with this judgment, including openly gay *Detroit News* media critic Michael McWilliams, who argued that

> outing should be used only in extreme cases. . . . Some cause-and-effect relationship must be established between a gay person doing his or her job and doing damage to other gay people. Does Williams qualify? I think he does . . . [because] he puts polish on the facade of perhaps the most systematically anti-gay organization in the United States. And since he's so good at his job, he covers up the suffering of every gay and lesbian who's ever been driven out of the military. (1991: 12C)

The *Los Angeles Times* ran a set of opposing opinion pieces by gay writers. San Francisco journalist Randy Shilts, who had hugged the middle ground on outing, called a plague on both houses by citing Cheney's "awesome institutional hypocrisy" but also characterizing outing as nastiness committed by "bitchy queens . . . clawing each other. It's not a pretty sight" (1991). Taking the opposing side, Marshall Alan Phillips focused on the double standard of the media when it comes to gay people:

> If a public figure is Jewish or Jehovah's Witness or Hindu, divorced or married or single, Asian or Icelandic or Kenyan, those personal and private facts, if adequately verified, may be duly reported. No need for an on-the-record admission. Only in the case of gays does this silly rule of invisibility apply. It is based on the hackneyed straight assumption that, somehow, being a gay person is innately bad. (M. Phillips 1991)

The debate about outing and the Pete Williams story were the subjects of a column in the *Washington Journalism Review* by editor Bill Monroe, who decried those journalists who participated in "savaging the privacy of a public figure" he referred to as "John Doeson . . . [who] had no record of anti-gay actions" and congratulated those "editors and producers who elected not to crash into Doeson's personal life" (1991). Monroe's column inspired at least two letters to the *Journal* critical of what the writers called censorship. One writer cited Wil-

liams's statement in the *Advocate* story that he is "completely comfortable with everything I do in my job for the Pentagon" as contradicting
Monroe's claim that "Doeson" was innocent of any antigay actions.
The second, a journalism teacher from Texas, implied that reporters
who suppressed Williams's name might have been protecting their access to a source on whom they were dependent.

Marjorie Williams, a *Washington Post* reporter, published an article
in the *Washington Monthly* of September 1991 that reviewed two recent
books focusing on journalistic practices in covering scandals of all sorts
(Garment 1991; Sabato 1991). She covered such episodes as the Gary
Hart adultery case and the many uncovered stories of Washington al-
coholics and mentioned a "radical outing publication . . . trying to
interest the major media in a civilian Pentagon official who is gay," but
she gave her vote to those who decided to preserve his privacy: "It
does terrible violence to the ideal of a common interest to carry too far
the insistence that a particular person, by virtue of gender or sexual
orientation or color or any other index, has a greater responsibility
than others to address a particular issue" (Williams 1991: 42).

But, of course, this is precisely the heart of the issue of outing as it
is considered by gay people. While the mainstream media are preoccupied with the question of political hypocrisy, calibrating their meas-
uring instruments to determine whether a particular case reaches their
threshold of outrage, lesbian and gay activists and journalists are more
likely to factor into their calculations the question of communal responsibility. Living in the closet is understood by many gay people as more
than a purely personal decision. Alexander Cockburn, columnist for
the *Nation*, consulted gay media producer John Scagliotti about the Pete
Williams case, and received an answer that illustrated this point:

> "There's a difference between a passive closet, in which you simply
> survive and hope for the best, and the active closet, which involves
> putting on a heterosexual mask and promoting yourself as such,
> which is in ethical contradiction to your actual life. You've made the
> choice. You're living an actual lie, bringing girls to the company ball
> and so on. So, think about a gay actor who has made the decision to
> advance his career by pretending to be heterosexual. But by doing
> that he is insulting and oppressing all those who are out. Take Barry
> Diller, who is in a position of enormous power at Fox. Why doesn't
> he push for a gay and lesbian TV show, which I could produce,
> which would be a gay version of 'In Living Color'? Now, no one
> wants to out little people, gay teachers and so on—unless gay
> teachers are publicly anti-gay—but I would out people who are gay
> and yet are promoting heterosexuality.

"I believe as a proposition that people should come out. It would
be better for them. But at the same time I understand that such a
public coming out might hurt or confuse children, parents, etc. But
just as there's a difference between being passively and actively in
the closet, you can be actively or passively out. In the former case
you are publicly espousing a cause, and in the latter, passive case,
you are attempting to live a gay or lesbian life within the limits of
what's possible for you and not too hurtful to parents, children, etc.
*One of the reasons straight people don't understand outing is that they don't
understand what it's like to be gay.* It's all more complicated than they
think." (Cockburn 1991: 220, emphasis added)[77]

Identity Politics

Like a streak of lightning, the phenomenon of outing illuminates a
stormy landscape of contending ideologies and conflicting loyalties.
At the root of much of the dispute about outing are unsettled and un-
settling questions about the nature of sexual identity and the responsibilities, if any, that people who engage in homosexual relations have
toward one another.

Beyond the failure to actively oppose bigotry or promote progress,
the public officials, entertainment industry executives, celebrities, and
journalists who have been targets of outing are also faulted for their
unwillingness to publicly identify themselves with the gay community
or show any solidarity with this still much oppressed group. Running
through the articles on outing is the frequent invocation of comparisons between lesbian and gay people and other groups that have
suffered and continue to suffer from oppression, specifically racial
minorities and Jews. While David Geffen invoked blacks and Jews to
imply that stereotypical portrayals are an unchangeable fact of life, his
critics used the analogy in order to highlight the relative indifference
of media executives to the problems faced by gay people: "certainly,
record companies in 1990 wouldn't sign the Ku Klux Klan to do an al-
bum advocating genocide of Blacks and Jews" (Signorile 1990h). But
most frequently the comparison with other minorities is used to de-

---

77. Scagliotti got his show, but not through Barry Diller or Fox. In June 1992, New
York's public broadcasting station, WNYC, originated "In the Life," a gay-themed variety program produced by Scagliotti for distribution over PBS (Johnson 1992). Senate
Minority Leader Robert Dole attacked the show on the floor of the Senate before it had
ever been shown, falsely asserting that it had been produced with taxpayers' money
(the funds were raised privately)—as if lesbian and gay citizens do not pay taxes.

mand "the accountability by gays in high places to their own community, much the way that Blacks, Jews and women in high places are accountable to their respective communities" (ibid.).

The argument for outing is motivated by three related considerations. The primary stimulus that pushed outing from the realm of speculation into the public arena was, as we have noted, the realization of the costs of homophobia dramatically revealed by the AIDS epidemic and a rising tide of antigay violence. In Armistead Maupin's words, "Career and money are no longer sufficient arguments when thousands of people are dying from neglect and hatred and outright abuse. The bottom line is homosexuality is either okay or it's not" (Mallinger 1990). And, for most people in our society, the answer would seem to be that it is not okay. In other words, antigay bias—homophobia and the heterosexism and sexism it springs from—is real and it is life-threatening.

The second impetus for outing is drawn from the initial structure of gay liberation: the political and the personal importance of coming out. The belief that "we'll never have the freedom and civil rights we deserve as human beings unless we stop hiding in closets" (Marotta 1981: 170) is as fervent today as when it was expressed during New York's first gay pride march in 1970. Public opinion research supports this belief with data:

> The polls show that gay activists have not been misguided in their campaign to "open the closet door": personal contact with people who are openly homosexual consistently produces greater tolerance for homosexuality. . . . [In a 1983 poll] among Americans nationwide who personally know an open homosexual, 35 percent were "negative" on [an attitudinal] index. Among those who did not know an open homosexual, the figure was much higher—61 percent Knowing a homosexual also affected support for gay rights. Thirty-one percent of those who knew homosexuals—and 44 percent of those who did not—opposed gay rights, according to our index. What counted was knowing someone who was *openly* gay. Knowing a suspected homosexual made little difference. (Schneider and Lewis 1984)

In the early days of gay liberation it was often said that if all gay people turned lavender overnight, antigay oppression would end the next day. The sheer pervasiveness and distribution of gay people across all levels of society and within all ethnic, racial, and other groupings would, in this fantasy, overcome the biases that are born of the sense that gay people are fundamentally "other," not like us, not like anyone we already know, respect, love. The tactic of outing is thus a sort of selective "lavendering" of individuals who are already visible to mainstream society and therefore are known and often respected and even loved by millions who do not believe that they know any homosexuals. In the 1983 national survey cited by Schneider and Lewis in 1984, two-thirds of the respondents said they did not personally know anyone (family, friends, co-workers) who were "openly homosexual." It is likely that AIDS has lowered this percentage, just as it has vastly increased gay visibility in the media, but the majority of Americans would probably still answer the same way.

What has changed since 1970, obviously, is the conviction that the decision to come out must always be an individual choice. Outers argue that this choice can be made by others, for the greater good of the community. Those who wish to convince their fellow citizens that they do, in fact, know lesbian and gay people are faced with a formidable challenge. They can't very well simply go door-to-door all across the country and break the news individually—"Dear Sir or Madam: Did you know that your son/daughter/uncle/cousin/mother is gay/lesbian?" Using the media to bring to everyone at once the news that familiar and celebrated women and men are lesbian and gay is a way of short-circuiting this impossible individual task. Furthermore, outing proponents would argue that for media-fixated Americans, vicariously knowing openly gay celebrities would be the next best thing to personally knowing openly gay people. Some might even argue that it's better.

The third justification for outing rests on the dual claims that "those who engage in frequent, voluntary homosexual conduct, whatever their state of political awareness, are by definition gay" and that "gays are a real, inescapable minority marching towards increasing self-realization" (Rotello 1990: 52). These final contentions are the most far-reaching of the conceptual and political arguments made in the debate over outing, as they imply a set of assumptions about the nature of gay and lesbian identities and the lesbian and gay community. These contentions take a theoretical as well as a tactical position at one extreme of the "essentialist versus constructivist" dispute that has preoccupied much contemporary gay scholarship.[78]

---

78. The "essentialist versus social constructionist" debates raged throughout lesbian and gay scholarship for much of the past fifteen years (and have their analogues in feminist theory and theories of race as well; cf. Fuss 1989 and Spelman 1988). As someone who felt like a conscientious objector throughout the worst of the conflict—neither will-

Roles or Realities?

Briefly, what might be termed the *traditional* essentialist position as-
sumes that homosexuals are a category of humanity existing in all cultures and throughout history:

> Homosexuality existed in ancient Egypt, in the Tigris-Euphrates Val-
> ley, in ancient China, and in ancient India. Many American Indian
> tribes had institutionalized homosexuality, at least the male variety,
> into the role of the *berdache* (the male woman), while other primitive
> groups have chosen their shamans from among them. Some societies
> in the past have idealized homosexual love, as did the ancient
> Greeks, while others have harshly condemned it, as did the ancient
> Jews. (Bullough 1979: 2)

There are two important components of this perspective on homosexuality: "For the essentialist, homosexuality is a universal, a form
found across cultures and throughout history: and the 'homosexual'
of ancient Greece is directly comparable to the 'homosexual' of modern
London" (Plummer 1981: 94). Writing in this tradition tends to celebrate the tracing of a continuous, if often hidden, thread that unites
contemporary lesbian women and gay men with their counterparts
across time and place. These celebrations have often been political, as
in Jonathan Ned Katz's pioneering *Gay American History* (1976), which
opens with these words:

> We have been the silent minority, the silenced minority—invisible
> women, invisible men. Early on, the alleged enormity of our "sin"
> justified the denial of our existence, even our physical destruc-
> tion. . . . Our existence as a long-oppressed, long-resistant social
> group was not explored. We remained an unknown people, our
> character defamed. The heterosexual dictatorship has tried to keep us
> out of sight and out of mind; its homosexuality taboo has kept us in
> the dark. That time is over. The people of the shadows have seen
> the light; Gay people are coming out—and moving on—to organized
> action against a repressive society.[79]

---

ing to accept the dominant social construction position in its full-blown excess, nor adhering to the often romantic and politically regressive alternative camp—I do not believe
it is necessary to rehearse here the entire argument. For a comprehensive set of alternative positions, and some encouraging moves toward synthesis, see Stein 1992 (especially the chapters by Boswell, Epstein and Stein) and Roscoe 1988.

79. By 1983, when Katz published a sequel, *Gay/Lesbian Almanac*, he had become converted to social constructionism and now noted that he was adopting a "circumspect use
of terms and concepts" in order to "correct my own earlier usage in *Gay American History*

These celebrations have also had a more spiritual focus, as in Judy Grahn's evocation of myths and language to connect past and present:

> The Gay culture I have set about to describe is old, extremely old, and it is continuous. The continuity is a result of characteristics that members teach each other so that the characteristics repeat era after era. I have found that Gay culture has its traditionalists, its core group, that it is worldwide, and that it has tribal and spiritual roots. Gay culture is sometimes underground, sometimes aboveground, and often both. . . .
>   The position that Gay people take in society, the function we so often choose, is that of mediator between worlds. We transfer power, information, and understandings from one "world" or sphere of being to another. In a tribal environment, this means shape-shifting into wolves, birds, stones, the wind, and translating their wisdoms for the benefit of the people of the tribe. In a modern urban environment it may mean living in a port city, helping to absorb and translate new arrivals of all kinds; in the long patriarchal history that has gradually enveloped the world's people, the Gay function has been to make crossover journeys between gender-worlds, translating, identifying and bringing back the information that each sex has developed independently of the other. (1984: xiv, 269)

As might be imagined, objections have been made to these celebratory schools of lesbian and gay history, on grounds of both conceptual rigor and empirical evidence. The primary objections have come from sociologists and historians who describe themselves as social constructionists. These scholars argue that "there are no objective, culture-independent categories of sexual orientation—no one is, independent of a culture, a heterosexual or homosexual" (Stein 1992: 340). Therefore, in this view, homosexuality is not a transhistorical phenomenon that takes on somewhat differing form and coloration under varying local conditions. According to some social constructionists, the homosexuality that exists in the modern Western world is a conceptual product of the late nineteenth century, when "the spread of a capitalist economy and the growth of huge cities were allowing diffuse homosexual desires to congeal into a personal identity" (D'Emilio and Freedman 1988: 226). At this point, responding to "real changes in the social organization," medical writers came to describe homosexuality "not as

---

where the word 'homosexual' was employed in reference to phenomena of the early colonial era, and the specific historical character of early colonial 'sodomy' was thereby obscured" (1983: 14).

a discrete, punishable offense, but as a description of the person, encompassing emotions, dress, mannerisms, behavior, and even physical traits" (ibid.). In the influential phrasing of Michel Foucault, "The sodomite had been a temporary aberration; the homosexual was now a species" (1978: 43).

Other social constructionists take a more extreme position, which Stein terms the "empty category version of constructionism," according to which it is inaccurate to talk about sexual orientations at all because they are merely figments of our society's need to categorize people. In illustration of this view Stein quotes Gore Vidal's statement that "there is no such thing as a homosexual, no such thing as a heterosexual. Everyone has homosexual and heterosexual desires and impulses and responses" (Stein 1992: 342). For this camp, the categories heterosexual and homosexual might be akin to the medieval category of witch: "There were people in the 17th century who were claimed (sometimes by others and sometimes by themselves) to be witches but we now know that there were no witches (i.e., there were no women with supernatural powers who had sex with the devil) and the category witch . . . did not properly apply to any person" (ibid.).

Whereas constructivist positions present a radically historicized view that emphasizes the *discontinuity* of socially defined roles and labels, what is termed the essentialist position suggests a contrasting focus on *similarities* of patterns of sexual attraction.[80] As John Boswell put it, in response to a constructivist view:

> Would it not be more economical to hypothesize that a percentage of human beings in all societies prefer their own gender sexually, that they are sometimes able to institutionalize this preference, and that the majority of human beings are sufficiently flexible to be able to derive sexual satisfaction from either gender under institutional pressure, whether or not that gender is their first choice? (quoted in Mass 1990: 220)

Boswell accepts the proposition that every person's experience, including sexuality, will be determined in a "largely irresistible way" by

---

80. I say it is termed the essentialist position because this is a characterization applied by its constructivist opponents. As John Boswell, a prominent scholar who has been so characterized, responded, "It seems to me that the common understanding of essentialist is a kind of stereotype presented by constructionists as a target rather than a position ever outlined by anyone who actually believes it" (Mass 1990: 213). As Charley Shively put it, essentialism is really a construction of the social constructionists (quoted in Stein 1992: 326).

"the social matrix in which she or he lives," and that this includes "creating (or not creating) opportunities for sexual expression and possibly even awareness of sexual feelings and desires" (Boswell 1992: 135). Yet he points out that "agreeing on this, however, hardly begins to address the problematic underlying questions, such as whether society is itself responding to sexual phenomena that are generic to humans and *not created* by social institutions" (ibid.).

In contrast to the radical "empty category" social constructionists, the view proposed by Boswell might be analogous to pointing out that human beings in all cultures and periods have had blood types, even though the awareness and classification of blood types is a modern phenomenon. Identifying and naming blood types did not bring them into being and, in this analogy, there may have been people we might reasonably call homosexuals in the premodern past and in non-Western societies, even though we would acknowledge the vast variety of ways they would have experienced and described their own sexuality.

Many important theoretical and political differences flow from these two positions. Most crucial among them are their implications for the question obsessively asked (by heterosexuals): What causes homosexuality? (translation: What went wrong? Whose fault was it? How can it be prevented?). The strong versions of social constructionism that deny biology a role in the determination of sexuality would be seriously undermined by a demonstration that, say, "a predeliction for sexual activity with one gender could be shown to be innate in all humans or fixed in childhood in all (or even many) known cultures" (Boswell 1992: 138). Social constructionist David Halperin acknowledges that "if it turns out that there actually is a gene, say, for homosexuality, my notions about the cultural determination of sexual object-choice will—obviously enough—prove to have been wrong" (1990: 49). Thus, it was only to be expected that neuroscientist Simon LeVay's claim to have found evidence of biological determinants (or, at least, correlates) of sexual orientation (1991) would set off a barrage of counterattacks from the strict constructionists (cf. Gallagher 1991c); similar responses awaited the publication of a study of twins by psychologist Michael Bailey and psychiatrist Richard Pillard (1991), purporting to show support for a genetic basis of homosexuality (Gessen and McGowan 1992).

In contrast to the suspicion voiced by many lesbian and gay scholars, the mass media loudly trumpeted the findings of these studies, proclaiming them as evidence for biological determination of sexual orientation and sex roles. The cover of a February 1992 issue of

Newsweek featured a close-up photograph of a baby's face, over which is superimposed the stark headline "Is This Child Gay?" Whatever the status of the theoretical and empirical debates waged by researchers and theoreticians, the public discourse concerning sexuality and sexual orientation is overwhelmingly essentialist. That is, despite the tireless repetition of the fundamentalist jingle "God created Adam and Eve, not Adam and Steve," fewer and fewer people seem convinced by the argument that homosexuality is merely a perverse choice of "lifestyle" adopted in order to—what? Irritate our parents? Frighten the horses? The official media sex educators, Ann Landers, Dear Abby, Dr. Ruth, and their ilk, have long since abandoned the "it's a phase" and "perhaps she will meet the right man" phrases of comfort to worried parents and adopted such "liberal" alternatives as "they're born that way" and "sexual orientation is determined early in life, and is not a matter of choice." Likewise, the preponderance of lesbian and gay political rhetoric, both within the community and externally, reflects an essentialist position, insisting that one doesn't "choose" to be gay, but "recognizes and accepts" that one is.

In an important sense, however, both the constructionist and the essentialist positions assume that there *are* at present, in our society, persons who can be appropriately labeled homosexuals (and, conversely, heterosexuals)—whether they are seen as the latest metamorphoses of universally recurring orientations or as completely novel, "modern, Western bourgeois productions" (Halperin 1990: 8). That is, however these theoretical perspectives may vary in assigning ontological causes for the appearance of homosexuals in our midst, they both seem to agree that such people *do* exist here and now.

This brings us back to the claims made by the proponents of outing: first, that those who engage in "frequent, voluntary homosexual conduct, whatever their state of political awareness, are by definition gay"—an implicitly essentialist position; and second, that "gays are a real, inescapable minority marching towards increasing self-realization" (Rotello 1990: 52).[81] Whatever position one takes on the issue of the "reality" of homosexuality, the next question that must be addressed is whether the term "lesbian and gay community" (or lesbian

---

81. That these two claims are not identical can be illustrated by analogy with handedness: one can believe that left-handedness is a real attribute (i.e., not merely a form of laziness or recalcitrance) yet not wish to claim that left-handed people should constitute themselves as a minority on the model of an ethnic group, sharing a fundamental, encompassing identity.

and gay communities) has anything more than a convenient rhetorical status.

Coming Out and Coming Together

Sexual acts between members of the same sex occur in all societies, but only in some instances have they become the organizing principle for distinctive subcultures, and only in recent times have these subcultures achieved a level of public visibility comparable to ethnic and racial communities (Weeks 1981). The emergence of modern gay and lesbian subcultures (which are not necessarily or always the same) was made possible by the transformations and dislocations wrought by industrialization, which "brought rapid growth to the cities, often rupturing traditional family relations," and the movement toward "the privatization of sexuality, like religion, in the liberal philosophy of the growing bourgeoisie" (Adam 1978: 25). As unprecedented numbers migrated from rural to urban areas there grew up in these expanding cities a wide range of voluntary communities and forms of association:

> Homosexually inclined women and men, who would have been vulnerable and isolated in most pre-industrial villages, began to congregate in small corners of big cities. Most large nineteenth-century cities in Western Europe and North America had areas where men could cruise for other men. Lesbian communities seem to have coalesced more slowly and on a smaller scale. . . . Areas like these acquired bad reputations, which alerted other interested individuals of their existence and location. . . . By the late 1970s, sexual migration was occurring on a scale so significant that it began to have a recognizable impact on urban politics in the United States. (Rubin 1984: 286)

These are conditions for the emergence of deviant self-images, subcultural identities and argot. All of these have existed for centuries but have multiplied and become more widely visible in the past hundred years. At present most young lesbians and gay men get their first introduction to what it means to be gay, and how it's done, from mainstream mass media, as well as, for those with access, various gay publications, including pornography. This is one reason why the pervasive negative stereotyping of gay people in the mass media has been consistently singled out by the gay movement as a major source of oppression and self-oppression (see Dyer 1977; Russo 1987; Gross 1989).

Unlike ethnic or racial communities into which people are born and in which they are reared, sexual subcultures are joined much later in life. They are also joined secretly, at least at first. Most gay people believe, probably correctly, that those closest to them—family, friends, institutional authorities—will not be pleased to learn the truth about their sexual identity. This initial stage of "coming out" tends to be a private, individual recognition that often occurs long before any physical homosexual experience.[82] It requires confronting the prejudices that everyone acquires as a member of a sexist and heterosexist society: "We learn to loathe homosexuality before it becomes necessary to acknowledge our own" (Hodges and Hutter 1974).

The next stages of coming out are more social and public, within the confines of whatever gay subculture the person can find and can muster the courage to join. At this point, there are skills to learn and codes to master: where to locate potential partners, how to identify likely candidates, how to negotiate with them, and, if successful, where and how to conduct these potentially dangerous activities (as of 1992 homosexual acts were illegal in 24 states and the District of Columbia; they are capital crimes in many countries).

Beyond coming out into a gay subculture are the stages John Alan Lee (1977) termed "going public," and these also can be categorized in phases, although there is no standard sequence followed by most people and few traverse the entire territory. Typically, the person who is going public begins by revealing his or her homosexuality to family, friends, and co-workers. Even within this relatively restricted public there are many variations and degrees of coming out. Because so many lesbian women and gay men move to large cities with concentrations of gay people, they may be quite out at work and where they live and yet still be closeted to their parents and others in their hometowns. Becoming associated with a lesbian and gay movement group and becoming an "activist" is often an important part of going public, although Lee's 1977 projection of at most 1 percent of Toronto's gay population is probably still a reasonable estimate of the proportion of lesbian and gay people who are active in such organizations. An even smaller number end up being publicly identified in the media—occasionally before filling in the typically prior step of coming out to family members: on more than a few television talk shows a guest

---

82. A gay journalist writing about contemporary gay life describes a twenty-year-old he met in a San Francisco gay bar. "He tells me that he wouldn't even think about telling his parents that he is gay; in fact, he adds gravely, he's never had sex before, with a woman or a man" (Hayes 1990). If you're thinking "then how can he be sure that he's gay?" that only proves you haven't been there. To put it another way, how many twenty-year-old virgins are asked if they're really sure they're heterosexual?

who was asked, "Do your parents know that you're gay?" has answered, "They do now!"

Gay people who begin the process of coming out to the straight world often find themselves held back at the threshold by others. "I'm glad you've told me, and you know it won't make any difference to the way I feel about you," many a lesbian or gay person has been told by a parent, "but let's not tell your father (or mother, or grandparents). It would kill him (or her, or them)." Or, "I suppose it's better that you've told us, but please don't tell anyone else, or I don't know how we'll be able to face the neighbors." As a member of the organization Parents and Friends of Lesbians and Gays put it, gay people coming out of the closet meet their parents going in. An openly gay journalist recently wrote about his experience with his family in a way that many gay people would find familiar:

> The last time I went home, five years ago, it took a total of 32.7 seconds (I timed it) from the moment I left baggage claim to the moment when my uncle Luis asked if I was getting married. So I came to this conclusion: As honesty is one of those moral imperatives that was instilled in me by my parents, whom I love, I decided to tell my Mom that, since having to lie about my life has led to the biggest traumas in it, I am not willing to do it again for her, or anyone else's, peace of mind. Simply put, if she is prepared for me to be completely honest when all of our relatives ask me why I haven't met "some nice girl" and gotten married, I will gladly go. If she isn't, it likely isn't me they want to see. (O'Neill 1991a)

All of these responses, of course, merely reinforce the presumption that homosexuality is a dirty secret, best kept discreetly out of sight of those who, to paraphrase Jack Warner's "closeted" Jewish executive, think they don't like gay people and would be disconcerted to learn that someone they know, like, and perhaps even love, is gay.

The pre-Stonewall gay world had much of the flavor of a secret society—a fraternity (and a sorority) bound together by its common bond of reciprocal keeping of confidences. The dangers of this secretive existence also had their attendant pleasures. The in-group knowledge and solidarity of locations and codes, the excitement of shared risk, and the pleasures of gossip—all of these have been challenged and denigrated by a movement that insists on openness and visibility. The growth of something that might, with any semblance of accuracy, be called a gay community came about through the symbiotic processes of coming out and coming together: "Visibility was the precondition for the establishment of lesbian and gay communities that resembled the urban neighborhoods of the immigrant groups in the late nineteenth and early twentieth centuries" (Escoffier 1985: 145).

But concentrations of gay people in particular neighborhoods, along with businesses and organizations created for and by gay people, do not in themselves constitute a community to which all people who engage in homosexual relations can or will feel a sense of belonging or obligation. Going out to a gay bar, despite Congressman Gunderson's retort to Michael Petrelis ("I am out! I'm in this bar, aren't I?"), is not what the gay liberation movement means by coming out. Although the rhetoric of community is widely used by gay activists and their political allies, and often used by their opponents as well, its conceptual and practical fragility is also readily discernable. As one unfriendly observer put it:

> I have to say that I've never really understood the definition of the "gay community." Presumably, some unemployed gay drug addict would be a member of this community. So would a wealthy gay polo-playing socialite. But other than how they choose to use their sexual appendages, I don't see that they have much in common, and it's unlikely the socialite would invite the gay drug addict to cocktails. So how close-knit a community can it be? (Royko 1990)

Association with other members of a "subaltern" group (Spivak 1988), including vicarious association with prominent figures, can provide the soil for the cultivation of a self-image that is less determined by the values of the dominant culture. But this requires an identification with the subaltern group, "the translation of commonality into community" (Adam 1978: 12). For many oppressed groups the experience of commonality is largely the commonality of their difference from, and oppression by, the dominant culture. Within the social construction paradigm, Foucault suggested that the labeling taxonomies elaborated by nineteenth-century professional "discourses on the species and subspecies of homosexuality . . . made possible the formation of a 'reverse' discourse: homosexuality began to speak in its own behalf" (1978: 101). Similarly, it has often been claimed that anti-Semitism may hold together a Jewish identity after religion and tradition are no longer experienced as part of one's selfhood. As Isaac Deutscher put it, "To me the Jewish community is still only negative. . . . Religion? I am an atheist. Jewish nationalism? I am an internationalist. In neither sense am I, therefore, a Jew. I am, however, a Jew by force of my unconditional solidarity with the persecuted and exterminated" (1968: 51).

The experience of Jews offers illuminating insights for understanding gay people because of their similar positions on a "rank order of visibility [which] may be constructed from almost entirely visible, e.g., women, through to almost entirely invisible (blacks through to Jews and gay people)" (Adam 1978: 14). Relative invisibility creates the possibility of *passing*, an option exercised by some people of color and Jews (and, as we've seen, often enforced by external institutions such as Hollywood studios).

The analogy of passing Jews or blacks with closeted lesbian women and gay men requires some critical qualifications, however. In contrast to the former category, as Richard Mohr points out, "it is not the passing gay person who is perceived as a major threat (since from gays who pass there is no fear of pollution through undetected miscegenation). Rather the normal-appearing person being out is a major threat and source of cultural anxiety. For that the normal can be queer means that anyone—father, brother, even you—may be gay" (1991: 26).[83] In most cases passing is not a full-time or totally absorbing role. In fact, as we've seen, all gay people start out by passing, first unconsciously, as we rarely think of ourselves as gay early on, and then consciously, before deciding to come out. And most gay people pass some of the time, because no one can come out over and over, day after day, in opposition to the universal assumption of heterosexuality:

> The [person who is passing] is likely to be somewhat integrated into the subordinated community; his denial of identity continues on a part-time or ambivalent basis. To other inferiorized people, the [person] reveals a more "authentic" identity, discarding a pseudo-identity constructed for superordinate audiences. The former identity is experienced "at ease," the latter as inhibited—an act. (Adam 1978: 95–96)

Among assimilating Jews in turn-of-the-century Europe this strategy was characterized by the advice given by Hebrew poet Y. L. Gordon: "Be a Jew in your tent, and a man when you go out." But, as the private identity was a stigmatized one, the privilege acquired through the public identity was always fragile. As Theodor Herzl wrote, "The emancipated Jew lives in a ghetto of illusions."

Wealth and social position can insulate gay people from the costs

---

83. There is a genre of Hollywood films that might be called "passing films": "Ostensibly they explore the frustrations of light-skinned blacks attempting to jump the color line and pass unnoticed into the white world of privilege. Underneath all the melodrama, they are cautionary tales about race mixing, and ultimately integration and black parity" (Jones 1991).

associated with their stigmatized identity, as they were able to insulate many assimilated Jews from the cruder forms of anti-Semitism in pre-Nazi Germany. But even without the advent of an officially oppressive regime, the cost of this insulation could be counted in the form of self-denial and constriction. Writing in 1926, Richard Bernstein described the assimilated Jew in Weimar Germany, who "trembles for the revelation of his real origin; he keeps himself under constant observation lest he betray himself by a word, a gesture, a look; his life has no more than one aim and purpose: successful camouflage" (quoted in Adam 1978: 96).

Hodges and Hutter in the 1970s wrote about similarly assimilated gay people, who choose to see themselves as part of the "whole human race, refusing to be identified with just one small part of it. 'I'm not joining any liberation movement,' they cry, clambering on to the nigger end of the bus. 'I'm part of the wide, wide spectrum of humanity' " (1974: 36).

Passing also raises the difficult question of definition: who decides who is a member of a subordinate group, and on what basis? Despite the horrendous example of Nazi racial laws that determined that one Jewish grandparent was sufficient to constitute a death warrant, Israeli political parties have struggled mightily over the criteria for determining who is a Jew and thereby eligible for immediate citizenship, among other privileges. In the case of race, Americans have traditionally assumed that any black ancestry made a person black. As Gunnar Myrdal put it, "The definition of the 'Negro race' is thus a social and conventional, not a biological concept" (1964: 115).[84]

Gay identity is more fluid than racial or ethnic identity. As we have noted already, it is a realization one typically comes to as an adolescent, and coming out means abandoning the taken-for-granted heterosexual identity imposed on all infants by society. Thus, coming out has much of the flavor of a conversion experience.[85] For many gay people it is both a confirmation of and an explanation for one's distance from the roles society expects everyone to adopt (this is sometimes labeled

---

84. Under the apartheid system in South Africa, racial identification was a highly significant matter, and a special court existed to adjudicate requests for changes in people's official racial status.

85. Many parents react to the coming out of their children as they might to their children being converted to a "cult" religion, and have even been known to hire "deprogrammers" to kidnap and restore their offspring. On the other side, there is a substantial literary genre of coming-out stories that have a clear resemblance to accounts of religious conversion.

"gender nonconformity"). Coming out entails sacrifice and danger; it often means facing hostility, rejection, and even violence from family, friends, and total strangers. Thus, it is not surprising that many gay people strive to maintain membership in the dominant culture even while participating in the gay subculture. That is, they live double lives.

Often the ability as well as the desire to live in two worlds is a function of social class. In her account of gay male subcultures in Chicago and Kansas City in the mid-1960s, Esther Newton described two categories of homosexuals:

> The overts live their *entire* lives within the context of the community; the coverts live their entire *nonworking* lives within it. That is, the coverts are "straight" during working hours, but most social activities are conducted with and with reference to other homosexuals. These overts and coverts together form the core of the homosexual community. (1979: 21)

Newton's characterization of the two facets of the gay subculture of the 1960s parallels Leznoff and Westley's description of an urban Canadian subculture in the mid-1950s. In both instances the covert homosexuals occupied higher-status positions and had more to risk by being known to be homosexual, while the overt gays were in lower-status occupations "where the homosexual is tolerated . . . and confine[d] most of their social life to homosexual circles" (Leznoff and Westley 1956: 257). Not surprisingly, there was—and is—palpable tension between these two worlds. The overt gays derisively label the coverts "closet queens," while the secret gays are fearful of being too visibly associated with their open counterparts. As one lawyer put it to Leznoff and Westley:

> I know a few people who don't care. They are really pitiful. They are either people who are in very insignificant positions or they are in very good positions but are independent. . . . I can't afford to know them very well, and I try to avoid them. . . . From their point of view it means living completely outside of society and they are no longer interested in people who they consider hypocrites. (ibid.: 259)

The primary tie that binds members of both groups together across the class and social divide is sexual activity itself: the search for sexual partners "forces the secret homosexual out into the open. . . . Thus it is the casual and promiscuous sexual contacts between the . . . secret and the overt . . . which weld the city's homosexuals into a community" (ibid.: 263). In Erving Goffman's dramaturgic terms, the members of both groups were all part of the same performance team. "Each teammate is forced to rely on the good conduct and behavior of his fellows, and they, in turn, are forced to rely on him. There is then, perforce, a bond of reciprocal dependence linking teammates to one another . . . [and] the mutual dependence created by membership in the team is likely to cut across structural or social cleavages . . . and thus provide a source of cohesion" (1959: 82).

Writing in the early 1970s, Newton acknowledged that the term "community" might not be appropriate to characterize gay people, though by the time she was preparing the 1979 edition she noted that "homosexuals are much closer to constituting a political force than they were in 1968," thanks to the emergence of the younger generation of gay activists (1979: 23n.8). But it is far from clear that the cohesion Goffman referred to has erased the distance between the upper and lower echelons of the gay community. The willingness of the young gay waiters and bartenders who were the objects of Malcolm Forbes's forays across the line dividing the covert and overt provinces of the gay world to divulge his secret in the interest of gay liberation does not suggest that two decades of post-Stonewall activism have done that much to erase that line.

Proliferating Identities

The North American lesbian and gay movement has been built on the model of racial and ethnic minorities and has consistently stressed the concept of a gay community: "This 'ethnic' self-characterization by gays and lesbians has a clear political utility, for it has permitted a form of group organizing that is particularly suited to the American experience, with its history of civil rights struggles and ethnic-based, interest group-competition" (Epstein 1992: 255).

The rhetoric of ethnicity adopted by the lesbian and gay movement presents an essentialist definition of an identity assumed to overlay or even supercede other categories of identification such as race or gender or traditional ethnicity. But, as I have already implied in the case of class, these other aspects of personhood and social being do not conveniently fade away once the discovery of a lesbian or gay identity has been proclaimed. Women and people of color, as well as working-class people, have had grounds to complain that this newly celebrated identity was largely molded in the image of white male middle-class experience and aspirations.

An early division within the post-Stonewall gay liberation movement came about when lesbians insisted on the distinctiveness of their experience, and their oppression. An influential formulation of this stance was Adrienne Rich's concept of the "lesbian continuum" of woman-identified experience that can be found throughout each woman's life and throughout history (1980). In Rich's view, lesbian existence is denied not only by the institutionalized heterosexuality of patriarchal society, but also by dissolving lesbians into a generalized gay population. On the contrary, Rich insists, lesbian experience is, "like motherhood, a profoundly *female* experience, with particular oppressions, meanings and potentialities we cannot comprehend as long as we simply bracket it with other sexually stigmatized existences" (1980: 81). Many lesbians who did not share Rich's essentialist belief in a transhistorical, pan-cultural lesbian continuum nevertheless agreed that lesbianism should be defined in terms of identification with women, and thus they preferred to see themselves as lesbian feminists:[86]

> For contemporary lesbians, feminism is *the* language of explanation, legitimation, and, ultimately, redemption. Because gay liberation does not effectively analyze the status of women, even those women who identify primarily with the gay movements recognize a debt to feminism. The power of feminism for lesbians has lain in its ability to link an analysis of gender oppression to critiques of the social construction of sexuality so as to provide a new set of understandings and meanings for lesbians. (Phelan 1989: 112)

But just as lesbian feminists could justly condemn the rhetoric of gay community as male-defined, so, too, they were criticized for painting a portrait of "woman" drawn too narrowly in their own image: "the focus on women 'as women' has addressed only one group of women—namely, white middle-class women of Western industrialized countries . . . [and treated] the differences of white middle-class women from all other women as if they were not differences" (Spelman 1988: 3). Race and class presented alternative claims to be the primary basis on which identities are forged.

For many lesbian women and some gay men, therefore, the pull of competing identities complicates their relationships to an overarching lesbian and gay community, however much they may resonate to its

---

86. Television talk shows seem incapable of understanding the meaning of woman-identification, as witnessed by their constant use of the phrase "lesbian who hates men" to describe guests who identify themselves as lesbian feminists.

claim of an underlying basis for membership. And these alternative identity categories themselves are not without their own complexities and internal divisions. The currently used term "people of color" was adopted in order to accommodate the various groups whose identities were submerged by the earlier "white" versus "black" opposition, while avoiding the definition-by-negation suggested by "white" versus "nonwhite" (the term "colored people" might have made for easier syntax, but was discredited by its earlier racist usages). But it is surely problematic to lump together in this way such a wide variety of racial and ethnic groups, trivializing or denying the tensions and differences that might divide them (as, for instance, Korean and African-American communities in many inner cities). Even the narrower term "Asian Americans" irons out the significant variations in experience and perspective of Chinese, Japanese, Korean, and Philippine cultures, just as "Native American" collapses into one camp diverse and often mutually antagonistic peoples (the Hopi and Navajo, for example, do not appreciate the gesture). In fact, the contemporary world scene is one of rapidly exploding ethnicities, each expressing separatist aspirations based on essentialist national identities.

The proliferation of ethnic and national identities has a parallel within the sexual minority community. The possibility of a unified lesbian and gay identity has been further challenged in recent years by the emergence of groups claiming a distinct identity and equal billing under the larger umbrella of sexual nonconformity. Leading the way in this latest labeling campaign are bisexuals. No longer willing to be seen as occupying a halfway house in the coming out process, or as being a hybrid category occupying positions one through five on Kinsey's zero-to-six scale of sexual behaviors, women and men who insist that they are attracted to members of both sexes have claimed an independently valid identity. "When asked why their struggle is emerging now, some bis draw comparisons to the late '60s, when lesbians and gays who had apprenticed in the civil rights and peace movements grew radicalized enough to make their own demands. Today, bis who apprenticed in the gay movement claim a similar awakening. Their movement is strongest where experimentation and the focus on identity politics is greatest—on campus" (Rotello 1992).

In the late 1980s on campus after campus across the country student groups were challenged to reflect the diversity of alternative sexual identities. At my own institution, the University of Pennsylvania, the group that began life in the mid-seventies as Gays at Penn and changed its name in the early eighties to Lesbians and Gays at Penn was by 1989 called the Lesbian, Gay and Bisexual Alliance.[87] Similarly, at the fifth Lesbian and Gay Studies Conference, held at Rutgers in 1991, a motion was adopted that henceforth there would be Lesbian, Gay and Bisexual Studies Conferences. But it doesn't stop there; it wasn't long before demands were heard for further expansion to include transsexuals and transgendered people. It is easy to see why many have been attracted to the simple inclusiveness of the "queer" label to gather all nonconformist sexualities under one big tent.

Nostalgia for a Place One Has Never Seen

"Rumor and gossip constitute the unrecorded history of the gay sub-culture" (Weiss 1991: 283). Writing about the emergence of lesbian identities in the 1930s, Andrea Weiss cites Patricia Spacks's analysis of gossip as an alternative discourse through which "those who are otherwise powerless can assign meanings and assume the power of representation . . . reinterpreting . . . materials from the dominant culture into shared private meanings" (ibid.). The gossip that Weiss is concerned with, however, is not the exchange of stories about one's friends and acquaintances, but the circulation of rumor and speculation about the lives of movie stars and other celebrities. Lesbian and gay media scholars have demonstrated the central importance of stars in gay ghetto culture and the special relationship gays have had to film (see Dyer 1977, 1979, 1986; LaValley 1985). Living in a world that despised and rejected their feelings, gay people found both escape and affirmation in the darkness of the theater and the luminance of the silver screen.

The crystallizing of lesbian and gay identities is somewhat akin to the rediscovery of their "ethnic roots" by third-generation Americans whose parents had successfully assimilated into the mainstream. But for gay people there were no grandparents to visit, and the stars and stories of popular culture often took the place of the "old country." As Vito Russo put it, "In *Queen Christina*, Garbo tells Gilbert . . . 'It is possible to feel nostalgia for a place one has never seen.' Similarly, the film *Queen Christina* created in gay people a nostalgia for something they had never seen" (1987: 65). "For a people who were striving to-

---

87. Founded in 1973 as the National Gay Task Force and expanded in the mid-1980s to the National Gay and Lesbian Task Force, the most visible national lesbian and gay political organization has so far resisted adding "bisexual" to its name.

ward self-knowledge," Weiss writes of lesbian women in the 1930s, "Hollywood stars became important models in the formulation of gay identity" (ibid.: 288):

> The sexually ambiguous, androgynous qualities that Marlene Dietrich and Greta Garbo embody found expression in the emerging gay sub-culture of the 1930s. Garbo and Dietrich were part of the aristocratic, international lesbian set which was this subculture's most visible and influential component; as such, they played a role in defining the meaning of androgyny for the small, underground communities of lesbians across the country who saw their films and heard about them through rumor. (Weiss 1991: 291)

Despite the explosion of lesbian and gay visibility since the late 1960s, the nearly total absence of openly gay celebrities insures the continuing importance of gossip in the crafting of gay subcultural identity. Insider gay gossip has always focused heavily on the exchange of names of famous people who are secretly gay, just as Jews (and, I'm told, Canadians, or Hoosiers) have told each other with pride about rich and famous people who are, but are not generally known to be, Jewish (or Canadian, or Hoosier).[88]

The denial and erasure of lesbian women and gay men in the formal curricula of our schools and in the informal but even more influential curriculum of our mass media leads to the understandable desire to discover and celebrate the contributions of lesbian and gay figures. Just as African-American activists and educators have brought out the often obscured achievements of people of color, and just as feminist art historians have uncovered the accomplishments of women artists whose work had been misattributed to men (Nochlin and Sutherland 1976), so too have lesbian and gay scholars assembled lists of famous people who were homosexual. These range from the "great queens of history" school of celebratory catalogues (from Sappho and Socrates, to Leonardo and Michelangelo, to Frederick the Great and James Buchanan, to Marcel Proust and Gertrude Stein, and so forth) to the rosters of more contemporary celebrities that are compiled and traded

---

88. A full-page article in Toronto's *Globe and Mail* in August 1992 was devoted to the Canadian fascination with revealing the hidden roots of famous expatriates. The article listed several dozen former Canadians, including intellectual heavyweights Saul Bellow and John Kenneth Galbraith, but, in true outing fashion, focused mostly on show business luminaries from Mary Pickford and Fay Wray to Dan Ackroyd, William Shatner, and Raymond Burr (Freedman 1992).

through gossip networks (from Cole Porter and Mary Martin, to Cary Grant and Barbara Stanwyck, to Merv Griffin and Jodie Foster, to Lily Tomlin and John Travolta, to Martina Navratilova and Greg Louganis, to . . .). Such lists present scholars, journalists, and activists with important issues of evidence and ethics: what constitutes proof of someone's sexual identity, especially when evidence is likely to have been suppressed or destroyed (Duberman [1986] discusses this question), and what considerations should influence the decision to reveal a person's previously hidden homosexuality? Are historians the outers of the past, or are outers the historians of the present?

It is lists like these that are meant when outing proponents talk about role models to help gay people as well as the rest of society counter the stigmatizing images fostered by invisibility and stereotypes. The lack of lesbian and gay role models has been cited as a factor contributing to the alarming statistic that "up to 30 percent of completed adolescent suicides annually" may be accounted for by gay teens (Gibson 1989: 110). *Village Voice* columnist Michael Musto, defending outing in response to a hostile letter, claimed to "get letters from formerly suicidal lesbian teens who now feel empowered" by the knowledge that an outed celebrity is also gay (Musto 1991b).

This is a *celebratory* form of outing, good for building internal morale and easily translated into a public tactic, as when marchers in annual June gay pride parades carry signs with the pictures and names of famous lesbian and gay "ancestors." The more political form of outing that focuses on exposing hypocrites who actively work against gay interests while hiding their own homosexuality has also been a commonplace of gay gossip, and its move into the public arena is the least controversial aspect of outing. But the most radical aspect of outing is the argument that all homosexuals are members of a community, whether they admit it or not, to which they owe a measure of accountability and allegiance:

> Whether gay public figures have an obligation to the gay commons is at the heart of the outing debate. By proclaiming that they do, we redefine the concept of a gay and lesbian community. Because such an assertion presupposes that the gay community is a genuine, inescapable minority like the Black or Latino community, into which one is born, from which one derives advantages and disadvantages, and to which one owes inherent allegiance. It brands as immoral the attempt by powerful gays to escape the social penalties of homosexuality, and asserts a claim of moral kinship where none existed before. (Rotello 1990: 52)

But even gay activists who would not subscribe to such a radical statement are caught in the web of rhetoric spun around the concept "that gay men and women were an oppressed minority and that, like other minorities, they possessed a culture of their own" (D'Emilio 1983: 248). If gay people constitute a *minority* in this sense then the rhetoric of allegiance and accountability is not as far-fetched as it sounds to many who respond to outing as an unwarranted invasion of privacy. Criticizing outing, the co-chair of the Iowa Lesbian and Gay Political Caucus refers to an *ethic*, "and that ethic is that we protect each other" (Johnson 1990); but the concept of an ethic is clearly rooted in the sense of a community. Conventional notions of a community include the expectation that the community will protect its members, and may on occasion sacrifice some members to protect or further the interests of the group. Outing would appear to be an example of such a sacrifice. In traditional political liberalism, the members will, it is assumed, offer themselves voluntarily for possible sacrifice, but there are cases, such as the military draft, where the community compels members to sacrifice themselves. The question, therefore, is whether the present embattled conditions—AIDS, antigay violence, virulent political attacks—override the "longstanding tradition that required sodomites to keep each other's secrets" (Goldstein 1990).

Those threatened with outing are likely to invoke images from our contemporary rogues' gallery of villains, as in writer Fran Lebowitz's characterization of *OutWeek*'s actions: "It's damaging, it's immoral, it's McCarthyism, it's terrorism, it's cannibalism, it's beneath contempt. . . . To me this is a bunch of Jews lining up other Jews to go to a concentration camp" (Lewin 1990). But the analogy to Jews and concentration camps is also used by the proponents of outing, who see powerful closeted gays as analogous to the assimilated Jews who never believed that they would be touched by the crude anti-Semitism directed at the ghetto dwellers. To such people gay liberationists might well reply by citing Hannah Arendt's account of her experience as a Jew expelled from Germany:

> For many years I considered the only adequate reply to the question, Who are you? to be: a Jew. That answer alone took into account the reality of persecution. . . . The statement: I am a man—I would have considered as nothing but a grotesque and dangerous evasion of reality. . . . The basically simple principle here is one that is particularly hard to understand in times of defamation and persecution: *the principle that one can resist only in terms of the identity that is under attack.* Those who reject such identifications on the part of a hostile world may feel wonderfully superior to the world, but their superi-

ority is then truly no longer of this world; it is the superiority of more or less well-equipped cloud-cuckoo-land." (1968: 17–18, emphasis added)

Even without focusing on the present crises of AIDS and right-wing antigay campaigns, however, as the achievements of the lesbian and gay movement steadily expand the possibilities of being openly gay in many places and occupations, there is a corresponding increase in the resentment and hostility toward those who choose to remain closeted while they reap the benefits of expanded psychological and social breathing space created through others' efforts. This resentment is not directed indiscriminately. Just as no one has outed such nonpublic citizens as our hypothetical lesbian gym teacher, no one is blaming the truly vulnerable for remaining in the closet, even though militants who have themselves taken the risks and suffered the costs of being out might wish everyone would follow their lead. On the other hand, to cite an example used by Richard Goldstein, why should a candid performer confined to gay cabaret look kindly on a closet case who gets to chat with Arsenio Hall? Lesbian writer Victoria Brownworth turned the ethical question around, saying that

> every gay man and lesbian woman who "passes" (and tries to) oppresses me further and reaps the benefits of my activism while hiding the strength of our numbers from the people to whom those numbers would make a difference. . . . Is it ethical to stay in the closet, pass for straight, assume the mantle of heterosexual privilege and enjoy its benefits while those who are openly gay suffer the oppression of their minority status? (1990)[89]

It might be objected that the closeted celebrities and media "big fish" who have been the targets of outing are not harming anyone, and not obviously taking advantage of other gay people merely because they are living "private" lives. We may be amused by the disingenuousness of the claim of privacy when it's made by show business celebrities who "share" their lives with millions of television viewers along with Jay Leno, Arsenio Hall, and any other talk show host who will have them, or invite *People* magazine into their home. But, beyond

---

89. For any heterosexual reader who is wondering what is meant by heterosexual privilege, here are two simple educational experiments: by yourself, carry a gay newspaper (with the name clearly visible) in public, and at your workplace; with a confederate of the same sex, hold hands in public (but be careful where you do this, or you may learn a more graphic lesson than you want).

the shallowness of the argument that celebrities deserve to have their privacy protected—when they're not parading their "private" lives before the media—there is the fact that stars not only take advantage of the presumption of heterosexuality but actually promulgate the assumption of the ubiquity and normality of heterosexuality. In other words, their very public pseudoreal lives, endlessly circulated by the gossip media, are cultivating the images and undergirding the ideology that oppress gay people. No one is obliged to make a fabulous living as a movie, television, or recording star, and those who do take on this burden can be held accountable for the images they promote.[90]

Quite aside from the question of the ideological consequences of their public personae, closeted celebrities and public officials are disingenuous in another way when they claim that their private lives are unrelated to the larger lesbian and gay community. There are important ways in which they benefit from the accomplishments of the lesbian and gay movement, even if they lack a sense of political engagement or responsibility. This is not exactly the same as the "minority community" claim that parallels the claims made on prominent Jews or blacks.[91] Any analysis of the changes wrought by the gay liberation movement would note the emergence and flowering of a fully elaborated subculture and suggest that these people are indeed enjoying the fruits of others' labors. In a book written just before the onset of the AIDS epidemic, Toby Marotta described the changes to be seen in Greenwich Village and beyond after the first decade since Stonewall:

> Gay bars, discos, restaurants, bathhouses, sex shows, porn shops, novelty stores, art galleries, and hustling bars, as well as homoerotic books, newspapers, and magazines and gay clothing styles, now abound everywhere. So many sections of the city have been populated densely by gay men and by lesbians that *gayification* may be a

---

90. Although I have concentrated, as have the outing activists, on entertainment celebrities and moguls and establishment public officials, similar claims might be made about the responsibilities of public figures identified with oppositional politics and ideologies. As Richard Mohr asks, "Why would one want to invest one's energies into institutional arrangements which oppress gays unless one had a less than robust sense of self as a gay person so as always to think it proper to defer one's dignity for The Cause?" (1992: 35). In this light, Angela Davis, for example, might consider the political contradictions implied by her guarded personal life.

91. An *OutWeek* writer noted that "Chris Edley, who left his post as head of the United Negro College Fund, recently spoke of successful African Americans who won't contribute to the fund: 'If I had my way, I'd ask them for money and publish in the paper the next day whether or not they gave' " (Goff 1991). This is a technique long ago perfected by the United Jewish Appeal.

more appropriate term than *gentrification* for the renaissance taking place in some local neighborhoods. . . . It is easy to see the same pattern of change . . . in most every sizable American city and in many resort areas. (1981: 327)

The successful gay and lesbian figures who live in well-appointed closets are able to enjoy much fuller gay lives than their counterparts in past generations. Although the upper classes have always been able to indulge in private tastes behind the high walls of their preserves, today's rich and famous have the option to partake of private pleasures in the semipublic precincts of the gay world. Until recently they have done so in the security of knowing that we kept each other's secrets (although we certainly gossiped about them among ourselves). Assistant Secretary of Defense Pete Williams and Congressman Steve Gunderson were two of the many closeted gay men who frequent the gay bars in and around Washington, D.C., and elsewhere. Such people can be condemned as tourists who exploit the freedoms provided by others' efforts and risks while refusing to use the power provided by their positions and visibility for the good of the community, and even occasionally using that power in ways that directly hurt gay people. The response of openly gay people in many instances, understandably, is resentment and, sometimes, outing.

This resentment is deeply felt by many activists, and probably by others less vocal, and it needs to be set beside the measured criticisms of outing given by the leaders of gay movement organizations when they are queried by the press. Eric Rosenthal, the political director of the Human Rights Campaign Fund (a gay political action committee with a closeted name for those reluctant to write checks to openly gay groups), told the *New York Times* that "privacy is a fundamental tenet of what the gay movement is all about" (D. Johnson 1990). Rita Addessa, executive director of the Philadelphia Lesbian and Gay Task Force, told the gay paper *Au Courant* that "people who chose to remain in the closet directly or indirectly do retard the social and political progress of the movement. At the same time, the matter of individual self-determination suggests that each individual has to make that decision for him or herself" (Mallinger 1990).

Thomas Stoddard, then head of the Lambda Legal Defense Fund (a quasi-closeted name for the largest lesbian/gay public interest legal organization), told *Newsweek* that the worst thing about outing is that "it looks mean and nasty. That doesn't advance the gay movement at all" (Gelman 1990). Note, however, that Lambda Legal Defense Fund, as Stoddard and his associates pointed out in a letter to the *Advocate*

(March 12, 1991), has a full-time staff of eighteen, including six lawyers, and an annual budget of $1.6 million. That is to say, without any
invidious intent, Lambda and its peer lesbian and gay organizations
are not radical or extremist. As Michael Bronski put it:

> Acutely aware of their tactical dependency on those in power and
> their economic dependency on broadbased, heterogeneous, donor
> populations, they are forced to always take the most prudent, least-
> extreme position on any given debate. No matter what they might
> really think or feel about outing—and their personal thoughts are as
> varied as their politics—their public opinions reflect the more conser-
> vative end of the discussion. (1990)

The reliance by the mainstream press on these "official" spokespeople is not only a function of the media predilection for limiting their
research efforts to the confines of the Rolodex. It is also a control mech-
anism through which they suggest that outers—or other "extremists"
in other instances—are viewed with hostility and disfavor by the "gay
community." But there is neither any reason to assume nor any way
to determine what the consensus among gay people is, or even if a
consensus exists.

It is likely, however, that such a consensus would be favorable toward *selective* outing: analysis of 549 survey forms returned by readers
of the lesbian and gay quarterly *Out/Look* in late 1990 revealed that 69
percent favored outing "elected or appointed officials who obstruct the
fight against AIDS"; 73 percent favored outing "government officials
who support policies that perpetuate homophobia and obstruct les-
bian/gay rights";[92] and 22 percent favored outing "well-known individuals (not politicians) because they deprive the lesbian and gay
movement of visible role models." Among respondents who said they
were HIV positive, the figures were 83 percent, 88 percent, and 45 percent, respectively (Escoffier and Rocchio 1991). An *Advocate* survey
taken in 1990 was divided 55 percent for to 45 percent against outing
(Rouilard 1991c). It is also important to note that these surveys were
taken long before Pete Williams changed the face of outing.

---

92. As the Connecticut Senate moved toward a vote on a statewide gay rights bill, one
of the most effective proponents was Representative Joe Grabarz, whose courage in coming out in a speech on the Senate floor proved significant to the passage of the bill. The
Hartford gay paper *Metroline* wrote an editorial commending Grabarz, encouraging
"those closeted gay legislators who voted for the bill [to give] serious consideration to following Joe's example," and warning "those closeted gay legislators who voted against
the bill . . . *we know who you are*" (*Metroline* 1991). But they didn't out them.

What is certain is that extremists have always pushed beyond the boundaries respected by the moderates and thus instigated the process of radical change that eventually redraws those boundaries. Just as the young radicals of the gay liberation movement of the early 1970s outraged many of the older "homophile" leaders who stressed education and assimilation, so too today's outers are denounced by the leaders of the established gay movement. But they have nevertheless cracked the code of conduct, and have broken some prominent eggs in the process of making their new sort of omelet.

A Kinder, Gentler Hollywood

"Nineteen ninety-one will be known as the year that altered Hollywood's relationship with gay and lesbian people as never before" (Sadownick 1992: 62). The year began with the furor surrounding *The Silence of the Lambs*, and the fires were further fueled when the Gay and Lesbian Alliance against Defamation (GLAAD) obtained copies of the script of the film *Basic Instinct*, due to be made in San Francisco that spring. The activists were outraged by the depiction of every one of the female characters in *Basic Instinct* as a lesbian or bisexual psychokiller, and they demanded changes. In meetings held in San Francisco as the filming was set to begin, members of GLAAD and Queer Nation were able to persuade the scriptwriter, Joe Eszterhas, that there were serious problems with the screenplay, for which he had been paid a record $3 million. But Eszterhas's proposed changes were rejected by producer Alan Marshall, director Paul Verhoeven, and star Michael Douglas (who was reportedly being paid $12 million for his participation). The filming proceeded and was immediately disrupted by Queer Nationals loudly protesting. The producers obtained a restraining order, and subsequently demonstrators were arrested as both filming and protesting continued for several weeks (Bronski 1992).

Coming on the heels of the opening of *The Silence of the Lambs*, the anger over *Basic Instinct* led Michelangelo Signorile and other activists to call for a march on Hollywood in 1992, to call showbiz gay and lesbian power holders and celebrities to account (Sadownick 1991). The march never took place, but the calling to account taking place in the gay press, in protests and threats of protests, began to have an impact. The much-decried homophobia of the show business capital came into focus in 1991 in two ways that related to AIDS: the embarrassing silence of the studios when it came to dealing with the epidemic and the revelation of the scandalous treatment of actors who were known or thought to be suffering from the disease.

It has often been noted that Hollywood dotes on fatal diseases as a never-failing theme for three-hankie movies. From *Love Story* to *Terms of Endearment* (to use only fairly recent examples), the film industry has had an affinity with the hero who dies young—but not from AIDS. Most recently, in fact, the film *Dying Young* was widely seen (but not, as it turned out, by audiences) as a transparent translation of AIDS into more acceptable (and heterosexual) leukemia. It isn't difficult to come up with theories to explain the aversion to AIDS in the movies and network television (there was a made-for-TV movie, *An Early Frost*, in 1985, and another, *Our Sons*, in 1991). Gay journalist Randy Shilts—whose books *The Mayor of Castro Street: The Life and Times of Harvey Milk* (1982) and *And the Band Played On* (1987), a history of the AIDS epidemic, have long been "in development" as a movie and a TV miniseries respectively—says that "for the movie industry, AIDS is still spelled g-a-y, and most studios believe that anything gay is box-office poison" (Lew 1991). Although Howard Rosenman, executive producer of the 1990 Oscar-winning documentary *Common Threads: Stories from the Quilt*, denies that "there's any homophobia in Hollywood; a good script is the bottom line," others suggest that the major studio executives may "never bring themselves to find that 'good script' about AIDS" because they "are afraid they may be labeled homosexual if they approve a project with gay themes or characters" (ibid.). Despite his obsessive fence-sitting when he writes about outing, Shilts sounded a lot like Signorile when he complained to the *New York Times* about closeted Hollywood executives who "are so terrified of being exposed, they'll get in the way of a project"—in this case, *his* books. "There is no industry in which there are more gay people in powerful positions who are more homophobic" (ibid.).[93]

The news of Rock Hudson's illness in 1985 had stirred up a tabloid frenzy of concern because Linda Evans, in the role of Crystal Carrington on "Dynasty," had kissed the secretly ailing Hudson in his last dramatic role. Although all were eventually assured that Ms. Evans was quite healthy—it was Hudson's last lover, Marc Christian, who eventually collected millions from the actor's estate—Hollywood had developed a bad case of the disease songwriter Tom Wilson Weinberg has labeled AFRAIDS. No group was more affected by this fear than ac-

---

93. There are those who claim that popular music is even more homophobic. "Hollywood . . . can't match the squeamishness and overt hostility with which pop music regards homosexuality—or its capacity for rendering gay men and lesbians invisible" (Weisel 1992).

tors, whose careers could be destroyed by even a suspicion of illness. John Glover found that rumors spread about him after he played a person with AIDS in the TV movie *An Early Frost* and then showed up at an awards ceremony with his hair shaved for another role: "for months after that, there was what my agent called a 'whisper circuit' on the street. It's very destructive . . . and it's very paranoid-making. There is fear we won't get hired" (Chunovic 1992).

The open secret went public when actor Brad Davis died of AIDS in September 1991, leaving behind a posthumous indictment of "an industry that professes to care very much, that gives umpteen benefits and charity affairs," but, in fact, "if an actor is even rumored to have HIV, he gets no support on an individual basis. He does not work" (Sadownick 1992: 66). Davis had tested positive for HIV six years earlier (he said it was contracted through needle use) but had kept his illness so secret that he had declined to take advantage of insurance benefits provided by the actors' unions he belonged to (Ryan 1991). Although David Geffen asserted that fears such as Davis expressed were unnecessary because "the industry as a whole is run by . . . people who are extraordinarily sympathetic who would not be disinclined to employ people either because they are gay or HIV-positive" (ibid.), others disagreed, claiming that AIDS phobia is even stronger than homophobia, and that Davis was right to err on the side of caution. Still, many actors and activists regretted the pervasive silence on the part of "people with HIV working on every movie-set, every TV show, behind and in front of the cameras. It's not a question of, Can they work? or Do they work? but, Would they work if we knew?" (ibid.). But the only actors who were coming out were, to put it delicately, neither at the start nor at the peak of their careers. Michael Kearns, a little-known actor who has long been openly gay, revealed his HIV-positive status following Davis's death, as did Dack Rambo, who had once played Jack Ewing in "Dallas." Around this time, retired actors Dick Sargent, once Darrin on TV's "Bewitched," and Sheila James Kuehl, Zelda on "The Many Loves of Dobie Gillis," revealed their homosexuality as part of National Coming Out Day in October 1991.[94]

---

94. When Anthony Perkins died at age 60 in September 1992, it was revealed that the actor, who never shook off the image of Norman Bates in Hitchcock's *Psycho*, had suffered from AIDS. The death announcement noted the presence at his bedside of his wife and sons, and in a posthumously released statement Perkins avoided any mention of AIDS-related stigma (or the persistent rumors of his homosexuality) and attributed his silence to modesty: "I chose not to go public about this because, to misquote *Casablanca*, I'm not much at being noble but it doesn't take much to see that the problems of

Davis's accusations followed on the heels of protests over *The Silence of the Lambs* and *Basic Instinct* and printed attacks on the industry, such as the cover story of the *Advocate* in March 1991 that detailed "Homophobia in Hollywood" (Ryan and Whitington 1991), in addition to personal criticisms directed at closeted moguls like Barry Diller (David Geffen's coming out was heralded in the *Advocate* article). According to Diller, Davis's posthumous letter crystallized a plan he had already conceived to start an organization to combat AIDS discrimination, a plan he said was inspired by a Fox Entertainment News series on AIDS and homophobia in Hollywood. As difficult as it might be to believe, Diller later told *Advocate* writer Jeff Yarbrough that this 1991 series opened his eyes to "a climate here that has to be changed." He showed the tapes to his buddies Sid Sheinberg, president of the giant entertainment conglomerate MCA, Inc., and Motion Picture Association head Jack Valenti, who exclaimed with similar astonishment, "My God! What can I do?" (Yarbrough 1991: 40). Of course, there was quite a bit they could do, once they put their minds to it. Diller and Sheinberg met with Gay and Lesbian Alliance against Defamation (GLAAD) and AIDS Project Los Angeles (APLA) leaders, and at a September 15, 1991, APLA fund-raiser they pledged more than $125,000 to form Hollywood Supports, an organization devoted to fighting homophobia and AIDS discrimination. Hired as its head was activist Richard Jennings, former executive director of the Los Angeles chapter of GLAAD, who had previously criticized the new organization's sponsors.

The founding of Hollywood Supports followed another pathbreaking event for the entertainment industry: a high-profile fund-raiser that raised $80,000 for the National Gay and Lesbian Task Force on August 10. Whereas, following Elizabeth Taylor's lead and frequently sheltering behind her indisputedly heterosexual image, AIDS-related benefits had become a Hollywood standby, this was the first turnout of Hollywood's big hitters for a lesbian and gay rights fund-raiser. The event was organized by four of "Hollywood's most powerful out-of-the-closet gay men," among them two producers and an entertainment lawyer who got "Tinseltown's most central player, Mike Ovitz, chief executive officer of Creative Artists Agency" to sign on as a spon-

---

one old actor don't amount to a hill of beans in this crazy world" (Bowles 1992). Others might have wished that the example of Humphrey Bogart's character in that classic movie would have moved Perkins to some actions that might have benefited others fighting AIDS.

sor, thus guaranteeing the success of the event (Murphy and Mars 1991). Although no one was saying so, it appeared to many observers that the industry—including its few openly gay major players—was beginning to yield to the pressure of the activists.[95]

The 1991–92 television season gave more evidence that Hollywood was starting to listen to lesbian and gay voices. Gay characters and themes appeared on many series ("L.A. Law," "Coach," "Roseanne," "Designing Women," "Seinfeld," and "Dear John," among others), and producer Esther Shapiro claimed that "awareness about AIDS has made the sleeping liberals more awake, creating a more relaxed attitude about gay themes" (McConnell 1992). But movies were a still a different story. In 1990, *Longtime Companion*, a story about a group of gay men dealing with and dying from AIDS that had been financed by public television's "American Playhouse" series, was picked up for theatrical distribution by an independent company. While it was not a smash, the film, which cost $1.5 million, brought in over $4 million and garnered a Golden Globe award and an Oscar nomination for actor Bruce Davison. Meanwhile, major studio executives were still waiting for "a script [to] come along that will tempt them" (Lew 1991).

As March 1992 rolled around, Hollywood began bracing for an onslaught of gay activism. *Basic Instinct* was scheduled to open around the country March 20, and lesbian and gay groups from coast to coast were planning demonstrations at which they promised to loudly reveal the thriller's ending in order to discourage potential audiences. At the same time, activists were also angry at the handling of the lesbian relationship that is at the heart of *Fried Green Tomatoes*, an unexpected hit at the box office. As GLAAD and Queer Nation saw it, Hollywood was happy to be explicit about lesbian psychokillers but became coy when it came to loving and happy lesbians. A third cause for gay outrage was the depiction of a cabal of degenerate gays at the heart of the conspiracy to kill the president in Oliver Stone's *JFK*; their sleaziness was accentuated in contrast to the portrayal of New Orleans District Attorney Jim Garrison's wholesome nuclear family.

Neither the fuss and the protests surrounding *Basic Instinct* nor the

---

95. Possibly even more widely remarked than the NGLTF benefit was a fund-raising banquet marking the twentieth anniversary of the Los Angeles Lesbian and Gay Community center at which Lily Tomlin was a featured speaker. Tomlin, who has long topped the lists of stars lesbians and gays want to come out, sat next to Michelangelo Signorile at the dinner (he behaved himself, though he did, as expected, encourage her to come out), and in her remarks congratulated "all of us for being gay for the past 20 years."

mostly negative reviews it received dissuaded the audiences attracted by the unprecedented flood of hype and publicity preceeding the film's release, mostly focusing on its graphic sex. But they did have an impact on the news media, which devoted an unprecedented amount of attention to the questions raised by the activists about the portrayals of lesbian women and gay men in movies and television. Major feature stories were run by newspapers—the *New York Times* even commissioned gay novelist and ACT UP member John Weir to write a lengthy piece on "Gay bashing, villainy and the Oscars" for the Sunday Arts and Leisure section (1992)—as well as by CNN, "NBC Nightly News," and "Entertainment Tonight."[96]

One reason for all the media attention to the issue of Hollywood homophobia was that shortly following the opening of *Basic Instinct* was the Academy Awards ceremony, and this annual orgy of movie-mania became the focus of queer action. By early March word was spreading that Oscar night would see all sorts of protests. *USA Today*, which kept a close watch on developments, informed its readers that "a march is planned. There is talk of a stall-in: trucks and cars stalling all aproaches. . . . Protestors with signs and t-shirts saying *Make Queer Film* will line the limousine corridor. Maps of closeted gay and lesbian stars' homes will be handed out" (Trebbe 1992). Other reports promised disruptions inside the Oscar ceremonies themselves, which might thus be seen by a worldwide audience in the scores of millions. The producers promised tight security and said they would cut to a commerical if an interruption occurred on the air.

The Silence of the Lambs had been nominated for most of the major awards, and the movie and its star, Jodie Foster, were the focus of both protests and media handwringing. The *Star* brought to supermarket aisles around the country the news that "Gays Plot to 'Out' 60 Stars at Oscars" and that "Militants Smear Best Actress Nominee Jodie Foster" (March 21, 1992), thus making sure that few were unaware that

---

96. Liz Smith contributed to the pre-opening discussion by quoting *Basic Instinct* star Sharon Stone on the protestors: "Their position was that the only characters who were bad in the film were homosexual, and that the film showed this minority group in an unfair, derogatory way. Well, *Roxanne* showed firemen to be inept and stupid, but you didn't see firemen demonstrating" (March 11, 1992). Once the film opened, Liz Smith told her readers that it "has about as much to do with real homosexuality as it has to do with real psychiatry. . . . The movie is nothing more than a blood-soaked hetero-sexual *Playboy* fantasy," and went on to criticize the outing activists' "self-aggrandizing scare tactics," which would only drive "these stars—many of whom have raised a lot of money for AIDS research—deeper into the closet" (March 25, 1992).

Jodie Foster had been outed. *National Enquirer* alerted its readers to the fact that "Hollywood celebrities are scared out of their wits because a gay terrorist group is plotting to destroy the Academy Awards by exposing stars they claim are secret homosexuals and lesbians."

The night of March 30 came, and the ceremonies went off with a minimum of disruption from the protestors demonstrating outside— kept far away by a phalanx of mounted police—and none at all inside. *The Silence of the Lambs* swept the top honors, and Jodie Foster accepted her second Best Actress Oscar with a speech full of heavily coded language, thanking "all the people in this industry who have respected my choices."

Still, there were visible signs of the changes that had been going on during the past year. In 1991 ACT UP/LA sent 400 letters to Academy members, asking them to wear "Silence = Death" buttons; only Bruce Davison and Susan Sarandon wore theirs. In 1992 nearly every lapel sported a red ribbon, the new symbol of AIDS awareness, which host Billy Crystal and presenter Richard Gere explained to the audience. Short-documentary award winner Debra Chasnoff thanked her "life partner Kim Klausner" in her acceptance speech,[97] and the male lover of deceased composer Howard Ashman accepted his award for Best Song.

The threatened outings never happened, but Hollywood's lesbian and gay closet door was standing a bit more ajar than ever before.[98] Suddenly, it seemed that good scripts were being found, and by some

---

97. Millions of lesbian and gay members of the television audience at that moment wished that Chasnoff's lover had a more traditionally female name. Backstage, a reporter asked, "When you thanked your 'life partner' Kim Klausner—was that a woman?" "It sure was," Chasnoff responded. "I'm sorry if that wasn't clear." That remark showed up in *USA Today* the next morning, but most of the media missed—or ignored—the precedent (Stevens 1992: 34).

98. By the end of 1992 David Geffen, who told *Vanity Fair* in 1991 that he was bisexual, made headlines in the gay press and was profiled as the *Advocate*'s "Man of the Year" after he told a crowd of thousands at a major Los Angeles AIDS benefit, "As a gay man, I've come a long way to be here tonight." In his "Man of the Year" interview, Geffen attacked outing as "wrong and unconscionable" (except in the case of "people who are doing things that are contrary to the interests of gay people"—which is what many thought promoting Guns N' Roses was), and characterized Michelangelo Signorile as a terrorist (Lemon 1992: 39). His own progress from the closet to saying he was bisexual ("That was as much as I could do then") to coming out as a gay man ("This is what I can do now") he attributes to that fact that he is "loving [him]self more and more" (ibid.: 38). Liz Smith, on the other hand, chastised those who implied that Geffen's earlier bisexual image had been disingenuous, claiming that, "like so many people, [Geffen] went through a formative period" (November 30, 1992).

of the very people who had been in the queer spotlight: *Silence of the Lambs* director Jonathan Demme announced plans for a movie about a lawyer fired because he has AIDS; Oliver Stone, whose *JFK* set off protests by gay activists, was slated to coproduce the long-delayed *Mayor of Castro Street*; and *Basic Instinct* author Joe Eszterhas told gay reporter Doug Sadownick that "there has to come a day when there's a hero on screen who happens to be gay. And I can tell you I will do my all to write that script" (1991: 32). As Michelangelo Signorile pointed out in an *Advocate* column, the threatened protests inside the Oscars ceremony hadn't really been necessary by that point: "If the purpose of the protest was to focus attention on our issues and get the powers-that-be to respond, that had already occurred. As one Queer National explained, 'This is a postmodern demonstration: We announce the action. The media creates it. And then whatever happens happens.' Or doesn't" (1992a).

Out of the HIV Closet

The political map of New York City took on a new look in 1991 when the city council district lines were redrawn, and among the more notable developments was the Village-Chelsea-Clinton district in lower Manhattan that everyone knew would elect a lesbian or gay council member. The race quickly turned into a two-person contest between longtime gay activist Tom Duane and the daughter of former Congresswoman Bella Abzug, Liz Abzug, who came out as a lesbian "after it was announced that the third district had been redrawn with new, 'gay-winnable' lines" (Minkowitz 1991a). Most lesbian as well as gay activists supported Duane, who was considered to have paid his political dues and earned the position, while Abzug had no track record in lesbian and gay politics.

In early August Duane announced that he was HIV positive and a new controversy arose. The *New York Post* reported that his decision to come out of the HIV closet had been spurred by pressure from AIDS activists Roger McFarlane and Larry Kramer, and quoted McFarlane "comparing Duane to Jews who kept silent during the Holocaust" (Massa 1991). Suddenly, arguments were reigniting the fires of earlier outing disputes. McFarlane and Kramer defended their actions—and their support of Abzug—in letters to the *Village Voice* that spelled out their views about the responsibility of people to be public about their HIV status. Kramer, gloating that Duane had been "shamed" into coming "out of the closet about his HIV+ status," said that he had been "disgusted by Tom's dishonesty in keeping his 'secret' for so

long" and drew an analogy between this issue and the outing of Pete
Williams by Michelangelo Signorile. McFarlane referred to Duane's
"cowardice in the middle of an epidemic that is killing his and my
brothers and sisters" (1991).

Donna Minkowitz and fellow *Voice* writer Robert Massa countered
McFarlane's and Kramer's attacks by citing the long fight to protect the
confidentiality of people's HIV status, even quoting McFarlane's recent statement to Liz Smith that he would never "out" any HIV-
positive celebrities (Minkowitz 1991b). Massa reported that AIDS activists they called said that "outing people with HIV had never occurred to them" and that they would oppose it except "when politicians actively campaigned against the rights and interests of people
with HIV" (1991).

Gabriel Rotello, founding editor of *OutWeek*, joined the debate in
the letters column of the *Voice*, noting that outing activists had never
proposed "the outing of people with HIV disease" and firmly distin-
guishing between the disclosure of sexual orientation and the disclosure of health status:

> Outers oppose a double standard that permits publication of straight
> celebrities' secrets while vigorously suppressing any mention of gay
> celebs' homosexuality. But there's no double standard surrounding
> HIV disclosure. Illness is one of the few instances where public
> figures' right to privacy is still respected by the press. The media re-
> main uniformly silent about celebrities' medical problems until the
> celebs themselves go public. HIV is treated like every other serious
> medical condition—as a private matter until the sufferer says other-
> wise. (Rotello 1991b)

On November 7, 1991, basketball star Earvin ("Magic") Johnson
went before a nationally televised press conference to announce that
he had recently learned that he was HIV positive and that, despite being in good health, he was retiring from professional sports effective
immediately. (Somewhat later he decided to join the U.S. Olympic
basketball team for the 1992 Barcelona Games and subsequently re-
joined his former team for a brief period before withdrawing in the face
of AIDS-hysteria-induced fears of contagion expressed by potential
opponents.) Magic Johnson's "coming out" as HIV positive was the
most explosive moment in AIDS-related media coverage and public
discussion since Rock Hudson's illness was revealed in 1985, and it
served once again to remind AIDS activists of the degree to which
Americans were able to distance themselves from the epidemic that
had already killed more than 125,000 people.

Magic Johnson's revelation spurred predictable speculation about his sexuality, and rumors were soon flying that he was actively bisexual—rumors that had previously circulated when he publicly kissed another player, Isiah Thomas, during the 1988 National Basketball Association playoffs (Brigham 1992: 37). The rumors may have been squelched, but so were the feelings of many gay people and AIDS activists, when Johnson firmly assured Arsenio Hall that he is "the furthest thing from being a homosexual," to loud applause from the studio audience. Johnson's disclosure had raised consciousness about the dangers of HIV transmission and the need for safe-sex education, but it did little to mitigate the heterosexism rife in the world of professional sports. Tennis star Martina Navratilova, the most prominent openly gay athlete in the world, was asked by a *New York Post* reporter what would have happened if she had been the one to test HIV positive. She answered, "They'd say I'm gay—I had it coming" and went on to point out that a heterosexual woman would also have been condemned as "a whore and a slut and the corporations would drop her like a lead balloon," referring to the well-publicized announcements that corporations would keep Johnson as a spokesman for their products.

Rotello's faith that HIV disease would be treated like every other serious medical condition—as a private matter until the sufferer says otherwise—was not put to a test by Magic Johnson's voluntary announcement. But a few months later tennis great Arthur Ashe learned to his dismay that this faith was misplaced. On April 8, 1992, Ashe called a press conference to reveal that he had known he had AIDS since 1988, and that he was probably infected through a tainted blood transfusion in 1979 or 1983. The drama of Ashe's announcement was intensified by his reason for going public after such a delay: he had been told by *USA Today* that they were going to publish the story, and he decided to scoop them himself. In the next few weeks the story, which started as front-page news across the country, remained in the media spotlight as a debate raged over whether Ashe's privacy should have been respected.

Editors and reporters were quoted on both sides of the issue, some defending Ashe's right to keep his condition secret if he so chose, others claiming that Ashe was a public figure and that his illness passed the test of newsworthiness (Jones 1992a, 1992b). AIDS activists felt that Ashe had the right to remain quiet about his health but that, as Larry Kramer put it, "he has a moral responsibility as a public figure." I would go further and note that Ashe's public stature derived from his status as a role model for black youth. As *Philadelphia Inquirer* columnist Claude Lewis put it, "You became the U.S. Open champion in 1968 and won Wimbledon in 1975 when you surprised the world and defeated the seemingly invincible Jimmy Connors. . . . You were on a mission to prove that blacks could compete successfully. It wasn't a role you sought but one that was imposed upon you" (1992). But then I would ask what Ashe's responsibility as a role model for black youth was: was it sufficient to inspire them to achievements in tennis and other sports, or was it his moral duty to use his misfortune to open their eyes to the dangers of HIV and the need for safer sexual practices? After the revelation of Ashe's illness, black commentators like Virginia Governor L. Douglas Wilder and Claude Lewis made revealing and despicable statements like "Because of you, AIDS is perhaps a bit more respectable today" (Lewis 1992).[99]

By the end of April 1992 many in the press and the public were ready to agree with the sentiment expressed by George Bernard Shaw in the 1930s that "an American has no sense of privacy. He does not know what it means. There is no such thing in the country."

Whose Right to Privacy?

The concept of a right to privacy arose out of nineteenth-century Victorian morality, which created an ideology of distinct public and private spheres and confined women to the private, domestic sphere (cf. Wolff, 1988). As this ideology was articulated by one of its foremost proponents, the influential critic John Ruskin, women are not only protected by their confinement to the home, they also thus maintain a safe refuge for men:

> The man, in his rough work in the open world, must encounter all peril and trial:—to him, therefore, must be the failure, the offence, the inevitable error: often he must be wounded, or subdued; often misled; and *always* hardened. But he guards the woman from all this; within the house, as ruled by her, unless she herself has sought it, need enter no danger, no temptation, no cause of error or offence. This is the true nature of the home—it is the place of Peace. (quoted in Wolff 1988: 120)

---

99. Ashe pledged to devote some of his time to AIDS-related efforts, and he called Magic Johnson. But it was also revealed that "he has been a director of the Aetna Life and Casualty Company since 1982 and plans to remain on the board despite the company's refusal to sell new policies to people with AIDS or to people who test positive for the virus that causes AIDS" (*New York Times*, "Sportspeople," April 11, 1992: 38). We can only hope that Magic Johnson wasn't planning to apply for an Aetna policy.

By the late nineteenth century, however, the growth of mass media and recently invented communications technologies threatened to invade the place of Peace and disrupt the tranquility of the domestic sphere: "With the advent of the telephone and other new media came relatively sudden and unanticipated possibilities of mixing heterogeneous social worlds—a useful opportunity for some, a dreadful intrusion for others" (Marvin 1988: 107). In 1890 the popular press in Boston wrote about the parties and dances of elite society in ways that seemed dreadfully intrusive, at least to Mrs. Samuel D. Warren. Mrs. Warren's outrage "prompted her husband, a professor of law at Harvard University, to join a colleague, Louis D. Brandeis, in devising 'the right of the individual to be left alone.' A Warren-Brandeis law journal article on the right to privacy became the fountainhead of later law and social policy in the United States" (Smith 1980: 3).[100] Warren and Brandeis singled out the new technologies and the media they served:

> Recent inventions and business methods call attention to the next step which must be taken for the protection of the person, and for securing to the individual . . . the right "to be let alone." Instantaneous photographs and newspaper enterprise have invaded the sacred precincts of private and domestic life; and numerous mechanical devices threaten to make good the prediction that "what is whispered in the closet shall be proclaimed from the house-tops." (Warren and Brandeis 1890: 195)

In the period following World War II the defense of the private realm became the primary focus of liberal efforts to reconcile the "interests of society" and the rights of the individual. The "right to privacy" first expressed in an effort to protect the sanctity of the Victorian domestic sphere would now be invoked as a defense against the enforcement of Victorian morality.

In the arena of sexuality the ground was broken by the publication of the Kinsey report, *Sexual Behavior in the Human Male*, in 1948 and its companion volume on females in 1953 (in both cases the human species studied consisted of white Americans), which lifted a curtain to reveal a much more active and varied sexual life than Americans were supposed to enjoy. Notable among its scandalous findings was the high proportion of males who had engaged in same-sex "contact to orgasm" on at least one occasion—37 percent of adults—and the figures

---

100. Recent scholarship cast doubt on this origin myth and suggested that the Boston press has been falsely accused of violating the Warren family's privacy (cf. Barron 1979).

that have ever since provided the underpinning for the standard estimate of 10 percent of the population being, in some sense, homosexual. Taken together with the success of the psychiatric profession in supplanting the previously dominant religious and legal perspectives on sexuality (Weeks 1981), the stage was set for a reevaluation of public morality and individual rights.

In 1954, following a sensational trial for homosexual offenses in which "there was no evidence of 'corruption'; no suggestion that the acts were anything but consensual and in private" (ibid.: 241), the British government established the Wolfenden Committee on Homosexual Offences and Prostitution. The *Wolfenden Report*, issued in 1957, was a landmark in the postwar evolution of a new standard for policing sexual behavior. Although generally seen as a victory for liberalism and individual freedom, the report must also be seen as a strategic retrenchment rather than an abdication of the desire to control the expression of sexuality.

The key to the *Wolfenden Report* is in the distinction between public and private. The purpose of criminal law, it argued, is to preserve *public* order and decency, not to enforce *private* morality. "There must be a realm of private morality and immorality which is in brief and crude terms not the law's business. . . . It is not in our view the function of the law to intervene in the private lives of citizens or to seek to enforce any particular patterns of behaviour" (*Wolfenden Report* 1964: 23f). But there is an important corollary to the report's hands-off stance toward private morality: "The logic of the distinction between private and public behaviour was that the legal penalties for *public* displays of sexuality could be strengthened at the same time as private behaviour was decriminalized" (Weeks 1981: 243). The recommendations of the report regarding homosexuality, therefore, focused on who was doing it, and where: homosexual acts between consenting adults in private should no longer be a criminal offence. But, it was emphasized in the report, "it is important that the limited modification of the law which we propose should not be interpreted as an indication that the law can be indifferent to other forms of homosexual behaviour, or as a general license to adult homosexuals to behave as they please" (1964: 87).

Interestingly, the recommendations to tighten controls over public prostitution were enacted into British law by 1959, while the recommendation concerning homosexual acts did not become law until the Sexual Offenses Act of 1967 decriminalized male homosexual activities in private for adults over twenty-one (although the age of consent for heterosexual acts was much lower). This act "was never intended as a clarion call to sexual liberation" (Weeks 1981: 274). The advocates of the new law urged discretion on the part of those who stood to benefit from it, asking them, in the words of Lord Arran, "to show their thanks by comporting themselves quietly and with dignity" (ibid.). For legal purposes "public" was defined as meaning not only a public toilet but anywhere where a third person was likely to be present. In the first few years after decriminalization the number of prosecutions actually increased as the police sought to increase "the 'privatization' and moral 'segregation' of homosexuals" (ibid.: 275). On the whole, however, the *Wolfenden Report* did much to promote the "right to privacy" as the rallying cry of liberal reformers as Western culture moved into the "permissive" sixties.

In the landmark case of *Griswold v. Connecticut* in 1965 the U.S. Supreme Court first recognized a constitutional right to privacy. The Court voided Connecticut's prohibition against the sale or use of contraceptives, because the law could only be enforced if the police were allowed to "search the sacred precincts of marital bedrooms for telltale signs."

The right to privacy extended to married couples and, in later decisions, to unmarried persons wishing to use contraceptives, unmarried women wishing to terminate a pregnancy, and people wishing to watch dirty movies in the privacy of their homes (Smith 1980: 269). But, it is important to note, the Court in *Griswold* stressed that "it in no way interferes with a State's proper regulation of sexual promiscuity or misconduct." It was soon made clear that the Supreme Court was not about to interfere with the state's desire to regulate *some* expressions of sexuality: in 1976 it upheld a Virginia decision punishing sodomy between consenting male adults, and later in the same year it left standing another Virginia decision that punished a married couple for engaging in oral-genital sex. As one privacy law expert commented, "Individuals have the right to watch all manner of sexual goings-on in a movie within the home, but not to engage in those very same sexual activities themselves within the home!" (ibid.: 270).

In 1986, in the infamous *Bowers v. Hardwick* decision, the Supreme Court stripped the right to privacy argument of its last vestige of credibility as a defense of gay sexuality. Diverging from the logic of sexual liberty implicit in *Griswold* and many subsequent decisions, and showing what Justice Blackmun in his dissent termed an "almost obsessive focus on homosexual activity," the Court asserted that the right to privacy does not extend to homosexual acts, even those committed by consenting adults in private: "The Constitution does not confer a fundamental right upon homosexuals to engage in sodomy. . . . Any claim that . . . any kind of private sexual conduct between consenting adults is constitutionally insulated from state proscription is un-supportable."

The Duty of Sexual Secrecy

The homosexual rights movement that appeared in the United States during the 1950s began to form alliances with sympathetic heterosex-ual liberals who agreed with the position that "the sex variant is no different from anyone else except in the object of his sexual expres-sion" (D'Emilio 1983: 81). The leaders of the first homosexual organiza-tion to emerge in this period, the Mattachine Society, had no argu-ment with the mainstream liberal position that focused on the right to sexual freedom in private. As a Mattachine leader said to Mike Wallace in the first network television "special" on homosexuals, "The Homo-sexuals," broadcast by "CBS Reports" in 1967, "In our view the en-forcement of laws which forbid public sexual behavior or overt demon-strations of affection and so on that lead to a sexual stimulus in public view, laws against that are appropriate and should be maintained" (Wallace and Morgan 1967: 11).

By the late 1960s, however, the gay liberation movement had ex-ploded and suddenly what was whispered in the closet was being proclaimed from the housetops, or at least in the streets. From this mo-ment there was no longer any consensus among either homosexuals or their allies that gay rights should be confined to the right to privacy.

On the one hand (the right hand, as it were), there were gay rights advocates who argued that the primary issue for the gay movement (perhaps the only issue) was the protection of the right to privacy. On the other (the left) hand, were the gay liberationists, arguing that "gays today are exercising much more than their right to be let alone; they are exercising their right to create communities and their right to publicity" (Tucker 1982: 32). As the latter understood, limiting the goals of the gay movement to the right to privacy would play into the strategy of the sexual counterrevolution: "It is primarily our *public* exis-tence, and not our right to privacy, which is under assault by the right" (ibid.). The ironic lesson that was being drawn—or resisted—was the one already implicit in the limited liberalism of the *Wolfenden Report*: "The right to privacy is a double-edged sword. Privacy can be *enforced* as well as pursued" (ibid.: 31).

As the gay liberation movement advanced in the early 1970s, scor-ing such victories as the 1973 decision by the American Psychiatric As-sociation to delete homosexuality from its official catalogue of mental illness and the passage of "gay rights" bills by cities around the country, there was a predictable backlash.[101] Much of this backlash focused on the growing *visibility* of lesbian women and gay men. By the mid-seventies the public emergence of gay people had begun to be reflected in mass media programming. A few network television series introduced nonstereotypic gay (male) characters in single-episode appearances, generally focusing on the reactions of the straight leads to the gay character's coming out. But tentative and limited as these forays were, they aroused the ire and drew the fire of mainstream America. Nicholas Von Hoffman, in his syndicated column of November 4, 1976, headed "Out from TV's Sit-Com Closet: The Presentable Gay," lamented what he termed the Year of the Fag. "It began," he said, "with one presentable gay in Doonesbury" (incidentally, that first gay character introduced in a mainstream cartoon strip in 1976 "died" of AIDS in 1990) and from there "it was but a hop, skip and a jump to television where the flits are swarming this year."

In the late 1970s Mayor Ed Koch proclaimed Gay Pride Week in New York City and was taken to task by prominent liberal journalist Murray Kempton in a column entitled "A Week That Should Go Back to the Closet" (unfortunately, I have an undated photocopy). Kempton felt that the proclamation was in bad taste "because public discussions of sexuality are always in bad taste," and he informed his readers that "the closet happens to be the single human invention whose consequences have been universally benevolent." Kempton also argued that the proclamation was "a cheat" because the reluctance of witnesses to a gay-bashing in Central Park to come forward and testify, at the risk of "becoming a social suspect," demonstrated "what pathetic hypocrisy it is to proclaim Gay Pride Week when gay shame remains an open wound all year round." Kempton seems oblivious to the obvious relationship between the timidity of those witnesses and a public atmosphere in which a famous "liberal" columnist would greet a gay pride proclamation by opining that "the vagrant impulses of the loins are matters of occasional comedy and more frequent

---

101. The victory involved in the APA's vote to "declassify" homosexuality was a dubious one: first, because it was partially replaced by a newly minted category of "gender dysphoria," created to placate the hard-liners, and it took several more years before this, too, was discarded; second, because gay people should beware "science by voting," which could also turn around and put them back on the disease rolls. If homosexuality is a disease, it can't be voted out of existence anymore than the Catholic Church could make the sun revolve around the earth; if it isn't, as most thinking people now agree, voting only acknowledges that reality. It is this last point, of course, that made this vote a political victory in 1973.

tragedy, but in no form are they ever proper subjects for celebration by mayoral proclamations."[102]

By the late 1970s and the early 1980s, even before the AIDS epidemic fueled the fires of homophobia, the sexual counterrevolution was in full swing, and homosexuality, along with abortion and pornography, was a prime target. The attack on homosexuality has consistently focused on its more public manifestations. As early as Anita Bryant's successful 1977 crusade to "Save Our Children" by repealing a Florida county's gay rights ordinance, and as recently as the passage in November 1992 of an amendment repealing—and prohibiting—gay rights protections in Colorado, the right wing has tried to roll back gay liberation and push us back into the closet.

A new wrinkle in the backlash against gay visibility are the "straight pride" rallies held at the University of Massachusetts as well as other universities. The founder of the Massachusetts effort was quoted as "saying the gay rights law enacted in Massachusetts and other gay rights activists were distracting attention from more important issues, like the decline of the traditional family. 'They don't want rights, they want to force a sexuality on me. . . . Keep it in the closet!' " (*New York Times*, March 11, 1991).

In this struggle it was—and is—increasingly irrelevant and counterproductive to hide behind the shield of the right to privacy. As Scott Tucker warned in 1982, "the right to privacy [is] easily translated into the duty of sexual secrecy. . . . A standard statement made by both gay rights advocates and anti-gay bigots is that *sexuality is a private matter*. Each side means something different: *Let us live our lives in peace*, and *Get back into the closet*" (1982: 32).

Keep It in the Closet!

In April 1991 a Minnesota judge's ruling dramatized the extent to which gay visibility threatens the defenders of traditional morality. The case in question began in 1983 when a car accident inflicted terrible injuries on Sharon Kowalski, who lived with her lover, Karen Thompson, in the home they had jointly purchased in St. Cloud. Kowalski

---

102. Lest you think that such querulous heterosexism went out of fashion in the seventies, note an article by Pete Hamill published by *Esquire* in 1990 titled "Confessions of a Heterosexual," featuring Hamill's complaint that he is "tired of listening to people who identify themselves exclusively by what they do with their cocks." Hamill and his editors seem oblivious to the fact that this describes many straight men (*Esquire* readers in particular?), and no lesbians I can think of.

was left unable to speak or walk, suffering major brain damage, including seriously impaired short term memory. Thompson's petition to be appointed her lover's guardian pitted her against Kowalski's parents, who had not known before the accident that their daughter was a lesbian. The legal struggle between the parents and the lover of Sharon Kowalski dragged on for years, and for much of this time Karen Thompson was denied all contact with her injured lover. By 1988 Thompson had succeeded in having her moved to a more neutral nursing facility, where Kowalski was able to communicate by typing on a special keyboard that she wanted to live in "St. Cloud with Karen" (Hunter 1991: 410). In 1990 Donald Kowalski resigned as his daughter's court-appointed guardian, and it was Thompson's renewed petition for guardianship that gave Judge Robert Campbell a chance to enforce his values. Campbell astounded those who had been involved in the case when he denied Thompson's petition and instead awarded custody to a friend of the parents, a woman he described as "a neutral third party," who proposed to move Kowalski back to a nursing home that a court had previously ruled was unable to provide for her needs (Yang 1991).

The key to the surprising decision "seemed to be the judge's anger at Thompson for ever telling Kowalski's parents (in a private letter), and then the world at large, that she and Kowalski were lovers" (Hunter 1991). In a prominent section of his opinion titled "Outing," the judge wrote that "the right to privacy protects the essence of the human individual. Privacy is a right deeply entrenched, yet transcendent beyond the moral shell of the body. . . . This disclosure . . . known colloquially as 'outing,' constituted an invasion of privacy" (quoted in Kopkind 1991: 59). The judge went on to suggest that Thompson might be legally liable to an action for her violation of Kowalski's privacy rights. In fact, "the judge's concern seemed to be more for the outing of Kowalski's parents. He described the Kowalskis as 'outraged and hurt by the public invasion of Sharon's privacy and their privacy" (Hunter 1991).

The struggle of Sharon Kowalski and Karen Thompson finally reached an end in December 1991, when the Minnesota Court of Appeals overturned Judge Campbell's decision and appointed Thompson as her lover's legal guardian. But the deeper implications of Judge Campbell's decision are not as easily set aside. Campbell and, it must be assumed, many of his fellow citizens do not want the love that dare not speak its name to break that silence, and are willing to take action to keep homosexuality securely locked in the privacy of the closet.

Among those who felt as Campbell did, it turned out, were the editors of the *Houston Post*. Early in 1991 the paper had appointed its first Hispanic columnist, Juan Palomo, and given his thrice-weekly column a prominent spot on the front page of the metro section. Palomo was quickly acclaimed one of the city's most controversial and best columnists for his hard-hitting columns on "Hispanic issues, Black issues, and all sorts of other issues that other columnists don't cover in Houston" (Palomo 1992: 23), among them gay issues. In early July 1991 Palomo wrote an impassioned piece about the murder of a twenty-seven-year-old banker by gay-bashing teenagers, and about the silence of the media, the police, and the public concerning antigay violence. "Paul Broussard died because we are cowards," the column concluded "The gay activists are right: Silence does equal death" (quoted in Fleck 1991: 54).

The column evoked hundreds of letters and phone calls from readers, mostly supportive, but Palomo's readers had not seen the entire column as he wrote it. The original column ended with a paragraph in which Palomo expressed a personal sense of responsibility not only to speak out but also to come out as a gay man, in order to help educate the public. The editors of the *Houston Post* felt differently, and they forced Palomo to remove the personal portion. As one of the editors later put it, "I feel that the edited version of the column made the point much stronger than the earlier version" (ibid.). The matter didn't stop there, however, because Palomo had shown the original column to friends at the paper, and somehow it had ended up in the hands of the alternative weekly *Houston Press*, which ran a story on the whole episode that was then picked up by the trade paper *Editor and Publisher* and the *Washington Post*. The *Houston Post* fired Palomo when the story of the column became public, because, as the editor put it, "the best interests of the *Post* come before the personal agenda of an individual" (Suro 1991).

The firing of Juan Palomo only served to amplify the incident as a national news story. The Houston Hispanic community rallied to his defense, and the local Queer Nation chapter put "out of order" stickers on the paper's vending machines and marched in front of the editor's condominium chanting, "Re-hire Palomo, who cares if he's a homo?" Within a week the paper was forced to back down and rehired Palomo, although he was now assigned to the paper's editorial board, and his column was moved to the op-ed page on a twice-weekly basis.

The *Houston Post* editors did not realize that they were enforcing a code whose due date had recently passed. Lesbian and gay journalists all over the country were beginning to open their closet doors by revealing their sexuality in the newsrooms and, in a very few cases, in print (radio and television journalists are still far more guarded, and perhaps with good reason). In April 1990 the American Society of Newspaper Editors (ASNE) released a ground-breaking report prepared by its Human Resources Committee (Ghiglione et al. 1990). "Alternatives: Gays and Lesbians in the Newsroom" revealed both their widespread presence and the often poor treatment they encountered from colleagues and superiors. The coordinator of the report was Leroy Aarons, senior vice president and former executive editor of the *Oakland Tribune*, who came out as the report was released (as did Lee Stinnett, executive director of ASNE) and subsequently founded the National Lesbian and Gay Journalists Association. By June 1992 the organization had chapters in cities across the country. Juan Palomo is a member of the association's board, as is Linda Villarosa, who made history of another sort when she came out in her position as senior editor at *Essence*, the country's largest magazine for black women. Villarosa's public coming out in the May 1991 issue took the dramatic form of an article co-written with her mother entitled "The Mother-Daughter Thing: Love, Loss and Coming Out."

When the new association held its first convention in San Francisco in June 1992 it was attended by nearly 300 lesbian and gay journalists working in the mainstream and the gay media. The newly legitimate status of the issues represented by the organization was evidenced by the presence of "leaders of some of the country's most powerful news organizations . . . among them Robert Kaiser, managing editor of the *Washington Post*" (Gross 1992b). The conference opened with a videotaped message from *New York Times* publisher Arthur Ochs Sulzberger, Jr., whose ascension to the throne of the nation's leading paper is widely considered one of the primary reasons (along with the replacement of managing editor Abe Rosenthal with Max Frankel) the *Times* has recently become startlingly gay-positive (Signorile 1992b, 1992c). Sulzberger set the tone for the new era by saying "we can no longer offer our readers a predominately white, straight, male vision of events and say we're doing our job" (Gross 1992b).

Whatever common sense of accomplishment the participants at the San Francisco conference may have felt, they were also divided on the issue of outing, "the question discussed most often . . . with several big-name journalists squaring off for some noisy, and sometimes vicious, jousting. It was easy to tell who was on which team by the uniforms: those in favor are most often clad in multiple earrings and sassy T-shirts. Those opposed wear suits and ties" (ibid.). The outing debate featured Michelangelo Signorile, who argued that "it is time to develop new ethics of reportage because the old ethics were created a long time ago by straight, white men," and, on the other side, *San Francisco Chronicle* writer Randy Shilts, referring to outers as "lavender fascists who would force their ideology on everyone" (ibid.). Allied with Shilts was Andrew Sullivan, the recently appointed openly gay, and conservative, editor of the (once liberal) *New Republic*. Sullivan, a personal friend and defender of Pete Williams, is a member in good standing of the Washington closet circuit, and has argued against outing (in a conversation with me) that closeted gays like Williams can do more good working from within the system, although he was hard put to point to any examples of their achievements along these lines.

Thus, in the early 1990s, mainstream lesbian and gay journalists in greater numbers are insisting on being visible at work and even occasionally in print, but the issue of outing is one to which they respond like traditional journalists. With few if any exceptions they proclaim the primacy of the right to privacy when it comes to gay people who are not egregiously hypocritical, conveniently ignoring the double standard revealed by singling out this one area in which to protect a right to privacy that is routinely trampled in the interest of the public's "right to know" everything about the private lives of celebrities and public officials.

The Cultural Front

As the 1980s drew to a close, the right wing broadened its focus to encompass the domain of elite culture. Although the political struggles of the 1980s had often been fought on the field of culture, it was the lowlands of mass and even marginal media — television, rock and roll music, pornography — that drew the attention of moral enforcers. Signaling the opening of a new front, journalist and 1992 presidential hopeful Patrick Buchanan called for "a cultural revolution in the '90s as sweeping as the political revolution in the '80s." In terms that Carole Vance (1989) compared to Nazi cultural metaphors, Buchanan warned that "just as a poisoned land will yield up poisonous fruits, so a polluted culture, left to fester and stink, can destroy a nation's soul" (Buchanan 1989).

The most visible of the battles on the new cultural front were the attacks by Senator Jesse Helms and his allies on the National Endowment for the Arts (NEA) for funding arts programs that included Andres Serrano's photograph "Piss Christ" and Robert Mapplethorpe's explicitly sexual photographs of gay men. The subsequent furor and maneuvering once again brought out Helms's favorite political tools, embarrassment and threat. He circulated selected Mapplethorpe photos, informed his Senate colleagues that Mrs. Helms had skimmed the exhibition catalogue and exclaimed, "Lord have mercy, Jesse, I'm not believing this," and carried the catalogue onto the Senate floor to clinch his point with senators such as Robert Byrd, who took one look and said, "Good gosh, I'll take your amendment." Even Howard Metzenbaum, one of the staunchest liberals in the Senate, went along with the amendment, saying, "Nobody thinks you ought to be able to be using funds to promote or disseminate pornography. I'm not going to oppose it, because it's hard to oppose an amendment of this kind because it sounds so right." As Helms boasted to Maureen Dowd of the *New York Times*, when it comes to denying funds to anything with explicit homoerotic content, "Old Helms will win every time."

Helms's attacks on the NEA are a central part of the right wing's cultural campaign, using a moral panic to fuel the political blackmail begun earlier with moves to deny federal funds for explicit safe-sex education to counter AIDS. Running through these various attacks, as we've already noted, is the familiar charge of "promoting homosexuality" leveled against any form of visibility that is not coupled with an attack on gay people. Just as every senator who spoke on the Helms amendment expressed his personal disgust with Mapplethorpe and Serrano, so it generally is the case with such moral campaigns: "fundamentalists select a negative symbol which is highly arousing to their own constituency and which is difficult or problematic for their opponents to defend" (Vance 1989: 41). No politician can comfortably defend "avant-garde" art or elite tastes, and this reluctance gives the right a powerful weapon.

In October 1990, the NEA won a three-year extension (previous renewals had been for five years) with minimal restrictions, but a distinct chill remained in the air. During the period of uncertainty and struggle after Helms opened the anti-NEA hunting season, newly appointed NEA chair John Frohnmayer overruled a peer-review panel and barred grants to four performance artists. This gang of four, not surprisingly, consisted of three openly gay artists whose work is overtly political (John Fleck, Holly Hughes, Tim Miller) and sex radical Karen Finley.[103] The "NEA four" sued the Endowment on the grounds that the law Frohnmayer cited, requiring the NEA to take into con-

---

103. Finley commented in an interview that "although I am straight, I think it would be wrong to say that the attack on me isn't about homophobia. My work is pro-gay . . . [and] I believe the foremost issue here is dread of homosexuality" (Sadownick 1990: 51).

sideration "general standards of decency," violated the First Amendment. In June 1992, a federal judge agreed with the artists and invalidated the "decency standard" that had been worked out as a compromise to forestall Helms in 1990 (Honan 1992b).

Even though the NEA survived the assault by Helms and his associates in Congress, "the issue has already proved to be a political and fund-raising boon for the Republican right. . . . 'It's been a good issue, and the longer it stays around, the better,' says Bruce Eberle, a leading Republican mail consultant . . . who has sent out several million solicitations on the endowment issue" (Berke 1990). When Patrick Buchanan embarked on a challenge to George Bush in the 1992 presidential primaries, the NEA was among his first targets.

Tongues Untied, Marlon Riggs's innovative, award-winning documentary about a black gay man's struggle for identity, received a lot of less favorable attention from right-wing crusaders when it was shown on public television's "POV" (point of view) series. The film's budget, like those of most independently produced documentaries, was a patchwork of support from many sources, including a $5,000 subgrant from the NEA. As the March Georgia primary approached, Buchanan released a television spot that showed a clip of dancing leather-clad men taken from *Tongues Untied*, over which was superimposed a small picture of President Bush and the words: "Bush used your tax dollars for this" (Berger 1992).[104]

The Bush administration's response to Buchanan's ad was swift and forthright: on February 21 John Frohnmayer, a personal friend of the president, was fired as NEA chair. Frohnmayer's tenure had been rocky from the start, as he tried to steer a moderate course between the conservative White House and the arts professionals both inside the NEA and around the country who were resisting attempts to impose ideological constraints. Despite a handwritten letter of support from the president, which he received in the spring of 1990, Frohnmayer had been under steady pressure from then White House Chief of Staff John Sununu, "who told Frohnmayer that the chairman's vision of the agency's mission conflicted with the administration's determination not to fund homoerotic and politically objectionable art"

---

104. The full text of the Buchanan spot: "In the last three years, the Bush Administration has invested our tax dollars in pornographic and blasphemous art too shocking to show. This so-called art has glorified homosexuality, exploited children, and perverted the image of Jesus Christ. Even after good people protested, Bush continued to fund this kind of art. Send Bush a message! We need a leader to fight for what we believe in. Vote Pat Buchanan for President."

(Lichtenstein 1992: 36). Buchanan's television ad may not have been expected, but the firing of John Frohnmayer was certainly in the cards, as he was proving not to be the team player Bush and Sununu wanted. Days before his abrupt dismissal, Frohnmayer told a friend that when he took the NEA job he was "a moderate on the First Amendment, but will leave an absolutist" (ibid.).

Not Worth an Outing

The White House had prepared the way for a more flexible NEA when Bush appointed a senior deputy—Anne-Imelda Radice, a former U.S. Information Service official with close ties to conservatives in the administration—chair in March 1991. A hard-line right-winger, Radice was widely assumed to be in place as Frohnmayer's replacement, "the last act in the play to bring the NEA under the kind of control that Sununu had wanted from the beginning," according to a *Los Angeles Times* reporter (Lichtenstein 1992). Thus, no one was surprised when Radice was appointed acting chair in March, and the *Village Voice*, long critical of Frohnmayer's flip-flopping, ran an article headed "Here Comes the New Boss, Worse Than the Old Boss" (Carr 1992a).

Radice lost no time proving herself to be the right person for the job, at least from the perspective of the White House and Jesse Helms. Testifying before an appropriations subcommittee, she pledged that the NEA would no longer fund works deemed "too controversial or sexually graphic. . . . Sexually explicit material—if that's the only thing that leaps out at you from a work of art, even though it may be done with the highest intentions—we can't afford that" (Salisbury 1992a). Although she was criticized for her testimony by arts professionals— the executive director of the National Association of Artists Organizations said that Radice's "vision is one that pleases the far right and congress first and the American public and artists last" (ibid.)—and by the subcommittee chair, Representative Sidney Yates (one of the Endowment's earliest and strongest supporters), who regretted the increased restrictiveness she promised, she was praised by conservatives such as Jesse Helms. Radice told the subcommittee that "she had been given no precise instructions from the White House . . . but that 'it wouldn't be necessary because those people know me and my work' " (Honan 1992a: C14).

It didn't take Radice long to live up to her self-styled billing of "decency czar": she vetoed two grants that had been strongly recommended by the National Council on the Arts. "Both rejected grants were for exhibitions that incorporated rather innocuous sexual references," one of these a work "that includes over 100 tiny photographs of body parts, including one 2-by-3-inch picture of a penis" (Wallis 1992: 27). Beyond the expected demonstration of conservative values being imposed on public funding for the arts, Radice's action also set another precedent by

> overturning the balance of power at the endowment in one fell swoop. . . . Frohnmayer compared his former job as NEA chair to that of a judge presiding over a jury. "The chairman should only act if the jury proceeds directly against the evidence," he said. "Radice is acting like a judge who has discarded the jury. She's saying that one person has the power to decide what is aesthetically appropriate." (Roshan 1992: 25)

The point was not lost on the jury, either, and within days of Radice's vetoes another unprecedented action occurred: "a panel of artists and art experts walked out in the middle of their deliberations . . . [when] members of a sculpture panel said they could not continue judging applications because the reviewing process had been 'severely compromised and placed in great jeopardy' " by the chair's actions (Salisbury 1992b). When a second panel walked out the following week after Radice refused to answer their questions concerning the criteria she was applying in judging artistic merit, many observers thought that these developments were a not-unwelcome part of Radice's campaign to undercut the peer-review system used to evaluate applications.

So far the story is much like many others in the Washington of Reagan, Bush, and Helms. But there is a novel twist to this story, because Anne-Imelda Radice is a lesbian, "a fact that has for years been an open secret in the insular circles of Washington society, though she . . . kept a considerably lower profile in the year preceding her appointment" (Roshan 1992). As the plan to replace Frohnmayer with his senior deputy became obvious to Washington observers, the question of outing Radice became a frequent topic of conversation within the confines of the capital's closet circuit—it occasioned much fretting at Pete Williams's birthday party—as well as among lesbian and gay activists, whether proponents or opponents of the tactic. Given the centrality of homoerotic art to the controversies swirling around the NEA since Jesse Helms first struck political paydirt with Mapplethorpe's photographs, it was inevitable that Radice's sexuality would play a part in the culture wars:

> "In NEA terms, sexually explicit has often been a code word for gay," notes Randall Bourschiedt of the Alliance for the Arts. "The battles that have raised the most opposition in the past few years

have always been related to sex, and with few exceptions they've been overwhelmingly related to lesbian and gay sex." (ibid.)

It was widely assumed that Radice's lesbianism was no secret to the White House—it was reported on reliable authority that the *Washington Post* possessed a memo she had written, alerting them that her lesbianism might become "an issue" (Jacobs 1992a). Cynics even speculated that being a lesbian had helped her get the NEA job, as the administration might have calculated that this would protect her, and them, from the charge of homophobia. As one gay NEA insider put it, "There are a lot of people who believe that Anne Radice is the lesbian Clarence Thomas." Washington constitutional attorney David Cole noted that "Helms and Buchanan might be very happy to have a lesbian government official who is working to suppress lesbian and gay speech, the same way corporate law firms sometimes use attorneys who are female or people of color to defend against sex- and race-discrimination suits" (Minkowitz 1992: 45). Nonetheless, when she vetoed the two grants on the grounds that the works were "sexually explicit," the consequences were predictable. On Friday, May 15, a small group of Queer Nationals, nearly outnumbered by reporters, demonstrated in front of the NEA offices and publicly outed Radice as a lesbian.[105]

The story of Radice's outing was carried by a number of newspapers, including the *Philadelphia Inquirer*, which had been giving the NEA story prominent front-page coverage, the *Los Angeles Times*, and the *Oregonian* in Frohnmayer's hometown of Portland. The *New York Times*, which consistently placed its NEA stories back in the third section "culture pages," did not report the outing.

The *Village Voice* had it both ways: outing opponent C.Carr, who had previously written about Radice's impending appointment, wrote an account of her actions as chair without mentioning her lesbianism

---

105. Two days before she was outed, Radice met with staff members of the National Gay and Lesbian Task Force, who expressed grave concerns over the implications of her words and actions. Radice told them that she was not homophobic and was hurt by the accusation, and reiterated her determination to deny funding to art with sexual content, suggesting that "perhaps we don't want to show America only the stereotypic image of gays and lesbians" (Minkowitz 1992: 45). The NGLTF staffers told Radice that "sexuality is a part of our lives and community, and just as viable and important as any other aspect." Their conclusion after the meeting was that Radice "may not be homophobic but she is sex-phobic, and because the oppression lesbian and gay people face is based on our sexuality, we will continue to face the brunt of the new restrictions" (NGLTF 1992).

or her outing (Carr 1992b), while Robert Atkins's arts news column in the same issue casually referred to the "on-again, off-again coverage of Radice's outing" (Atkins 1992); the following week another *Voice* columnist quoted a former NEA panelist calling Radice "Washington's new Roy Cohn" (P. Anderson 1992). A few weeks later, the *Voice's* press columnist, James Ledbetter, remarked on the contradictory performance of the *New York Post*, which outed Radice in a June 8 news story and then ran an editorial June 9 attacking the "homosexual thought police" for outing her, claiming that "we, frankly couldn't care less about Anne-Imelda Radice's sexual orientation" (Ledbetter 1992). Ledbetter didn't comment on his own paper's inconsistency.

The lesbian and gay press was less divided on outing Radice: the news was reported by New York's *QW* weekly, by Philadelphia's two gay papers, and by *Gay Community News*, distributed nationally from Boston. The most widely distributed lesbian and gay publication, the *Advocate*, which had made outing history when it published Signorile's Pete Williams story, seemed conflicted about how to approach the Radice outing. Apparently willing neither to say this case called for another "singular" exception to their anti-outing policy nor to pass the story by, they ran an unsigned piece titled "Not Even Worth an Outing." The *Advocate* may not have deemed Radice worthy of outing, but it did quote Jesse Helms's paean of praise—"a lady with good sense and guts to match"—as well as a lesbian activist's less enthusiastic "she's a lesbian from hell," and concluded that "Bush's lesbian Clarence Thomas has always had the politics of a Neanderthal" (*Advocate* 1992).[106] Two weeks later, the *Advocate* published an analysis of Radice's appointment in the context of Bush administration politics, concluding that "the growth of the lesbian and gay movement has made the fates of gay and lesbian activists, George Bush, the far right, and one Helms-befriended HRCF [Human Rights Campaign Fund] contributor named Anne-Imelda Radice entwined in a way Roy Cohn and Joseph McCarthy could never have imagined" (Minkowitz 1992).[107]

---

106. The next issue of the *Advocate* featured the publication's annual humorous awards for antigay actions, which included six references to Radice. One of these came in an "award" to Pete Williams, said to have been "seen . . . on the arm of NEA generalissimo Anne-Imelda Radice. . . . Who says the Republicans are homophobic?"

107. Despite Jesse Helms's approval, Radice was viewed with suspicion by portions of the Christian right. Andrea Sheldon of the Traditional Values Coalition was quoted in the *Christian American* as conceding that Radice "has done the right thing now and we appreciate that," but warning that "I don't know if we can trust her. . . . Our con-

The Guns of August

Patrick Buchanan's 1992 Georgia primary ad, which used images of gay men to accuse Bush of spending "our tax dollars [on] pornographic and blasphemous art" did more than grease the skids under NEA chair John Frohnmayer; it signaled the central role that gay people would play in the presidential campaign. As *Time* magazine put it even before the Republican National Convention in Houston, "After Willie Horton, Are Gays Next?" (Painton 1992).

The Democratic National Convention in New York that nominated Bill Clinton in July was notably more gay-positive than previous national political conventions (though hardly to a degree that should satisfy legitimate lesbian and gay concerns). Openly lesbian San Francisco supervisor Roberta Achtenberg addressed the convention as a member of the platform-drafting committee and said that, "as a lesbian and [a] Jew, I have had to live with fear for my physical safety and that of my peoples." Bob Hattoy, a gay man with AIDS who served as an environmental adviser to Clinton, gave an eloquent speech about AIDS, while the cameras zoomed in on delegates holding signs demanding AIDS funding. Speeches by Paul Tsongas and Ted Kennedy referred to gay teenagers, cabinet members, and military personnel. And, although it required last-minute behind-the-scenes politicking to insure that his acceptance speech made even a subtle reference to lesbian and gay people, Bill Clinton did promise to end the military's antigay policy, adopt the recommendations of the National AIDS Commission, and ban antigay bias in the federal government.

In early August a gay man named Taylor Franz appeared on ABC's "Nightline" and charged that he had been forced to resign from his job at the Republican National Committee because of his sexual orientation. In response, Vice President Dan Quayle claimed, to CNN talk show host Larry King and ABC News, that the Bush administration had a policy of nondiscrimination against homosexuals, thus setting off a charge by the Southern Baptist Christian Life Commission that the administration was soft on gays (Penn 1992a). It didn't take long to

---

cern is that if she's given the permanent position that she would flip flop" (Thoburn 1992). Sheldon and her colleagues were probably pleased, although many in the arts community were not, when Radice denied funding to three lesbian and gay film festivals. The action, announced two weeks after the November 1992 election, was widely perceived, in the words of one NEA panel chair, as "a politically motivated and mean-spirited parting gesture by the acting chair" (Coward 1992).

resolve the suspense: the Bush administration decided to cast its lot with the bigots.

The Republicans were quick to seize on the Democrats' overtures to gays as further evidence of cultural decay. The Republican platform committee was dominated by the party's far right, and the result was a platform that explicitly opposed efforts to provide antidiscrimination protection for gay people — as signs carried at the Republican Convention proclaimed, "Family Rights Forever, Gay Rights Never!"

By the time the convention opened in Houston, the scene was set: lesbian and gay Americans were defined as a prime target as Patrick Buchanan declared in his opening night prime-time speech that "there is a war going on in our country for the soul of America. It is a cultural war, as critical to the kind of nation we will one day be — as was the cold war itself." Buchanan set the tone for much of the convention, attacking the Democratic platform for endorsing homosexual rights, among other changes "we [cannot] tolerate in a nation that we still call God's country," and characterizing Clinton and Gore as "the most prolesbian and progay ticket in history." Other prominent Republicans were more subtle, preferring to use the euphemism of "family values," although

> privately top Bush campaign officials said they would hit the issue hard in the campaign, portraying Mr. Clinton as an advocate for homosexuals. Campaign aides said radio ads were being considered that would run only in the South and would portray a Clinton victory as sure to lead to more gay teachers in the schools. (Schmalz 1992: A21)

In the long run, it seems likely that this strategy backfired, that more Americans were appalled than were attracted by the blatant bigotry displayed in Houston. Moderate Republicans were quick to distance themselves from their party's platform (although Massachusetts governor William Weld was the only convention speaker to say anything that might be interpreted as a defense of the rights of gay people), and the Log Cabin Federation, a struggling gay Republican group, refused to endorse Bush. Whether the Republicans' antigay pogrom won or lost them votes in November, it did lead to the outing of several party members.

Shortly after the Houston convention, the New York lesbian and gay weekly *QW* outed the author of George Bush's acceptance speech. Ray Price, "a speechwriter for Richard Nixon, . . . is also a longtime friend of President Bush. During the Nixon years, Price was said to have sent a White House limousine to Washington's Union Station to pick up his New York-based lover on Friday afternoons" (Nobile 1992). The Republican National Committee refused comment on the report, and the story didn't travel beyond the gay press. The outers did a lot better on the next try.

In his 1987 book on the AIDS epidemic, Randy Shilts told the story of an encounter that took place at a party given by gay Republicans at the 1984 convention in Dallas. According to Shilts's account, gay journalist Larry Bush ran into "the son of a prominent anti-feminist leader, a woman who had earned a national reputation for spearheading opposition to the Equal Rights Amendment" (1987: 473). Recalling that this woman had recently argued that the ERA would increase the spread of AIDS, Larry Bush asked her son, "Does [your mother] know you're gay?" to which he replied, "I'd never do anything to embarrass Mother." He excused himself and left the party when Bush asked how he felt about "people dying of a disease while your mother makes political capital off it." (ibid.).

Even those who were not well connected to gay gossip networks probably figured out who the unnamed anti-ERA crusader was, but neither Shilts nor Bush would confirm the identity of Phyllis Schlafly's son John until after the Republican Convention, at which Patrick Buchanan introduced her "as the woman who saved the nation from having homosexual rights guaranteed by the Constitution" (Cohen 1992). Despite the tacit agreement among pro-outing activists that gay relatives of celebrities are not appropriate subjects for outing (it was the tabloids, not the gay press, that wrote about Cher's daughter), John Schlafly had become an irresistible target.[108] For one thing, the 40-year-old tax accountant lives with his mother and advises her organization on financial matters. But the writers of the *QW* cover story on "Phyllis Schlafly's 'Deep Dark Secret' " cite a more persuasive reason:

> Many homosexuals are unfortunate enough to have homophobic parents. But Phyllis Schlafly wears her homophobia as a badge of honor. She has turned it into a pernicious national crusade, and a career. And though she lives with her gay son, works with him, and is

---

108. At about the same time that they outed John Schlafly, the editors of *QW* withheld the name of "an influential ally of President Bush [who] was arrested in July in Maryland for non-consensual sexual contact with an undercover police officer" (Penn 1992b). An anonymous source sent copies of the arrest record to the *Washington Post* and CBS News as well as *QW*, but none chose to identify the man, "who currently holds a prestigious appointment with no policy-making powers. Previously, he held positions in both the White House and on Bush's campaign staff," and his attorney assured *QW* that "this is a guy who's never taken [an antigay] position" (ibid.).

aware of his sexuality, her anti-gay rhetoric has only escalated
through the years. (Roshan and Hilditch 1992: 23)

The *QW* writers had spoken with John Schlafly while they were
working on their story, but he "politely refused to directly confirm or
deny the questions about his sexuality . . . [and] defended his
mother against charges that she is anti-gay" (ibid.). Shortly after the
article appeared, Schlafly and his mother agreed to an interview for
the *San Francisco Examiner* conducted by Larry Bush, the journalist
who had told Randy Shilts about the 1984 Dallas party. In the *Examiner*
interview and in a subsequent interview with the *Philadelphia Inquirer*,
John Schlafly confirmed that he is gay, and said, "I support and endorse everything my mother's doing. I hold her in great esteem." He
also said he felt gay men and lesbians were being "too sensitive" if they
felt offended by the tenor of the speeches at the Republican National
Convention (Adams 1992). The story was transmitted by the Associated Press and covered by the *Boston Globe*, the *Chicago Tribune*, the
Washington Post, and *Newsweek*. Writing in the *Washington Post*, columnist Richard Cohen noted Phyllis Schlafly's claim that she never went
in for gay bashing, "but then she never went in for bashing the gay
bashers, either. She runs with an ugly crowd. . . . They are the people who provide the white noise of silent approval when a gay is
treated shabbily" (ibid.).

The political gay bashing of the Republican party was a primary
motivation behind the *Advocate*'s decision to engage in a second cover-
story outing. In an editorial titled "Homosexuality, Honesty, and Hypocrisy," *Advocate* publisher Niles Merton quoted Martin Luther
King's analogy of the importance of running a red light to get a fire
truck to a raging fire or an ambulance to the hospital:

> In this issue of the *Advocate*, we run the red light of outing and cast a
> very bright beam on the lies and hypocrisy of Republican representa-
> tive Jim McCrery of Louisiana. We open his closet door and reveal
> him for what he is: a homosexual. A liar. A hypocrite. An oppor-
> tunistic exponent of what the Republican Party dares to call "family
> values." (Merton 1992)

McCrery, a two-term congressman who "has worked diligently to
establish conservative credentials, . . . has voted with opponents of
gay rights on issues ranging from AIDS funding to the National Endowment for the Arts" (Bull 1992: 40). When rumors about McCrery's
sexuality were raised by a 1988 opponent in a televised debate,
McCrery, prepared for the question, responded by denying that he is

gay, joking, "And I wish you'd stop calling me at home." The incident seemed to work in McCrery's favor, and his marriage in 1991 to a Shreveport television reporter would seem to have cemented his heterosexual image. But McCrery's antigay politics eventually moved a former lover, Gary Cathey, to expose McCrery's hypocrisy.

The *Advocate* story, which included Cathey's account of his relationship of more than a decade with the closeted politician, had what Michael Petrelis referred to as a "smoking dick" who could provide detailed first-person testimony to McCrery's homosexual activities, and at least one other man told the *Advocate* that he had had sex with McCrery. The story thus met the stringent requirements set by journalists for reporting such revelations: testimony of reliable witnesses who were willing to be identified; a "high level state official" is quoted as saying "Gary Cathey has an excellent reputation in the state. . . . I know he wouldn't do anything like this without having the truth behind him" (ibid.). The story also met the primary criterion for revealing someone's hidden homosexuality: political hypocrisy. As Barney Frank put it, McCrery is "one of the hard-core homophobes in Congress. [If he's gay] it's like if [gun-control activist] Sarah Brady owned a gun" (ibid.: 45). Despite all this, the story was not picked up by the national media; even newspapers that had covered the outing of Pete Williams ignored the exposure of McCrery's hypocrisy. The Shreveport ACT Up chapter, of which Gary Cathey was a founder, called a press conference in order to draw local media attention, and the Shreveport papers did carry the story. Nevertheless, McCrery was elected to a third term.

The lessons to be drawn from the McCrery story are not entirely clear. It may be that the *Advocate* made a strategic error by not releasing the story during the Republican Convention, when the legions of reporters swarming through Houston might have welcomed such a dramatic example of family-values hypocrisy. It certainly does seem that meeting standard journalistic criteria for exposé stories will not guarantee mainstream media attention to an outing. Closeted politicians with similarly antigay records may well have sighed with relief that they might not have to take to heart *Advocate* publisher Merton's warning that "we may just run another red light—right through your closet door" (ibid.).

Ethics, Tactics, and Prospects

When I began to write this book, in the winter of 1991, Mikhail Gorbachev was president of the Soviet Union and George Bush was scor-ing record highs in public opinion polls. As I finished, in the fall of 1992, George Bush was still president of the United States, the nation still had no coherent AIDS policy, and the Pentagon continued to insist that homosexuality is incompatible with military service. It now appears likely that by the time you read these words the facts will have changed at home as they have abroad. Truly, we live in interesting times. If there is anything we can take for granted at the end of the twentieth century it is the certainty of change, and no amount of preaching or political speechmaking will revive a mythical past in which all people knew their places and kept to them. The majority of the population that is made up of "women and minorities" is restless and dissatisfied. All segments of our society have become disenchanted with the institutions that define, carry out, and report on the nation's agenda.

In this time of rapid change, the standards and practices of journalism are no less vulnerable to challenge than those of any other institution. When the history of journalism is written, the story of the last decade of this century may be the eclipse of journalists and journalistic routines. The satellite-carried live coverage of dramatic events—the 1991 Gulf War, the 1992 Los Angeles riots—permits us to witness important events without the journalistic mediation and interpretation made necessary by previous technologies. Live coverage reduces journalists to the role of sportscasters commenting on a game they are watching along with the audience. The television talk-show circuit that flourished as a part of show business's celebrity industry cultivated a "rhetoric of authenticity" in order to (falsely) imply "privileged access to the star's 'real' personality" (Dyer 1992: 136), and this circuit has now begun to supplant the "official" arenas of public political discourse. When H. Ross Perot declared his openness to a 1992 presidential candidacy on CNN's "Live with Larry King" show, it marked a sea change in American political campaigning and the role of the media in the political process.

Among the journalistic norms and routines challenged by recent developments is the sense of a clear boundary between the private and the public. The public's taste for sensation is never sated, and the audience-seeking media that feed it a steady diet of gossip (some of which is even true) have a difficult time drawing a line and saying—to themselves and to their audience—beyond this point we have no right to intrude. Even those who would like to stay on the polite side of the line are driven across it by "journalism's two ultimate imperatives: 'Don't get beaten to a story by another media outlet,' and, 'If we don't break this, someone else will'" (Sabato 1991: 56). The competition between network news programs and the local news programs broadcast by their own affiliates (now equipped with satellite access), and the growing array of syndicated tabloid TV "news" shows, only raises the stakes and confuses the professionals as well as the audience. Yet there are instances of restraint that illuminate the murky terrain of journalistic principles. Despite the extensive posthumous accounts of John Kennedy's sexual exploits (and FDR's), sitting presidents seem to benefit from one of the few remaining taboos on tabloid-style journalism. In the same period in which the American public was introduced to Donna Rice and Gennifer Flowers, the press exercised nearly total restraint by barely reporting on the very widely circulated rumors that George Bush has had mistresses.

Although the name of at least one of George Bush's alleged mistresses has been known for years—as R. W. Apple, chief Washington reporter for the *New York Times*, put it, "It is not a name that is unknown in any newsroom in Washington. . . . It is known everywhere, and it is not used" (Conason 1992: 32)—the story was barely touched during the 1992 campaign. During the storm over Bill Clinton's possible affair with Gennifer Flowers, Hillary Clinton complained to a *Vanity Fair* reporter about a double standard in media treatment of the candidates' personal lives. She mentioned the name of the "other Jennifer," and the public uproar forced her to apologize for raising the issue of Bush's purported mistress (Sontag 1992). The issue surfaced again when a footnote to a book about a Washington lobbyist quoted a deceased diplomat as saying that he once arranged for Bush and Jennifer Fitzgerald to use a guest house in Geneva. This published note gave a reporter from CNN "permission" to ask Bush about the story during an August 11 televised press conference. Bush angrily denied the report, declaring, "I'm not going to take any sleazy questions like that from CNN" (he later repeated his refusal to "take any sleaze questions" in an Oval Office interview with NBC News reporter Stone Phillips), and the story died after a few days. According to journalist Joe Conason, whose cover story on Bush's alleged mistresses in *Spy* magazine also failed to ignite the issue, "Regarding Bush, the respectable press has set itself a standard of proof so high— the 'smoking bimbo'—that the story literally can't be done unless an ex-girlfriend steps forward to talk on the record" (ibid.).

In this era of rapidly shifting (declining?) standards, the willingness, even eagerness of most journalists to respect the privacy of the closet stands out almost as glaringly as their deferential treatment of presidential secrets. But the grounds surely differ in these two instances. The managing editor of the *Washington Post* explained that he didn't see the homosexuality of a public figure "as something we need to inform people about" (Sabato 1991: 88).[109] And, indeed, the *Washington Post* did not inform its readers that Assistant Secretary of Defense Pete Williams is a gay man, despite the fact that the military spends over $27 million each year ferreting out and expelling lesbian and gay members of the armed services (O'Neill 1992); or that acting NEA head Anne-Imelda Radice is a lesbian, despite her role in denying funding to arts projects that express homoerotic sexuality. It should hardly be necessary to ask whether the *Post* would exercise similar restraint were the issues involved the race or gender of a public figure.

Writing more than a year after the outing of Malcolm Forbes opened a new page in journalism, *OutWeek* editor Gabriel Rotello argued that "what we have called 'outing' is a primarily journalistic movement to treat homosexuality as equal to heterosexuality in the media." Rotello agreed that many people, gay as well as straight, would like to believe that the "tacit agreement that queerness is unfit to print . . . is done by a sympathetic media eager to avoid damaging the lives or careers of famous gays," but he insisted that "such has never been the case," citing the willingness of the media to expose most other celebrity secrets as well as the names and addresses of "every chump in Podunk who gets arrested on a morals charge" (Rotello 1991a: 10). The solution proposed—and practiced—by Rotello and by Michelangelo Signorile and others who agreed with them was "equalizing homosexuality and heterosexuality in the media," and Rotello set out four guidelines for the practice he preferred to call "equalizing":

> Number one: Because the privacy of the non-famous is usually respected by the press, there is no double standard in maintaining that private lesbians and gays have a right to stay private. . . . Equalizing is only concerned with public figures, people who have accepted the benefits and should accept the liabilities of fame.
> The second guideline is to confine equalizing to those celebrities

---

109. When the *New York Times Magazine* published a cover story on the new president of the National Organization for Women (NOW), Patricia Ireland, which included the fact that she has a female lover as well as a husband, the article alleged that Ireland revealed this only because the *Advocate* threatened to out her (J. Gross 1992a: 38). However, besides the *Advocate*'s denial that they made any such threat, Ireland herself told an *Advocate* writer that she had voluntarily told the *Times* reporter about her lover, "but it was for all the world like it passed over her head" (Minkowitz 1991c). Most mainstream press attention to Ireland's election as NOW president seemed preoccupied with the question of whether "stories like the *Advocate*'s fuel a serious image problem for NOW" (Voboril 1991).

who are already out in their private lives, a category which includes
most gay public figures—indeed, that's usually how we know they're
gay. . . .

Third, we should avoid disclosing the sexuality of those whose
careers would likely be destroyed [presumably, an exception would
be made here for rank hypocrites]. . . .

Guideline number four applies to all journalism: Know your facts.
(ibid.)[110]

Rotello defined equalizing as telling the truth, thus defining the
routine journalistic treatment of closeted gays as lying. "Those who
call us immoral for speaking truthfully about celebrity homosexuality
imply that it's moral for journalists to lie, at least when the issue is being queer" (ibid.).

Rotello's arguments against concealing or lying about others'
homosexuality are reminiscent of the imperative of the gay liberation
movement that every aspect of stigma must be rejected, and every
facet of one's identity proclaimed. As sociologist Roy Cain has shown,
the early success of the movement in persuading the American Psychiatric Association to remove homosexuality from its list of patholo-
gies was part of a fundamental reorientation:

> When homosexuality was considered pathological, secretiveness
> about one's homosexuality was widely viewed as normal and desira-
> ble; openness, conversely, was seen as an expression of personal and
> social pathology and as a political liability to gays in general. In con-
> trast, when homosexuality was normalized, openness about one's
> homosexual preferences came to be viewed as desirable, while secre-
> tiveness came to be seen as problematic. Disclosing one's homosex-
> ual preferences, especially to nongay others, is now considered to be
> psychologically advantageous to the individual gay person and politi-
> cally advantageous to the gay community. (1991: 25–26)

The ethic of disclosure and authenticity has come to be widely accepted in most domains of contemporary life—probably contributing

---

110. It is important to note that Rotello's criteria would not support the outing of gay
people who are the relatives of public figures but not themselves celebrities. In fact, such
instances of morally dubious outing—Cher's daughter, Spiro Agnew's son—have been
committed by the tabloid press and by mainstream journalists, not by gay activists. Journalist Brit Hume, who was working with columnist Jack Anderson in 1970, recalled the
outing of Agnew's son as "something I'll be sorry for all the rest of my days" (quoted
in Sabato 1991: 140). On the other hand, there is no moral injunction against enjoying
cosmic justice when the son of rabidly antigay psychiatrist Charles Socarides becomes
an openly gay activist.

to, as well as being promoted by, the ubiquitous availability of celebrities' real or pretended private lives. One of the stranger phenomena, at least to my mind, exhibited daily on television, is the seemingly endless supply of noncelebrities willing to share their unusual and often bizarre personal lives with millions of strangers. In Michel Foucault's words, "We have become a singularly confessing society" (1978: 59). Foucault associates the Western penchant for confessing with the elaboration of discourses that control us in the guise of seeking truth:

> The obligation to confess is so deeply ingrained in us, that we no longer perceive it as the effect of a power that constrains us; on the contrary, it seems to us that truth, lodged in our most secret nature, "demands" only to surface; that if it fails to do so, this is because a constraint holds it in place, the violence of a power weighs it down, and it can finally be articulated only at the price of a kind of liberation. (ibid.: 60)

Whether Foucault was applauding or decrying this state of affairs,[111] it does seem to be the case that we have adopted a view of personhood that favors authenticity and disclosure in self-presentation, and that homosexuality stands out as a rare exception to this rule. We do generally acknowledge a right to keep much about our private lives just that—private—but for most people that does not include their sexual orientation (otherwise sales of wedding rings would plummet). Only gay people, it seems, are applauded for keeping hidden the very sort of information others are congratulated for sharing. Keeping pictures of one's spouse on display at the office, for example, is a familiar and respectable practice (notice the family pictures in the background the next time you subject yourself to a presidential address from the Oval Office), but lesbian and gay people rarely can afford such openness.

As Richard Mohr points out, concealing or dissimulating one's sexual orientation is an act of secrecy, not privacy. One can keep one's private life out of the public eye as, say, theater producer Cameron Mackintosh seems to do (Rothstein 1990) without keeping it secret. Nor is communicating the fact that someone is gay a violation of that person's privacy because one is making his or her sex life public. As Vito Russo put it, "When I say my brother and his wife are heterosexual, that

---

111. Given Foucault's "discretion" concerning his own homosexuality and his concealment of the AIDS-related disease that killed him, it seems that he was not well disposed toward the confessional imperative that, in any case, he managed to evade.

doesn't mean I'm talking about their sex lives. Likewise, when we say someone is gay, we're talking about their *sexual orientation*, not their sexual activity" (1990). Mohr concludes that "it is sexual acts, and derivatively talk of them, not sexual orientations that are protected by privacy. The reporting of sexual orientation does not violate any of the senses of privacy that are legitimately invoked in sexual matters" (1992: 17).

Mohr carries his argument one step further, and closer to the question of outing, when he says that a "right against outing" amounts to the imposition of "a gag order, that is, [it] calls for squelching speech." In other words, the alleged moral duty to keep someone else's secret is an imposition on my freedom. As he notes, the unwritten rule that gays protect each other's secrets is just that, an unwritten rule:

> No one signs on to this code, rather one is born into it. . . . Gays simply find themselves immersed in the presumption of protecting each other's closets. Individual consent has nothing to do with it. And this presumption is quite entrenched in gay social custom. Not maintaining the Secret is not easy. I have found that even if one has consciously decided to abandon the convention, one still finds oneself unwittingly acting in accordance with it. Abandoning the convention, like speaking in non-sexist English, requires unlearning automatic responses. (ibid.: 27)

One reason for the difficulty Mohr describes in abandoning the convention of respecting other people's closets in almost all circumstances —and I can testify from my own experience to the accuracy of Mohr's characterization—is that we are aware of the danger that our motives will be misunderstood and our actions will play into the hands of our enemies. Eve Sedgwick warns that the "selective utterance of open secrets whose tacitness structures hierarchical enforcement" is a risky move, "depending as it does for its special surge of polemical force on the culture's (though not on the speaker's) underlying phobic valuation of homosexual choice" (1990: 245).

Yet for all the dangers of confirming antigay biases or appearing to support the bigoted view that homosexuality should be a dirty secret, I see no way to move beyond these attitudes without accepting and acting on the presumption that homosexuality must be seen and treated the same as heterosexuality. To invoke another point made by Sedgwick, for the most part only gay people are pleased at the prospect of there being more gay people in the world—even the most tolerant nongays would just as soon there were fewer of us, if only to spare us the suffering we face from the intolerant. "The number of persons or institutions by whom the existence of gay people is treated as a precious desideratum, a needed condition of life, is small" (Sedgwick 1991: 23). If this is so, and I believe it is, then it behooves those of us who count ourselves in this small number to act accordingly, and outing—or, as Rotello prefers to call it, equalizing—is a means to this end.

In his defense of outing, Rotello notes that in the 1950s "it was social and professional suicide for straights to live in out-of-wedlock arrangements" (1990: 53). And so it was. In 1950 Ingrid Bergman was drummed out of Hollywood and denounced on the floor of the Senate as "a powerful influence for evil" for having an illegitimate child (Friedrich 1986: 410). In the early 1960s it was considered politically impossible for a divorced politician (e.g., Nelson Rockefeller) to aspire to the presidency. Cut to the 1980s, when once-divorced Ronald Reagan presided over a country in which celebrities routinely discussed their unmarried romances and out-of-wedlock babies on "Entertainment Tonight." Rotello argues that this change in societal tolerance was lubricated by changes in journalistic practices, as "writers, biographers and, especially, gossip columnists began honestly reporting the sexual lives and live-in arrangements of the stars" (1990).[112] True, some of these stars "were financially damaged" (especially the women, although even Ingrid Bergman returned in triumph to Hollywood and two more Oscars), but

> everyday people, liberated by the press from the hypocrisy of silence, reconsidered their earlier disapproval. The young, always eager to experiment with premarital sex, now pointed to movie stars and pop stars as sexual examples and role models. Parents, at first horrified, loosened up. Society grew tolerant. And finally the 50s "out-of-wedlock/living in sin" became the 80s "domestic partnership." (ibid.)[113]

---

112. Rotello's example of progress becomes an exhibit in Patrick Buchanan's case for the prosecution against secular culture: "A sense of shame presupposes a set of standards. In the Old America, Ingrid Bergman, carrying the child of her lover, fled the country in scandal. Today, she would probably be asked to pose naked—and pregnant—on the cover of Vanity Fair" (1992).

113. An analogy might currently be drawn with abortion. If there's nothing shameful about abortion, then women should be willing to be public about having had one. Like being gay, it's not visible, and it crosses class and ethnic lines. If women who have had abortions start going public about it—or are outed, although certainly no one is making an argument that these women constitute a minority community, despite their common experience—then people might be forced to confront the fact that the numbers are large, and that people they know and trust and like, and who are very different from one an-

In the same way, Rotello argues, unwilling celebrities may find themselves leading the way in doing to homophobia what was done to heterosexual prudery. Thus, the arguments for outing go far beyond the exposure of hypocrites to the goal of confronting America with "gay reality . . . thousands of famous, popular, respected gay notables" (ibid.), however reluctant most of these notables might be to play the roles in which they would be cast.

Up until now the advocates of outing have been remarkably restrained, despite their belief that to respect the rights of the celebrity closet is to respect homophobia (as I noted at the start, but it may bear repeating, *no one* has advocated or engaged in indiscriminate outing of indisputably private and vulnerable individuals). Given this logic, it is hard to avoid asking why it is that outing has so far been both extremely limited and narrowly focused on a small number of public officials and show business performers and executives. If the goal is the dramatic raising of a curtain to reveal a societal cast of characters star-studded with hitherto unsuspected lesbian women and gay men, is it really sufficient to concentrate so much on an industry already widely considered to be rife with perversion and immorality?

The dual focus of outing exposés so far—a few politicians faulted for their actions, or inaction, relating to AIDS and other issues, and a handful of entertainment stars and tycoons—may, as I have suggested, be a result of the demographics of the outers. For activists largely drawn from a younger generation steeped in mass media and politicized by the AIDS crisis, these two groups are the most obvious and appropriate targets. If they follow the logic of their own arguments, however, it is unlikely that they will stop there. We may yet see closet doors unhinged to reveal a much wider swath of society's notable figures.

If outing is the public claiming for our community of exceptional people who are lesbian and gay, and not merely the exposure of hypocrites who "fuck us by night and fuck with us by day," then why have we not been deluged with divulged sexual identities of politicians, captains of industry (the late Malcolm Forbes was hardly the only tycoon with a well-appointed closet),[114] military leaders, eminent scien-

---

other, have had abortions. And here, too, celebrities could play a powerful role, as Betty Ford and Nancy Reagan did in the case of breast cancer.

114. In a two-part interview with the *Advocate*, AIDS activist Larry Kramer bemoaned the outers' concentration on show business, saying, "I always go after Michelangelo Signorile. I say, 'Why are you always writing about Barry Diller and David Geffen? Why aren't you writing about the people in business, starting with Dick Jenrette?' who is president of Equitable Life Assurance Society. He has more power to do things than a

tists, prominent clerics (by some accounts the Catholic and Episcopal priesthoods are the heaviest concentrations of gay men this side of Fire Island), artists of all sorts (painters, composers, conductors, dancers, architects), doctors, lawyers (and Supreme Court justices?), and other notables?

Of course it is possible that efforts to out such prominent people would meet with media unwillingness to go along with the game—as the mainstream and gay press both refrained from printing the names read out on the Capitol steps by Michael Petrelis and Carl Goodman, and as many refused to name the "high Pentagon official" or the "head of a government agency" who had been outed. To succeed as a political tactic outing requires the amplification only the mainstream media can provide; without that megaphone we may merely be felling trees far off in the forest where few can hear. Undoubtedly, as we attempt to seek the validation of lesbian and gay identity through public acknowledgment of our numbers and our manifold contributions, the media will play their familiar role of enforcing norms and marginalizing anything that threatens the status quo; thus their relative openness to cooperate with outing in the singular case of rank hypocrisy. But, by the same token, recent media treatment of the military's antigay discrimination and the NEA's moves toward censorship, as well as Hollywood's newfound enthusiasm for gay-related scripts, demonstrate that the ground broken by outing can prove fertile.

What seems certain is that gay visibility will continue to provoke a reactionary backlash, and that the gay movement cannot afford to maintain a narrow focus on the right to privacy: "Emphasizing this right plays right into our enemies' hands. Private is, after all, exactly what they want us to be . . . I believe we are in the long run fighting less for the right to privacy than for the right not to have to be private" (Schatz 1991). While not without its ethical complexities, outing is not an isolated outbreak of petulance; it is a natural progression in the evolution of community consciousness and political struggle.

Lesbian and gay people are the last remaining group against which public displays of bigotry are respectable, from the high school locker room to the floor of the U.S. Senate. We are a group whose right to

---

Barry Diller does in a certain kind of way. When we're talking about outing, we shouldn't let these people off the hook. It's just that they're not as romantic to write about as heads of studios" (quoted in Zonana 1992: 45). Kramer didn't comment on the *Advocate*'s choice of prominent photographer Annie Leibovitz to shoot his dramatic cover portrait, although he is presumably aware of her frequent appearance as a target of outings by Signorile and Armistead Maupin.

love as we choose is criminalized in half the states of the union, and we are officially discriminated against by our government. For more than a decade we have been fighting an epidemic, with thousands dead or dying and many more living with a life-threatening disease, while public responses to AIDS both reflect and reinforce pervasive homophobia, creating a climate that promotes a rising tide of antigay violence. Harvey Fierstein summed up the underlying sentiment: "I don't know anybody who just happens to be gay, especially now. You're either on the cutting edge or you're not. You're either political or you're hiding" (Stuart 1991). In such times it is easy to understand why so many of us knew what authors of the "I Hate Straights" broadside meant when they wrote "that lesbians and gays live in a war zone, that we're surrounded by bomb blasts only we seem to hear, that our bodies and souls are heaped high, dead from fright or bashed or raped, dying of grief or disease, stripped of our personhood." It is easy to understand why so many of us, after listening to Jesse Helms and Patrick Buchanan and George Bush and Dan Quayle and so on, ad nauseam, want to tell the straight world to shut up and listen: We're here! We're queer! Get used to it!

I. Before the Revolution

Naming Gay Names

Larry Bush
(*Village Voice*, April 27, 1982)

For gays, the aftermath of the arrest of Representative Bob Bauman for homosexual acts was an intense soul searching. Should gays protect gays, as they had Bauman, no matter how antigay their public politics?

That is the question increasingly on the minds of many in the gay community, and it was not the first time I had wondered what the right answer is. Shortly after Reagan was elected, I attended a number of parties welcoming the gay Reagan staffers to Washington. As I looked around the room I wondered how these people could be openly gay in here and still be allies with the Moral Majority. If I were to write an article, I thought I could call it "A Night in Weimar, A Day in Berlin." Only days before, I had interviewed top Carter aides at the White House about their forecasts for gay issues. Their grim assessment had led them to box up and remove the names of all their gay community contacts, rather than leave them for Reagan's staff. Now I saw that at least some of those men going into the White House or publicly allied with the Moral Majority were walking in the door with boyfriends on their arms.

When is it responsible—if ever—to disclose the homosexuality of someone who has not volunteered that information? In today's political climate, are there obligations to make that information public about various New Right and New Christian Right leaders allied in a campaign to severely curtail the rights of gay citizens? What was once only a gay political slogan—"We Are Everywhere"—is increasingly being accepted as a fact of life.

Once gays knew those who have remained deeply closeted and publicly antigay because we shared the homosexual demimonde, a life of dark bars, adult bookstores, and public places where sex could take place furtively and anonymously.

But in 1982, something entirely new is going on—it is that in some of the most important ways gay liberation has succeeded. Being gay is not something to keep hidden and compartmentalized in one's life, but can be integrated into a sense of identity. Inevitably a sense of gay community has been created as gay people reach out to one another in an effort to connect in ways where sexual contact itself is a minor theme. Gays who are conservative, or who are locked into tightly closeted lives, have not been immune to the example the openly gay community has been setting. They too are reaching out to discover their connection to this community.

In Washington today members of the openly gay community have contacts throughout the city no matter what the political season. I knew of no presidential candidate in either 1976 or 1980 who did not have a gay staffer at a high level, staffers who believed their gay identity was unknown to the candidate. In many of those cases, the staffer quietly passed on the private musings of presidential aspirants on gay civil rights, musings that sometimes were more liberal than their public utterances and sometimes more conservative if not almost homophobic. It has been just such glimpses that often have led to gays being very cautious allies with the liberal politicians who appear publicly committed to gay civil rights goals, just as such glimpses leave gays uncertain about Reagan, who privately opposes antigay views.

Members of Congress discreetly let it be known that they can be relied upon, and one gay member of Congress joked with another that perhaps they should launch the "fruit fly" caucus. There are gays known to the gay community in the leadership of the New Right, in the liberal leadership, the antiabortion movement, the Pentagon's "E" Ring of inner sanctums, the CIA, the FBI. Increasingly they recognize the role the gay activist community plays in creating a more tolerant climate, and the result is often a new consideration for what obligations they should accept in return.

It is not that gays have become free to "flaunt" their "perversions," nor is it that a fifth column is quietly shaping up in Washington that one day will overthrow the current patterns of discrimination. It is simply that the idea that gay people are related in some ways to each other is taking hold, and bringing with it such relief to those who have felt isolated and alone that virtually no barrier can stand in its way. Not even the barrier of virulent homophobia that surrounds the New Right and the New Christian Right is impervious.

As heartening as this may be to politically active and open gays in theory, the reality has been to create considerable anguish. The frustration goes right to the guts. Gays refer to this inhibition that keeps them from speaking publicly and naming names as "The Code," and what is amazing is that despite all the provocations, that code of silence has never been broken.

Gay activist and Democratic Party official Jim Foster told me about the time he traveled to Miami to help fight Anita Bryant's crusade against the Dade County gay rights ordinance only to learn from gays that one of Bryant's aides was a homosexual. When Foster himself was involved in a public debate with that person, Foster says he was unable to make a strong case for gay civil rights because he was completely distracted by the question of how a closeted person would dare lead such a crusade. Still, Foster and other gays said nothing publicly.

In a medium-sized city in a mid-Atlantic state, the mayor last year publicly urged his police department to begin cracking down on gays who were using adult bookstores for sexual trysts. The entire panoply of antigay rhetoric soon spread, with the mayor joining in. There was no sizable gay community there, and virtually no organized gay group. But the mayor was homosexual, and was known personally by gay activists in another city he visited for private encounters with other gays. Again, the debate about what to do was kept entirely in gay circles.

In a southern state, a candidate for governor is a closeted homosexual. He has previously used public position to ridicule gay rights claims as "bizarre," and refuses as a candidate to meet with gay groups. Members of those same groups find him at closed gay barbecues and small dinner parties, where he smiles indulgently and pleads that his position is "just politics." What some people call "just politics" can have a devastating impact. An American Psychological Association study documented the link between antigay rhetoric and antigay street violence. Last year in San Francisco 17 gay men were murdered in separate attacks; nationwide the toll could be as high as 40. The anger gays feel is as much personal as it is political. "If our opponents don't stop telling lies about us," said Adlai Stevenson in 1952, "we're going to start telling the truth about them." So far, gays have remained silent.

Just as the gay community is being forced to confront its silence, journalists find themselves questioning their own silence. The accepted practice about publicly disclosing someone's homosexuality has always been to report it only when it became a matter of public record. Almost invariably, the public record was an arrest record. It was by this criteria that such well-known conservative leaders as Representative Bob Bauman, Republican of Maryland, and Representative Jon Hinson, Republican of Mississippi, had their homosexual conduct disclosed. A similar list of less well known individuals, prominent in their local communities for promulgating conservative causes, have also figured in recent news stories.

It is arguable, however, that the process of the general media disclosing homosexuals has been underpinned by a close relationship with police officials. In many cities, police officials immediately notify the press when arrests for homosexual conduct are made, and urge that the arrests be treated as newsworthy.

In Houston, a local television crew in the summer of 1980 accompanied police for a raid on a popular gay bar for 61 arrests no more serious than public intoxication, a typical pattern of police-media cooperation.

In 1981 in Clarksville, Tennessee, the *Leaf Chronicle* ran at least eight articles about the arrests for public sex. Peter John Wenger, an Austin Peay State University professor and one of those named, committed suicide last March. The *Leaf Chronicle* editor said afterwards, "We're trying to do our job, fulfill our responsibility of presenting news to the public, and it's the other individual's responsibility not going out and killing themselves."

Last Thanksgiving, NBC ran a story after the FBI leaked a rumor to an NBC correspondent that a male escort service in Washington, D.C., might be serving as a vehicle for Soviet KGB infiltration to discover the names of closeted senior American officials, diplomats, and military officers believed to be numbered among the clients. In late March, police confiscated 13 boxes containing the names of 500 to 1,000 "preferred customers." The *Washington Blade*, the local gay newspaper, responded with the question on the minds of most gay people: what happens to those names?

The effect of this "police blotter" journalism has been traditionally to treat homosexuality as something one did—often illegally—that fell somewhere between shoplifting and armed robbery. And the tradition lingers on, perhaps the greatest inhibition keeping gays from naming gay names.

Gays are successfully changing police attitudes in many cities, however; where resistance continues gays have gone far in challenging the image of police impartiality. Both approaches are bound to have an effect on journalists' use of police as a source on homosexuality.

Perhaps the most significant reason the media is reexamining its "police blotter" approach is, again, the success of the gay liberation message; it argues that being a gay goes to a core sense of identity that can have many meanings and which cannot be isolated as a crime or aberration. The implications are profound. Already this has affected biographies, where the past reluctance to dismiss the central character's homosexuality and its relevance is being overcome, and it certainly long ago became acceptable in fiction.

What the public has not yet seen in print, or in front of a camera, are the private discussions of what this issue may mean for living persons. If being gay is important to understanding a person's character, or his actions, is the absence of that information a critical distortion that misleads the public? That is the issue that lies just beyond the question of hypocrisy in the New Right: what if homosexuality is relevant on its own merits alone? But it is the question of hypocrisy by closeted gays who are publicly antigay that is the current focus and that is an issue debated long and hard in the gay communities themselves.

"There's a lot of moral anger involved in this issue," answered Vito Russo, a longtime gay activist and author of *The Celluloid Closet*. Disclosing names is something Russo has at times been urged to do by the media in writing about Hollywood, and also something he has occasionally been angry enough to want to do.

"Every star who is in the public eye does the community a disservice by pretending to be straight," Russo said. "By their silence, they are reinforcing the idea that America is straight. Their silence alone is treason. On one hand, one wants to say, 'Let the battle rage and let 200 libel suits bloom,' just take out an ad in the *New York Times* and name everyone who is gay and then rot in jail with a smile on your face. But then the human side of you takes over, and you see how fascistic that can be, in the sense that you are dealing with people's lives, and they have a right to do with it what they want no matter how repellent to you." It produces a tremendous, tremendous amount of anger and frustration because it is literally a no-win situation.

"What's significant is that we had these questions 15 years ago, when we had these fags working against us, and these people are still around."

Yet Russo himself blocked an effort to use his book to make innuendos about who in Hollywood might be gay. "*US* magazine, instead of excerpting my book, originally requested the right to excerpt my acknowledgements, so that they could perhaps suggest the people in Hollywood I credited were gay. That was the smarmiest thing I ever heard of, and of course I wouldn't allow it."

Russo's feeling of being pulled apart on the issue is typical of many gay people. One person who is rethinking the question is Virginia Apuzzo, director of the Fund for Human Dignity, a nonprofit gay educational group, and a prominent Democratic Party activist in the 1976 and 1980 campaigns.

"I think the gay community has been extremely patient, and behaved with responsibility," Apuzzo said. "I know gay men who have stood in bars with Congressman Bauman, when that man contributed to an atmosphere that has resulted in the kind of violence that we see in the gay community today. They rely on our silence, and respond by abandoning all reasonable responsibility to protect our basic civil rights. My feeling is that there is a tacit contract among gays where we do respect the right to privacy that so many of us need in order to survive. However, when a public official who is closeted uses his or her power in a way that hurts gay people, I feel that tacit contract has been broken."

Veteran gay activist Frank Kameny, whose campaign for a congressional delegate seat a decade ago laid the groundwork for the remarkable influence of the gay community, would take Apuzzo's position even further.

"I think Bauman's the perfect example," Kameny said of the duplicity he sees. "I would have had no compunction about using the fact [of his homosexual experiences] to blackmail him to modify his political action. To say, 'Back off, or I'm going to start publicizing you're gay.' But except for one passing moment in the night, I never met the man."

Kameny said he would require rigorous evidence that an antigay person was in fact homosexual before making a public statement, and also cautions that closeted gays who "passively ride the tides" of antigay efforts in their organizations should not be exposed. "But if I found some Moral Majority leader who was rabidly and effectively being antigay, I would have no compunction about using that and destroying him with it," Kameny said. "You deal harshly with traitors, and that's really what it amounts to."

Kameny is no stranger to strong political actions on behalf of gay rights — he was a major player in the gay protests against the American Psychiatric Association's once steadfast refusal to reconsider homosexuality as an illness, disrupting meetings, and in 1980 threatened to chain himself to the Tomb of the Unknown Soldier unless the Pentagon relented on its ban forbidding gay groups from laying a wreath there — but in his 25 years as a public advocate, he admits that he has never used the tactic of disclosing someone's homosexuality.

Steve Endean, director of the Gay Rights National Lobby, which fights the antigay initiatives that the New Right seeks in Congress, said that he had been approached "numerous times" with information on the homosexuality of gay rights opponents, "and in a number of those cases they were people who were dire enemies of what I view to be the community's best interests." It is an issue, Endean said, "that may hit me and a few others who deal with Congress quicker, because we saw firsthand people who are both opposed to the community and are also members of it."

Still, Endean numbers himself among those who say that it is his policy, and that of his organization, never to make public the homosexuality of anyone who does not choose to be identified, even when it is an active gay civil rights opponent.

The *Washington Blade* has established an enviable reputation both within the gay community and in the capital as a responsible newspaper devoted to good journalism. Publisher Don Michaels is a member of the National Press Club and sits on the mayor's Press Pass Committee, and has had to confront the issue of naming gay names.

"We would be unwilling to be the pioneer in breaking this code," Michaels said. "There is still enough pain and agony about dealing with being gay that, in spite of effort to hurt the gay community, I feel we should abide by that code. It's an agonizing decision to make because revealing public officials who are gay would certainly tell the public we're not just a small segment, but I would have to fall on the side of saying no. It's just not fair, given what just about every gay person goes through. It's no sense fighting fire with fire. There's a big part of me that would love to wreak revenge on the New Right people who are gay, but the strongest part of me says I'd rather live by the code that recognizes the agony."

Former Gay Activist Alliance president Jim Zais, who has turned down invitations to dinner parties that included gay New Right leaders "because it would have been impossible for me not to talk politics and confront them, and I was being invited for a social occasion," also draws the line at speaking publicly.

"People's sexual orientation is their business, and it would be a contradiction to what gay liberation stands for to consider that public business. That's an ethical position, but there's a more practical position, and that's that once you start down that path of beginning to expose people, where does it end, and how many people suffer?" Zais asked. "If responsible gay leadership give to the crazies of the world the example of beginning to expose gay people, where does this all end?"

Dan Bradley, who capped off his term as president of the Legal Services Corporation by publicly disclosing in the *New York Times* that he his gay, spoke directly to how he would have felt about having his private life revealed by others.

"I don't know what I would have done," Bradley said. "I'm not going to be melodramatic and say I would have committed suicide, but I would have been destroyed. I subconsciously was so protective of my own sexuality and hiding that would have destroyed me personally and professionally."

Dan Bradley personifies the flip side of the issue, where the question is whether an individual's private life does have a bearing on public policy issues. Bradley's agency was under attack in Congress for assisting gay clients, and Bradley did not back away. His position was solidly based in legal precedent and had the backing of all legal experts, but was his commitment an outgrowth of his own life?

The fact is that suggestions about private homosexual lives are traditionally asked more often of those who support gay civil rights than of those who oppose them. Bradley was never the target of rumor campaigns that he supported his agency's work with gay clients because he was gay, but other politicians have been.

Ed Koch is probably the best-known example of a politician who was baited for supporting gay civil rights, a fact that still could make him angry four years after his 1977 mayoral campaign. In an interview in the *New York Native*, the city's gay newspaper, Koch took out against his detractors in the gay community by pointing out the difficulty he had in publicly supporting gay rights as a man who had never married.

"You know, it is very difficult for someone who is himself single — and therefore subject to the innuendos that were used in the race which I ran in '77 — to be up-front and supportive as I have been," Koch said in that interview.

The same type of innuendo dogged the campaign of California governor Jerry Brown during his first election, and it wasn't until he was well into his second term of office that he publicly embraced gay civil rights.

New York City Council members also faced down rumors as a result of their support for this year's gay rights bill.

"The last time around on the measure, City Council members told me of being accused of being gay because they supported the measure," Vito Russo said. "Straight people are scared off from helping gay rights." The irony is that among gay activists it's almost axiomatic that it is the closeted politicians who hold back on gay rights, no matter how liberal their other positions.

Representative Ted Weiss, Democrat of Manhattan, serves as the chief sponsor of the federal gay civil rights bill and has also been confronted with this issue among his colleagues. He did not state whether he was aware, as many in the Washington gay community are, that the large majority of gay members of Congress consistently vote against gay civil rights measures.

"I think it is extremely difficult for somebody who is single and never been married to support gay rights and not to have rumors that he is himself gay, and self-serving," commented Weiss.

He also numbers himself among those who are extremely uncomfortable with the idea of revealing which antigay leaders are themselves gay.

"Once you start this," Weiss said, "once you say it's valid to expose people who are hypocritical, then you start to have shadings, and you end up removing the privacy aspect of the issue, and that bothers me. You have a right to take a substantive position without regard for your own personality."

If one finds the argument coming around full circle, it is a circle with a central focus. The key issue in the debate is simply who will control how gays are accepted into society. Will the New Right succeed in imposing its definitions of homosexuality and then levying a price against all those who are indicted? Or will gays succeed in the self-determination effort, arguing that it is their voices that should be heard about the meaning of being gay?

This, finally, is the relevant issue. It is an issue that does not require that others, either in the gay community or in the press, step forward to reveal information about the private lives of public figures, whether they are for or against gay civil rights. The voices that need to be heard are already out in the open, available to any who will listen and, if anything, their silence on gays who are publicly antigay only imparts greater integrity to their message. It shows the New Right claim about "militant homosexuals" to be the lie that it is and replaces it with the truer image of people simply seeking the right to decide what their own lives mean. The public knows these gay voices best by their calls for justice but it is time to acknowledge the essential humanity that is there as well.

This is what is to be found in the thoughtful voices of people like Don Michaels and Jim Zais, in the anger and humor in Frank Kameny and Vito Russo, and [in] the sense of profoundly difficult choices heard from Virginia Apuzzo and Steve Endean. Voices like those gave Dan Bradley and others the courage to come out and create a sense of community that draws gays even across the gulf of the New Right and the New Christian Right. These are people who have a lot more to say than just who might be gay. What a shame if that were all the world wanted to hear from them.

Celebrity AIDS

Edwin Diamond

(*New York*, March 2, 1987)

AIDS isn't a disease anymore, the playwright Harvey Fierstein has been quoted as saying, "it's a media event."

He's being theatrical, of course. Fierstein knows as well as anyone that acquired immune-deficiency syndrome has reached epidemic proportions and will have killed 179,000 Americans by 1992, according to a report last month by the U.S. surgeon general. Still, Fierstein's comment has the shock of recognition. Since AIDS the epidemic has become major news, AIDS the story has made troubling news. We've had Celebrity AIDS coverage (Rock Hudson and Liberace), Mystery AIDS (the cases of Roy Cohn and Perry Ellis), and Ideological AIDS (the handling of the death of new-right activist Terry Dolan).

More than any recent breaking news story, the AIDS epidemic has exposed questions of journalistic standards, confidentiality, and privacy. Both *People* and the *National Enquirer*, for example, were on the newsstands and supermarket racks with cover stories about Liberace's "secret battle with AIDS" before the Riverside County, California, coroner had in fact concluded that the entertainer suffered from AIDS. AIDS was mentioned in fashion designer Perry Ellis's obituaries in the *Washington Post, USA Today, Newsday,* and *Newsweek.* It was not mentioned in the *New York Times, Los Angeles Times,* or *Time.* Terry Dolan's death got extensive page-one coverage in the "conservative" *Washington Times*—with his death carefully attributed to congestive heart failure—a day before the "liberal" *Washington Post* reported that Dolan had died.

In many respects, coverage of the last days of a Rock Hudson or a Liberace is no different from other celebrity-centered journalism. Celebrity Drugs and Celebrity Divorce also command ink and airtime. Celebrity AIDS, though, offers an extra sensation: To the "drama" of death by incurable affliction—even the rich and famous aren't immune —is added the shiver of sexual ambiguity. As long as AIDS kills prominent public figures, there will be media exploitation of celebrity deaths.

The more disturbing media issue revolves, perversely, around the *under*reporting of AIDS. A generation ago, the word *cancer* almost never appeared in obituaries or news accounts of deaths. Because of ignorance and fear, an implicit social stigma was attached to the disease. Today, in many minds, AIDS registers an explicit—and stronger

—aversion. It started out, after all, as "the gay plague." As a result, journalists are rethinking such previously routine tasks as writing about deaths, while readers and viewers must learn how to decode many news stories. Some recent cases:

• *What the Doctor Said*: Because John Terrence ("Terry") Dolan had been so identified with the "family values" agenda of political conservatives and with the Reagan administration—his brother is the chief White House speechwriter—his death at 35 in late December [1986] did, in fact, become a media event. Dolan had denied that he was a homosexual, despite contrary reports. When he died after a long illness, a kind of news management—familiar in Washington—took place. The front-page tributes in the *Washington Times* were accompanied by a phone campaign to the *Washington Post* by Dolan's friends and colleagues. As a *Post* editor recalls it, "Everyone who knew anyone's number here called." The message was that Dolan's doctor had listed the cause of death as congestive heart failure, and that if the *Post* reported Dolan had suffered from AIDS, it would be wrong and a disservice to his memory. The *Post*, however, did its own phoning around and ran a 22-inch story the next day, stating flatly and with no attribution that Dolan had had AIDS.

According to *Post* people, several factors influenced the decision. "An undisputed source" said that Dolan suffered from AIDS. Further, Dolan's doctor acknowledged that he had never tested his patient for the AIDS virus and that he wasn't the only doctor treating Dolan. Also, no one "dies of AIDS": It's a condition, not a disease, that allows *other* diseases to kill.

• *The "Authoritative" Source*: The *Post* remains confident about its source. The Washington bureau of the *New York Times* had less success with the Dolan story. Pressed by New York editors to match—or shoot down—the *Post* account, the bureau came up empty-handed. The bureau had heard the rumors—a lot of people in Washington had. But, says Allan M. Siegal, a *Times* assistant managing editor, "we don't print scuttlebutt." Without an authoritative confirmation of the kind the *Post* had, or believed it had, "the *Times* to this day has not said Dolan had AIDS," says Siegal.

Liberace and his friends and family also sought to control the news. As *People* wrote in its cover story, "Liberace's homosexuality had been one of the worst-kept secrets in show business, but he had guarded it until the end." Liberace had been the target of a so-called palimony lawsuit brought by Scott Thorson, his "personal chauffeur," and there was a presumption in the media about Liberace's sexual preferences. Two weeks before Liberace's death, Hank Greenspun, the publisher

of the *Las Vegas Sun*, ran a story declaring that the "longtime showstop-
per on the Las Vegas Strip is terminally ill with AIDS." The *Sun* cited
"informed sources." Greenspun, himself a major figure on the strip,
had known Liberace for decades; he also said he'd had access to medical records—documents supposed to be confidential—in Las Vegas
and elsewhere.

When the end came, Liberace's doctors gave the cause of death as
cardiac arrest due to heart failure. It was true as far as it went—ultimately, we all die when our hearts stop. The doctors also acknowledged—after the coroner's report—that AIDS virus was present in
Liberace's blood. But a lot about AIDS is "far from defined," the doctors said, adding that they chose to go with the narrowest interpretation of the facts to protect the privacy of Liberace and his family. Many
papers, the *New York Times* among them, carried both the doctors'
statement and the *Sun*'s report.

• *Private Rights, Public Rights*: Unlike most papers, the *New York
Times* doesn't run many obits (as opposed to death announcements,
prepared and paid for by the deceased's survivors or funeral home,
and set in a different typeface). *Times* obits invariably involved relatively well known or clearly prominent people; three to five a day
typically appear. When the deceased is, in Siegal's words, "a reasonably private figure," the *Times* will ask the survivors for the cause of
death but won't aggressively pursue it. "We don't beat up on people,"
Siegal says.

But because of questions of news judgment raised by the *Times*'s
coverage of certain deaths in the past year—notably Cohn's and
Ellis's—Siegal put down some guidelines for the staff. "If we know or
can reliably learn a specific cause of death, we print it," his memo of
last December 10 states. "If we lack the information, we try to learn it
through all normal reporting methods. . . . If we suspect we are being given only a partial truth, we print it, with pointed and specific attribution to the source."

At the *Washington Post*, policies are different, and stories reflect it.
The *Post* regards itself as a hometown paper. When a Washington resi-
dent dies and the survivors phone, the paper tries to run an obituary,
according to Richard Pearson, one of four reporters in the paper's obit
"bureau." Stories have a required format: age, cause of death, and survivors. Pearson and his colleagues insist on printing the cause of death
for private and public figures alike. If callers—the deceased's family,
or friends or coworkers—resist, they are asked to reconsider; if they
still hold back information, there will be no obit. With prominent
figures, the "bureau" pursues stories as any reporter would. Pearson

wrote the story on Roy Cohn's death. Cohn had denied having AIDS—to Mike Wallace on "60 Minutes," no less. But in Cohn's last days, he was being treated at NIH with an experimental drug whose sole use, says Pearson, "was to fight AIDS, and we said that in our story."

• *Drawing the Line*: Some sufferers and their families see beyond the AIDS stigma. The day that the *Times* carried an AP [Associated Press] item describing the California coroner's concern about a Liberace cover-up, it also carried a short obit on the death of a 45-year-old TV producer who had died of AIDS, "according to his family."

Not everyone is so enlightened. Complex interests—institutional as well as familial—may come into play in AIDS coverage. In the current *Vanity Fair*, a two-page photo spread commemorates AIDS victims in fashion and the arts. Editor-in-chief Tina Brown writes that she knows of five creative people who are infected with AIDS. Brown explained last week that she would not identify them, as the magazine did the deceased. To do so might damage their ability to continue to earn a living and pay their medical bills—"a sad commentary on the world."

Yet even distinctions between the living and the sick don't always work. Perry Ellis may have died last May, but Perry Ellis designs remain a $260 million-a-year enterprise. Again, there had been gossip about Ellis's sexuality. When he died at 46 (of viral encephalitis, according to the hospital), the *Los Angeles Times* obit was written by its fashion editor, Bettijane Levine. According to Levine, she omitted any mention of AIDS, because after at least 45 calls, she couldn't get anyone to confirm "authoritatively" that Ellis had had AIDS. Friends protected Ellis's memory, and—not so incidentally—a prestigious label. Last summer, however, Patricia Morrisroe spent two months researching the Ellis story (*New York*, August 11, 1986), interviewed 52 people, and concluded, "Many people believe Ellis had AIDS, and given the evidence, it seems likely."

The obit page has become a new battleground. Gay groups ask for a full reporting of AIDS deaths, if for no other reason than to give heterosexuals a sense of the magnitude of the epidemic, and spur more support for AIDS research and treatment. The cases of stonewalling have led some gay writers to point out that there may be a distinction between being "gay" and being "homosexual": Gays identify socially and politically—and therefore publicly—with their sexual orientation. Homosexuals choose to suppress that identity, to control a carefully cultivated public image, in life and—if possible—in death.

The media have to protect their own image. The most open way is by avoiding sexual politics of any kind, thus steering clear of being perceived as squeamish or part of a cover-up, gay or straight, left or right. Energetic but lawful reporting, together with full disclosure of the causes of death when public figures die, creates fewer ethical problems than avoiding mention of AIDS. As Siegal says, "It's journalism to print what you can find out." In short: Put it in the paper.

II. The Wall Springs a Leak

Michelangelo Signorile, "Gossip Watch" columns (*OutWeek*, October 1, October 8, and December 17, 1989)

Steve Warren, "Telling 'Tales' about Celebrity Closets," an interview with Armistead Maupin (*Au Courant*, October 23, 1989)

William A. Henry III, "Forcing Gays out of the Closet" (*Time*, January 29, 1990)

Michelangelo Signorile, "The Other Side of Malcolm" (*OutWeek*, March 18, 1990)

Gossip Watch
Michelangelo Signorile
(*OutWeek*, October 1, 1989)

Last week we spoke of columnist Liz Smith (*Daily News*) and all those detestable "ladies who lunch." How ironic then that in the very same week *OutWeek* was mentioned in *W* magazine, the glossy fashion rag published by megalomaniacal, fascistic John Fairchild and read by all of those same rich, lunching women who scour it for their names and faces. In *W*'s "In New York . . . " column, it read: "Pick up an issue of *OutWeek*, the city's most with-it new publication spotlighting a mix of culture, politics and vicious gossip." We thought it a hoot that the belly of the beast, so to speak, would be recommending its readers to buy *us*, though it's quite disturbing how it simply slipped their minds to mention that *OutWeek* is a gay and lesbian publication. But maybe it's better off: I'm getting a kick out of the thought that terminally trendy, monied hets are having fashion attacks, running off to newsstands, picking up *OutWeek* and getting the shock of their day.

However, I'd like to discuss what *W* calls "vicious gossip." This term conjures up the thought that this column exists simply to be mean—for the sadistic readers and for the vanity flash it may provide its writer. I'm not going to say that these factors are nonexistent—that this column isn't fun to read and that I don't love writing it—but there truly is a larger mission here.

Gossip columnists reach millions of people. Suzy, Cindy Adams and Page Six are the three most powerful slots at the *New York Post*. Liz Smith *carries* the *Daily News*, making more money for the paper than any other person on the publication. She has a megafigure contract. Her column is syndicated to hundreds of papers around the country. When she quotes a dangerous line from the *New Republic* without making a comment, millions of people in towns and cities across the U.S. read it. More people read gossip columns each day than read the *New York Times* and the *Washington Post* and *Time* magazine put together. People won't always admit it, but you closet gossip suckers know who you are.

Gossip columnists have a scary, *God-like* image; a sort of *special* role in the eyes of the public. They are considered by the reader to be *all-powerful* and *all-knowing*. Frightening, but true. No one dares to question their sources. Unlike anyone else on a newspaper, gossip columnists are not required to attribute anything; it's part of their mystique not to.

This "image" was actually created by Hollywood back in the '30s and '40s. It was the movie moguls, presidents of the film companies, who "placed" the first columnists in their jobs at the papers (either by actually paying their salaries or by literally owning the papers) so as to have them constantly write about the films and therefore generate publicity. The film companies helped create and perpetuate the aura of the gossip columnist and constantly supplied them with dirt on all of the stars. But the moguls didn't retain control for long. Hedda Hopper and Louella Parsons realized their immense power and soon began dishing the companies and the moguls themselves. The independent—but equally fascistic—gossip columnist was born.

Why did I go into all of this? Because some people think I'm just playing games here; that this is all frivolous fluff to help me stroke my ego. Others think I go too far; that printing William Norwich's (*Daily News*) telephone number and having a gossip phone zap was outlandish and wrong.

Meanwhile, these monster columnists are oppressing us each day in their spaces—and half the time they are gay or lesbian themselves! But that doesn't stop them from deeming us invisible, making homophobic remarks or schmoozing and worshiping the people who are killing us. When William Norwich (*Daily News*) tells us that Liz Taylor and Malcolm Forbes are "dating," millions of people get the wrong impression, though Norwich knows better. When Liz Smith writes glowing praises of Donald Trump, millions are convinced that he's wonderful, and would find it hard to understand that he's in bed with this city government, that he's getting all sorts of tax breaks, that he's soaking up city property—while the city claims that there's just no housing available for thousands of people with AIDS who are dying on the streets! How about how Liz and Billy worshipped the ground that Ronnie and Nancy walked on for eight fucking years while my friends died and the Prez did nothing? How about how Liz and Billy now foam at the mouth over George and Barbara, while millions are infected with HIV, don't have access to health care, and don't hear a peep out of our *leader*? And I'm supposed to just let Liz write her ass-kissing bullshit, without saying anything? Fuck her! And when Billy Norwich purposely omits facts about parties or about a controversy because it might deal with gay issues, am I supposed to just let that go?

Some people say I shouldn't have printed Norwich's telephone number. Hell, I don't care if he's getting calls at three in the morning. I don't care if he's cowering in the corner of his apartment. I don't care if it's making his life miserable. People are dying, and this idiot is going to a million parties and forgetting what he really is!

Some people have said that it is *unprofessional* of me to give out Norwich's home number, but that it would have been okay if it was his work number. Who ever said there were rules to a Gossip Zap? Besides, Norwich works *at home*. That is his office.

It's funny, because the people who are complaining are people who are in similar positions – gays and lesbians who are sitting pretty and sucking crumbs in the hierarchy of the social elite. They say that everything in this magazine is great except for this column. I find that observation interesting because this magazine is pretty uniform in tone and politics. It's militant throughout – not just here. What they're saying is: "It's okay to yell and scream and rant and rave and fight for your rights. But just don't do it in *my* backyard, don't ruffle *my* feathers." And I say to them and every other writer, columnist, artist, designer, etc., who's whirling with the oppressors: I realize you're oppressed just like the rest of us (which is why you're hiding in the first place). But don't react to it by oppressing *us*. It's much easier for you to break the chain of homophobia than it is for me. You are in enormous positions of power. Use that. And don't excuse yourselves by telling us that these rich people donate money and that you write about AIDS benefits, etc. Yes, money is important, but this community cannot be bought off! We need you to voice your opinions. We need you to attack the monsters and build up the heroes. This is a crisis! SOMETHING HAS TO BE DONE AND IT HAS TO BE DONE FAST. AND YOU ARE IN THE POSITIONS TO DO IT. Be part of the solution instead of part of the problem. If not, then get the fuck out of our way. Because we're coming through and nothing is going to stop us. And if that means we have to pull you down, well, then . . . have a nice fall.

Gossip Watch
Michelangelo Signorile
(*OutWeek*, October 8, 1989)

Well, the shit hit the fan.

It's probably not necessary for us to recap what happened last week when the *New York Post*'s Amy Pagnozzi interviewed us and then the paper ran a story headlined: MAGAZINE DRAGS GAYS OUT OF THE CLOSET. Of course not, since you all probably read it (and I just explained it, anyway). As usual, the "mainstream" media distorted the entire situation, blowing it up and likening us to Senator Joseph McCarthy. We find this pretty ridiculous considering that McCarthy was a *right-*

winger trying to "expose" *communists* (with Roy Cohn – A CLOSETED GAY MAN! – by his side, I might add) in an attempt to *squash* their movement, while we are *radical fags* trying to get a message through to *our own kind in power* so that we can stop an epidemic and *further* a movement. But what can we expect from a knee-jerk liberal reporter, especially one whose editors are reactionary right-wingers (it's quite a bizarre scene nowadays at the *Post*)?

Anyway, the *Post* story did cause quite a stir. We were contacted by every slimeball media outlet in town from the *National Enquirer* to the Phil Donahue show. Of course, *their* motives are completely different from ours, but I suppose it's healthy that everyone – in both the straight world and the lesbian and gay community – is now screaming at each other and debating this issue 'til kingdom come. After all, that's what *we're* for, aren't we?

But sadly, none of this really seems to have changed things yet, dear friends. William Norwich (*Daily News*) hasn't learned from all of your educational phone calls, as can be seen by the current mini-interviews he did with – you guessed it – homophobic artist Mark Kostabi and that monstrous wife of the fascist, Pat Buckley, in the current issue of *HG*. Meanwhile, in the *Daily News*, William F. Buckley made another horrific attack on fags and dykes regarding censorship and the Helms amendment while Norwich, just a few pages later, wrote glowing things about his spouse Pat. A few days later, Norwich wrote all about a party thrown by Pat and Bill in a column headlined: IT WAS SAMBA ENCHANTED EVENING À LA BUCKLEY.

Is it *me*, dear friends? Or is this just plain sick shit?

I do think, however, that we are getting a rise out of Liz Smith (*Daily News*). In last Sunday's column she writes another puff piece about *New York* magazine's Julie Baumgold and ends her fawning with this: "It is writer Baumgold's overview, her satirical eye and her genial humor and understanding of human nature that put her head and shoulders above so many of today's suddenly quite vicious members of the Fourth Estate. There's a nasty new breed out there operating with no restraint. They only want the blood and guts of anybody in the public arena." Well, dear Liz, if it is me you are referring to, you should know that it's not your blood and guts I want; it would be enough for me if you simply stopped fucking us over.

And just to point out that it is not merely I – or The Queer Nation, for that matter – who is upset with these two columnists, pick up a copy of *New York Press*, which can be found in a gross green dispenser on any corner in the city. In their *Best of Downtown 1989* issue, the "Best

Reason to Be Embarrassed about NYC Journalism" award goes to—
you got it!—Liz Smith. *New York Press* explained: "The damage that Liz
Smith inflicts on all NYC journalists can't be overstated. Six days a
week Smith, or her ghostwriters, fill a half page in the *News* with press
releases, paybacks, favors for friends, shameless plugs for upcoming
magazine articles, thinly veiled pleas for acceptance from the rich and
powerful, paeans to overpublicized creeps like Donald Trump and
roars of approval for everyone and everything that comprises the status quo. That she's apparently teaching her younger colleague Billy
Norwich that it pays to kiss ass all over NYC bodes ill for the future
of gossip columnists in this city. And because she's taken seriously,
unlike the *Post*'s Suzy, who's so deep into a weird fantasy society
world that her ravings seem almost quaint, her clout is even more dangerous. This is, after all, the woman who allegedly cautioned *Vanity
Fair*'s Tina Brown to tread lightly on New York's ruling elite lest her
child be denied admission to the right public school, advice Brown
seems to have taken to heart. Liz Smith's brand of journalism is so
fawning, so obsequious, so provincial, that you'd swear she was a
scribe for the *Mayberry Herald* and not the proud *Daily News*, a paper
with a circulation of over one million. The reputation of every New
York journalist is sullied each day her column appears."

Need we say more about these two jerks, dear friends?

Gossip Watch
Michelangelo Signorile
(*OutWeek*, December 17, 1989)

An open letter to all of *you* (and *you* know who *you* are):

At least three of *you* have told me the story about the famous *not-so-out-
of-the-closet* lesbian photographer. As it goes, when she was working
at a rag that is less glamorous but as equally well known as the current
one she shoots for, she flew on the *wings* of love with a famous movie
actress. They met and had a torrid affair while Ms. Photographer was
snapping pics of Ms. Movie Actress for a story the magazine was doing. Ms. Movie Actress became quite curious as to what direction the
story was taking. So, Ms. Photographer, caught up in the passions of
romance, snuck in and got the galleys and gave them to Ms. Movie Actress to peruse—a naughty thing to do. After reading it, Ms. Movie Actress and her agent were furious with the not-yet-published story,

which portrayed Ms. Movie Actress in a bad light. They made a major stink to the magazine's editors. And, oh, boy, was Ms. Photographer in BIG trouble.

Why did three of you tell me this story? For the same reason that lots others of you are suddenly telling me even more scandalous stories about your co-workers, your bosses, your friends, your lovers and your ex-lovers who are climbing alongside you in the hierarchy of the social elite and are, like you, getting a few crumbs in return for staying quiet about homophobia. All of you are self-serving megalomaniacs; the filth and garbage that stains this city but ultimately rises to the top via shamelessness. In your slime-pit world in which you all GNAW AND CHEW YOUR WAY UP, you've been worried about saving your own asses ever since we began revealing things about people at *Vanity Fair*. See, in your world, everyone can be bought. So you figure that if you give me a piece of gossip about someone else, we'll leave you alone. It also helps you deal with your own guilt by "telling on" others, and it's always good to put the person down the hall a few spaces back. It's the nature of the game. Meanwhile, all of you just keep empowering us with MORE AND MORE AND MORE information. It's all ammunition for us to fire back at you. And that shot does get heard around the world.

You tell me you got a laugh out of the *Vanity Fair* column, when, in some cases, you were laughing at yourselves, your friends or even people in your own office; even your own boss. Some of you gave me information about a co-worker or a friend, not even knowing that that same person had given me information about *you*. CANNIBALS! And then there are the others of you, some at publications I don't even read (but I guess I should), feeding me gossip in a desperate attempt to appease your own guilt. It's amazing that you would all care so much about all of this, but I guess no one wants to be called an UNCLE TOM FAG or UNCLE TOM DYKE—especially when it's true.

Now there's even a guy who spies on people and calls me up every couple of days from a pay phone on the street while he's doing his dirty work. He tells me how many drinks Pat Buckley has at Mortimer's during lunch—and tells me lots else about where other people go. Then there's the famous magazine editor's ex-chauffeur, who has plenty to say about her and her carryings on. Of course, for them, and for quite a few others who are giving me dirt, the rationalization for gossiping is that it's for a higher cause since they're giving it to the person one of them calls "the activist gossipist." That's fine. But what you all should realize is that when people are gossiping with a higher cause in mind, they feel NO REMORSE. They don't care about getting down and dirty since the ends justify the means. And, quite frankly, I feel the same way.

So now, we have enough trash to write a book about Liz Smith (*Daily News*) (sharks always gather when they smell blood), and to write quite a few chapters about lots of other people who've been mentioned (or alluded to) in this column. Oh, and lots of stuff on those who've not yet been in this column but who most certainly will be in the future.

Why am I doing this?

Well, I'll not deny that in the process I get some sort of kick out of it. Yeah, it's satisfying; even fun. But there is another, bigger reason. See, FOR ABOUT TEN YEARS WE HAVE TRIED TO MOTIVATE YOU FUCKING IDIOTS. We have tried to EDUCATE you. We have tried to make you see that we are all—including yourselves—being wiped out. We have tried to make you realize that we're being murdered by a negligent government. And your response has been to buy a new outfit and go to another benefit while you wait for your next job promotion. Those of you who have spaces to voice your opinions have decided that your contribution to ending the AIDS crisis is in merely writing about Elizabeth Taylor and the glitzy benefits.

And so now, realizing that "conscience" is not the way to get to you people, we've decided to peddle your own shit, and throw back at you all the garbage you spew out.

Of course, you can all disempower us instantly if you'll just break the chain of homophobia and give us nothing to write about. I promise, I'll go get a job at the pennysaver or something, I'll stay out of trouble for a while, honest.

For starters, if you're gay or lesbian you can come out of the closet, publicly. You can make sure that we're visible and included. You can voice your opinions loudly and clearly. You can attack the homophobes, instead of glorifying them. YOU CAN TELL THE AMERICAN PEOPLE ABOUT THE INJUSTICE THAT HAS OCCURRED DURING THE PAST TEN YEARS INSTEAD OF TELLING THEM ABOUT HOW WONDERFUL THE '80S WERE BECAUSE "OPRAH WINFREY EPITOMIZED THE EXCITEMENT OF THE MEDIA DECADE." Maybe, you can even—heaven forbid!—get off your asses, go into the streets and scream and yell your heads off WITH THE REST OF US?!?!

It's really up to all of you. Perhaps you should look to your colleague Billy Norwich (*Daily News*), who is slowly beginning to change, saying more about AIDS and even glowingly writing up ACT UP just a couple of weeks *after* the activist group protested his dear friend Pat Buckley (a clear message to Pat). He even seems to be straining, trying to write less and less about Pat and her vain, cosmetic attempts at clearing the Buckley name. And in an upcoming issue of the *Advocate*, in a story written by Chris Bull all about the *OutWeek*/Buckley controversy, "a columnist" responds to my implications that he is gay by practically coming out: "I understand what [Signorile] is trying to do. Sexuality is very complicated. I know silence equals death. I'm not as stupid as you might think." (As Liz Smith has said to you, "Way to go young Billy!")

Honestly, all of you don't have the time to deal with our jabbing you. You're much too busy moving UP, UP, UP (which is fine, since we need you there). So why not do it the right way? You'd not only save yourselves a lot of headaches (i.e., having us expose you), but you'd actually be doing some good.

Love & Kisses,
M.

"Telling 'Tales' about Celebrity Closets," an interview with Armistead Maupin
Steve Warren
(*Au Courant*, October 23, 1989)

Armistead Maupin recalls a Hollywood maxim from the period when multimillionaire Merv Griffin had a daily talk show: "You don't get on 'Merv Griffin' unless you get *on* Merv Griffin!"

Maupin is the author of the *Tales of the City* series, of which the sixth and last, *Sure of You*, has just been published. When he and his lover, Terry Anderson, stayed at the Griffin-owned Beverly Hilton recently, Maupin says, "The place was under construction, it was really somewhat of a mess. As we were leaving we found a comments card on which we were asked to place any suggestions . . . about how the hotel could be improved. And Terry wrote, 'Hotel is under construction and Merv is in the closet; so finish hotel and have Merv come out.'

"We left the card and two weeks later we received a [form] letter from Baron Hilton himself, saying, 'Thank you very much for your comments about the hotel. We have spoken to our staff and we are taking measures to correct the situation.' . . . I was imagining the staff being lined up and told, 'Now listen, we've got to do something about Merv taking Eva Gabor to events.' "

Maupin has been friends with a number of gay celebrities, both open (Quentin Crisp, Christopher Isherwood and Don Bachardy) and otherwise. He says he began urging Rock Hudson to come out in 1976: "I think it would have been quite possible at that point. He had all the money in the world, he was already playing older leads. And I've always believed that if this sort of thing is orchestrated properly the fears they have about it just go up in smoke.

"Ian McKellen will tell you this is the happiest time of his life. He's not creeping around in fear anymore, he's in charge of himself. People can't say nasty things about him in the tabloids because he's already exploded the sensationalism of it by announcing himself in a calm and happy manner."

Maupin thinks all gay men and lesbians should come out, for their own good and the good we can do each other; but celebrity closets are his pet peeve.

"If the gay press has any function at all," Maupin believes, "it's to tweak the conscience of famous people who are in the closet; and certainly we shouldn't continue to lionize those among us who are making a success of themselves in the mainstream while remaining so determinedly in the closet . . . even if they are doing all the benefits and everything."

The author says he no longer has a double standard for "good" and "bad" closeted celebrities: "There are people who say if they're in the closet and they're behaving like Jesse Helms, then I think we should bring them out; but if they're attending AIDS benefits and they really like us, then we shouldn't. I'm taking the hard line on it and saying homophobia is homophobia. If you're Lily Tomlin and you've got your manager telling the press, 'Don't bring up her private life,' you are being homophobic. I guess I'm harder on those people because I know they do have a conscience. . . .

"I don't buy this 'working for us on the inside' line," Maupin continues, "because they've been doing that forever and the world isn't getting any better. Hollywood still creates the impression that homosexuals do not exist. I guess I've become more strident about this as I've become more famous because I see more and more instances of hypocrisy. I didn't know who was gay years ago, I was buying the line that Hollywood was giving me; but the more contact I've had with the people who run things the more I realize to what degree this is an enormous lie that's being told to all of us.

"What it boils down to is, the message that is being communicated is that there is something wrong with us. . . . If you are being secretive about the people you love, you are conveying the impression that you are ashamed of who and what you are. . . .

"We have to get beyond the point where homosexuality is regarded as a detriment to one's career," Maupin stresses, "because if we don't, the general public is still going to regard it as a dirty little secret which should be kept under wraps. If gay people themselves act ashamed of who they are, then the straight people around them have no choice but to believe that there must be something wrong with it."

Told that the late puppeteer Wayland Flowers once said to a close associate, "If I said those three little words—'I am gay'—it would cost me a million dollars a year," Maupin responds, "He's got no choice in the matter [now]. . . . That combination of greed and self-loathing is not particularly attractive. . . . The man was working gay cruises . . . making money off the fact of his homosexuality.

"I've worked the same bookstore circuit as Lily Tomlin. She has as many homosexuals standing in line at her book signings as I do. But God help you if you ask her why. . . .

"For Wayland Flowers to say he'd lose a million dollars if people found out he was gay is no more acceptable than for an actor to say, 'If they knew I was Jewish I wouldn't make as much money as I do, so please keep quiet about it.' Imagine a Jewish person saying that to another Jewish person, and imagine the response of that second Jewish person. That's the way I feel when [closeted gay people say] they have the right to stay in the closet to protect their career.

"We have to go to the very source of this problem," Maupin maintains, "which is the homophobia itself; and the only way to attack the homophobia is to refuse to maintain the secret of homosexuality, either your own or anyone else's. And that means expressing your impatience to other gay people who are in the closet, telling them you feel that they have a moral responsibility to be more honest about their lives because it'll make the world a better place for everyone.

"I realize that that's a process that takes some people longer than others, and I'm willing to wait, as long as I see some movement on the part of my friends."

Slated to appear on "Oprah Winfrey" on National Coming Out Day, Maupin refers to the event when he says, "The whole premise of National Coming Out Day is 'Take the next step.' What I'm saying is: Take the next step, Lily and Jane. Take the next step, Barry Diller. Take the next step, Merv Griffin."

The author of a recent *Playboy* interview, Maupin notes, spent half a page trying to draw Barry Diller out about his sexuality, but Diller kept the door firmly closed.

"I feel someone should be in a position to put pressure on the people who are really in power," the writer goes on. "Homosexuals are not some sort of oppressed minority. We are in fact in charge of a lot of places. Eddie Murphy's boss is a gay man. [Actually, Barry Diller has left Paramount for the top spot at Fox, Inc.] Someone could have told Eddie Murphy 'This is inappropriate' when he made those horrid AIDS jokes, but we have an enormous number of gay people out there who have no conscience when it comes to the issue of homophobia. They're perfectly willing to let it ride because they're afraid of blowing their own cover and making less money.

"The pressure can't be put on by Joe Blow on the street," Maupin says, "but if I were in a room with Barry Diller I would tell him that. I do this. I made the same speech to Tim Curry last year after reading [in an interview by this writer] that his private life involves watching ducks on the Thames.

"Tim looked me up when he came to town because he had read the books, and I was flattered because he's a certain cultural icon to me. We hit it off tremendously, had dinner on three or four occasions and partied together. One night I made it clear to him I felt he should be open about his sexuality, and I didn't hear from him again. Here is a man who spent the greater part of the '70s running around in a garter belt and a merry widow—I don't know what he's trying to protect, but he doesn't have half the guts Ian McKellen does.

"Ian had trepidation about coming out," Maupin acknowledges. "He had people telling him not to do it. Now I've actually heard people saying, 'Oh, it's easy for him because he's at the top of his field. Then I hear quite the opposite—they say, 'I can't do it because I'm not famous enough yet.'

"I've heard every excuse in the world," Maupin sneers. "It really just boils down to coming to grips with your own life."

Peppering his diatribe with anecdotes, Maupin tells of a young, little-known actor friend who once called excitedly to say he had a date with John Travolta, who had invited him out through a mutual acquaintance. The excitement was gone when the actor called back with the postmortem: Travolta had taken him to a Scientology presentation! "They've got him pimping for them," Maupin laughs.

The writer/activist had hoped AIDS would make things better in the movie industry. When Rock Hudson died, for instance, "I thought that Hollywood's sensible response to that whole situation would have been to gather 30 of its top stars in a room and have someone step forward and say, 'Half of us are gay and half of us are not. It doesn't matter to us and it shouldn't matter to you.' But we haven't even gotten that close."

Instead, Maupin says, there seems to have been a rash of Hollywood marriages. His friend who had gone out with Travolta called a couple of years ago and told him he " 'might have to get married' as a cover. Isn't it funny? That's what 'having to get married' means today." Tom Selleck, Jamie Lee Curtis and other stars got married around that time, Maupin says, just as Rock Hudson got married in the 1950s and Cary Grant got married in the '30s, '40s, '60s and '80s.

Maupin considers Selleck "today's Rock Hudson," tracing his career through adventure films and light comedy to his current serious drama, and recalls an advertisement the actor appeared in shortly before the success of "Magnum P. I." "He was the perfect clone," Maupin says. "People couldn't believe they'd use someone so gay-looking in an ad."

Reminded that he's speaking for the record, Maupin has no desire to censor himself. He is skeptical, however, that his words will ever be published: "What invariably stops a story like that from even making it into print is that a lawyer comes along and says this is libelous. Why is it libelous? If I'd said they were Jewish or black, would it have been libelous? . . .

"I'm deeply offended by the idea that the fact of someone's homosexuality is considered libelous. What's so terrible about homosexuality? We're talking out of both sides of our mouths in this country. We have a liberal press that's gotten to the point that they say 'Well, yes, it's okay for them to be gay, *but* we can't say that about someone else because after all it really is a terrible thing.' Which is it?

"Malice is usually required to prove libel," Maupin points out. "I would challenge anyone to find malice in my action, because I'm happy about being gay and I celebrate the other people that are gay — and most gay people do. That's why we have something like *The Gay Engagement Calendar* that brags about the people who are gay, because we're proud of these people."

Unaware that Tom Hulce has joined the short list of openly gay actors, Maupin is happy to hear it and not too surprised: "He seems to be the kind of character that would make that possible."

Putting the situation into historical perspective, Maupin notes, "For years the function of gay society was to maintain a safe and secret brotherhood which would protect its members from the glare of notoriety. We're so much in the habit of hiding and altering our behavior, we continue to perpetuate the problem that makes life miserable for the average 14-year-old trying to deal with his own homosexuality. No one out there above a certain level can represent wholesome images of homosexuality to new generations of children coming along.

"One of the unwritten laws of gay life," Maupin sighs, "is where you reach a certain level of fame you shut up about your homosexuality. You're not told this by straight people, you're told it by other famous homosexuals who are ushering you into the pantheon of the right.

"And for somebody like me who's relatively new on the scene and who's making a big noise about it, you make people extremely uncomfortable. . . . Everyone compromises at one point or another, and I've resolved to be the one who doesn't. If my career doesn't go any further than this, I don't give a damn. The joy I'm having is in living my life completely openly and sharing everything about myself that I want to share."

Forcing Gays out of the Closet: Homosexual Leaders Seek to Expose Foes of the Movement
William A. Henry III
(*Time*, January 29, 1990)

Gays have long gossiped about which public figures of past and present might be secret homosexuals. Publications from the scholarly to the semi-scabrous have speculated about the likes of Alexander the Great, Shakespeare, Willa Cather and James Dean, with hundreds of others cited along the way. This name dropping is defended as a way of giving the gay community role models and a sense of continuity. When the rumors involve living people, however, discussion about who is "in the closet" has generally been held to a discreet murmur — partly in deference to libel laws but mostly in defense of privacy. That consensus is fast breaking down with the spread of a phenomenon known as "outing," the intentional exposure of secret gays by other gays.

Frustrated at the slow pace of gay civil rights legislation and what they consider governmental indifference to the AIDS epidemic, growing numbers of gay activists now claim a moral right to "rip people out of the closet"—either to force them to help the movement or to nullify them as opponents. The main targets are elected officials and religious leaders who may enjoy a gay life in private but who endorse antigay measures to safeguard their careers. Radical gays go further, pointing the finger at entertainment and media figures and even ordinary citizens.

Among conspicuous victims within the past year have been an East Coast big-city mayor, a Midwestern Governor and a West Coast U.S. Senator, none of them incontrovertibly known to be gay. In each case, the official was identified as a homosexual via leaflets or noisy demonstrations. The rationale for exposing the politicians' alleged secret lives was that they were guilty of malicious hypocrisy on matters of life and death. One outing victim had endorsed legislation allowing hospitals to test patients for AIDS without their consent. Another backed a ban on funding to school programs that describe homosexuality as normal. A third supposedly failed to provide adequate public AIDS services. Yet in an odd twist that underscores the uneasy position of gays in society, the demonstrators were attacking enemies by embracing each as one of their own.

Similar action against leaders of the Roman Catholic Church hierarchy has been threatened, although not yet taken, by prominent members of a gay Catholic group. Whereas the political leaders have been under attack for specific personal acts, the clergy is a potential target because of the church's general, institutional opposition to gay sex.

While the idea of outing a fellow gay used to be considered repellent under any circumstances, the tactic has become increasingly acceptable to mainstream homosexual leaders. It is practiced by some gay publications, and its propriety has even been debated in the corridors of Congress. Last June, when Republicans falsely implied that House Speaker Tom Foley was gay, Representative Barney Frank threatened to expose Republican officeholders who really are homosexual. Few in Washington doubted that there were such officials, or that Frank, an acknowledged gay, would be able to name them. Republicans were already keenly aware of the ironic fates of two of their most prominent antigay voices, Maryland Congressman Robert Bauman and conservative fund-raiser Terry Dolan. Bauman's political career ended in 1980, when he was charged with soliciting a teenage boy for a paid sex act; Dolan died in 1986 of AIDS complications. Republicans backed off, so Frank did not carry out his threat, and he was at pains to underscore the limited circumstances in which he would apply it: "I referred only to those gay people who shamefully use the fact or accusation of homosexuality as a weapon against others."

Still, many gays and sympathetic straights remain troubled by the idea of outing, even if [it is] used only against the movement's avowed enemies. Says Sarah Craig, an associate editor of Chicago's gay-oriented *Windy City Times*: "Really, you're only using the same bludgeon used to injure you to injure someone else." As a practical matter, moreover, if outing a closeted gay ends his or her career, there is rarely any reason to believe that the target's successor will be more sympathetic to the gay cause. Nonetheless, some prominent gays favor forcing every closeted person to come out, holding that being gay is nothing to be ashamed of and that there is strength in numbers. Novelist Armistead Maupin, a leading gadfly of San Francisco's gay community, was one of the first to confirm Rock Hudson's homosexual life after Hudson announced he had AIDS, and in interviews Maupin has named many other entertainers, some of them married, whom he knows or believes to be gay. Says Maupin of those he would drag out of the closet: "Their embarrassment and self-loathing makes me lose respect for them. It also indicates to me they find my life repugnant."

The debate points up a fundamental division that has burdened the gay-rights cause for decades. Notes Thomas Stoddard, executive director of the Lambda Legal Defense and Education Fund and an adjunct professor of law at New York University: "The gay movement is actually based upon two principles that collide. One is privacy, and the other is disclosure, the process of coming out." Those focused on privacy are responding to society as it exists, with its emotional and sometimes physical perils for overt homosexuals. Those favoring disclosure are more concerned with society as they hope it may become, with tolerance for all. The political "causists" are prepared to sacrifice their present lives for future good. The problem with outing is that it claims an unjustifiable right to sacrifice the lives of others as well, whether they agree or not.

The Other Side of Malcolm
Michelangelo Signorile
(*OutWeek*, March 18, 1990)

A short, plump woman dressed in black feverishly gave programs to reporters and photographers outside the church. As the flashbulbs popped and the TV cameras rolled, Le Cirque owner Sirio Macioni played doorman in front of St. Bart's on Park Avenue, pointing to those whom the 50 aggressive police officers should clear a path for.

"Oh yes, that's Claudia Cohen. . . . Yes, yes, that's Diane von Furstenberg. Let her in!"

The next day, the *New York Times*—which had previously published an obituary implying that Malcolm Forbes was romantically involved with Elizabeth Taylor and said he had once planned to marry her, only to mysteriously strike the reference in the paper's later editions—had this to say about the event: "Some worldly mourners said they had never seen such a splendid mix of people—not even at another somewhat heterogeneous gathering, Truman Capote's fabled Black and White Ball at the Plaza Hotel two decades ago."

It was a splashy memorial service indeed. Lots of pretty boys, Hollywood agents, publishing magnates and celebrity beards, as well as Richard Nixon and quite a few other staunch conservatives. But did the homophobes know that they were coming to pay homage to someone who embodied what they ultimately detested? Did notoriously anti-gay Bill Buckley, who only a week before wrote a syndicated *Daily News* column headlined "Forbes—A Man Larger than Life Itself," know that he was laying praise upon a "sex-driven gay" whose ass he might have wanted to tattoo? Did *USA Today* founder Al Neuharth, who a few months ago made anti-gay remarks about male flight attendants, know that his dear friend "Chairman Malcolm" was one of those dreaded perverts? Did *Newsday*'s Dennis Duggan—who still refuses to believe Father Ritter toyed with boys—know what his "Peter Pan with dough" did with his capitalist tool? Did Forbes's own son Steve, who now takes over the empire and whom the *Wall Street Journal* describes as an "ideological, conservative Republican," have any idea that his own greenback-conscious dad was as queer as a three-dollar bill?

Dan (not his real name) worked for two years as a waiter at the Forbes townhouse and galleries, which adjoin the *Forbes* offices on lower Fifth Avenue.

"It's the homoerotic art that hit me when I first got there," he recalls. "There's this one painting on the wall called 'Sailors and Floozies,' in which all the floozies look like drag queens. Then there's this one called 'Manhole'—it's the top view of a manhole with construction workers toiling inside."

Dan had great respect for Forbes. He says he was always treated exceptionally well. Although he never engaged in sexual activities with Forbes, he watched the comings and goings of many men.

"He really went after the waiters. I mean he did it a lot—as much as he possibly could. If he liked them he'd ask them to show up the next time early—at the townhouse. He'd ask them to go in the Jacuzzi with him. Then, of course, they'd have sex. He'd give them a hundred-dollar bill when he finished—they used to love to talk about it. They got the money even if they refused the sex."

Troy, Hal, Andy and Mitch (not their real names), all waiters, each separately described the same scenario. In each case Forbes would ask the young man to come up to the house. He'd ask him into the Jacuzzi. Forbes would then begin to stroke the man's legs slowly. He'd then proceed to masturbate him before going on to perform oral sex on the young man, if indeed the man desired it (not all of the four had let him). After the sexual encounter ended, Forbes would hand the man a hundred-dollar bill.

"Of course, if you were lazy you had to put out, otherwise you were gonna get fired or you had to start working harder."

Actually, some of the people present at the memorial service *had* to have known that Malcolm Forbes was gay, no matter what they may actually say. They, after all, were privy to the same information that the rest of us were. But their hypocrisy is easily rationalized.

Malcolm Forbes was a rich and powerful man and if he wanted to be secretly queer, well, then, none of them would be the first to stop him. Besides, that was all *his* business and he kept "quiet" about it, a highly praised quality in wealthy and ultraconservative circles. Bill Buckley, for instance, probably finds it highly commendable that certain individuals who float about in the same social arena as he and his wife, Pat, remain "discrete" about their sexual orientation.

It becomes increasingly clear that while the thought of our big, macho, American publishing tycoon being a homo comes as a shock to many, lots of others knew for a long time of Forbes' secret gay life and simply *excused* his being a fag. Others, no doubt, were in denial, sloughing off any rumors or stories they'd heard.

Georg Osterman is playwright-in-residence at The Ridiculous Theatrical Company, the company made famous by the late Charles Ludlam and now being carried on by Ludlam's longtime companion, Everett Quinton. Osterman has received quite a bit of publicity for his current adaptation of *Dr. Jekyll and Mr. Hyde* for Quinton at the Ridiculous.

But before becoming a near-well-known playwright, Osterman worked as a communications manager at *Forbes*. That was in 1982.

"I was personally involved with Malcolm," he says flatly. "I was impressed with him. He worked that business into something amazing. And his art collection was bizarrely eclectic. But to be honest, I thought he was very self-centered. The times I spent with him, he'd spend 15 minutes or so asking 'how are you?' then from there on it was 'me, me, me, me, me, me. . . . '

"How it starts is—it's the same with everyone; he's done it with others in the office—he notices you working there and he starts to follow you around.

"I'm delivering something and there's Malcolm following me, and asking, 'How are you today?' and I answer, 'I'm in a hurry, Mr. Forbes.'

"I'd heard from other people that he tries things. My friend who worked in the art department had a bad experience. Malcolm was very persistent. Things became very difficult for him when he didn't want to do it.

"He invited me to the townhouse for drinks. I went to the townhouse. I think he thought it would be some idiot who would just pop into the sack with him right away. We talked awhile. There were all these beautiful paintings all around. It was beautiful. There was a lot of work, and I knew all of these painters. He just sort of sat there and stared at me. I don't know if he was impressed or appalled.

"We then watched a Colt gay porn video, and got around to *the business* after that—and after some of the best strawberry daiquiris I've ever had!

"It continued a few times after that. To a degree, he was very charming. I did it for the experience. I mean, I was having sex with a millionaire. It was an experience. It was fine."

Osterman says that, though Forbes' marriage to the former Roberta Remsen Laidlaw ended in divorce in 1985, the two had been living separate lives for years. The marriage was, in his opinion, for cosmetic purposes and for the sake of creating heirs.

"They only got together during the holidays to take pictures and such and they hadn't had sex in ages," he claims.

Throughout the marriage, it seems, Forbes never stopped engaging in homosexual activities, which as the years went on would become his predominant, if not exclusive, form of sex. Trapped within the confines of family and big, big business, Forbes found himself trying to fit gay sex into his daily routine—trying to incorporate it somehow into his life. For him, that meant hiring men as chauffeurs, waiters, captains and houseboys with whom he could have sex on a daily basis. It meant putting some of his staff in charge of scouring the town to find hired help that would also potentially put out. It meant propositioning people on staff he might not know were gay or who he did not originally seek out for strictly sexual purposes. (Sometimes these people were writers and other employees of his magazines. And many times the sex took place inside his office at *Forbes*.) It meant engaging in practices which many have described as exploitative, coercive, and tantamount to on-the-job sexual abuse. Many times—or even most times—it meant paying for the sex, carrying around a stack of hundred-dollar bills and slipping one to each employee after the sexual encounter took place. It meant also passing a bill to those men who were insulted, outraged or just plain said no so that they would keep their mouths shut.

"If you were a waiter, or anybody, and he liked you, he might ask you to be his chauffeur," says Dan. Ernest (not his real name), who briefly worked at the townhouse, confirms this. He was at one point asked to be a chauffeur, but refused. As the men point out, Forbes would have easier access to the chauffeur and a better chance of having regular sex with him since they could do it in the car. It was considered a "special" position.

Peter (not his real name) had arrived in New York from a European country a few years ago.

"A friend had set me up on a date with a rich man the week I arrived in the U.S.," he recalls. "He said his name was Malcolm Forbes. I had never heard of him. I asked another friend if I should go. He said, 'Of course, are you crazy?!'

"[Forbes] picked me up on his motorcycle. We went to dinner and then to a nightclub. And then we spent some time together later."

The two saw some more of each other in the next two weeks. Peter is extremely coy when it comes to talking about sex and about discussing just what they did "later," but does not deny that they had a physical relationship.

Within weeks of first meeting Forbes, Peter left New York for Los Angeles to become "an actor." But he was back within a year.

"I went back to Forbes and became a chauffeur for him," he says. "I was driving around people like Elizabeth Taylor. It was very exciting. And I spent a lot of time with him. Sometimes we'd go out on the motorcycle. I liked him a lot. He was a great person."

Evelyn (not her real name) remembered hearing all of the rumors at the magazine about certain young men in the office having flings with Forbes.

"Half the people in the office were totally blind to what was going on. If you told them, they would never believe it," she says. "I mean, I think they'd think you were crazy if you told them. The other half, well, I think they just sort of knew everything that was going on and talked about it a lot. I certainly knew that some of the guys were fooling around with him."

Victor (not his real name) had had encounters with Forbes in the editors' offices at the magazine.

"I remember when he'd call me up to the office. Everyone would be impressed, thinking it was business. I mean these people were so stupid. They really didn't know what was going on.

"Those closet doors are six-foot lead. This is before the renovation. His office was on the end. Just 30 feet from his desk was where his son Steve was sitting.

"The door would always be wide open. And the secretary would be sitting there. There was no way she could see in though. And she would never just come in. She'd always call first.

"Anyway, he'd just start going down on me. I would get so nervous. And every now and then he'd pull his head up and ask me some sort of business question so that they would hear us talking outside the office. Then he'd go back down on me and I'd be answering the question. He did this—leaving the door open—because it was safer. No one would think anything. He was very careful. He wouldn't shut the door because he didn't want it to look weird. And, also, I really think he liked the intrigue and excitement.

"When it was over, he'd slip me a hundred bucks."

While many of those who knew Forbes spoke highly of him, others were much more critical. Some employees felt seriously coerced and even abused.

Richard (not his real name) was one of quite a few men who worked for Forbes as cater waiters and felt angry about things that went on.

"When you start working there the other waiters tell you what to expect," he explains. "They tell you that he asks you to strip and to go in the hot tub. Or to escort him to dinner as his 'bodyguard.' It's not that he hid that. He was always on his motorcycle with hot boys. Everyone knew. It's surprising that nobody mentioned that—people like Liz Smith—but they didn't.

"One night I went into work and the captain said, 'The old man wants to see you.' So I went up to his office. He said, 'I admire the work that you're doing.' He asked me to come up to the townhouse after the cocktail party and see some pictures from Tangiers. I said to myself, 'Well, why not?' I was curious. I wanted to see the pictures.

"It was ten o'clock and I was up there. He made me a drink. Then we were sitting there and he put his hand on my knee and said, 'You don't mind an old man liking you, do you?' He was rubbing his hands up and down my thighs. I said, 'I gotta go.' He gave me a copy of this book—some hot air balloon book, one of those self-indulgent books he wrote. He said, 'I don't give this book out to many people.' In the elevator, he slipped something in my pocket and said, 'Keep this between you and me.' And then he said to give his secretary a call if I wanted to go to dinner and rate restaurants with him. 'We'll go to dinner and you can be my bodyguard,' he said.

"I got outside and found a hundred-dollar bill in my pocket and thought, 'This is hush money. Fuck this!'

"In general I think he was really a very nice man. I don't fault him at all for trying to pick up boys. He really meant well. He certainly was not as bad as a lot of other rich people. However, I have a lot of trouble with people who have money and have to put on this major charade. When you have so much money who gives a shit? He was trying always to worry about his image in Peoria.

"What did bother me was his saying 'this is between us,' I find that offensive.

"He's exploitative. He thinks he could just give some boys money and they'll do what he wants. It's not good. I don't think anyone should need to feel pressured to do it. I think some people thought, 'Hey, I might be fired if I don't do it.' I know people who have had sex with him and that's probably why they did. That's the most egregious part of the whole bargain. It wouldn't occur to him that he was taking advantage of them. But people I know thought that they were taken advantage of.

"The whole thing kind of sickens me. This man with all of this power feeling that he could do all of this as if it's not a big deal.

"It's pathetic that in order to be a happy man he'd have to go out and humiliate himself and do all this secret stuff.

"I always wanted to say to him, 'if you would just come out you could be so beneficial to gays instead of being this pathetic, secretive person.' "

From what can be surmised based on the available information, Forbes rarely had any long-term relationships with men since any attachments would naturally make it all that much more difficult to stay in hiding. He steered clear of gay establishments, having once even approached the disco Mars on a Sunday night only to leave immediately, realizing it was gay night. His closeted lifestyle kept him from mingling in any way within the gay community. And, of course, he had to keep this side of him a secret, hidden from his friends, his business associates and his public.

But still the stories were everywhere. Judging from information uncovered it's probably true that Forbes had been with hundreds of men, not all of whom would stay quiet. People talked and, in quite a few segments of the gay male community at least, it seemed that *everyone* knew *someone* who'd done it with Malcolm Forbes. He was also quite showy, liking to ride around with his "dates" on his motorcycle. It was not uncommon to spot Forbes on Christopher Street taking a break next to his bike with a hot, young, leathered bikemate by his side. He also would show up—often with young men—at such mixed clubs as Love Machine and Celebrity Club at the Tunnel, where the crowd was predominantly gay but was never listed as such or considered a gay club per se. Thus the contradiction of Forbes: While he tried to keep it all very hush-hush, he behaved many times in a sloppy, seemingly deliberate way, yearning to have fun, and testing the limits of living a closed life.

The result was that, unlike the cases of other, more cautious millionaires, lots of people got wind of Forbes' escapades. Certainly many of those who moved in his circles had been told a thing or two. And that meant people in the media.

"I'd heard all of the stories. You always heard the stories," says *Newsday*'s James Revson. The *Daily News*' Billy Norwich reiterates: "Like anyone who traveled the circuit, I heard the rumors." And Michael Musto of the *Village Voice* wryly comments, "I always knew he was a friend of Dorothy—and I don't just mean Kilgallen." But the *Daily News*' Liz Smith, in a one-page statement faxed to *OutWeek*, claimed to be "too square" to have been privy to information regarding Forbes' homosexuality. Without addressing what she might or might not have been informed of regarding Forbes in the past, Smith speaks only of her personal relationship with the man. "The subject never came up at any time. I never saw any evidence of it. In fact, it never occurred to me," she states. "I must say he and I were both at an age where sex never came up as a topic of conversation." Smith goes on to refute claims that Forbes purposely used Elizabeth Taylor as a "beard" to make him appear heterosexual. "I never saw any evidence of such pretense. Both of them said to me on several occasions that they were just friends. The romance was completely in the minds of the tabloids." But Smith herself has never stated that fact in her own column; she has never said these two were *just friends*. Quite to the contrary, she was one of the major perpetrators of the false Forbes/Taylor romance two years ago, trying to convince readers that they were a hot item.

But if Smith appears to be nervously fence-sitting, others are downright indignant. Many columnists, writers and editors, as well as others who worked for Forbes who knew of his gay life, became quite upset upon being approached by *OutWeek*, and refused to comment for this story. (The Forbes children, having been tipped off early on about this story, never returned my calls. Neither did editors at *Forbes* and *Egg*.)

"Why dig up all of this stuff?" angrily asked a one-time columnist who'd enjoyed a friendship with Forbes over the years. "I mean, what does it matter now?"

This was the attitude encountered from many both within the gay and lesbian community and among those straights who claim to be "liberal," "understanding" and "pro-gay."

"He was as good as gold," says Dan. "It didn't matter whether you were a fling or you meant something more. He treated people right.

"Actually, he rarely, if ever, had really long or involved relationships with men. From what I could gather he lived in such a medieval way. He was the King, who married the Queen just for purposes of siring offspring. And then he went about just having quick flings and affairs. Of course, with men, I mean. I never, ever, ever heard of him having sex with women."

Dan, as well as Ernest, independently identified one man by name who worked at the townhouse and who they say acted as a "headhunter" for Forbes' male sex partners. This person is described as being immensely good-looking. Part of his job, according to these sources, was to always be on the lookout for attractive young men who might work at the townhouse and be persuaded to have sex with Forbes.

"He always got great people," says Ernest. "Some really hot guys."

According to Dan, Forbes treated the "headhunter" extra specially.

"He got Malcolm his boys," he says. "He was responsible for getting that fresh meat. So he was important. Malcolm had a special place for him." According to Dan, at one point a couple of years ago, the headhunter had left Forbes' employ and moved to another state. This, he said, left Forbes so lost that when the headhunter decided to come back, at Forbes' behest, Forbes sent out his private jet, the *Capitalist Tool*, to get all of his furnishings and belongings and get him back as soon as possible. Once back, he was given a better position in Forbes' empire, which he now occupies.

Is our society so overwhelmingly repressive that even individuals as all-powerful as the late Malcolm Forbes feel they absolutely cannot come out of the closet?

It would seem so. Much like Congressman Barney Frank before he came out, Forbes was the victim of a virulently homophobic society which he too fed into regularly. He was forced to lead a life of secret pursuits and dark, dirty doings; of exploitation and abuse. His own internalized homophobia far outweighed the commanding authority that any amount of money could possibly wield.

And what is the significance of bringing all of this out now?

First, for the sake of posterity the truth must be told. All too often history is distorted. One of the most influential men in America just died, and regardless of how we may or may not see him as a proper public figure, he was gay. And that must be recorded.

Second, it sends a clear message to the public at large that we are everywhere.

Third, perhaps gays and lesbians at all levels of society can learn a great deal from the story of Malcolm Forbes. In researching this piece, in an attempt to try to obtain more information about Forbes and get to people who were close to him, I came upon someone who knew the family very well and who would have been able to discuss intimate details about the man; not merely about sex, but about the real inner workings of Forbes' mind. It was a person who could perhaps provide an insight into what Forbes thought about such issues as gay rights and AIDS. But, after considerable thought, he decided not to speak to me. Currently living a closeted existence with regard to his own family and business, he said, "My choice in speaking to you is between myself and the greater gay community. And—at this moment—I have to go with myself."

Ultimately, that was the tragedy of Malcolm Forbes' entire life. Under the guise, perhaps, of doing the best for "himself," Forbes initiated a senseless, self-imposed prison sentence which benefited no one.

III. After Forbes, the Deluge: The Mainstream Press

David Tuller, "Uproar over Gays Booting Others Out of the Closet" (*San Francisco Chronicle*, March 12, 1990)

Dirk Johnson, "Privacy vs. the Pursuit of Gay Rights" (*New York Times*, March 27, 1990)

Mike Royko, "Antsy Closet Crowd Should Think Twice" (*Chicago Tribune*, April 2, 1990)

Randy Shilts, "Is 'Outing' Gays Ethical?" (*New York Times*, April 12, 1990)

Uproar over Gays Booting Others Out of the Closet

David Tuller

(*San Francisco Chronicle*, March 12, 1990)

To most people, the late Malcolm Forbes was the ultimate capitalist. The multimillionaire head of a publishing empire, he reveled in his public roles as an extravagant party-giver and a motorcycle and hot-air balloon enthusiast. Gossip columnists wrote extensively about his close friendship–and rumored romance–with Elizabeth Taylor.

Within New York's gay and publishing circles, however, other rumors had circulated for years that the divorced grandfather of eight was gay. And this week, a cover story in a New York gay magazine liberally quotes unnamed waiters and other male employees at the publishing company who claim to have had sex with or been propositioned by the 70-year-old magnate.

A spokesman for Forbes refused to comment on the subject, but Michelangelo Signorile's article in the weekly magazine *OutWeek* is already intensifying an emotional debate within the gay community about "outing"–the practice of forcing public figures out of the closet by revealing their homosexuality.

The Issue Stated

On one side of the debate are increasingly militant gay rights advocates who say gay individuals in positions of power and influence have an obligation to the community to come out of the closet. On the other side are those who argue that the right to privacy must be respected at all costs.

"It's an ethical dilemma, because for a long time there's been this gentleman's agreement that you don't bring people out–but now that agreement is unraveling," acknowledged Bob Smith, a member of the San Francisco chapter of the AIDS Coalition to Unleash Power, which has not taken a formal position on the issue.

For years, gay men and women have gossiped among themselves about famous people, both living and dead, who were known or thought to be homosexual. Now, several factors are spurring the call by some gay leaders to make such rumors public: continued frustration at the government's response to AIDS, the impatience of a younger generation of homosexuals with the closeted lifestyles of older lesbians and gay men and a gnawing sense that an anti-gay backlash is threatening civil rights gains achieved during the past decade.

Those who approve of outing argue that closeted public figures, by posing as heterosexual, are actively helping to perpetuate society's oppression of homosexuals and are robbing the gay community of valuable role models. Others, including a great many within the gay community itself, are horrified by the disclosures.

"It's a tragedy for the individual and the community that people lead their lives in hiding, but we believe that coming out is a decision [individuals need] to make for themselves," said Urvashi Vaid, executive director of the National Gay and Lesbian Task Force, a Washington-based civil rights group.

Recent Incidents

In the past year, several incidents have forced the gay community, as well as journalists, to grapple with the issue:

—Publishing magnate C. K. McClatchy, the chairman of the Sacramento-based McClatchy newspaper chain and a closeted gay man, died of a heart attack last April. During the autopsy, the coroner discovered that McClatchy also was infected with the AIDS virus, although that played no role in his death.

When the *Sacramento Union*, the local rival of McClatchy's *Sacramento Bee*, broke the story the next month, journalists debated the ethics of reporting such a finding against the wishes of the deceased. Tom Goldstein, dean of the journalism school at the University of California at Berkeley, said the disclosure was "despicable."

—Last summer, after the Republican National Committee released a memo implying that Speaker of the House Thomas Foley was homosexual, openly gay Massachusetts Representative Barney Frank threatened to expose closeted gay Republicans.

"If they don't cut the crap, something's going to happen, and I'm going to happen it," said Frank, who is embroiled in his own sex scandal.

—During street demonstrations, gays and AIDS protesters have taken to carrying signs and chanting slogans denouncing as gay those politicians who they believe are pursuing policies detrimental to gay or AIDS-related causes.

Among the targets of such protests in the past year was former New York Mayor Ed Koch, whose sexual orientation has long been the subject of rumors. During Koch's tenure, many gay leaders felt he was slow to provide funds and services for people with AIDS because of fear that, if he responded quickly to the epidemic, the general public would assume he was gay.

—In his popular "Gossip Watch" column in *OutWeek*, Signorile regularly blasts what he sees as collusion between the mainstream gossip columnists and gay figures in the entertainment and fashion worlds. The columnists, he charges, are often themselves closeted homosexuals who help other gay celebrities cover up their sexual identities by frequently writing about their "dates" with members of the opposite sex.

Subjects of recent Signorile columns have included designer Calvin Klein, who is married, and Cher's daughter, Chastity, whose sexual orientation has been the subject of fevered articles in supermarket tabloids. "At a time when people are dying of AIDS all around us, I just have no sympathy for a designer who is trying to build an empire and convince us he is heterosexual so he can sell more clothes," said Signorile, whose blistering columns have caused a stir in New York social circles.

In the case of Forbes, Signorile invokes the principle of correcting the historical record. "History is all too often distorted," he said. "The bottom line is that a huge media celebrity has just died, and he was gay, and that should be reported now rather than 500 years later, like with Leonardo da Vinci and Michelangelo." Many historians say that both Renaissance artists were homosexual.

Soul-Searching

Within the gay community, the debate over outing has caused extensive soul-searching because it cuts to the heart of what many gays have long cherished as a fundamental privilege: the right to privacy.

"I think that the right to privacy is so basic that it shouldn't be abridged," said Steve Morin, an openly gay aide to Representative Nancy Pelosi, D-San Francisco. "Most every gay person has at some point in their coming out been closeted in at least some circumstances, and you would therefore expect great sympathy for that situation."

Opponents say that gays who expose closeted homosexuals are guilty of the same smear tactics used for years by heterosexuals against the gay community in general. They argue that as long as homosexuality remains a stigma, the practice of outing might serve only to reinforce society's prejudices.

"Forcing someone out of the closet publicly is feeding into the public perception that there's something wrong with homosexuality by suggesting that it's hidden and shameful," said Debra Chasnoff, executive editor of *Out/Look*, a San Francisco magazine covering lesbian and gay issues.

However, many of those, both heterosexual and gay, who are generally opposed to outing make a clear exception in the case of gay right-wing public officials hypocritically engaging in verbal or political gay-bashing.

Ben Bagdikian, former dean of UC Berkeley's Graduate School of Journalism and a media critic, said that outing might be appropriate in such situations. "I think it's legitimate if there was a well-known person who was homophobic or whose public position on sexual preference was contrary to what he did in his personal life," said Bagdikian. "But, if it became a standard thing, I think there could be a great deal of harm done with no particular purpose."

Privacy vs. the Pursuit of Gay Rights
Dirk Johnson
(*New York Times*, March 27, 1990)

A faction among American gay people, in an effort to battle stigma against homosexuals, has adopted a tactic that many find an alarming invasion of privacy: unmasking prominent people who it says are secretly gay.

In some instances, as a way of showing the widespread achievements of homosexuals in American society, gay publications print articles declaring certain figures in entertainment or business to be gay. In other instances, demonstrators picket politicians, asserting that the officials are secretly gay but are pursuing policies harmful to other homosexuals.

Proponents of this tactic, known as outing—as in "out of the closet" —say homosexuals in positions of power have a responsibility to acknowledge proudly who they are and provide positive role models, particularly in an era when many homosexuals believe they face rising discrimination as a result of the epidemic of AIDS. But this argument is viewed by some gay organizations as a betrayal of privacy.

"A Code of Silence"

Gabriel Rotello, editor of *OutWeek* magazine, a gay publication in New York that has identified prominent figures as homosexual, favors outing. "It's taken for granted that other minorities deserve to have role models, so why not gays?" he said.

"The media talks about the private lives of famous people in great detail," he added. "But when it comes to somebody being gay, there is a code of silence. Why? It's because being gay is perceived by many people as just about the worst thing somebody can be. And by imposing this code of silence, we are perpetuating that notion."

That assertion fails to convince the Human Rights Campaign Fund, the largest lobbying group for gay rights. "We believe privacy is a fundamental tenet of what the gay and lesbian movement is all about," said Eric Rosenthal, the fund's political director.

Criticism of the practice is echoed by many experts on civil liberties. "This only furthers the unfortunate process that's gone on for the last few decades: Society's diminishing respect for the rights of privacy," said Dr. Eric Plaut, vice chairman of psychiatry at Northwestern University, who has written on ethics. "We've already given up privacy in so many ways. And one's sexuality is the most private aspect."

Ghosts of Nazi Horrors

The issue is being confronted by all gay rights groups. Robert Bray, a spokesman for the National Gay and Lesbian Task Force, said: "What do we do about homophobic homosexuals in positions of power? It's been a problem since Nazi Germany."

Many civil liberties experts say the debate is particularly wrenching because of the historic irony involved: the threat of disclosure, which has traditionally been used as blackmail against homosexuals by their heterosexual enemies, is now coming from other homosexuals. Further, they say, if it proves to be an effective political pressure tactic, what is to keep false accusations from being used against heterosexual politicians?

Other complex questions arise, gay rights advocates said. Who is to determine that a public figure is gay? What is an anti-gay vote or position?

"Reasonable people will differ about where the line should be drawn," said Thomas Stoddard, executive director for the Lambda Legal Defense and Education Fund, which supports equal rights for gay people. "To my mind, a politician should not be held to cede the right to privacy simply because of a vote. On the other hand, when a politician goes out of his way to harass gay people, his private conduct can become a matter for discussion."

Foley Rumors Recalled

The movement gained impetus last year when Representative Barney Frank, who is openly gay, became incensed by the innuendo surrounding the election of Representative Thomas S. Foley of Washington as Speaker of the House. Mr. Frank threatened to reveal the homosexuality of some Republican Congressman who he said had participated in a campaign of whispers that Mr. Foley was gay.

"There is a right to privacy, but not hypocrisy," Mr. Frank, Democrat of Massachusetts, said in a recent interview. "If politicians are gay or lesbian, and then use that against other people, they have forfeited their right to privacy. I resented very much that there were gay Republicans using gayness as an accusation."

Others agree. "Outing is ethically justified in a situation where a gay politician is openly pursuing an anti-gay agenda and building a career on that kind of dishonesty," said Nan Hunter, director of the Lesbian and Gay Rights Project at the American Civil Liberties Union. "If, on the other hand, it's a person who is not anti-gay, and merely wants to be left alone, then it's wrong to force that person's private life into the open."

Ira Glasser, executive director of the ACLU, said the overall organization has no position on outing. He said Ms. Hunter's statements reflected her personal views and not necessarily those of the ACLU.

Among those who approve of outing, there is no agreement on what actions by politicians justify exposing them. An array of issues — appropriations for AIDS research, efforts to exclude homosexuals from teaching or being foster parents, and many others — may be invoked.

An Incident in Illinois

Some members of the group ACT UP, which has staged protests in its efforts to focus attention on AIDS, demonstrated with pickets near the home of an Illinois politician who they said was homosexual.

The politician had "acted poorly" on AIDS issues, said Daniel Sotomayer, who participated in the demonstration, "so that was good justification for trying to bring him out."

He added, "We'll leave them alone, as long as they vote well on our issues."

Some homosexuals contend that outing should not be limited to politicians, or even those secretly gay people who have spoken out against homosexuals. They argue that prominent business people, writers and athletes who hide their sexuality are depriving gay people of role models.

When *OutWeek* recently published an article declaring as homosexual a famous businessman who had recently died, several readers wrote in to applaud. "He was a powerful person," one reader said, "and it must be reported to the public that such individuals can also be homosexual, whether we think they are good representations of homosexuals or not."

Another reader, adamantly opposed, pronounced the article "the sleaziest piece of tabloid trash disguised as journalism I have ever encountered," and asked, "Who are you to humiliate his family and destroy the memories they might have had of him?"

Gay people who reject outing say that "coming out" is a personal decision, and that forcing sexual disclosure can imperil gay people who have remained silent for self-preservation.

"It's a technique fraught with danger," said Linda J. Yanney, cochairwoman of the Iowa Lesbian and Gay Political Caucus. "We should not lower our standards by resorting to the same kind of invasive behavior that anti-gay and -lesbian people have employed for so long. Simply because a Congressman or somebody else has betrayed the ethic does not give us a mandate to betray the ethic. And that ethic is that we protect each other."

Staking Out Middle Ground

Mr. Bray, of the National Gay and Lesbian Task Force, said he supported "the middle ground in this debate," a tack based on personal suasion.

He cited as an example a Congressman he observed one night in a gay bar, dancing with a male friend. The politician had recently voted against gay-rights legislation.

Without causing a ruckus, Mr. Bray said, he approached the man, introduced himself and asked the politician to reconcile his vote in Congress with his presence in a gay bar.

"I privately confronted this member of Congress and as a gay man, I talked to him about the damage he had done," Mr. Bray said. "It worked. The next time around, we got his vote. And he's voted right ever since."

Others, like Mr. Rotello, express concern about such quiet lobbying: "We should not use it as a weapon. We should simply be open about it. We can talk about all the other things about the life of a famous person. Why not homosexuality?"

Antsy Closet Crowd Should Think Twice
Mike Royko
(*Chicago Tribune*, April 2, 1990)

Some militant homosexuals have come up with a new idea for improving their self-esteem, increasing political power, exaggerating their importance and getting themselves invited on TV shows that are in need of addle-brained guests.

These militants claim to know the identity of many homosexuals who go through life posing as heterosexuals. In other words, those who choose to stay in the closet.

But the militants want them to come out of the closet, whether they want to or not, and become visible members of what is known as the "gay community."

At this point, I have to say that I've never really understood the definition of the "gay community." Presumably, some unemployed gay drug addict would be a member of this community. So would a wealthy gay polo-playing socialite. But other than how they choose to use their sexual appendages, I don't see that they have much in common, and it's unlikely the socialite would invite the gay drug addict to cocktails. So how close-knit a community can it be?

That question aside, the homosexual militants are now using something called "outing." This means that if they have reason to believe, or even strongly suspect, that someone is a homosexual, they reveal it in one of their newspapers, picket his residence and make his sexual preferences public. That's where the word "outing" comes from. They drag him out of the closet.

This has created a controversy, which delights the militant homosexuals. With bumbling Andy Rooney off the hook, things have been quiet on the gay front. There is always AIDS, of course, but it has slowly sunk into the consciousness of most Americans that far more people die of cancer, heart disease and other afflictions. And that few non-homosexuals or drug-needle users are in danger. But when the

President makes a speech, you don't see many cancer victims showing up to screech that he is insensitive to their needs. Those who practice or favor "outing" provide two motives. One group says that it wants to punish secret homosexual politicians who are not sympathetic enough to homosexual causes. The other says that it wants to expose prominent, successful homosexuals to provide ordinary homosexuals with "role models."

The opposing view is that under our system of law, an American's home is his castle. Even a cop has to obtain a search warrant before barging in. So if a secret homosexual's home is his castle, his closet is a nook in his castle, and if he doesn't want to be dragged out of his closet, that's his right.

But the "outing" practitioners say that closet homosexual politicians are hypocritical and have no right to privacy. And that it is the duty of prominent gays to serve as "role models."

In other words, what they do might appear to be an invasion of privacy, but as the saying goes, you have to break a few eggs to make an omelet. Or, as Slats Grobnik might put it, you have to peel a few fruits to make a fruit salad. (Look, don't accuse me of being insensitive. You're the ones who are poking into someone's closet.) This controversy is stirring strong feelings and growing debate, but I can't make up my mind.

On the one hand, I believe that what a couple of consenting males choose to do with their genitalia is their own concern, so long as they don't do it on my front porch, in the company lunchroom, in the middle of Michigan Avenue or at home plate during the singing of the National Anthem. In other words, they should be discreet and respect the sensibilities of those who are indifferent to their leering, panting and moaning. After all, the rest of the nation doesn't hold parades and cry: "Impotent pride" or "Premature ejaculation power."

On the other hand, it might be interesting—at least for Geraldo and Oprah—to see what happens if the militants pursue their policy of "outing."

I would guess that what we'll see is a show in which the proud militants are sitting there with a few of those who have been dragged from their closets, and the conversation will go something like this:

"Bill, you were a successful corporate executive and a pillar of your community and had a wife and three kids before it was disclosed in the *Boys Will Be Boys News* that you secretly stopped for drinks and other activities at the Swell Guys Lounge. How has your life been affected by being dragged out of the closet?"

"Well, my wife was very understanding and said she would have her lawyer take only the house, the summer home, the cars and 90 percent of our savings, as well as full custody of my children.

"The CEO at my company said he is very understanding and said he would write a glowing reference letter to the school of hair styling of my choice.

"All three of my children are now in therapy. The last time I saw them, they said that I have been replaced as their role model by Chuck Norris.

"Other than that, things are going OK. I'm still a member of my golf club, although there is a debate whether my locker should be in the men's or women's locker room."

But are you more at peace with yourself now that you are no longer living a life of deceit, duplicity and sham?

"Not quite. But I'm approaching a feeling of tranquility and will be there after I make one more move."

What's that?

"When I shoot that little sumbitch that opened my closet door."

Is "Outing" Gays Ethical?

Randy Shilts

(*New York Times* op-ed page, April 12, 1990)

In more polite times, gay organizers and journalists generally agreed that homosexuals in the closet had a right to stay there if they didn't choose to publicly acknowledge their sexuality. It was an unspoken rule.

With the AIDS epidemic now causing a significant depopulation of gay men in major urban areas, however, the times have become less congenial for covert homosexuals. Both gay newspapers and militant AIDS activists have launched a campaign of "outing": publicly revealing the sexual orientation of people who'd rather keep it quiet.

The controversy over outing recently erupted in force when the sexual activities of a famous, deceased millionaire were documented in a New York City gay newspaper. Over the past year, various AIDS groups have also circulated fliers announcing that several national and local politicians were gay. They did this after the officials took actions that the activists considered inimical to the fight against AIDS.

For journalists and gay leaders themselves, these tactics present a panoply of ethical quandaries.

Most mainstream daily newspapers have refused to name those exposed in gay newspapers and AIDS protests. In most cases, this has made sense. The outings of politicians, for example, were based on nothing more than gossip and did not contain the factual substantiation that would warrant reporting in a legitimate news story.

Moreover, none of the politicians thus far exposed by outings have engaged in rabidly anti-gay politicking. By the standards of most journalists, such hypocrisy would warrant a public outing, because the politicians themselves would have already asserted that homosexuality was an issue that demanded intense public scrutiny.

The outing of the dead presents a different dilemma. There are no privacy issues here: under American law, the dead have no right to privacy. That's how it should be.

Some newspaper editors maintain that they would not reveal even a deceased person's homosexuality because they always refrain from discussing sex lives. But that just isn't so. In the most recent case, the late millionaire's heterosexual affairs with some of the world's most celebrated women were the stuff of news coverage for more than a decade. Many newspapers included the information in their obituaries.

It seems then that the refusal of newspapers to reveal a person's homosexuality has less to do with ethical considerations of privacy than with an editor's homophobia. In my experience, many editors really believe that being gay is so distasteful that talk of it should be avoided unless absolutely necessary.

This has left us with newspapers that often are more invested in protecting certain people than in telling the truth to readers. In Hollywood and New York, hundreds of publicists make their living by planting items in entertainment columns about whom this or that celebrity is dating. Many of these items are patently false and intended only to cover up the celebrity's homosexuality.

Moreover, many newspaper writers and editors know full well that this is the case and merrily participate in the deceptions. Editors who would never reveal a public figure was gay are routinely lying to their readers by implying the same person is straight.

It is in rage against this hypocrisy—and in desperation over the ravages of AIDS—that the trend of outing was born. In major urban areas across the country, the homosexual community must watch helplessly as AIDS decimates the gay male population. Meanwhile, just about every eminent body studying the Government's response to the AIDS crisis has agreed that it is woefully inadequate.

Just about everyone also agrees that the response to the epidemic is so pathetic because gay men comprise the largest population struck by AIDS—and gay men are largely viewed as degenerate reprobates. In truth, of course, lesbians and gay men are to be found among the most respected public figures in every field of American society.

Gay organizers hope that if more Americans knew this, the nation might see a better response to the AIDS epidemic. Fewer people might die. That's a major reason why outing started. That's also why it will become more pronounced, as more people die and frustration among AIDS activists grows.

At the same time, outing presents gays with their own moral quandaries. In outing politicians, gay activists often have acted more from vindictiveness over a particular vote than from a genuine desire to enlighten the public. Outing threats are political blackmail. And what happens if religious conservatives threaten to reveal a politician's homosexuality if he or she doesn't vote a certain party line? Outing is a powerful political weapon that can cut both ways.

Gay activists counter that young gay people have a right to role models of successful gay adults. That's true, but someone who is only public because he or she has been hauled from the closet is certainly no paragon of psychological integration.

As a journalist, I cannot imagine any situation in which I would reveal the homosexuality of a living person who was not a public official engaged in voracious hypocrisy.

Yet, as someone who has chosen to be open about being gay, I have nothing but disdain for the celebrated and powerful homosexuals who remain comfortably closeted while so many are dying. Most of these people have nothing to lose by stepping forward and they could do much to instruct society about the contributions gays daily make to America.

As I watch my friends die all around me, a certain part of me hopes against all hope that the outing stories now appearing in the press may do something to stop the avalanche of death around me.

IV. The Insiders' Debate:
Gay and Alternative Press

Stuart Byron, "Naming Names" (*Advocate*, April 24, 1990)

Michelangelo Signorile, ed., "Smashing the Closet: The Pros and Cons of Outing," a symposium (*OutWeek*, May 16, 1990) including:
Hunter Madsen, "Tattle Tale Traps"
Steve Beery, "Liz Smith Mon Amour"
Ayofemi Folayan, "Whose Life Is It, Anyway?"
Victoria A. Brownworth, "Campus Queer Query"
Andrew Miller, "Malcolm Forbes, Malcolm X and Me"
Sarah Pettit, "On Glamor and Parochialism"
Gabriel Rotello, "Tactical Considerations"

Michael Bronski, "Outing: The Power of the Closet" (*Gay Community News*, June 3–9, 1990)

C.Carr, "Why Outing Must Stop" (*Village Voice*, March 19, 1991)

Gabriel Rotello, "Why I Oppose Outing" (*OutWeek*, May 29, 1991)

Naming Names

Stuart Byron
(*Advocate*, April 24, 1990)

Since the birth of the gay-liberation movement 20 years ago, we gay journalists have adhered to a fairly rigid code of conduct on the matter of bringing people unwillingly out of the closet. With the possible exception of closeted political figures who were actively working against the movement (such as the late Terry Dolan and Roy Cohn), it was strictly verboten, an absolute no-no.

Not that a celebrity's coming out willingly wasn't something to be devoutly wished for. One famous role model, it always seemed to me, was worth five gay rights bills. In 1982 I told *American Film*, "I have this fantasy that this gay actor wins the Academy Award and the next day he gives an interview aimed for the front page of the *New York Times* in which he announces he is gay." But I—and every other gay journalist and editor—would have been appalled at the idea of bringing that actor out involuntarily.

"In terms of benign people who are just old-fashioned or protecting their careers, I don't believe in [bringing them out]," Vito Russo told a *Mandate* interviewer in 1987. "It's a moral issue. I believe in trying to convince them to come out. I don't think my purpose is served in exposing them. Also, because I still believe that the act of coming out is a personal political act, it loses its value unless you know why you're doing it. You have to have the courage to do it on your own; otherwise, what does it mean?"

Now this relative consensus has been shattered. Naming names—known as "outing" in *Time* magazine, called an "outage" by others, and termed "dragging people out of the closet" by an indignant columnist in the *New York Post*—is now all the rage in the gay press.

One of the prime instruments for this change has been novelist Armistead Maupin, who, in a series of interviews last fall related to the publication of his latest novel, *Sure of You*, named names and dared the publication to print his remarks. (Maupin has since declined to discuss the issue further, stating that he doesn't want to be labeled as an outing activist.)

Far more publications than I would have expected met his challenge, including the Washington-based *Lambda Rising Book Report*, Los Angeles's *Frontiers*, San Francisco's *Sentinel*, Philadelphia's *Au Courant*, Miami's *Weekly News*, *El Paso Style* and Chicago's *Outlines*—all gay community papers. Mainstream papers have also recently gone to

233

press with feature stories on the outing issues, although none have gone as far as the gay press in naming names.

In a separate development, the New York gay weekly *OutWeek* last summer ran "what is apparently a list of allegedly closeted homosexuals," as Rex Wockner (in a triumph of legalese) put it in a story in the September issue of *Outlines*. Titled simply "Peek-A-Boo" (and explained nowhere in the magazine), the August 7 listing of 66 names was followed on September 11 by "Peek-A-Boo II," consisting of 31 more.

Robert W. Peterson, the *Advocate's* western regional news correspondent, told the *Los Angeles Times* in a March 22 story on outing that "there's going to be an incredible reaction within the gay community at these tactics and their destructiveness. There's nothing to be gained from outing. And the public at large will never respect a group of people that cannibalizes its own."

But others would disagree.

A Tragic Dilemma

"I don't believe in the age-old code that one doesn't bring another person out of the closet without their consent," Maupin told *Lambda Rising Book Report*. "Career and money are no longer sufficient arguments when thousands of people are dying from neglect and outright abuse. The bottom line is: homosexuality is either OK or it's not."

Of the legal implications, he told syndicated gay writer Steve Warren, "Malice is usually required to prove libel. I would challenge anyone to find malice in my action, because I'm happy about being gay, and I celebrate other people that are gay."

But is there any moral difference between bringing out a celebrity and calling up the boss of some unknown and saying "Your employee is a faggot"? Yes, argues *OutWeek* editor Gabriel Rotello. "The trade-off you make if you want to be a celebrity, if you want to be rich and famous, is that you give up your privacy," he said. "Why is it OK to bring out Roseanne Barr as a woman who had an abortion in her youth, and OK to bring out Gary Hart as an adulterer, and not OK to bring out gays? Why is there a double standard? Why is it acceptable to open heterosexual closets but not homosexual [ones]?"

Every closeted gay celebrity would probably agree with the old gay-lib axiom that there would be no further need for gay liberation if everybody woke up tomorrow colored lavender. There's safety in numbers. It's being the first one out that's frightening, and that can destroy a career.

When people like me or Russo—or the editors of the *Advocate*—took the old-fashioned line, it was because we thought that people in the positions that really matter in this celebrity-driven culture—big movie stars, big politicians, big business executives—would come out one by one until the floodgates opened. But that strategy hasn't worked. After 20 years, almost none of them have come out. The bottleneck still remains stopped up. As the recent spate of tabloid stories on Malcolm Forbes proves, only death brings celebrities out of the closet.

Few would disagree that Rock Hudson's illness and death marked the turning point in opening up funding for and public sympathy to the AIDS epidemic. How many lives might have been saved had there been many more truly important uncloseted stars and athletes testifying before congressional committees and leading AIDS marches?

I used to think that "dragging people out of the closet" was unacceptable under all circumstances. Now that Maupin and *OutWeek* have made me rethink the question, I've moved somewhat to the left. I see the issue as presenting a tragic dilemma to the gay community and the gay press, and it is one for which every answer is equally troubling. No matter what position one takes, someone's going to get hurt.

Smashing the Closet
The Pros and Cons of Outing
Essays by:
Steve Beery : Victoria Brownworth
Ayofemi Folayan : Hunter Madsen
Andrew Miller : Sarah Pettit
Gabriel Rotello

(*OutWeek*, May 16, 1990)

NEWSFLASH: Outing Seizes America!

Not too long ago, some of us at *OutWeek* decided that we could no longer participate in helping rich and famous gays and lesbians stay in the closet. We felt an obligation to tell the truth.

In one such case—that of Malcolm Forbes—all of the editors of *Out-Week* decided that we would frankly discuss his homosexuality in the magazine. That cover story hit the stands three weeks after the famous multimillionaire died, and sent shock waves throughout the media.

Telling such truths is now called "outing," named, of course, by

heterosexuals who had to put a quick McDonald's-like label on our behavior. It's a term that suggests something negative; something active,
aggressive and evil. And it makes a silly metaphor seem only more
real. Lest we forget, there is no closet, no door, no hinges. There are
just individuals who've told a lot of people that they're queer, and individuals who've told fewer people that they're queer. And the whole
thing is pretty arbitrary. (How many people must one confide in to be
"out of the closet"?)

But we're stuck with calling all of this "outing," a term neatly coined
by *Time*. And we're finding ourselves in a raging, but productive and
much-needed, debate. This is a controversy that seems to have no
boundaries within a political framework. Even within that sliver of the
spectrum we call "the far Left," there are at least 20 different positions
about it, running the gamut.

The same is true here. Believe it or not, there is no official *OutWeek*
position on outing. As the following essays will show, editors of this
magazine have widely divergent views on the subject. To help clarify
all of the complex issues raised by outing, we asked them and other
writers from around the country to offer their diverse opinions on the
subject.

Though wide and various in their scope, all probably agree: Something big has happened—something from which there is no turning
back. As some have said, "The genie is out of the lamp." And, as for
myself, I think it's all exciting, wonderful, fabulous, powerful,
progressive and truly great.

But that's just me.

—Michelangelo Signorile

Tattle Tale Traps
Hunter Madsen
(*OutWeek*, May 16, 1990)

Once during my book tour last summer for *After the Ball*, a reporter
posed a question that stopped me flat. He said Armistead Maupin had
suggested this question to ask me: If I possessed a big, thick computer
list naming every gay person in America, would I be willing to *publish*
that list for straights to see?

The idea had appeal. Isn't it publish or perish, these days? Doesn't
my own book, in the macho cause of political pragmatism, urge every
gay American to leap from the closet, and pronto? Wouldn't the sheer

bulk of the homolist instantly add heft to our demand for civil rights? Wouldn't the list sextuple my prospects for a date on Saturday night? Wouldn't it be heroin-pure pleasure to rout all the gay community's sneaky cowards, quislings and hypocrites at once? Isn't the list already familiar, anyway, to gay gossips far and wide?

I answered each of these questions to myself with a qualified yes. But I told the reporter *no*, I simply couldn't publish the homolist.

Since last summer, the idea of gay-listing has been rechristened "outing" and retrofitted with several rationales. Outing has attracted a noisy gang of tattlers who've gone rampaging through others' closets, looking for frightened queers to drag into the icy spotlight of public bigotry, where they'll either learn to like it or else die of exposure.

I still think outing is wrong and impractical, in nearly all cases. In *After the Ball*, we make it Rule Nine of our preferred social code for gay America: "I'll encourage other gays to come out, but never expose them against their will."

Why not? To see what's wrong with tattling, let's start with the case of closeted gays who are not public figures, then consider those who are.

Exposing the Privates of Private Figures

No evangelist is more heedlessly dogged than a new convert. Some gays—particularly the recently arrived—have found it such a relief and joy to come out of the closet that they simply *insist* upon the same for all their gay acquaintances. No more hiding for them . . . or anyone else! If straights ask who's who (and sometimes even when they don't ask) these gays lunge to clue them in. Top of their tattle list: closeted gays they especially like, and those they particularly despise. I'm troubled by such disclosures for four reasons.

(1) Being out is good, but coming out is better. We must cherish the process of coming out. No gay person should deny another the incomparable, irreplaceable, once-in-a-lifetime opportunity to come out of the closet under his or her own steam, as the fruit of deep personal reflection, courage and conviction. For each individual, self-confrontation runs by its own internal clock; to the exasperation of onlookers, the moment of truth is often evaded or postponed for months, years, a lifetime. But, for many a closeted homosexual, the moment does eventually arrive when she steps forward to affirm her own character openly, and thereby becomes the author of it. This rite of passage is far too important to the development of a positive gay identity for

someone else—some venal or irrepressible blabbermouth—to callously preempt it, to steal it away.

(2) To be closeted is bad, but to be outed can be worse. Being flushed into the open by others before one is ready—before one has overcome shame and guilt, before one has constructed a solid personal alternative to society's mores—can crush a person. Indeed, the effect is doubly crushing because one has lost forever, at that terrible instant, the single thing that makes coming out socially bearable: the dignity one may claim from having at least *chosen* to come out, chosen to be different.

And, of course, when you take it upon yourself to force others out of the closet you may wreak havoc in unintended ways as well. Your intentions may be good, but your timing atrocious. Your high-handed intervention might expose them to real hardships and discrimination that they should have had a chance to weigh for themselves—keeping in mind, after all, that coming out isn't *everything* in life. Or you might prematurely pigeonhole a bisexual as a homosexual—in the entire town's mind—before he himself had decided against the option of living a straight lifestyle.

(3) It's better to live in a society that respects your right to privacy than in one where the world is a fly on your bedroom wall. Exposing the private sex lives of others to public rumor, and asserting that it's perfectly fine to do so, is a needlessly risky strategy for gays. Here's why: For decades, gays have been squawking, in courtrooms and to the press, that what they do in bed, and with whom, isn't anyone else's business; that sexual activity among consenting adults should enjoy a special right to privacy—implicit in the Bill of Rights—that bars scrutiny and interference from society and the state.

I happen to agree with those squawkers. But our benighted Supreme Court does not: It doubts both the notion of a "constitutional right to privacy" and our claim that gay sex is protected by such a principle. Consequently, the right to be left alone in sexual matters will not be enforced from the top down in America. This means that a tolerant respect for sexual privacy can only be cultivated—by gays, if no one else—from the bottom up, among the citizenry itself. Yet how can we hope to teach straights to mind their own damned business when they see us relentlessly sniffing out one another's homosexuality and then squealing to the neighbors?

Ironically, this recent appetite for outing other gays "for their own good, and ours" takes its meddlesome spirit from the conservative contagion of our times. As the late Henry Fairlie observed, "America too is becoming a nation of informers. We are encouraged to go around

checking on everyone else's eating, drinking, smoking, sexual procliv-
ities, and general hygiene." (Alas, as co-author of a book that pokes
and prods the gay community's welfare without mercy or restraint,
I'm in no position to press this point too far!)

(4) It's better to live in a gay community that operates on mutual
trust rather than mutual finking. This point is simple but important:
what kind of gay subculture do you prefer to live in—one with an atmosphere of trust, or one of gimlet-eyed suspicion? The latter is what
develops when everyone is outing everyone else.

Not all gays can or will come out fully at the present moment, so
I'd rather that our demimonde continue to be a refuge for them; an in-
viting place where they can let their hair down and dance, confident
that the waltz is *entre nous*. This goes for closeted gays both famous
and unknown; as a rule, their secret should be safe with us until they
deem otherwise.

Going Public about Public Figures

I have detailed at length the demerits of outing private figures for a reason. Many readers would quickly agree that snitching on other hap-
less nobodies is mean, pointless and bad for the gay community in the
long run. On the other hand, they feel that exposing the sex lives of
famous people—who, after all, live in a fishbowl already—is somehow
more acceptable.

Their distinction is callous, as can now be seen: My four complaints
still apply. The outing of closeted celebrities can—as with the rest of
us—rob them of that precious, irreplaceable chance to grow personally
by coming out. Outing can damage them emotionally and materially.
It dramatically undercuts the gay community's claim that sexual
preference should be a strictly private, not a public, concern. And it
fans the atmosphere of whispering mistrust within the gay community.

The benefits of outing big shots must, therefore, be so very compelling that they can outweigh these hulking drawbacks. Are they? Consider the common rationales.

(1) Young gay people need positive role models, so famous people
should be outed if they haven't the civic decency to come out on their
own. Gabriel Rotello, the editor of this journal, recently justified outing for the *New York Times* in this way: "It's taken for granted that other
minorities deserve to have role models, so why not gays?"

The only possible reply is yes, gays *should* have their own uncloseted role models, and one wishes that the nation's many covertly

gay "success stories" had the gumption to do the right thing, drop their elaborate covers and come clean. But a positive role model who has to be outed simply isn't one! Closet cases—however accomplished they might otherwise be—hardly set a good example for young gays once they've been exposed as cowardly lions.

Next, think of the impression outing makes on the general public. After centuries of straights bullying and queerbaiting homosexuals, now gays are turning *each other* in. The image of homosexuality as a furtive, sick, shameful thing is amply reinforced by the spectacle of otherwise prominent closet cases being driven out from their dark hiding places into the blinding light of day, only to suffer (as they usually do) an immediate fall from public grace. Role models, indeed.

(2) The straight press's double standard against reporting the homosexual intimacies of celebrities should be smashed. Here's a truly peculiar argument, again issued by Rotello: "The media talks about the private lives of famous people in great detail. But when it comes to somebody being gay, there is a code of silence . . . because being gay is perceived . . . as just about the worst thing somebody can be. And by imposing this code of silence, we are perpetuating that notion." In other words, if the press is going to descend to trash-tabloid standards by invading the sexual privacy of straights, then it darn well ought to do the same for closeted homosexuals—with the gay community's help, if necessary. Evidently, to paraphrase Oscar Wilde, the only thing worse than being talked about is *not* being talked about.

Now, this reasoning is so patently cockeyed that, if you can't already see the problem, I'm not sure I can explain it to you. Certainly, the more the straight press discusses gay issues in a matter-of-fact way, the more desensitized the public will become on the issue (my book speaks at length about this process). But deliberately encouraging the trampling of gay people's privacy rights just to serve this purpose is ill-advised. Might it not make more sense to encourage media discussion of gay *issues* instead of gay personalities?

Moreover, the press never treats the stories of forcibly outed celebrities in a matter-of-fact way: It's always a sensational scandal! And who really believes the press observes a double standard nowadays, anyway? The prestige press still considers celebrity sex lies basically off-limits—being the stuff of libel suits—and so declines to monger straight or gay tattle. The tabloid press, on the other hand, digs into both with gusto. (Just check out the tabloids' recent exposés on Forbes, Chamberlain and Schwarzenegger.)

Speaking of Forbes, I should add in passing that I'm less distressed by the outing of deceased celebrities than of living ones. In the case of the dead, of course, our concerns about the heartache, stunted personal growth and career damage that outing can cause are moot.

(3) The more gay leaders who are out, the more powerful the gay movement becomes. This is true, and only sometimes, if the famous gay person has come out under his or her own steam—as in the case of Congressman Barney Frank. My own guess is that outing prominent gays will, by embarrassing them and rendering them targets of bigotry, tend to diminish their power within the mainstream and marginalize their position. We'd never wish to do that to the gay community's closeted but otherwise supportive *friends* in government—who can, perhaps, do us more good than harm by remaining undercover for the time being. On the other hand, those conservative creeps who acted as our enemies before their outing will have little reason (or power) to help the gay community thereafter—Robert Bauman's example notwithstanding.

(4) Some closeted enemies of the gay community must be neutralized through exposure. Outing does have its merits as a form of political castration and psychological terrorism, but this is a dire remedy to be reserved for the most diabolical hypocrites, which are few. I have in mind those cases where one observes a consistent pattern of malignant attack on gay rights and interests, by someone who—in his private hours—enjoys the gay life he publicly abhors.

But resort to outing in these instances entails setting aside our general ethic of privacy in order to attack another for lacking such ethics. This contradiction Barney Frank deflects well: "There is a right to privacy but not hypocrisy. If politicians are gay or lesbian and then use that against other people, they have forfeited their right to privacy."

Even so, this tactic puts us on a slippery slope to a bad habit of coercion, and validates the kind of exposure-blackmail long favored by the other side. First, you'll out a public figure only for being aggressively anti-gay; next, for supporting a gay civil rights bill only tepidly; and eventually, for taking conservative stands deemed "politically incorrect" on all manner of issue within the Rainbow Coalition. That goes much too far.

Outing's Last Inning

What, in the end, is behind the outing craze (apart from the gay intelligentsia's perennial need for something new to bicker over)? A big part of the answer, as Randy Shilts noted some time ago, is AIDS. Frustration over failure by the nation's governmental and commercial elites to assume full leadership in fighting the disease has boiled over, first, into rancorous public demonstrations—ACT UP-style—and, lately, into the threat of outing gay leaders who presumably could do much more. As an expression of valid rage, then, one must grant outing its share of moral justification even though it is impractical and ultimately self-defeating.

My hope and expectation is that, within a decade, the outing debate will be swept into utter irrelevance by a sea change in the sheer number of gays, in places high and low, who surge out of the closet. For it won't be long before the real benefits of being openly gay outweigh the perceived costs. Even now we are close—perhaps *very* close—to tipping the scale in that direction. In the meantime, may the bitter tacticians of outing do nothing that inadvertently makes coming out seem more frightful than it actually is.

Liz Smith Mon Amour

Steve Beery
(*OutWeek*, May 16, 1990)

Take it from me, an experienced "outer" who's been telling the truth about closeted celebrities for years now. Outing is a tactic whose time has come. But I'd like to step back a minute and explain what it is we're talking about here.

Editorials from coast to coast have tried to cast the outing debate as a battle between the gays. It's more accurately characterized as a battle between the mainstream media and those of us who feel they've been allowed to get away with telling lies for far too long.

A staggering double standard exists. We're invisible and the irrational fear of homosexuality has resulted in a massive conspiracy of silence. This outing controversy will be valuable even if it only alerts the press that we expect more—more than the lies they've deliberately manufactured, more than the contempt, the dishonor and the public indifference they've condemned us to.

Since the dawn of time, we've talked amongst ourselves about who is and who isn't, and nothing is going to prevent us from continuing to talk. What's at stake here is what the press is willing to print.

Why is homosexuality the only thing we aren't allowed to write about? Drug addiction, childhood sexual trauma, teenage abortions, rape, incest and patricide are the lifeblood of popular journalism. The columnists never demand privacy for Marla Maples or Donna Rice, both of whom were "private citizens" before everybody got curious. The private lives of Roseanne Barr and Elizabeth Taylor are laid more open for public consumption than the Freedom of Information Act. But dare to tell the truth about Malcolm Forbes, like my colleague Mike Signorile did, and every commentator comes up with a two-bit reason why society is supposed to be better off not knowing.

The principle is really very simple. Either being gay is OK or it isn't. And allowing homosexuality to take its place as a normal part of the human sexual spectrum requires ceasing to treat it as a dirty little secret.

Outing is nothing new to me. I first took Liz Smith to task in October 1984, in my film column in the *Advocate*. She had expressed disgust at Harvey Fierstein for thanking his lover on the Tony Awards show, all the while continuing to report such unlikely romantic pairings as Tommy Tune and Twiggy, and Richard Chamberlain and Linda Evans. I couldn't believe her hypocrisy, and said so.

Defending her position, Smith wrote, "May I ask who are you to judge what Tommy Tune and Twiggy are doing with their lives? Their romantic involvement happened to be very real while it lasted. It amazed everybody I knew. I certainly would have been remiss not to write about it when they were all over New York entwined, clutched in each other's arms and she was living in his apartment, madly in love with him." I need hardly add that this sense of astonishment never found its way into print.

But I must have hit a nerve. This was better dish than any Liz Smith column I'd ever read. "Richard Chamberlain and Linda Evans *do* go out together," she concluded. "I have no idea what they do or don't do in their private moments. I don't believe I ever said they were madly physically in love because I don't know. Do you? . . . Don't these people (even or especially the gay ones) have the right to change their minds, experiment, practice bisexuality or fake it? . . . I like to let my intelligent readers draw their own conclusions about the depth, sincerity and veracity of public liaisons. I am evidently not so judgmental as the *Advocate* of these things."

Not judgmental? By her own admission, Smith prefers reporting "changed minds," experimentation and bisexuality—however "fake"—to telling the truth about gay men and women.

Smith was doing what she's done all along: keeping the lid on, covering for her friends, conveniently reporting heterosexual "dates" to help mask the truth, which is that many of these actors and actresses, directors and movie stars—popular celebrities who enjoy the world's acclaim—are gay and lesbian.

I challenged her again the following year, when she insisted on having the last word on the Rock Hudson story. She wrote that she deplored the "media barrage" surrounding Hudson's illness, and revealed that she had once dreamily doodled "Mrs. Rock Hudson" in the margins of her notepad. I wrote that that particular column was nothing less than high camp to those who knew Smith personally.

This brought another, even more irate letter. "How dare you call my deep inner feelings about Rock 'high camp'?" she fumed, "I certainly was not part of any 'conspiracy' to misrepresent his sex life. I knew him very well for many years and he never once said anything about it to me or anyone else I knew. Was I supposed to repudiate his own position publicly? How well did *you* know Rock?"

Well enough to have been cruised by him one afternoon in 1980, at his house on Beverly Crest Drive. Was Smith honestly saying she hadn't known he was gay? I couldn't believe how ridiculous the woman was making herself. But she was caught, poor thing, and still hasn't figured out how to extricate herself.

It starts, Liz, with telling the truth.

Back came word from the *Advocate*. Smith's second letter had been opened by the editors before they forwarded it. I was bluntly told to lay off. Was there really any compelling reason for attacking . . . (gasp) . . . Liz Smith? The editors claimed that the kind of stuff published in gossip columns was too insubstantial to make a fuss about. And they didn't feel comfortable printing her letters, since she had written to me directly rather than to the *Advocate* letters page.

It was clear to me then that the gay press was neglecting its responsibility. This is an issue that needs to be discussed thoroughly, because the lies have been mounting for so long they're accepted without question. But no editor in the world wants to let us. Even the gay ones. Even those who claim to represent the gay press.

I knew some background that the *Advocate* didn't. Years earlier, back in 1981, I'd transcribed an interview with Smith for *Interview* magazine. She'd been interviewed at her Manhattan apartment, and on the tape her roommate, the archaeologist Iris Love, could be heard making comments in the background. But Smith trusted us to play by the same rules she applies to her own reporting. She automatically assumed that either I or the editor at *Interview* would discreetly edit Love out of the piece, to make it appear as though Liz lived there alone. She was right.

In the intro to that particular piece I went so far as to call Smith "America's best-loved gossip." The crazy thing is, at the time, I believed it.

What all this boils down to is the overwhelming hypocrisy of the press, and the double standard that keeps us invisible. Smith's favorite lament is "little, powerless me." If she really believes this, she underestimates herself and the power she wields. Those closeted lesbian and gay columnists play into the prejudices of their homophobic editors. Together, they keep the power structure firmly in place. They have the final say on how gay the world appears to be at any given moment.

Self-censorship is an odious instinct. Gay people do it all the time, whenever we decide to blend in and disappear. I was guilty of it myself, by editing Iris Love out of that interview.

The real question is: Who's writing journalism? Reporters or PR flacks? So much space is given over to promotion that we've turned into a nation of unpaid press agents, eager and willing to perpetuate the lies of the rich and famous, all for the sake of somebody else's "career."

There's a reason we're the most despised minority on the planet. Too many people, of all ages, in all walks of life, still don't know of anyone who's gay. We're either perverts and child molesters or nameless, faceless "gay militants," marching in the streets, wearing dresses when we're happy and throwing things when we're mad. We're repeatedly told we're making too big a deal about sex when what we really should be celebrating is our right to privacy.

Ask the press to take responsibility for their conspiracy and they get sanctimonious in a hurry. The *San Francisco Chronicle* declared in an editorial last month that outing goes against traditions of sexual privacy. The *Chronicle*'s editors say outing will result in an abridgment of liberty similar to that seen in Nazi Germany, where citizens were required to spy on their neighbors.

This is patently absurd, and the *Chronicle* knows it. What they're trying to do is codify a system that says Malcolm Forbes can be rich and powerful as long as he shuts up about being queer, and the "gay militants" will remain powerless because we insist on telling the truth.

What's needed is a test of the libel laws. When I say, as I do often, that someone is gay, I say it without malice. I'm gay myself, and I'm tired of being defined in terms of other people's prejudices. Most editors and publishers honestly believe that homosexuality is too disgusting to be written about. If you're famous enough, you're made an honorary heterosexual.

Since the burden of proof has been handed to us, I mean to make the most of it.

Those opposed to outing say we're defeating our own purpose. They say we should be celebrating our right to privacy, that outing breeds sensationalism, that those who are brought out aren't good role models anyway. And my favorite excuse: that prejudice is so deeply entrenched, there will always be someone, somewhere, who will rabidly hate gay men and lesbians.

What? Our hatred of this system of lies isn't enough? We're supposed to internalize the moral outrage of our enemies? I frankly don't care about role models being acceptable when we're fighting total invisibility.

The privacy argument is a lot of hot air. I have too much respect for the men I've loved—several of whom are now dead—to represent myself as anything less than what I am. Showing the world who we are will only humanize us, and we've been denied humanity. How often have you seen this photograph: two men, holding hands, shot from behind so their blue-jeaned butts show instead of their faces? This is the "acceptable" public image of homosexuals. It's easier to hate a cipher.

Is outing "ethical"? Since when are ethics dragged in to excuse lying? Where are the ethics of the press, in distorting the world to fit their image of reality? How ethical is it for Representative Dannemeyer to squelch a federal report showing that gay teenagers are three times more likely to commit suicide than straights, just because it doesn't jibe with "family values"? How ethical is it for Senator Helms to try to water down a badly needed hate crimes bill with an amendment that once again adds insult to injury by further depersonalizing gay men and women?

Where are ethics when the murderer of a gay man can get off on the "homosexual panic" defense—claiming that being cruised by another man was so terrifying, the only natural response was to kill him?

Wake up, folks. They're using their unfamiliarity with us as a club to beat us with. And when we try to declare ourselves, they lecture us about ethics. It's long past time to rip the closet doors off the hinges and let the world see who comes tumbling out.

Once you announce yourself, it ceases to be news. I'm just back from London, where I witnessed this principle in action. Some close friends of mine, frustrated by the abridgment of liberties that the Thatcher government is getting away with, have come out of the closet in a big way. What's more, they're actors, members of the profession Liz Smith has put herself in charge of covering for. Watch out for Michael Cashman; he's a renegade on the subject. He wouldn't mind seeing pictures of every closet case in Parliament plastered on billboards all over Piccadilly Circus.

When Ian McKellen asked me three years ago if I thought he should come out of the closet, I sat up until four in the morning telling him why I thought he should. Today, the man who's acknowledged as the greatest classical actor of his generation says he's happier, both personally and professionally, than ever before in his life.

By seizing the initiative, you set the rules about how the world responds. This is what David Hockney and Christopher Isherwood did; it's what W. H. Auden and Tennessee Williams did. Liberace and Halston never figured it out.

For years I grew up thinking I was the only person in the world attracted to my own sex. And while I was never victimized myself, I can't help remembering the power that older, small-town homosexuals hold over terrified youth. The power comes from fear of "exposure." The old gay-boy and gay-girl network has a vested interest in keeping the scene illicit and underground. Otherwise their hold over the scared young kids would evaporate.

Similarly, many of our so-called "gay leaders" have been co-opted by closeted fags and dykes in positions of power. They take the Byzantine layers of hypocrisy for granted; they pride themselves on knowing how to navigate. How many times have you heard this one: "We're more effective working *within* the system." Nonsense. By remaining invisible, they're perpetuating the system.

All the smoke and hot air won't change the fact that it's time to be open about who we are. The time for timidity is past. The world is finally curious about us, and I plan to speak up both for myself and for those "brothers" and "sisters" who are doing their best to prove to the world we don't exist.

Running for cover seems especially cowardly today. Remaining hidden has bought us a government that feels no sense of urgency to cure AIDS. We still have lessons to teach the world, in compassion and caring that transcend archaic sex roles. We won't teach these lessons by hiding those we love and insisting on a right to a private life.

As long as Eddie Murphy can insult "faggots" in front of an audience of millions, I don't feel timid about questioning the sexuality of Barry Diller, the man who greased the skids at Paramount for Murphy's rise to the top.

As long as there's such a thing as the "homosexual panic" defense — as long as they can kill us and get away with murder, as long as our very unfamiliarity is used to condemn us — I don't feel bad about doing my best to familiarize the public with homosexuality.

And I'm not alone.

Whose Life Is It, Anyway?

Ayofemi Folayan
(*OutWeek*, May 16, 1990)

I was asked to write on the subject of bringing celebrities out of the closet, particularly those who have been in positions where their being openly gay or lesbian could have positively affected our lives, for example, the members of Congress who have felt compelled to vote in response to their own internalized homophobia or the recent decision by this magazine to expose the hidden homosexual life of Malcolm Forbes. I have a number of responses to this issue that have come screaming forth from my insides, all of them strongly opposed to what the media has exploited as the term "outing."

I don't think it is either appropriate or ethical to categorize people on the basis of their prominence and then subject them to treatment that is somehow different or punitive. As a Black lesbian with disabilities, I have spent much of my life dodging the choices this society has historically made to treat me differently simply because I belonged to a group that was chosen as a target of oppression. The end never justifies the means, and how you do something is reflected in the result you accomplish. Using these same tactics of singling out someone for the supposedly more noble purpose of exposing that person as gay or lesbian is simply not acceptable.

While I recognize that powerful people have access to privileges that others lack, I do not think that gives us the right in a homophobic society to deliberately subject them to the oppression they have felt it essential to escape. The reasoning has been proposed that they have nothing to lose, precisely because they are prominent and bringing them out of the closet will not specifically jeopardize their income or celebrity status. The lessons of the McCarthy era and the guilt by mere implication that ruined the lives and careers of many alleged "communist sympathizers" are too fresh for me to assume that Jesse Helms and his hysterical response to "obscenity" (which includes homoerotic art) will not expand to a similar zealous purge of gay men and lesbians from public life. While I may personally resent the advantages that closeted celebrities enjoy, choosing to target them is not an appropriate way to address the inequities of privilege and class in this society. I see this argument as an example of the internalized homophobia that poisons our thinking, since no effort is made to equally disempower or jeopardize the status of renowned heterosexuals.

I also find spurious the argument that bringing celebrities "out of the closet" is important as a way to encourage young people to be open about their own sexual orientation. To me it is analogous to saying that one can learn a lesson about honesty by watching the police drag a shoplifter in handcuffs from a store. It is true that some deterrent factor may be imprinted in the subconscious. I would personally be more affected by the rare account of an individual who realized he or she had been given excess change or someone else's purchase and returned to the store to rectify this mistake. It is a far more powerful role model for someone to choose to voluntarily identify themselves as gay or lesbian than for someone to make that choice out of fear that it will be made for them.

I particularly resent that *OutWeek* chose to participate in what I view as journalism that smacks of sensationalism. When I walk in the supermarket and see a headline in one of the tabloids about Chastity Bono or Kristy McNichol or Richard Chamberlain being in a homosexual relationship, I assume that is probably true because of rumors that I have heard within the gay and lesbian community. However, I still resent the intrusion into those individual lives for the purpose of making a dollar. When I see the same type of headline about Malcolm Forbes in this magazine, I am no less convinced that the motivation is pandering to that prurient element in the readers who need a shot of sleaze in their lives. It offends me as a reader who is looking to the publications from within our community to model the values of pride and ethics that are lacking in the larger society.

My philosophy on this subject can be captured in the simple maxim "live and let live." I cannot decide what is right for anyone else, whether it be the choice to be gay or lesbian, the choice to be *openly* gay or lesbian or the choice to live the "lifestyle of the rich and famous." I don't want someone else making those decisions for me and will actively resist any attempts to do so.

Campus Queer Query

Victoria A. Brownworth
(*OutWeek*, May 16, 1990)

This year outing has become as popular as voguing. Everyone has a point of view on how or whether to do it, to whom, and the level of outrageousness involved. In the still-as-apathetic-as-the-'80s '90s, it's one of the few issues to goad liberal and conservative alike. Even college campuses are aware of outing, and students have big questions.

Last month I was a featured speaker at the Pride Week festivities of Haverford and Bryn Mawr Colleges. My topic was the subversion of gay culture by heterosexual society, and the talk was attended by a refreshingly large number of students—male and female, white and nonwhite in nearly equal numbers. Because much of the talk focused on denial of homosexuality—either by the heterosexual culture or by gay artists and writers themselves—many of the early questions in the period following the lecture focused on closeting and, by extension, outing.

So what do the students of two of America's most prestigious colleges think about outing? They love it and it scares them to death. After nearly an hour and a half of questions, the consensus was that outing is a good thing to do to people who are dead (Forbes), evil ([Father Bruce] Ritter and Roy Cohn) or working against us (oops, we haven't outed him yet) but not something to do to anyone gay who might ever do anything nice or helpful for other gays. Including themselves. For as one young Black woman said, "How can we be sure that as we're outing these people we can stay safe?"

In short, how do young gays and lesbians out the people they don't like—the gays they believe should be "exposed" for their internalized homophobia—while remaining safely cocooned in the closet themselves?

These students had serious questions about the long-range effects of outing and the ethics of it. They also wanted to talk about the techniques: how to out homophobic college administrators, for example. But the more questions they asked, the more apparent was their underlying fear: To participate in outing must you be out yourself?

I have been on both sides of the outing issue since before it was called outing. In the 15 years I've been writing for the gay and mainstream press I've had occasion to "out"—sometimes intentionally and sometimes by accident. When I was in my early 20s I had a lot of sympathy for closeted queers. When I hit 30 it stopped completely.

In telling these students the story of my own activism—being expelled from my high school for being a lesbian (in the enlightened '70s, no less); being arrested in "zaps" of anti-gay organizations, media and the like; being a token lipstick lesbian on television talk shows and basically taking on the day-to-day homophobia from a very public place—I also told them that I have no patience any longer for anyone in the closet. I told them that every gay man and lesbian woman who "passes" (and tries to) oppresses me further and reaps the benefits of my activism while hiding the strength of our numbers from the people to whom those numbers would make a difference.

When we talk about outing, what are we really talking about? We're talking about exposing the collaborationists, we're talking about exposing those who think they'll never get marched to the gas chambers because "nobody knows."

We know outing has arrived because it is suddenly a mainstream media topic. Outing has become a matter of "ethics" for the liberal left who liken it to McCarthy tactics and red-baiting; the neo-cons are gloating because they see it as the final feeding frenzy before we kill ourselves off. But outing is, in reality, a civil rights tactic. Radical yes, but then so was refusing to move to the back of the bus.

Talking with these students and listening to their fears of coming out, the threat they believe is posed to them specifically, individually, by the outing issue made me believe even more strongly in the need for just such tactics. Here are 18-, 19-, and 20-year-olds poised on the brink of the rest of their lives and they have the choice of being openly gay and facing the possibility of discrimination that is very real or hiding it and facing the reality of a double life for all eternity. Yet because they cannot look to the huge and compelling variety of gay and lesbian models—from the Hermann Goerings and Roy Cohns to the boys and girls next door—because they continue to be closeted from them, they think there is only one choice that makes sense. That choice is the one they see practiced most often: climbing into the closet, changing pronouns, faking heterosexuality and praying every day of their lives that no one finds out. This is the choice we offer our gay and lesbian youth.

Outing has become an essential in the quest for gay and lesbian rights, gay and lesbian equality. The big question is: Is outing ethical? Is outing politically correct?

These questions come from the same source as the oppression that fuels them. Let's reverse those questions and, instead of blaming the activists striving for equal rights, let's shift the blame to the self-proclaimed victims. Is it ethical to stay in the closet, pass for straight, assume the mantel of heterosexual privilege and enjoy its benefits while those who are openly gay suffer the oppression of their minority status? Is it ethical to turn a deaf ear to AIDS? Is it politically correct to ignore the fact that gays and lesbians have absolutely no rights under the law?

This is why outing cannot be equated with red-baiting and this is why outing should be welcomed rather than feared by the gay and lesbian youth of America. Outing represents a step toward freedom, a step toward acknowledgment of our diversity and our vast numbers. Gays and lesbians are the largest single minority in the U.S., yet because of the huge number who remain silent and closeted, we appear to the heterosexual society to be far smaller and, as a consequence, less strong, less politically powerful, less financially powerful, less self-determinant.

One student asked me if outing didn't represent a threat to the privacy of the individual. In one sense it does, most certainly, yet if we look at the history of oppression, the most virulent backlash has been directed toward those groups who were able to "pass" as members of the majority group—like the majority of Jews in Germany in the final days of the Weimar Republic.

Blacks, Asians, Hispanics and women cannot "pass." Gays and lesbians can. And as long as we perpetuate the theory that in passing we can augur change from within, we perpetuate the whole cycle of oppression. When we try to pass there is always the possibility we will be uncovered. Outing represents the refutation of that level of oppression, the oppression of passing. Passing only gives the illusion of allowing us access to power; yet by forcing us to pass, to be other than who we really are, the culture maintains its dominance over us. It has disallowed us ourselves.

One student asked what if we outed someone who really wasn't gay, wouldn't we destroy that person's life?

The answer to that is self-evident. As long as fear surrounds gayness, rather than affirmation, there will be denial. And until the gays and lesbians of the world begin to assume with the same level of arrogance that heterosexuals have assumed—until we operate on the assumption that everyone is gay until proven otherwise—we are not going to shift the balance of power.

There is a radicalism attached to outing that is different from any other gay rights activism. Because at the heart of outing is a refutation of internalized homophobia; participating in outing makes the statement that anyone can be gay and that as a group we can accept that. That's a major leap toward self-love and independence. And quite simply, until we believe and *act* like we are *worthy* of the same legal protections, rights and privileges awarded the heterosexual society, we won't achieve them.

This is the lesson I wanted to teach those students last month: That they are in charge of their own freedom. That outing should become a tool for them toward that freedom. That until heterosexuals can be presumed gay until proven otherwise, until being called gay isn't the worst thing that can happen to you, there is going to be a struggle. And the best way to participate in that struggle is to come out, acknowledge yourself and refuse to be placed in the closet.

We will not have equality and we will not have legal rights until the closet doors in this country—on every level—are ripped off their hinges and their occupants declared.

Malcolm Forbes, Malcolm X and Me
Andrew Miller
(*OutWeek*, May 16, 1990)

Since when did telling the truth become taboo?

As a journalist, I find it appalling that so many of my colleagues are tripping over each other to justify engaging in perhaps the longest ongoing media cover-up in the history of the fourth estate: hiding the homosexuality of the rich and famous.

It's as appalling as the libel laws that impinge on the free speech of lesbians and gay men by actually making the discussion of someone's homosexuality, whether actual or imagined, a crime.

Not that the topic itself isn't irresistible, particularly to writers in the mainstream media, who have, in their never ending search for a narcissistic approach to gay and lesbian issues, discovered one that dovetails nicely with their own world. Straight papers are only interested in outing because it means that some of them might actually be some of us. So don't expect to see anti-gay violence, or the battle against sodomy laws, covered with the reams of newsprint and hours of airtime devoted to outing any time soon.

But let's leave aside for a moment the objections to outing raised by straight people. Gay people as disparate and well-respected as National Gay and Lesbian Task Force chief Urvashi Vaid, Lambda Legal Defense and Education Fund director Tom Stoddard, Lisa Keen, editor of the highly acclaimed *Washington Blade*, and Richard Goldstein, arts editor for the *Village Voice*, have all gone on record opposing outing with well-defended, well-reasoned arguments.

Yet all are eager to abandon those arguments in the case of a closeted anti-gay public figure whose malice could be ended by exposing his or her true nature. Moral high ground or slippery slope? You decide.

I suspect that much of the opposition to outing coming from the lesbian and gay community, wreathed as it is in lofty arguments about the right to privacy, the higher need for gay unity and the dangers of appropriating the tactics of fascism, is actually a mask for deeper feelings that are no less legitimate, but are a whole lot less cool.

Fascinating, too, is the alacrity with which rabid conservatives have jumped on the anti-outing bandwagon. Always wary of finding myself in bed with the right wing (Catherine MacKinnon, are you reading this?), [I am made uneasy by] the vehemence with which the Mike Roykos and William Dannemeyers are proclaiming the right of gay people to stay in the closet.

But not as uneasy as [by] dragging people out, which for many gay people is in direct conflict with their picture of our community as a gentle, angry people, strumming guitars, perhaps blocking traffic when necessary, and never, ever ceding the perceived moral high ground to anyone at any time for any reason, not even the revolution itself.

In short, while it may be politically expedient, outing isn't a very nice thing to do. Indeed, I don't have an argument with the purported benefits of outing. I believe that once we're all out of the closet, and everyone knows that his six-term congressman and her favorite actress are gay, we will all be able to walk down the street holding hands without getting our guts stomped out. But the glee and vindictiveness that some bring to outing sickens me.

As a journalist working for the gay press for two years, I can personally appreciate the irony of closeted gay reporters who have landed jobs with well-paying, high-level daily papers speaking out against dragging people out of the closets that have enabled them to land those well-paying, high-level jobs that it will be a cold day in hell before I have access to because I can't (won't) go back into the closet. And that kind of pisses me off.

One of my gay colleagues in the mainstream press, whom I hold in high esteem, told me recently that while he would never out someone himself, "it doesn't mean that I wouldn't enjoy someone else doing it."

For me, I will never enjoy it—but I won't veil it in issues of right to privacy, right to secrecy or the right to anything else. There is no constitutional right to stay in the closet, and whether it's my gay colleagues at the *New York Times* or Malcolm Forbes himself, their closets are oppressing me and all our out sisters and brothers. And, in the words of Tracy Chapman, who has sung about revolution, "if not now, when?"

Nevertheless, I'm uncomfortable with the idea of a revolution by any means necessary, and in some ways the gay community is wrestling with the same tactical issues that our Black forebears struggled with in the tense days when both Martin Luther King and Malcolm X walked the earth.

The non-violence/by-any-means-necessary argument threatened to divide that movement, too. Perhaps it did. But when the Black Panthers got guns and followed the Chicago police around, it also moved their struggle for liberation and equality to a new, if uncomfortable, level. Now outing has shown the world that at least some of our numbers are willing to play hardball.

Journalists, who make careers out of printing secrets, should tell the whole truth, and I have no respect for reporters, including Liz Smith, who continue to lie about gay people. When a closeted lawmaker backs pro-gay legislation in the United States Senate, his or her sexual orientation is as much an issue as Justice Thurgood Marshall's race is when he writes an important civil rights decision for the Supreme Court. Or, for that matter, as relevant as Manhattan Borough President Ruth Messinger's heterosexuality [is] in the history of her pivotal support for New York City's lesbian and gay rights ordinance.

Most openly gay people remember the closet, where none of us asked to be, where society demanded that we stay. And we remember the terror of people guessing we might be gay, of our families finding out we were gay, of people telling other people we are gay as we teetered on the threshold of the very societal construct that tyrannizes our people through our own participation in it.

So while outing may be politically expedient and sometimes journalistically ethical, it is also undeniably painful, frightening and confusing for its targets. And while wrecking people's psyches in order to expose hypocrisy and tell the truth comes with a journalist's territory, I don't think it is ever something I will get used to, or take lightly.

On Glamor and Parochialism
Sarah Pettit
(*OutWeek*, May 16, 1990)

"Desperate times call for desperate measures," counsels the old chestnut. America in the early '90s is our desperate time, outing our desperate measure. It is appropriate that this issue should coalesce now and inevitable that the media be the place it occurs; our realities are focused by the lenses of TV and film and made audible through the radio waves. The time of disparate, contained discourse and morality is rapidly receding. As the seas on our political globe are made stormy by eyeballing from a bland lunar "spectatorship," manipulation of the means of communication is the order of the day. So the presidential debates are given a "spin"; so too do Gran Fury's campaigns toy with the images and language of popular culture.

High in the Hollywood Hills a languorous figure rests by a pool's edge. Her companion does laps in the azure water, the drift of the afternoon unchartable save the shifting shadow of palms. With all the effort she can muster, the languorous figure wipes a trace of sweat from between her Norma Kamali'd breasts. She is bored, bored by this outing business. "Fascists," she calls them, lunatic fringe desperados with pins at the ready. Ready to burst her bubble, Christian Lacroix, weekends in Gstaad, Spago and all.

But what becomes a queer star most? Not, as one might suspect, the closet, but rather that lofty ether somewhere beyond it. Being a gay or lesbian celebrity in the '90s is less the business of deep, dark closets than it is the reign of a subtle yet haughty club mentality. So Sandra Bernhard rolls her eyes, Pedro Almodovar becomes obtuse, John Waters hands Ricki Lake another cupcake. The articulate turn away, their mouths suddenly full of marbles. More often, they scoff. The question, they say, is irrelevant, parochial, literal minded, not to be dignified with an answer.

The question is, quite definitely, *not* irrelevant. But our attention to it is. "Role models," we cry, all the while feverishly hooking the cart before the horse. Outing is a red herring and those leading us with it are, unfortunately, too upwind to smell the rot. The gay and lesbian movement, having squeezed blood from stone for years, having sewn silk purses from sows' ears, having forged the dignity and strength we have with our own hands, ought to know better by now. Life, unlike theater, is sadly without a deus ex machina. In a time of great despair and exhaustion, as the hate crimes statistics rise and our friends die around us, it would be a relief to us all if there were one. The actuality is that our progress will be maddeningly slow. Activists of the '90s have learned that surprise demos change minds and agendas, but progress comes at a crawl with a lot of homework.

The notion that all we need is a rash of outing is wrongheaded. What happens once this invisible world is rendered visible? What happens when meat puppet matinee idol is exposed as pouting ponce? What transpires when leggy pop vixen is caught in a lezzie love-up? Not as much as we'd hoped, I'd venture. We are all perfectly aware that minority groups are not inured simply by being identifiable. Bigotry is not obliterated by having a witness. A glamor puss in Gaultier admitting to Sapphic digressions doesn't save a flat-topped dyke from a bashing on a dark street corner.

My question is not whether it is right or moral to dig through Tom

Cruise's trash can. My point is that I don't care if we come up with Crackerjacks or a copy of *Colt* magazine. My priorities are in finding the most expedient and practical political strategies for the future of this movement. My priorities are in recognizing the gay and lesbian heroes we already have. My priorities are, finally, in questioning the very construction and idolization of public figures. I would prefer to hand the youth of today a copy of *Giovanni's Room* or *Beebo Brinker* or *Nightwood* than a *People* article on Greta Garbo's secret life. I care more about my gay male peers educating themselves about the culture my sisters are building now than I do about them discovering that Liz Smith took her archaeologist to Tangiers. Are we so much in the twilight of reality that we dream of cinematic heroes who, skin all bronzed, pecs at the ready, sweep down and carry us off to a safer world? I ask that our movement recognize the fatuousness and danger of such fantasies. With our faces pointed towards the stars, are we missing the shifting sands beneath our feet?

Tactical Considerations
Gabriel Rotello
(*OutWeek*, May 16, 1990)

The unexpected emergence of the issue of forcing famous gays and lesbians out of the closet, or "outing," is causing us to reappraise basic assumptions about ourselves and our movement. For the first time, movement activists are declaring that powerful closeted gays, and perhaps by extension all gays, have an inherent obligation to their community. That obligation is, simply put, to come out.

Whether gay public figures have an obligation to the gay commons is at the heart of the outing debate. By proclaiming that they do, we redefine the concept of a gay and lesbian community. Because such an assertion presupposes that the gay community is a genuine, inescapable minority like the Black or Latino community, into which one is born, from which one derives advantages and disadvantages, and to which one owes inherent allegiance. It brands as immoral the attempt by powerful gays to escape the social penalties of homosexuality, and asserts a claim of moral kinship where none existed before.

Such an expected redefinition of gayness is being bitterly resisted by both straights who fear and loathe the concept of gays as a legitimate minority and by gays who are unprepared for the implications of such a redefinition.

Outing is subversive in other ways. It presumes that those who engage in frequent, voluntary homosexual conduct, whatever their state of political awareness, are by definition gay. This challenges a long-held philosophical conviction among many in the movement that being gay was different from being homosexual, that being gay was a political statement or a spiritual choice. Outers, by their actions, vividly reject the notion that being gay is a choice.

Outers are also declaring that the movement's four-decades-old strategic focus on the "right to privacy" has now become merely a quest for a right to secrecy, a right to hide one's homosexuality from a hostile world. Such a strategy, necessary as it once was to create the conditions whereby a gay community could come into being, is now destructive and reactionary when it conflicts with openness and honesty. Outing activists maintain that what homosexuals now need is the right to be openly gay, not the right to hide.

Outing is more than a response to frustration at the snail's pace and self-imposed limitations of much of the modern gay movement. It is also a tactic, a tactic which both proclaims a new reality and creates it at the same time. For by calling powerful closeted gays to account, such people have become accountable. In fact, by merely engaging in the outing debate, we alter forever the dynamic of the closet.

Gays who oppose outing cite many reasons, but their opposition essentially focuses on the brutality inherent in undesired exposure. It's a valid and humanitarian concern. By raising the stakes and calling for accountability, gay people are indeed bound to get hurt. This potential for hurt, especially to people who have not volunteered for the honor, represents a very uncomfortable escalation in a movement that has long prided itself on its gentleness. Many lesbians and gays, remembering their own pain at coming out and sensing the pain outing might inflict even on the famous or powerful, will never come to terms with the practice.

They don't have to. Logic dictates that if gays are a real, inescapable minority marching toward increasing self-realization *as a real, inescapable minority*, then such self-realization will inevitably assert itself as it has with every other emerging minority. As self-hate declines and self-awareness grows, demands that the powerful among us declare themselves will continue to increase. And the fact that such demands are easily enforceable by a simple newspaper headline means that outing is virtually inevitable.

The controversy surrounding outing is a reminder of how far we have to go in becoming a real minority, and how easily we have taken self-disrespect for granted.

For example, we live in an anti-Semitic and a racist society. There are very real penalties for being Jewish or Black. Yet it's inconceivable that Jews or Blacks would insist that their most successful members have an inherent right to actively lie, deny their own kind and pass for gentile or white. It's even more inconceivable that those minorities would demand that the press has a moral obligation to respect and reprint such lies.

Yet that is exactly what gays opposed to outing are arguing. Their excuses are numerous and obvious: "Outing can hurt a celebrity's chances to earn more millions," they say, "it doesn't produce valid role models," "it denies powerful people a chance to come out on their own," "it will divide us," "it will drive people further into the closet," "it's an invasion of privacy," "it's just plain embarrassing."

These reasons would be absolutely valid if gays had no obligation to their kind. They would be particularly valid if being gay were a choice, if our community wasn't a real minority which could exert claims of moral kinship, but instead a loose association one could join and leave voluntarily. Most straights, and many gays, think it is. If that were the case, the very idea of outing a millionaire or a senator or an archbishop would be immoral and indefensible. After all, by that definition, you're not gay unless you say you are.

But if gays in fact *are* a real minority, and if people who engage primarily in homosexual conduct are by definition members of that minority, such objections evaporate, as they would for any other minority. For no claim of expediency or embarrassment, privacy or financial gain, could ever excuse denying one's own kind and turning one's back on one's own people. Especially if by so doing one irreparably harmed one's people. No beleaguered minority, no threatened nationality, no oppressed religious group would ever respect such betrayal. Why should gays?

By accepting such betrayal, gays and lesbians have been demonstrating exactly how fragile our claims to minority status are. And by now rejecting the celebrity closet, we are finally asserting ourselves collectively as a true minority and contemplating ourselves as we really are in 1990. A people. A terribly oppressed people. A people who need visibility, role models and the power inherent in numbers. And a people who are being disclaimed, and thereby betrayed, by their most powerful members, those rich and famous grandees who deny us and hide from the consequences of their sexual kinship with us.

But even if all of the above is true and the gay community can now claim the allegiance of all its brothers and sisters, even those who would deny us, that still leaves these questions: Why? What is the point of outing? What is to be gained? And do the costs outweigh the benefits?

To answer, it's useful to look for historical parallels. They're not hard to find.

In 1959 it was social and professional suicide for straights to live in out-of-wedlock arrangements. Those old enough to remember know that "shacking up" was unacceptable to middle-class society. When a famous person like a movie star "cohabited" with a lover, it was covered up and ignored by the press; gossip columnists simply looked the other way. Such journalistic silence was the pillar of the double standard that then existed about a major facet of heterosexuality.

In the late '60s, however, things changed. Landmark Supreme Court decisions freed the press from the threat of libel suits. Writers, biographers and, especially, gossip columnists began honestly reporting the sexual lives and live-in arrangements of the stars. To a shocked public it suddenly seemed that practically everybody was "living in sin."

The celebrities thus "exposed" were outraged at this journalistic invasion. "Who are you in the press to violate our right to secrecy?" they and their lawyers argued. Some were financially damaged, as conservative producers and advertisers retaliated with moral indignation, particularly against the women involved.

But this flood of exposure to alternative domestic arrangements lubricated a glacial shift in public attitudes. Everyday people, liberated by the press from the hypocrisy of silence, reconsidered their earlier disapproval. The young, always eager to experiment with premarital sex, now pointed to movie stars and pop stars as sexual examples and role models. Parents, at first horrified, loosened up. Society grew tolerant. And finally the '50s "out-of-wedlock/living in sin" became the '80s "domestic partnership." Laws are now being passed giving legal sanction to relationships once deemed unspeakable. Celebrities, unwilling though they were, had taken the lead. Kids today can't even imagine how different things were for straights just 25 years ago.

Those of us who argue for journalistic honesty about gay celebrities feel that what happened to heterosexual prudery can now happen to homophobia. Once the press drops the double standard and the lies and starts dealing with gay reality, once Americans are confronted with thousands of famous, popular, respected gay notables, the world will change dramatically.

Conversely, homophobia will never disappear as long as the code of silence about real-life gays is maintained. As long as the celebrity closet is respected by the press, homosexuality will remain illegitimate, a shameful sad secret to be hushed up. To respect the rights of the celebrity closet is to respect homophobia. And like outing, such respect for the closet isn't just a philosophy, it too is a tactic: It creates and perpetuates the homophobic reality it reflects.

Paradoxically, those gay leaders opposed to "journalistic honesty" about famous gays universally agree that the world would be drastically improved if everyone famous were to suddenly come out. There seems to be no disagreement about that. Our leaders loudly lament that this hasn't even begun to happen 21 years after Stonewall. They wring their hands and talk of a little progress here, a bill passed there, one defeated somewhere else. They sigh and dream of a better world.

Yet outing, a tactic which could drastically hasten that better world's arrival, is something these leaders can't bring themselves to accept. Gay and lesbian leaders admit that openness is the cure for homophobia, admit that in outing they have it in their power to effect that cure, but then, alas, can't bring themselves to do it.

Why? Because, they say, outing is mean. Outing might hurt people. Because we don't want liberation on those terms.

The flaw in this argument is obvious: "We could spare millions of young and yet unborn gays and lesbians the agonies of growing up in a homophobic world," our leaders say, "but if it means that some powerful big shots might be embarrassed or hurt today, then it's not worth it."

Apparently, according to these leaders, it's more ethical to lie and thus perpetuate the wounding of millions than to tell the truth and free those millions, if that means a few VIPs get bruised. Why does the well-being of a few powerful celebrities overrule the salvation of millions? Why is this equation never expressed by the Tom Stoddards of the world?

The answer says more about the state of lesbian and gay leadership than it does about outing. Ours is a movement co-opted by well-intentioned gay conservatives who rely on networks of powerful closet cases for financial, political and organizational support. The self-perpetuating boards of major gay organizations, and the executive directors they appoint, have chosen to cooperate with the closet. Their very power base is threatened by any attempt to challenge the status quo. As such, they oppose outing as a direct threat to their "networks," their money and their "insider" status.

All social liberation movements need some insiders. But such insiders, while performing valuable clerical, legal or practical functions, generally oppose truly fundamental change. Fundamental change, after all, totally alters the framework in which insider relationships exist. Thus, when a liberation movement comes to be overwhelmingly dominated by insiders it ceases to liberate.

If nothing else, the outing debate has thrown the state of gay and lesbian leadership in 1990 into sharp relief. Those who are supposed to lead us into the future have fairly tripped over themselves to reaffirm the goals and tactics of the past. As the practice of outing becomes commonplace, and its revolutionary consequences become clear, the stage will be set for the next phase of our movement: the search for leaders who will lead.

Outing: The Power of the Closet
Michael Bronski
(*Gay Community News*, June 3–9, 1990)

Outing. First it was a verb, as in "to out someone from his or her closet." Then it became a media event as *OutWeek* magazine posthumously brought Malcolm Forbes from behind the closet door and publicly claimed him as a member of the gay community. Within weeks the practice became a cultural phenomenon. Joan Rivers kept mentioning outing with disdain on her television show in between grilling her guests about their personal lives; the *New York Times* published an op-ed piece by Randy Shilts, and William Safire explored the term's etymology in his *Sunday Magazine* column on language; the *Village Voice* ran an article by *OutWeek*'s Michelangelo Signorile defending his Forbes piece, which was then followed by a flurry of letters; *Time* threw in its two cents worth, and *Newsweek* did a full page news analysis, and most of the other straight media followed suit with their own pieces, never quite being able to decide if they were writing news, gossip or editorials.

Now the phenomenon seems to have escalated into a war. Gabriel Rotello, *OutWeek* editor, was physically attacked by an audience member on the "Geraldo" show; those claiming to be concerned with journalistic ethics have attacked outing—in no uncertain terms—as unethical; and heads of both local and national gay organizations are being besieged by reporters asking if the lesbian and gay community condones such a practice. That most skilled of noncombatant interviewees, Barbara Bush, has attacked outing: "I am not one of those people who believe in 'outing,' " she informed reporters recently. "I think there is no justification for that." Even the most innocent of gay gatherings has often become a battlefield as tempers flare, ideological lines are drawn, and serious arguing begins. And while it is unclear if outing is actually "in," there is no doubt that it is certainly hot.

But with all of the heat generated by the outing discussions, there is very little light forthcoming. The debate seems to be played out on the high emotional fringes, without political or historical contexts, and with little attempt to locate it in the actual—rather than the theoretical—world. The current wave of outing-as-political-act surfaced about 18 months ago when gay novelist Armistead Maupin— who has always placed a high value on *everyone* coming out—began writing articles in which he named famous closeted lesbians and gay men. A few gay papers printed the pieces; no straight papers would. Last June, when Republicans were gay-baiting House Speaker Thomas Foley, U.S. Representative Barney Frank sent shock waves through political ranks when he threatened to expose prominent gay Republicans. The gay-baiting stopped and Frank never had to show his cards.

Since that time, *OutWeek* printed its Malcolm Forbes story and has, sometimes expressly or in passing, mentioned the sexual orientation of such varied people as record industry mogul David Geffen and Greta Garbo. And ACT UP groups around the country have targeted officials such as Illinois Governor Jim Thompson and Republican Senator Mark Hatfield of Oregon, who they claim are closeted homosexuals with a history of voting against gay rights and progressive AIDS legislation. ACT UP members in Portland even altered a Hatfield campaign billboard to read "Hatfield, Closeted Gay: Living a Lie—Voting to Oppress." The gay Washington rumor mill, once filled with news of who was and who wasn't, is now buzzing with speculations about who is going to be brought out next. As one outing advocate pointedly put it: "Come out while you are still able to do it yourself."

Celebrities, whose lives have always been the basis for speculation, have also been touched by the debate. Richard Chamberlain recently drew ire when, after allegedly having come out in a French magazine, he allowed his press agent to deny the story.

The notion of outing as a political act did not originate with Maupin's articles, however. As early as 1972, writer and gay liberationist John Paul Hudson predicted/speculated in his 1972 manifesto/travel guide/history of gay life, *The Gay Insider USA*, that in the future a group of radical gays (known by various names including The Lavender Conspiracy, Operation Empty Closet and Mission: Possible) would launch a campaign to bring famous people out of the closet, either by persuasion or force. And although Hudson's nearly 20-year-old fantasy was not the blueprint for '90s outing, it speaks to the tension that has *always* existed between those who live openly lesbian and gay lives and those who remain closeted. There is no doubt that the emotional pain of the closet is also accompanied by considerable social privilege, and that this is going to engender anger and resentment.

This tension and anger is built into the very fabric of lesbian and gay life: the real pressures to remain closeted vs. the real pressures to come out. But because of AIDS and the increasing prevalence of conservative social policy (and when we are talking about access to AIDS treatments, *deadly* social policy) the stakes seem much larger: literally a matter of life and death. The anger that was once personalized or subliminal is open and seen as outrightly political.

One of the reasons that outing has been so difficult to discuss is that the straight non-tabloid press has, for so long, monopolized and distorted the very basic tenets of the debate. Whenever writers of the straight press have written about outing—and to the last one, condemned it—their arguments have been uniform. It is unethical, they claim, to bring people out of the closet because it is an invasion of privacy. What people do in bed is nobody's business. Even public figures deserve private lives. And many claim that printing information about someone's homosexuality will leave a newspaper open to charges of libel.

Such arguments may sound reasonable, but the reality of the actions of the straight press are so different and antithetical to both the spirit and the letter of their stated anti-outing stance that their "ethics" are nothing less than outright hypocrisy and duplicitous cant.

Although there is a general consensus in the press against outing, the fact is—as Kevin Cathcart of Boston's Gay and Lesbian Advocates and Defenders has pointed out—that almost *every* newspaper in the country does it, from the *New York Times* to the *Boston Globe* and most recently to the student-run *Harvard Crimson*. These papers have consistently printed the names and *addresses* of men who were arrested for sexual-related activities: certainly, a form of outing. And yet, while the apologists for media ethics decry the posthumous outing of Malcolm Forbes, they are silent on this.

But the hypocrisy about outing in the straight press goes even deeper than this obvious example. A person's homosexuality is often mentioned by the mainstream press when it wants to discredit a public figure. The *New York Times* had no trouble implying for years that red-

and queer-baiting McCarthy sidekick Roy Cohn was a homosexual, or mentioning in an obituary that right-wing fund-raiser Terry Dolan was gay. Yet no paper would ever print the rumors surrounding high-level presidential adviser Donald Regan or Nancy Reagan's best friend, socialite Jerry Zipkin.

The question of the newsworthiness of the private lives of public figures is a complex one, but the mainstream press has always maintained a double standard on it. The media have diligently imposed a complete blackout on all gay activity that was not of a damaging nature. On the one hand, it is fine to talk about the extraordinarily commonplace relationship problems of Donald and Ivana Trump and, on the other, never to mention Malcolm Forbes's (relatively open) gay social life. The press consistently covered up the widespread knowledge of Francis Cardinal Spellman's homosexual activities but was more than willing to broadcast the details of the early gay sex-related charges against Representative Gerry Studds. For the straight press, being gay has always been—and to a large degree remains—a dirty little secret only to be brought up in order to hurt people.

The notion of "privacy" that is so frequently used to denounce outing is one with very specific social parameters and uses. And while people always speak of "privacy" as a right, the actuality is that it is a form of protection for those with power: as a power broker in the straight media, you would want to protect the "privacy" of Cardinal Spellman, but not some man entrapped in a men's room. (The fact that doctors, lawyers and other professionals can very often bargain to keep their names out of the newspapers when they are arrested on morals charges only speaks again to the notion of selectiveness of "privacy.")

One of the more inventive and pernicious arguments for the "privacy" of sexual orientation is a comparison to rape promulgated in an article on outing by Suzanne Braun Levine in the *Columbia Journalism Review*. By comparing the disclosure of someone's sexual preference to that of the names of rape survivors, Braun Levine only reinforces the notion that gayness is a dirty little secret forced upon its "victims." (Coincidentally, this is the same argument used by the new "Today" show host Deborah Norville, to halt a dialogue on outing with guest Gabriel Rotello of *OutWeek*.)

Beyond Privacy: Gossip

But just past the boundary of the cultural notion of "privacy" lies the construct known as "gossip." "Gossip" allows the press an ethical trapdoor that gives the public access to the information in which they are truly interested: the unseemly, unvarnished "truth." But even in this idea of "gossip" there is a standard blackout on any gay information. Speculation on Liz Taylor's love life is open season in any newspaper, but speculation as to whom k. d. lang, John Travolta or Tracy Chapman may be dating is verboten.

This point was forcefully illustrated recently on an episode of Joan Rivers' morning talk show that focussed on gossip columnists: all of the dirt was being dragged out—the Trumps, the Helmsleys, Bess Myerson and most everyone in Hollywood. Suddenly Joan got very serious and said, "But sometimes people go too far. That New York paper [*OutWeek*] is saying those terrible things about a certain man who has just died, I won't even say his name [Malcolm Forbes], and it just makes me sick." This from a woman who built her stand-up comedy and talk show career recycling gossip and quizzing people on their personal lives.

Of course, Joan's message is clear and familiar: being gay is bad, it is a dirty secret, and it should be kept quiet. Positive gay sexuality is *never* a permissible topic in the mainstream media, not even as gossip. The irony of all of this, as pointed out by film critic Vito Russo in a recent letter to the *Village Voice*, is that the idea that someone's sexual activity is a private matter does not even apply to outing: "When we say someone's gay, we're talking about *sexual orientation*, not their sexual activity. It's not our fault that every time someone says *gay*, people think 'sex.' That's *their* twisted problem."

As constructed by the press—as well as the gossip network—the very fact of homosexuality is a problem, something bad, something to be hidden. For years the mainstream press has hidden behind the argument that to mention someone's sexual orientation would constitute libel. The concept of libel is based on the premise that the statement in question is both untrue and intentionally malicious. Recently, when Armistead Maupin has mentioned someone being gay or lesbian, he always points out that this is not an attack but a compliment. The eagerness of the press to hide behind the libel excuse only reinforces the overriding idea that there is never anything positive about being gay, and reinforces the blackout on open, positive gay visibility.

It is important to acknowledge the absence of lesbian and gay visibility in any discussion of outing. It is not just a lack of news coverage or a hesitancy to deal with gay issues, but rather a wholesale cultural attempt to conceal and lie about the existence of gay and lesbian people and culture. Outing does not occur in a morally, philosophically or politically neutral vacuum, but in a world that continually teaches people to hate homosexuality, to hurt homosexuals and—perhaps most importantly here—to hide and obscure homosexuality; to deny it both context and validity.

It is interesting that in all of the articles written about outing in the straight press, almost every one mentions that "there is an unwritten law among homosexuals never to bring anyone out of the closet." (One wonders where these reporters from *Time*, *Newsweek* and the *Wall Street Journal* had access to unwritten homosexual laws, but never mind.) And it is true that there has been a long-standing agreement among lesbians and gay men to keep a certain degree of secrecy—of protection—about their own. When I was coming out in the mid '60s, this was certainly an understanding that older lesbians and gay men imparted to me. But it is important to recognize that laws (written or unwritten) are socially constructed for a variety of reasons. It is also important to remember that this was not the only law. You were not to show affection in public. You were not to act too effeminate or too butch. You were not to be too obvious. You were not to talk about being gay. You were not to say anything against the straight world. You were not to complain about ill treatment at the hands of a hateful society. The list was endless. These were all unwritten laws and they existed for a very good reason: it was dangerous—physically, emotionally and psychically—to be known as a homosexual. It was called "living in the closet." And many times it devastated or killed people as much as if they had come out and been destroyed for it.

Sarah Schulman, in an eloquent letter to the *Village Voice*, stated: "To call [outing] an invasion of privacy is distorting and dishonest. Most people stay in the closet because to do so is a prerequisite for employment. Having to hide the way you live because of fear of punishment isn't a 'right,' nor is it 'privacy.' Being in the closet is maintained by force, not choice."

Because of gay liberation, most of these unwritten laws—a.k.a. repressions—have been repealed. Which is not to say that outing is fine or not without consequences, but the rules of 10, 20, 30, or 40 years ago are no longer the same. Gay and lesbian liberation has moved us forward, and it is this progress we must continue to chart, not what has been left behind.

So often it seems as though the discussion of outing in lesbian and gay social and political circles buys into the myths, mystifications and self-justifications that have been presented in the straight press. People don't seem to be addressing the complexities or the nuances of what outing is, or what it means in the context of movement history and politics.

And the politics of outing are complex. First of all, it is important to keep in mind that when we have spoken about outing we have actually been talking about a specific group of people. No one has ever suggested that grade school teachers, bus drivers and sales clerks be outed. The discussion has always centered on public figures, and then only on those members of Congress and state governments who affect public policy—as well as some celebrities who capture the public imagination. (This is especially true of celebrities. English actor Ian McKellen came out and no one would write about it, because there was no scandal involved. Comedian Judy "Sock-it-to-me" Carne came out in the *Advocate* and nobody cared.) It is important to keep in mind the social context there—hardly *anyone* who is a public figure *ever* comes out. For every Ian McKellen there are literally thousands of lesbians and gay men in the public eye who insist on not only hiding their sexuality but also inventing fake heterosexual lives to do so; joining—in the words of Christopher Isherwood—the ranks of the "heterosexual dictatorship."

It is also important to make distinctions within this small group. Some activists are only interested in outing those gay and closeted elected officials who have actively voted against progressive gay or AIDS legislation. Thus, they would out the closeted Mark Hatfield for his abysmal voting record on the Helms Amendment limiting explicit gay-positive text and images in government-funded safe sex information, as well as other legislation that would prohibit the use of federal funds for materials which would "promote or encourage homosexuality." Such a tactic would not only bring the official "out" but would presumably hurt his standing with a possibly conservative constituency. This form of outing—a clear, direct, political strategy—views those in the closet who work against lesbian and gay rights and AIDS legislation as collaborators and quislings who are to be punished. These activists would argue that such public officials were not being brought out as homosexuals but as hypocrites.

The other "trend" in outing has as its aim to bring out *all* public figures, including officials (regardless of their voting records) and celebrities. This is contrasted to the outing tactic that is set up to punish those who work against the community and instead concerns itself with lesbian and gay visibility. The motivation is the feeling that the more famous gay people there are who are "out" the more the press—and the culture—will have to deal with the existence, the very *fact* of gayness. And while the "outers" don't overtly call these closeted women and men "traitors," they do view them, quite rightly, as contributing in a major way to gay and lesbian invisibility and thus to the detriment of the community and movement. In a sense that is the more radical approach, using outing not for specific political expediency but as a way of addressing the position of lesbians and gay men in the whole culture.

It is interesting to note that for all of the uproar over outing, there has been very little of it actually done. There have been demonstrations against Illinois's Governor Thompson, as well as Oregon's Senator Hatfield, and while there have been rumors of threats against other anti-gay public officials, no action has been taken. As far as celebrities go, there has been almost no organized work done by lesbian and gay groups. It is true that the supermarket tabloids—*National Enquirer, Star* and *Globe*—have all printed stories about Richard Chamberlain, Malcolm Forbes, Kristy McNichol, and John Travolta, but these have usually been homophobic in slant and no different—although probably more explicit—than the expo-stories they have run for decades. It is not as though there is a shortage of closeted famous people but rather that, at this point in time, it is the establishment of outing as a social possibility that is important. This is why outing is occupying the public's imagination, and dominating so much discussion.

The Community Responds

The gay and lesbian community's response to outing has been varied, and to a large degree unreported. Some specific objections have been made, but these have not carried much weight in the straight press.

But it has been argued by some, for example, that it is the very "right to privacy" that has allowed the lesbian and gay community many legal gains these past 20 years. But the fact is that most of the legal battles have been won by arguing First Amendment rights of speech and assembly, or have focussed on traditional civil rights arguments. It is ironic that the major gay rights case that focussed on "privacy"—*Bowers v. Hardwick*, in which it was argued that Michael Hardwick had the right to have sex in the privacy of his own bedroom with whomever he chose—was a failure. (Interestingly enough, feminist theorist Rosalind Petchesky argued recently in the *Nation* that to succeed in the long run the reproductive rights movement will have to focus on the concept of "social rights"—that you have a right to do something, like the right to vote—rather than relying on the idea of "individual privacy.")

Still others in the gay and lesbian community have claimed that outing anti-gay politicians is blackmail. This is not, perhaps, an untrue statement but one which falls flat since most people realize that *all* politics are fought with threats and blackmail of some sort. Even the argument that it is "morally wrong" to drag people out of the closet does not go very far in a lesbian and gay world where people are more interested—and certainly more invested—in attacking the morality of the FDA's drug release programs, or the morality of a health care system based on greed and not compassion.

It is always difficult to gauge the response of the lesbian and gay community: there are so few venues for the varied expression of opinions that all too often those people with access to the press are taken as the spokespeople for the entire community. This, I think, is certainly the case when the straight press has constructed the debate about outing.

Most of the lesbian and gay people quoted in mainstream press outing articles have been the directors or board members of prominent lesbian and gay organizations such as the National Gay and Lesbian Task Force (NGLTF), Human Rights Campaign Fund, Lambda Legal Defense Fund, and the Massachusetts Gay and Lesbian Political Caucus. These people are in a very delicate position as they attempt the difficult task of working for change within existing social structures. Acutely aware of their tactical dependence on those in power and their economic dependence on broad-based, heterogeneous donor populations, they are forced to always take the most prudent, least extreme position on any given debate. No matter what they might really think or feel about outing—and their personal thoughts are as varied as their politics—their public opinions reflect the more conservative end of the discussion. But by only quoting these "leaders"—a [word] the press loves to use when it wants to invent/bolster support for its own agenda—the straight press can give the impression that outing is generally abhorred by the entire lesbian and gay community. The fact is that the straight press does not know—or, more to the point, care—what the gay and lesbian community thinks about anything.

One of the results—and probably one of the intentions—of the straight coverage has been to politically and culturally isolate anyone who speaks in favor of outing. Specifically, in most cases, this has meant *OutWeek* and its editors Gabriel Rotello and Michelangelo Signorile. By isolating such vocal proponents of outing as crazies or members of the lunatic fringe—creating the dichotomy of the "good gays" vs. the "bad gays"—the straight press can avoid examining not only the politics of the trend, but [also] the real social conditions that have brought it to the forefront of political action.

Outing is always treated in the mainstream press as a peculiar aberration of homosexual malice, a particularly vicious expression of nasty queendom. But the fact is that outing was born as a healthy response to an ever-increasing anger: anger at a government that continues to do little about AIDS; anger at a mind-set that still belittles the very *idea* of gayness; anger at a country that consistently condones violence against lesbians and gay men; anger at a culture that rewards people for staying in the closet and punishes others for coming out. There is also an insistent, ever-gnawing anger at all of the deaths that have happened and will continue to happen and happen and happen because of AIDS. For the straight press to acknowledge such immense anger, and the reasons for it, would be to indict itself.

It is not an accident that the current outing trend started in various ACT UP organizations throughout the country and in *OutWeek* magazine, a magazine that—in part—emerged and overlapped with New York's ACT UP movement. The anger that mobilized ACT UP is the anger that infused the notion of outing, an anger born of rage and frustration, of wanting to change the world and knowing that part of that cannot be done within the system. SILENCE = DEATH applies to the politics of the closet as easily as it does to the AIDS epidemic.

Going Too Far

One of the most common charges against outing (and ACT UP) is that both "go too far"; that they cross some accepted social and political boundary. And it is true. The aggressive direct actions of ACT UP—such as the raucous demo at New York's St. Patrick's Cathedral or the closing down of the Food and Drug Administration in Washington—are a new form of AIDS activism, as is outing. These techniques have not been used before and, in a very real sense, they are frightening: frightening to the culture they are aimed at and frightening for the people who put themselves on the line to use them.

But it is important to realize that the gay movement—and any political movement—has always had to continually "go too far" in order to get ahead. Harry Hay and the Mattachine Society went too far when they first organized. Phyllis Lyon and Del Martin went too far when they published the *Ladder*. Frank Kameny and Barbara Gittings went too far when they picketed the federal government in 1963 to protest discrimination against homosexuals. And certainly the queens, drags, dykes and street queers on Christopher Street went too far when they declared open war on the police at the Stonewall Inn. "Going too far" is not only a political fact, it is a political necessity.

One of the by-products of "going too far" is that it creates the political and social space for those not on the front lines to engage in more acceptable actions. The 75 executive directors of national gay and AIDS organizations (very few of whom had ever been involved in direct action before) who were arrested in front of the White House last year were able to [be there] because of the massive FDA protests a year earlier (which could only have come about with the evolution of the ACT UP movement). Urvashi Vaid of the NGLTF was able to stand up and disrupt George Bush's insulting "AIDS speech" because of all of the more vehement ACT UP disruptions that came before. Lobbyists who are battling on Capitol Hill for comprehensive health care have more leeway because ACT UP's demonstrations have widened the parameters of what is possible. It is conceivable that the very concept of outing—so startlingly new and provocative—might actually create the social space for people (not just the famous and the powerful) to think about coming out on their own. The power of outing has refocussed the coming out discussion, switching it from a personal to an innately political decision.

Although the politics of outing blossomed at the same time as ACT UP and *OutWeek*, it is a mistake to think that this is not just the tip of the iceberg; that the anger and the sentiment about outing is not a product of the more grass-roots sentiments running deeper in the community.

You see its manifestations everywhere. A few months ago at a k. d. lang concert at Boston's Opera House, several lesbians in the audience yelled to the performer between songs: "Why don't you just come out?" and "Come out, k. d.!" There was an encouragement and a resentment in these voices that would not have been heard so loudly and publicly two years ago.

In a recent bar discussion, I heard one man ask another if he thought Greg Louganis was gay. His response was immediate: "Fuck him, who cares? He's so closeted."

This is a startling change from years ago. I remember coming out in the pre-Stonewall late '60s and exchanging with newfound friends the endless names of who-might-be and who-certainly-was and who-probably-was. It all felt like a secret society, a selective in crowd of special people that we needed to know about because the fact was that we *didn't* know about anyone. But it feels as though that is gone now.

The security of secrecy has been replaced by an impatience and an anger at those who take refuge in privacy while the rest of us suffer the perils of being out of the closet. The anger is concentrated especially at those whose careers in show business would not really suffer if they came out, or those whose cults and reputations have been created by the lesbian and gay community, or those who are just not willing to take the chance—as we did, and do—to live more honestly. As Rita Mae Brown once said about not coming out: "I've heard all of the excuses, honey. And they're all shit."

I suspect that if you spoke to a large number of lesbians and gay men—not media-appointed leaders—you would actually find, if not widespread support for various forms of outing, a new anger and resentment at those who aren't out. If Stonewall taught us that we could be out and proud, perhaps AIDS has taught us that we can—that we *have to*—be angry. There is a new understanding that the very existence of the closet hurts the whole community and while some of us might choose to respect personal decisions to stay closeted, others are not going to. People can choose to lie about themselves, but they cannot expect that others will always join them in those lies.

The fighting and confusion over outing is a reflection of a tension that has always existed in the gay and lesbian liberation movement. While some have insisted that they just want to be accepted, like everyone else, others have demanded the freedom to be different. The first accepts social norms, the second challenges them. The Stonewall riots made earlier gay politics obsolete and loudly and clearly stated that it was important not to hide, to "come out." The personal was the political, we said, and the ultimate goal—the only way to effect true social change—was to break down the dichotomy between private and public life. *To come out.* In a very real way, outing is a direct result of this tension; an eruption of anger that the secrecy and enforced privacy of the '50s and '60s has not yet moved forward to deal with the more urgent, pressing, life-and-death politics of the present.

But after all of the arguing, all of the qualms, all of the theorizing, it remains to be explained why outing has become such a huge issue for both the gay and straight community. Like the mythical bra burnings of early 1970s feminism, outing has become a sort of shared popular-cultural symbol of two antagonistic communities. The image of bra burning, even today, represents feminist rage and anger as well as the anti-feminists' fear of rebellion. So, too, outing has become a potent symbol for both the gay and straight worlds. For lesbians and gay men it is the newest instance of "going too far," it refuses to accept the separation of the personal from the political, and it is an act of cathartic anger at a world that seems more and more intolerably homophobic.

And for the straight world, outing represents a fearful loss of power because the straight world—maybe even more than the gay world—knows the *power* of the closet and the enormous possibilities of social control that the closet can wield. To break down the closet's walls—either by coming out or dragging people out—destroys the power that now rests in straight society's hands. Outing is—for straight people—a direct, uncompromised challenge to their insistence on controlling our lives.

Why Outing Must Stop
C. Carr
(*Village Voice*, March 19, 1991)

Born in rage and hatred, directed exclusively at gay people, outing is gay bashing at its sickest. It has to stop.

A few weeks ago, posters of celebrities labeled "Absolutely Queer" appeared on a few Manhattan walls. It's no accident that they looked like Wanted Posters. That iconography goes to the heart of the matter. Gay people who practice outing must think homosexuality is criminal or they wouldn't be so passionate about attacking those who "get away with it." This is internalized homophobia run amok.

It used to be a given in the gay community that we had to *protect* each other from the homophobes, and while we often knew who the famous queers were, vicious gossip was as vicious as it got. Outing seems to be about *impressing* the homophobes by showing off our famous ones at any cost. When David Geffen admitted to being bisexual (and since when is that the same thing as being gay) in a recent *Vanity Fair* piece, *OutWeek* columnist Michelangelo Signorile crowed, "Geffen has finally let America know that queers are everywhere, including the upper-upper-upper crust of this society." I can understand this obsessive need to prove that we too are rich/famous/beautiful when straight society spits on us every day. But what homophobe is going to be persuaded by this? Let's stick to the self-asserting "We're here. We're queer. Get used to it."

Ostensibly, outers want closeted homosexuals to come out for the common good—consequences to their individual lives be damned. That's totalitarian thinking, a regime I can't live in. For me, gay liberation is still about individual freedom.

The more who *do* come out, the better. But I don't want to be told how to be gay. I've been through that before, back in the days of lesbian separatism. While I was living in Chicago in the mid-'70s, a political crisis developed in the community when a lesbian opened a "feminist restaurant" and decided to serve men. In separatist thinking, she was now "giving energy to the oppressor." Separatists began boycotting the restaurant and urged everyone to stop eating there—while they themselves ate at the hot dog stand down the street. (And guess who owned that joint?) Finally the feminist restaurant closed down, so we could *all* keep eating at places run by men.

Every liberation movement seems to develop this need to recreate the Victim/Oppressor paradigm within its own ranks. That's how the closet case became our enemy, while the real foe bashes all of us and gets away with it. I find it astonishing that Signorile urged people to phone/mail/fax-zap David Geffen, and protest at events he attended, "urging him to publicly come out." We have lost thousands to an epidemic which is far from over. We live in a world of Helmses and Dannemeyers. We are officially illegal in many states. We can't marry. We can't join the military. And we're out picketing David Geffen? How can we go on trivializing our oppression this way?

How can *any* liberation movement look to Hollywood for leadership? Or even role models? Outing will bring us neither. *We* are the vanguard. And no one who has to be forced from the closet is going to be my role model. Neither is some sacrificial lamb whose career has been ruined by the outers.

By the twisted logic he often applies in his *OutWeek* column, Signorile has insisted that he doesn't ruin careers; homophobia and straight people do that. In other words, "I just push 'em in front of the truck. The *truck* hits 'em." Signorile is the magazine's self-appointed ayatollah, who metes out the weekly scoldings and punishments, and a world of straight homophobes richly deserves his wrath. But outing gay celebs is his real passion, and an apparently unexamined one. Anyone who thinks, for example, that a lesbian can proclaim her sexuality in an industry as male-centered as Hollywood, where even straight women have trouble getting work (and no gay male actor has ever come out) has to be out of his fucking mind.

Time for a reality check. I asked a Hollywood producer who's a personal friend whether Geffen's revelations have made it easier for others to come out: "No. David Geffen is worth two billion dollars. He's a buyer, he's not out there selling his wares. I don't think anyone cares if a writer or director or studio executive is gay, because it doesn't affect viewing the movie. There *would* be consequences for actors. They're supposed to embody our fantasies. People in Hollywood imbue Middle America with ultraconservative values. They're always going to err on the side of conservatism."

Outing celebrities is a confusion of symbolic power with real clout. Like every woman, I've been harassed on the street, but "hey, babe" is nothing compared to a couple guys running at you yelling "dyke, dyke, dyke . . . " Now the outing cadre insists that such incidents wouldn't happen if a famous actress or two would have come out. Do they think these people have magic powers? Homophobia is an irrational disease from which no celebrity can save us.

I'm still waiting for the news of Malcolm Forbes's homosexuality to improve my life.

Anyone who's out knows that closet cases are often worse than straight people—in their furtiveness and confusion, and their need to not associate with the likes of us. But who has the right to decide that they should be exposed to homophobes? It is *never* right for gay people to use homophobia to punish each other. What about those closeted comedians who tell homophobic jokes? They make me sick, and so do straight comics who target queers. But why just punish the gay ones, while the straight bigots go free? It's so typical. I say, scream at them all, and don't see their movies.

Last summer, the *New York Times* reported on a study of bias-related violence. "In 'one of the most alarming findings,' the report found that while teenagers surveyed were reluctant to advocate open bias against racial and ethnic groups, they were emphatic about disliking homosexual men and women. They are perceived 'as legitimate targets which can be openly attacked,' the report said." People have a right to protect themselves from the hatred of others without being accused of hating themselves.

Signorile has written that "being gay is not a 'privacy' issue—unless you do believe that we are all harboring some dark, dirty secret." Well, the Supreme Court certainly agrees with him, as does Jerry Falwell. When a gay man from Georgia was arrested in 1982 for having sex with another man in his own bedroom, he decided to challenge the state's sodomy law on the grounds that it violated his right to privacy. In 1986, the Supreme Court decided that the right to privacy does not extend to homosexual conduct. Chief Justice Burger's concurring opinion, with its "crimes against nature" citations and history of sodomy laws since the fall of Rome, reads like a case study in officially sanctioned homophobia.

Privacy may not be important in the world we wish for, but it is in the society we're stuck with. Everyone—gay, straight and in-between —has an absolute right to decide that their intimate lives are nobody's business. As Justice Harry Blackmun wrote, in his dissenting opinion, "Depriving individuals of the right to choose for themselves how to conduct their intimate relationships poses a far greater threat to the values most deeply rooted in our nation's history than tolerance of nonconformity could ever do."

I find the outing campaign most upsetting in its affinity with the reactionary mind-set: the idea that there are authorities (mostly male) who know what's best for all of us, who are qualified to tell us how to present ourselves to the world and how to express our sexuality. It's easy to imagine religious zealots putting up posters of people with AIDS or women who've had abortions. We would regard such an act as moral terrorism, something at which the right excels. I see no reason to follow their lead if we don't want to land in their territory.

The goal of gay liberation has always been our autonomy. Abandoning that standard now, along with privacy rights and common decency—just so we can claim a few movie stars—is the most absurd excuse for political thinking I have ever encountered.

Theory and Practice: Commentary
Why I Oppose Outing
Gabriel Rotello
(*OutWeek*, May 29, 1991)

Outing is a disaster—the signifier, that is, not the political action it signifies.

Coined by someone who thought that the practice was deeply immoral, the word has a negative connotation that sounds both frightening and mean. And that, of course, was just the point.

The term "outing" derives from the idea of dragging someone out of the closet and conveys the image of a person being forced from a safe place into a dangerous one. Given the subtle power of words, every time we use the term "outing," we accept and convey that image.

Yet the closet is not a safe place at all, as anyone who has spent time there can attest. It did offer relative safety in the era before Stonewall, when it was wiser to hide one's homosexuality from the world, and it was in that dark era that the metaphor of the closet was invented.

Today, however, I've met not a single out person who says that life was safer when they were in. Indeed, if we were to abandon the metaphor of the closet and invent a new one, it's likely that those who are hiding their sexual orientation would be termed "out"—as in "out in the cold." Those who are publicly lesbian or gay would be described as having "come in," meaning into the safety of a healthy self-image and a burgeoning community.

Yet the image lingers of the safe closet out of which one ventures at one's own peril. From that mildewed metaphor, "staying in" and "coming out" persist as well. It's hardly surprising that a hostile straight person was allowed to coin a term that defined and distorted an essentially gay debate. We were sitting ducks for the word "outing."

So let's toss the term and take a fresh look at the phenomenon. What we have called "outing" is a primarily journalistic movement to treat homosexuality as equal to heterosexuality in the media. On a larger scale, that's the goal of the entire gay liberation movement: to raise homosexuality to an equivalence with heterosexuality in all spheres of life. The press doesn't hide heterosexuality or treat it as a private and unbroachable secret, so why should homosexuality be so treated?

In 1990, many of us in the gay media announced that henceforth we would simply treat homosexuality and heterosexuality as equals. We were not going to wait for a perfect, absolutely safe, utopian future to arrive before equalizing the two: We were going to do it now.

That's what outing really is: equalizing homosexuality and heterosexuality in the media. And that's why I'm abandoning the word "outing" for good, with its antiquated, slanted, pejorative imagery, and adopting the word "equalizing" instead. The imagery of "outing" is inaccurate, and I want to be clear about what it is we're espousing. I also want those who oppose the practice to be perfectly clear about what it is they're opposing.

Equalizers like me begin with the assumption that the media [have] perpetrated a damaging double standard by omitting homosexuality from the roster of those human facts and foibles subject to the scrutiny of celebrity journalism. Celebrity journalism in America is based on the concept that public figures surrender their right to "journalistic privacy" when they agree to become famous. Such people, in effect, make a pact with society: They accept fame, fortune and influence, and in return accept that their private lives may now be exposed in a way they cannot control.

The courts have repeatedly upheld the concept, ruling that a very different standard of libel applies to public figures than [to] ordinary folks. And the public, by elevating the unauthorized biography, the gossip column and the TV tabloid to the hottest commodities in journalism, has issued an overwhelming endorsement.

So we are bombarded with the divorces, separations, traumas, infidelities, substance abuses, illnesses and general trials and tribulations of the famous. From Nancy Reagan to Mamie Eisenhower to Mary Todd Lincoln, we've learned pretty much all of it, whether or not such revelations were devastating, damaging or just plain embarrassing to the people involved.

The big exception to this journalistic free-for-all has been homosexuality. There has been a tacit agreement that celebrity queerness is unfit to print, and that lesbian or gay public figures can count on the media to cooperate in maintaining their secrets. While many gays would like to think that this is done by a sympathetic media eager to avoid damaging the lives or careers of famous gays, such has never been the case. The media [are] rarely so concerned with the damage [they cause] celebrities and frequently report facts about famous people which cause serious harm. Just ask Nancy Reagan. For that matter, ask the small-town police beat reporter who makes sure that every chump in Podunk arrested on a morals charge gets his name in the paper, a practice that has damaged more people than an army of outers. Yet I've never heard any pundit complain about that, although in many countries such reportage is illegal and libelous.

Damage isn't the reason we've covered up queer. Most editors and publishers are simply homophobic, uncomfortable with the subject, and feel that their readers will object.

As a result of this double standard, homosexuality has been cast as the only unmentionable in a world of candor, giving it an inevitable patina as the worst possible human vice. Indeed, what other conclusion should the public draw when celebrity alcoholism, child abuse and adultery are openly discussed, but queerness is fervently hushed up?

In reaction, many of us in the lesbian and gay media have called for an end to this double standard, insisting that since public figures long ago traded their privacy for fame and routinely suffer embarrassing, even damaging, revelations in the press, it is hypocritical and damaging to exempt only homosexuality from that process.

Despite persistent jabs from detractors, I do not feel that equalization will instantly result in a golden age, and an end to homophobia, a thousand points of role-model light or even an immediate visible difference in our lives. But such benefits will never become possible until the ban on homosexual candor is ended.

If the goal of gay liberation is to raise homosexuality to a moral equivalence with heterosexuality, then equalization *is* liberation. It's practicing what we preach: treating our sexual orientation as a normal part of life.

All journalism operates on guidelines, however, and equalizing should be no exception. Number one: Because the privacy of the non-famous is usually respected by the press, there is no double standard in maintaining that private lesbians and gays have a right to stay private. They certainly do. Those who oppose us based on fears that every private homosexual is now at imminent risk of exposure by fellow queers are being paranoid. Equalizing is only concerned with public figures, people who have accepted the benefits and should accept the liabilities of fame.

The second guideline is to confine equalizing to those celebrities who are already out in their private lives, a category which includes most gay public figures—indeed, that's usually how we know they're gay. Since such people have already dealt with coming out, they're unlikely to face any particular psychic damage by extending the realm of those in the know. But targeting deeply closeted gays who aren't even out to their close friends or family would be cruel, possibly devastating —and would hardly advance anyone's agenda.

Thirdly, we should avoid disclosing the sexuality of those whose careers would likely be destroyed. Staunch outing opponents raise this objection in every case, but they're vastly overreacting. (I once considered doing a story on major celebrities who had come out or been outed, and whose careers had subsequently been destroyed. I had to abandon the idea when I couldn't find a single example, except for one right-wing, anti-gay, anti-choice Republican hypocrite.)

We live in a society in which hundreds of thousands of people are out, and yet very few lose their jobs because of it. Nonetheless, there are occasional cases among everyday people. And there are entire professions—the military, the diplomatic service—where such an outcome is certain. It would be cruel and unkind to target celebrities in such occupations, even in the name of liberation, and it hardly advances our goals to penalize our brothers and sisters by getting them fired.

Guideline number four applies to all journalism: Know your facts. The sloppy activist outings of straight people may be sensational, but they give the opposition ammunition to blast the entire process, and they're simply lies.

Finally, I do not believe—and here is where the word genuinely does apply—in outing politicians or others to force them to toe the line on lesbian and gay issues. The threat by a gay lobbyist to out a closet-case member of Congress unless he voted in favor of an AIDS funding bill smacks, to me, of using homosexuality as a form of blackmail. I might reconsider if the target were Jesse Helms, but I hope we can live without imitating our oppressors.

Although arguments against this process have been pursued relentlessly, opponents don't discuss the alternative, especially for us in the media.

Equalizing is almost entirely a media phenomenon. And because equalizing is, in essence, telling the truth, the alternative is to lie. Those who call us immoral for speaking truthfully about celebrity homosexuality imply that it's moral for journalists to lie, at least when the issue is being queer.

Imagine parallel situations—a politician who's actually Italian or Jewish masquerading as a WASP, a male celebrity who's actually a woman in disguise. There are few who'd advise reporters that they have a moral obligation to assist in maintaining such deceptions.

Yet assisting in deception is exactly what anti-outers insist we do. They say that journalists have a moral obligation not only to cover up the truth, but to assist the deceivers in their deceptions as well. And that if we don't, we're fascists or radicals.

That is the position of the *Village Voice*, the *New York Times*, and most lesbian and gay organizations in the United States. They tell us that—because queers are apparently not ready to be treated with equality—journalists, even gay journalists, have a moral obligation to lie.

I didn't go into journalism to lie. And the lesbian and gay movement has told me over and over that homosexuality is not the dirtiest little secret in the world.

But I didn't go into journalism to deliberately hurt people. And I didn't enter the movement to derail it. So I follow my guidelines, and urge others in the media, including the mainstream media, to follow them as well. And I draw a distinction between outing, which homophobes have been doing for centuries to destroy lesbians and gays and which I'm against, and equalizing, which is a powerful, positive, defining end in itself.

And I pray that others, particularly the leaders of our movement—even colleagues at my own magazine—can grasp this distinction too. If they can't, I'm afraid that it'll be business as usual in homo-hating American journalism, the single most powerful institution in society. And as journalism goes, so goes the nation.

V. The Pope of Outing

Michelangelo Signorile, "Gossip Watch" (*OutWeek*, April 18, July 18, and December 26, 1990; February 20 and March 27, 1991)

Gossip Watch
Michelangelo Signorile
(*OutWeek*, April 18, 1990)

I guess it's not surprising to find closet cases defending their fortresses of hiding. But it's still quite sad.

One of James Revson's (*Newsday*) columns a couple of weeks ago was truly pathetic. I feel so sorry for a man who still clings to something from the dinosaur era, standing up for such a rapidly diminishing position, and then desperately trying to shove this tired garbage down everyone's throat.

You see, an editor whom I respect at a major daily recently tried to explain to me why Liz Smith (*Daily News*) feels the way she does about queer things. He said that Liz had lived through times which—in many ways—were much worse than now, when homosex was NEVER discussed and when any hint of it might ruin one's entire life. For her, chatting frankly about sexuality seems unthinkable (though, like everyone, she certainly could change if she tried). It was this editor's opinion that change will occur in the future because younger columnists are much more open.

But, though that may be true in some cases, it's certainly not the case among those "younger columnists" from families with names to protect. No, it's certainly not true among THE KIND WHO FEED DESPERATELY OFF THE CLOSET LIKE VULTURES [OFF] THEIR PREY.

Revson wrote about what *Time* magazine a while ago dubbed 'outing,' which they had described as the practice of bringing prominent figures out of the closet (we've decided we like better the term 'inning' as in bringing people out of the closet and "into" the community). And the story, of course, that caused all the controversy was our recent piece about Malcolm Forbes' secret gay life.

Revson referred to a recent *Village Voice* story which I wrote about how the media responded (or rather, didn't respond) to the revelations in *OutWeek* about Forbes' homosexuality. He finds some of my statements about how we should TRUTHFULLY report on people's homosexuality as "truly frightening and offensive." I find this all so utterly strange and in direct contradiction to what they taught me in good old journalism school. You see, homosexuality seems to be the only area in which journalism in New York is mandated to pursue lies and cover-ups rather than the truth. If you write about a closet gay man's woman friend as his "lover," that is applauded. If you print the truth you are deemed "frightening and offensive."

This LYING is apparently rationalized by applying the term "right to privacy." So, when straight people's sex lives are written about, it's considered "news" in every publication from *People* to the *New York Times*. But if gay people's sex lives are written about, it's "an infringement of privacy." Well, I call it homophobia—from both straight people and gay people alike. When we say that our sex lives are "private," we immediately are opining that homosex is disgusting, vulgar and distasteful.

I saw Lambda Legal Defense's Tom Stoddard, another relatively "young" person, on the "Today" show babbling about that almighty "right to privacy" last week. And regarding my prodding of Liz Smith, Joe Dolce (*Paper*), a usually progressive writer who adheres to archaic principles on this topic, wrote: "[The choice to come out] is a question of privacy, a concept that lesbian and gay people have always held near and dear. Having weathered the witch hunts of the McCarthy era, we have as much right as any citizen does to protect what we do in bed." Well, I never said what Liz Smith does in bed (I honestly don't know what position she likes best or anything like that, so how could I print it?). I've said she's a *lesbian*, but I don't think that constitutes an invasion of privacy. When someone tells you he or she is *straight*, do you consider that they've just told you something private? By saying it is private, we are telling people that homosexuality is only about sex. And, of course, it's not. It's the way you look at the entire world, the way you read a book, or paint a picture. It's the way you think. As queers we have our own culture, and we're looked at by society in a certain way. Being gay or lesbian, like being Black or being a woman, is an entire existence. And like those groups, we know firsthand how it is to be victims of irrational hatred and violence. Surely this is all not *private*.

Of course I understand that the government should not be invading our homes or keeping lists of queers. And I certainly *demand* that the government uphold our—and all people's—right to privacy. But that's the *government*. In the public forum—the media—we should drop this Neanderthal notion because we're not going to get anywhere with it any longer. As gays and lesbians, we must advocate that our sex—and everyone else's sex, for that matter—be made AS PUBLIC AS POSSIBLE. How else are we supposed to kill the premise that sex is something dirty, gross, sinful and excessive and that homosex is an abomination? We must sensitize society, NOW.

Revson proclaims: "Outing only creates fear, and fear creates more repression." Oh, please. I would expect such reactionary drek—in which the basic premise is that we should continue LYING for another 700 years or so—from a man such as him.

For Revson and all of his namby-pamby, snobby friends who climb in the hierarchy of the social elite, the construct of the closet validates their very existences. Revson is a privileged white man from a family with a lot of money. YOU JUST DON'T TALK ABOUT THINGS LIKE MEN FUCK-ING EACH OTHERS' ASSES OR WOMEN EATING EACH OTHERS' PUSSIES. It is the closet that keeps your East 34th Street penthouse; the closet that gets you that house on the island; the closet that keeps that bank account full; the closet that keeps you doing your society column and getting you invited to lots of parties; the closet that puts you in good favor with all of the other closeted columnists; the closet that ultimately gets you what you want—a few measly crumbs and fastidious approval from the rich and famous.

Yes, the Revsons are far, far away in a different world; so out of touch with reality that they have no concern for the Black lesbian in the Bronx who gets raped and beaten to a pulp because she appears "butch." Nor do they know of the Latino drag queen who is terrorized every day of his life in the neighborhood where he grew up. No, Revson and his friends have no inkling of the fact that most gay people don't have the luxury of the closet. For the closet, you see, is really something *owned and operated* by white men with money. The Black lesbian and the Latino drag queen can't afford to leave the neighborhood in which they're attacked daily, and they don't have the opportunities, the skills or the education to build a closet.

So Revson and his friends go on and just worry about THEMSELVES. It doesn't matter to them that their coming out of the closet might help other queers. THEY HAVE TO PROTECT THEIR OWN FRAGILE LITTLE PRIVI-LEGED WORLD. And what I'm doing *definitely* must seem "truly frighten-ing and offensive."

But guess what, Jim? I think what *you* do is "truly frightening and offensive."

You spend most of your time going to boring parties filled with monstrous people. Then you tell us all about it in the form of drivel. (You don't even get invited to "A" list parties. There's only one thing worse than drivel and that's drivel about "D" list parties.) EVERYONE talks about how absolutely narcolepsy-inducing your column is; how it's by far the worst one around. They talk about how you once were on top—when you were fierce and strong back when you attacked Suzy (*New York Post*) for her slippery ways—but how you've now be-come a parody of Suzy yourself. Except you're a *third-rate* Suzy.

What a waste.

Meanwhile, you rarely write about gay issues. Yet you somehow think you're "out." You've even said this to people—that you're "out." That's funny. I remember when you scolded me when my editor— assuming you were "out"—wrote that you are gay. I remember when the *Advocate* approached you for an interview. You said you'd do it, until they stipulated that you'd have to say you were gay (after all, it's a gay magazine and that was their interest in you), then you declined. And you've never acknowledged your queerness in your column (in fact, why don't you take this as a challenge. If you're so "out," go ahead and write it).

Oh yeah, once in a while you do an "AIDS item" or talk about a benefit. And you did get arrested with ACT UP at city hall last year. You even wrote a column about it (which didn't address the issues but did record the songs people sang in jail). But Jim, getting arrested with ACT UP does not an "out" gay man make. In fact, getting arrested with ACT UP in front of lots of cameras and while wearing a suit can be a very "chic" thing for a "straight liberal" columnist to do, especially if he wants some press. I've never seen you back at ACT UP since that arrest over a year ago. And you have never, before or since the arrest, implored the government to do anything about AIDS. You don't ever discuss the many problems facing this community. Instead, you have defended Pat Buckley and dubbed William F. Buckley as merely "misguided." But, somehow, you do find space to talk about one particular gay issue: *OutWeek* magazine and those horrible people who work there. I believe this is your fourth or fifth time, isn't it, Jim?

It seems you even get a kick out of bashing us. It gets you a little press, gets you a bit noticed again. And it adds some sparkle and excitement to your otherwise dreary life. You probably even calculate my striking back, and even get off on that. Honestly, such masochism wouldn't surprise me.

You're so obviously unhappy doing that column (and everyone else is so unhappy reading it).

Wake up, Jim!

You're wasting precious time. Why don't you just do something really good with that space? Stop listening to those social-climbing idiots all around you, those blood-sucking creeps, those closeted cocktail queens, those up-again-down-again writers who swirl around but go nowhere. Take control. Scream and yell. Talk about what has to be done. Do it now, Jim. Fight for your life.

Gossip Watch
Michelangelo Signorile
(*OutWeek*, July 18, 1990)

Everyone's got a story.

Word from the Almighty Coast has it that EVERY big-time queer actor and actress in Hollywood is petrified — as in *scared shitless* — of *OutWeek*, of this column, of *moi*. Of course, instead of sitting around cowering, these pea brains could all come out, stand proud (thereby [rendering] me and anyone else powerless), challenge the hideous homophobia in that town and do the right thing for humanity. These people are selfish sewer rats, pursuing their own gluttonous needs, lying around in the sun and waiting for another million-dollar check, while their own friends die. Though I won't ever consider them halfway-decent human beings until they come forward for this community, they should know that, while I can't speak for the *National Enquirer*, *Star* or even the gossips at the major dailies (all of whom call me with excruciating frequency), the constant worrying about being "decloseted" by *me* is vastly exaggerated.

In fact, I think it's all pretty silly.

In the confusion of the media swirl, so many things get lost. For the record: Though I see nothing wrong in openly writing about ANY AND EVERY lesbian or gay man as such, this column does have certain parameters. As a media column of sorts, it is mandated to speak specifically about people who control, participate in and actively shape the popular media. What that means is that I'm much more inclined to write about, and to expose the hypocrisies of, the powerful columnists, producers, record company honchos, editors, publishers and everyone else behind the scenes — the power people. Of course, if you're a secretly queer performer actively and publicly engaged in homophobia and/or ardently trying to pass yourself off as a heterosexual by having your publicist match you up with faux het lovers, you will, without question, wind up here at some point. And, even if you're someone who is not necessarily doing anything *bad*, you many simply get mentioned in passing some time, since I see it as perfectly fine — if not my duty — to say that someone is queer if I happen to be writing about that person and if his or her homosexuality is pertinent to the story. But for the most part, just because of the way the chips fall, it's the big media fish who are fried up here.

And boy, do those fish squirm once you pull them out of the water. 20th Century Fox head Barry Diller, the supreme self-hater whom you all know has been heavily pounced on in this column regarding his movie company's rim-job of Andrew Dice Clay, seems to be flapping —just a little bit.

Word leaked out last week that Diller had decided not to release one of the films in a three-picture deal he'd signed with Dice Clay. The film, which is a live concert of Dice Clay's, was apparently so offensive that Diller felt Fox shouldn't handle it. This could very well mean that Diller has suddenly developed a conscience and feels that he must be accountable to his own community—or rather, it could have something to do with the fact that Dice Clay billboards around Los Angeles have been spray-painted in recent weeks with the words: BROUGHT TO YOU BY A CLOSET CASE, BARRY DILLER.

All that Diller's spokesperson, Dennis Potroskey, has to say is: "The concert movie is not on the release schedule and it is unlikely that it will be." Of course, there's no telling whether Diller will sell the film to another company—and make some cash on it, while it gets released anyway—or simply kill it.

But what we should really concern ourselves with is what the fuck Diller can do for us *now*. No, we won't be content with his dropping a film with some homophobe screaming out offensive remarks. We expect that. THE ASSHOLE SHOULDN'T HAVE BEEN SIGNED TO BEGIN WITH (as lots of other offensive acts are not signed because 20th Century Fox has certain standards and ethics). We're not asking for censorship. We're merely asking for treatment equal to that of other groups which Fox is mindful of and tries not to offend. What we want now is for Fox to scratch people like Roger Ailes and other homophobes whom they now have producing TV shows on the Fox network. What we want is for Fox to develop, back, distribute and release films about us—about the lesbian and gay community and about this horrific crisis we've suffered through for ten years. (Why did it take Craig Lucas so long to get a movie company to distribute *Longtime Companions*—it was, after an exhaustive search, finally picked up by the Samuel Goldwyn Company—while his soul mate Barry Diller is sitting up at Fox, and his fellow gay David Geffen is sitting up at Geffen Pictures?) What we want is for Diller to stand up for this community. WHY DOESN'T HE GET TOGETHER HIS FRIENDS DAVID GEFFEN AND LIZ SMITH AND MERV GRIFFIN AND HOLD A PRESS CONFERENCE IN WHICH THEY COULD ALL DECLARE THEMSELVES, HOLD THE GOVERNMENT ACCOUNTABLE FOR IT ACTIONS AND TELL THE AMERICAN PEOPLE WHAT IS RIGHT AND WHAT IS WRONG? Why don't they simply say that they won't stand for homophobia and won't back homophobes? None of these people is going to lose anything. Two are among the richest people in America. The other two rule the entertainment industry. No one is going to stop them. IT's AMAZING WHAT THEY COULD DO!

Did I mention Merv Griffin?

Oh, I guess that was because he's been on my mind.

Last week I got more than one call about rolling-in-dough honcho Merv and his appearance on CNN. Asked by a CNN reporter about his longtime relationship with Eva Gabor, Griffin reportedly replied, "At our age, what would *you* call it?" (Well, *I'd* call it a boy and his beard. I'm reminded of the old joke that used to circulate among young Hollywood actors who wanted a break in Hollywood at the time when Merv had his TV talk show: "The only way to get on 'Merv Griffin' is to get on Merv Griffin.") I began thinking back to a few months ago in *Vanity Fair*, and how, up to their usual tricks, they presented Merv and Eva and their "romance" to their readers without question. Why, I asked myself, would *Vanity Fair*—a publication which prides itself on being *someone's* version of cutting edge—choose to dabble in this mundane, heterosexual (and untrue) love-up, when it could have really revealed the mouth-watering excitement of Merv's numerous antics with chocolate candy bars and young, cute things?

Everyone's got a story.

Gossip Watch
Michelangelo Signorile
(*OutWeek*, December 26, 1990)

"[Cameron] Mackintosh has been quite skillful, in the midst of all the publicity surrounding him, at keeping his private life private. He claims that the circumstances of his public life have not changed his private ways. He has had, he says, a long-term relationship—nine years—with one man, a London photographer. Mackintosh is not a jet-setter who runs from party to party trying to get his name and photograph into the gossip and society pages."

So wrote Mervyn Rothstein in last week's *New York Times* magazine about the producer of the now-famous Broadway-bound *Miss Saigon*. What is wonderfully refreshing, both about Mackintosh's outlook and Rothstein's presentation, is the distinction between "private life" and being gay. You see, for the past year and a half I've been squawking like a madman, battling the notion that being gay is a private matter—

and even last week the *Times'* own John Rockwell tried to shove that same homophobic garbage down our throats regarding the late queer composer Aaron Copland. But here Mackintosh is, in essence, pointing out that the reality of his own homosexuality is not a *private* issue (it's simply a fact of life), even though he leads a quiet life and is very much a *private* person. Yes, gay public figures *can* have private lives and still be *openly* gay (just as straight public figures can retain private lives and still be openly straight).

But try telling all of this to that slimy slug from the bottom of the ocean, David Geffen. Oh, yes, having scored big in another Hollywood mega-deal, Geffen fawned, posed and gave good quote for the press last week for becoming Hollywood's biggest powermonger, opening up his stinking life like a can of wretched sardines. Yet one major facet wasn't forthcoming.

In *Newsweek*, we learned of Geffen's alleged affair of many years ago with Cher, but we certainly didn't hear about his liaison with, for instance, porn star Joey Stefano (who last year told a roomful of reporters about his and Geffen's steamy associations). *Newsweek* gave no homo details at all, depicting Geffen much like Malcolm Forbes – a jet-setting, rich, hetero bachelor who'd dated a movie actress. (John Schwartz, who wrote this story, was dumbfounded when I called him, responding, after some silence – and perhaps after realizing that there was *something* to what I was saying – that he is "sorry" if it made me "angry.")

At *Forbes*, where Chairman Malcolm once ruled from inside his Capitalist Closet and where son Kip now trembles at my every word, editors Lisa Gubernick and Peter Newcomb wrote a huge cover story on Geffen, "Getting Rich Is the Best Revenge." And, as reporters who are obviously well versed in such hypocrisy (having worked for closet cases), they tell us in the first paragraph: "Geffen is well on his way to achieving his well-known ambition of becoming Hollywood's first billionaire. And he's a bachelor to boot." Gee, sounds like the perfect man for any straight, female readers with that all-American dream of marrying BIG.

Well, my heart goes out to any of those hetero girls who might even be reading *this*, but you should know that GEFFEN LIKES TO SUCK DICK. (And it's terrible that *Forbes* is once again misleading you poor dears, but take my advice on this: Almost every rich, single man whom the media describes as a "bachelor" – and *especially* in *Forbes* – really likes to suck dick. Why, they even like to put other men's dicks up their asses, too, heavens to Betsy!)

And it is up to Geffen himself to tell that to the media. A simple "I'm gay" will do. HERE IS THIS ALL-POWERFUL QUEER GETTING HIMSELF ON THE COVERS OF MAGAZINES—AND HE CAN'T EVEN STAND UP, BE PROUD AND GIVE VISIBILITY TO THIS COMMUNITY. Meanwhile, as he revels in his $850 million, the rest of this community is in a shambles, with a disease ravaging us and while thousands are being beaten on the streets BECAUSE OF THE VERY HATRED THAT ONE OF HIS OWN FUCKING BANDS, GUNS N' ROSES, ENCOURAGES.

And after this deal, Geffen is untouchable. Who could stop him now from doing anything? What's keeping Geffen from coming out in a big way, condemning gay-bashing, attacking the government's response to AIDS, denouncing Guns N' Roses and what they've stood for, making a dent in the institutionalized homophobia that permeates Hollywood and taking some of his power and putting it toward this community's liberation? WHY CAN'T GEFFEN TAKE ONE FUCKING MINUTE OUT FROM HIS GREEDY, SELF-SERVING LIFE AND THINK ABOUT THE THOUSANDS OF PEOPLE BEING BLUDGEONED TO DEATH OR DYING IN HOSPITALS AND HOW THEY NEED SOMEONE AS POWERFUL AS HIM TO CONFRONT THIS MESS?!

I certainly know that many people *have*—ever since the first rantings against Geffen came from this space—approached the multimillionaire publicly. Some have run into him at Rounds, the uptown gay bar where lots of guys go to find cheap (and not so cheap) dates, and watched him spin into a frenzy when they've brought up these issues. Others have spoken to him at cocktail parties, dinners, fund-raisers and the like and confronted him about being responsible to this community—and not just by making a couple of drop-in-the-bucket donations. He needs people to tell him, and they should vigilantly continue to do so. It has so far forced him to drop Andrew Dice Clay from his roster—but that isn't nearly enough of what he can do.

EVERYONE must call Geffen *NOW* and ask him to confront Hollywood's homophobia, establish a public TV show about lesbians and gays and/or produce films about us—leave a message at (213) 278-9018—and we must also pressure all those who are close enough to him to put these issues before him. He is now the richest man in Hollywood, and whether or not he is the proper "role model," he is queer, and there is no denying that. HE MUST BE ACCOUNTABLE TO THIS COMMUNITY, IN LIEU OF WHAT HE IS AND IN LIEU OF WHAT HE'S DONE. He must also know that *we will not stop*—and if that means digging up and spewing out all of the revelations about him that have passed over my desk, if it means protesting him and zapping him and STICKING OURSELVES IN HIS FACE, if it means doing outlandish and incredible things to get attention, then so be it. Here is a horrifically wealthy man in a position to move mountains for us, and not only is he doing little (and yet benefiting from the gay rights movement), but he's ACTUALLY HURT-ING US BY PROMOTING—AND PROFITING OFF OF—HOMOPHOBIA AND DEATH. How could anyone thus call *us* the monsters in all of this for *any* actions we may take?

And a message to Mr. Geffen: Time is running out. Very soon I will be coming to that almighty coast. The goal is to break that logjam out there and show people that it is *self-loathing closet cases who are actually the culprits who have kept this vicious circle of heterosexism and homophobia churning away in Tinseltown.* I will be meeting with people and ex-changing information and talking with activists and coming up with plans and HOLDING PRESS CONFERENCES.

You see, David, now that you are much better known and more fa-mous, the media is *that much more* interested in ANYTHING we have to say about you—and about your buddies like Barry Diller, Merv Griffin, Michael Eisner and the rest of the gang. Yes, it seems that—unless you stop the chain of homophobia—you and I will be inextricably tied for-ever, David: The more powerful *you* become, the more powerful our newfound tools against you become.

Funny how the world works, isn't it?

Gossip Watch
Michelangelo Signorile
(*OutWeek*, February 20, 1991)

Of course I sometimes think that Larry Kramer is wacked out. (As I'm sure lots of people sometimes—or even most times—think that certain others of us are equally deranged.)

That's OK. It's the nature of the activism business.

But just think about it: Not long after Larry erupts with something hurtful and seemingly fabricated, not long after he blurts out some outlandish, freakish, appalling comment, not long after he appears to have flipped his queer little lid before your eyes, *you come to realize that just about everything he says is true.*

I love that man.

At Vito Russo's memorial service last December, Larry gave yet an-other passionate speech that left me in tears—while it sent many well-known queer media types angrily huffing out of the auditorium, mum-bling something about "how dare" Larry "blame" them for "killing" Vito. (Guilty? Possibly. Lazy? Probably. Literal-minded? Definitely.)

There was one thing about the speech, however, that bothered me at the time: Larry attacked Jodie Foster and her new movie, *The Silence of the Lambs*, branding the film "homophobic." He claimed that the serial killer in the film—who preys on young women—is a gay man. But it just didn't sound like Larry had his facts right—and he hadn't seen the movie himself. However, that very vicious attack, made at a highly visible queer event, was enough to scare the shit out of AmFAR [the American Foundation for AIDS Research], which was planning a benefit around a star-studded screening of the film. They pulled out as soon as they smelled controversy—and yet no one involved had actually viewed the thriller flick.

I'd previously heard about the Thomas Harris novel of the same name on which the film is based. The killer was a transsexual *who was not gay*, according to those who'd read it. And as reported by some who'd been to early screenings of *Lambs* in the fall, the movie apparently had the same story line. Then, last month, in an interview with director Jonathan Demme in *Interview*, *Voice* columnist Gary Indiana reaffirms that the killer "makes himself up in drag but is identified in various ways as someone who's *not* gay, *not* a real transsexual, *not* a representative of a minority group." Demme responds to any charges of homophobia by defensively laying the blame on "the presidency of this country," "our school system" and "a gigantic toxic problem." But he does say that "if *Lambs* is found—eventually, through debate on the subject—to be guilty to some extent, however unwittingly, of functioning as a tool of homophobia, then I will learn a lot from it."

All of this made it appear as if the film would not be so offensive. Demme seemed reasonable and sensitive. And once again, Larry seemed wacked out.

"Was Kramer acting as a censor, rabble-rousing about a vitally important issue but which has nothing to do with the film at hand? Is he a gay version of those pitiful nuns and religious zealots who stood outside cinemas twaddling on about Martin Scorsese's *The Last Temptation of Christ* or Jean-Luc Godard's *Hail Mary*? I'm afraid so." So wrote the proud, openly gay and usually on-target *Paper* columnist, Joe Dolce.

Obviously, I had to see this movie, so I caught a sneak preview last week. It's thrilling. It's frightening. It's mesmerizing. BUT—PROVING THE WACKED-OUT LARRY IS ONCE AGAIN ON THE MONEY—IT'S BLATANTLY HOMOPHOBIC. (And, sorry Joe, but you're way off base about the "censor" analogy—though I know it's hard to resist those reactionary buzzwords. Larry is *not* asking for any legal sanctions banning the film. He's simply exercising *his* freedom of speech by screaming about it. Get a grip.)

I'm really tired of people who, just because they like the stars or the story line or the author or the director of a film, either consciously or unconsciously whitewash it of its offenses, thus rationalizing anti-gay depictions. Dolce, like Indiana, claims that the killer is straight. Interestingly, both of these writers also read the book, where the killer's heterosexuality is supposedly explicit.

But—as someone who *only* saw the movie, with its flashing, quick images and its lightning-fast script—I can tell you that this character is definitely not depicted in any way as heterosexual. In fact, in one scene, we're told that he once had a lover, and that person's name is a male one. The last time I checked, that meant GAY. (And the *Los Angeles Times* last week confirmed this: "A reference is made to [the psychopath] having killed a male lover.") Throughout the film, the killer is in drag, and is playing up every known gay stereotype. TO THE AVERAGE, IGNORANT, AMERICAN MOVIEGOER—AND THIS *IS* A BIG-BUDGET HOLLYWOOD FILM INTENDED FOR THE MASSES—THE MESSAGE IS CRYSTAL CLEAR: THE KILLER IS A FUCKING QUEER!

And yet Dolce sadly tries to convince himself that it just ain't so: "Though one could infer homosexuality (statistically, most cross-dressers are, in fact, heterosexual), it's hardly the point, and it's the most simplistic reading of the character." Oh, really? Yeah, Joe, let's talk about "simplistic readings." First off, most filmgoers know nothing of the statistics on cross-dressers—a man dressing as a woman is simply a "faggot." Secondly, it really doesn't matter whether this character is gay or straight anyway. I MEAN, DOESN'T THE QUEER MOSAIC *INCLUDE* TRANSSEXUALS AND TRANSVESTITES—WHETHER THEY'RE STRAIGHT, GAY, BISEXUAL OR WHATEVER? SHOULD WE NOT BE STANDING UP FOR THE CROSS-DRESSERS AND DRAG QUEENS? AND DON'T MOST PEOPLE IN THIS COUNTRY LUMP US TOGETHER ANYWAY?

On the same night that I saw the film, in one of those chilling and nervous late-night incidents that we all know so well, a friend and I were physically threatened and called "homos" by three young men as we playfully walked the streets of the East Village—and I can assure you that we were not dressed as women. No doubt, those men would watch *Silence of the Lambs* and certainly call that killer the same thing: a "homo." They simply don't see the difference. AND THEY WOULD CHEER WHEN JODIE FOSTER SHOOTS THE "HOMO" DEAD—BECAUSE HE'S A DANGEROUS FREAK WHO KILLS WOMEN AND WHO MUST BE ELIMINATED. And then—who knows?—the next time they see me and my friend on the street, the next time they see a couple of "homos," they might just feel more validated and more empowered to BASH OUR FUCKING FACES IN! You see, they have *no other* example of gays to compare this to.

Where are all of the films from Hollywood showing *positive* images of gays to balance out this kind of stuff? I DON'T SAY THAT WE MUST SANITIZE ALL DEPICTIONS OF QUEERS OR ANY OTHER GROUP. BUT UNTIL HOLLYWOOD—PEOPLE LIKE JONATHAN DEMME AND JODIE FOSTER—FAIRLY SERVES UP THE *ENTIRE SPECTRUM OF EVERY COMMUNITY,* IT IS NECESSARY TO SCREAM LIKE THIS AT THESE DEPICTIONS.

Every single day in this nation, women are being raped and tortured by STRAIGHT, MACHO MEN. And 99.9 percent of serial killers who kill women are STRAIGHT, MACHO MEN. When was the last time you can even *remember* a drag queen/transvestite/cross-dresser/transsexual serial killer? (Truthfully, it is the transvestite and transsexual communities, as well as the lesbian and gay communities, who are also daily *under* physical attack by straight men.) But in our homophobic society, it certainly seems that it must be a common reality for such fruitcakes to be murderers. People like to see this kind of killer and want to believe it. It's exciting and scary and helps them condone their irrational hatred. *Presto!* Let's make a movie and make a fortune!

"We want to send a message to Orion [Pictures] and to the rest of the film industry that we're tired of being depicted in the movies almost exclusively as villains, murderers, and twisted psychopaths," said Rich Jennings, executive director of GLAAD/LA [Gay and Lesbian Alliance against Defamation, Los Angeles] to the *Los Angeles Times* last week. In California, the controversy has already heated up (and is no doubt heading East, where the film opens on February 14). The headline blared across the pages of the *L.A. Times*: "GAYS DECRY BENEFIT SCREENING OF *LAMBS.*" It was a story about how GLAAD/LA is furious that, unlike AmFAR, AIDS Project Los Angeles went through with a benefit screening of the film. And Jennings had some astute observations as to why the AIDS benefits were offered by Orion Pictures in the first place: "The moviemakers were obviously concerned about the movie. They attempted to launder the film by using [organizations] whose clients are mostly gay to deflect criticism."

HOLLYWOOD DISGUSTS ME! ALL OF YOU LYING FREAKS MAKE ME WANT TO VOMIT. Jodie Foster, TIME'S UP! If lesbianism is too sacred, too private, too infringing of your damned rights for you to discuss publicly, then the least you can fucking do is refrain from making movies that insult this community! Is that too much to ask of you? Jesus, you want to have your queer little cake and eat it too, right? NO WAY, SISTER!

And all of you queer writers who caressed dear Jodie in your interviews, why didn't you bring up the subject? Jonathan Van Meter, why didn't you ask Foster about this issue in your *New York Times Magazine* piece on her? And what about you, Cindy Carr, Ms. Openly Lesbian

Village Voice columnist? Why didn't you address this in your *Mirabella* piece? Certainly you saw a screening of the film before doing a cover story for a major magazine. (And, by the by, why couldn't you even bring yourself to ask Jodie if she's a dyke in that interview?)

Everyone tells me that I'm too mean, so I'm going to try to say this in the nicest way possible: Why is it that, while we are beaten up and killed and defamed and denied drugs and left to suffer in hospitals, these writers are prancing their way across the glossy pages of glamour rags, without even challenging the people who are not only hiding in the closet BUT ARE ACTIVELY HURTING US BY MAKING MOVIES LIKE THIS? You writers are on the front lines, talking to the powers that be. It is up to you to confront them and get all of this shit out into the open (and, politics aside, it's also part of your jobs as journalists, period). I mean, we've got to get moving here, folks. We've suffered long enough, and we've taken too many losses.

You can call me wacked out. Or you can get with the program—QUICK.

Gossip Watch
Michelangelo Signorile
(*OutWeek*, March 27, 1991)

Just as the Gulf war supposedly came to an end, everybody's favorite leftist weekly—which had spent the whole time correctly condemning the big, bad United States for abuses of power—began dropping its own bombs on little ol' *OutWeek* and several gay activists. This is a tale of hypocrisy, a narrative of self-delusion, mass deception and egos which frighteningly loom ever larger by the minute.

This is the story of the *Village Voice*.

It all began with a debate about a film. But it has since dredged up long-standing issues regarding the *Voice*'s complacent predictability, it's pandering self-indulgence and its desire to maintain a stranglehold on the whole wide world of lefty arts criticism.

Now the last thing we all want to talk about again is *that movie*. But I promise: We're not going to discuss the film so much as we're going to take a look back at the events leading up to how the *Voice* got itself into another sloppy mess, from which it then attempted to extricate itself in the most disingenuous way.

Months ago, sources say, top editors of the *Voice* saw *The Silence of the Lambs* and decided that it wasn't homophobic. Never mind that several gay writers and film-industry people had charged that the movie was anti-gay, urging editors to proceed with caution. It was, after all, a Jonathan Demme film, and he is a favorite director of *Voice* critics, who wanted to champion the film, since it had, they claimed, a strong feminist edge, and—perhaps more importantly for their commercial interests—because it was going to be a huge blockbuster. A mega-hit film with good feminist politics and a top director, it was, for sure, MAINSTREAM, MAINSTREAM, MAINSTREAM. (Lest we forget, former *Voice* film editor Howard Feinstein was fired last year because he wasn't "mainstream" enough, as reported by New York *Newsday*.)

No, *The Silence of the Lambs* was something that the *Voice* just couldn't refuse to hype. The homophobia? Well, it wasn't *that* bad, I mean, it could be construed as such by some, but others wouldn't think so. It's *debatable*—that magical and wonderful word that makes everything OK.

It was back then, when the *Voice* first pushed the film, that it should have been acknowledged that homophobia might possibly be a problem in an otherwise unusually interesting film. But it didn't. Instead, the paper stupidly got behind a problematic project, put its head in the sand, and waited for the explosion.

Why? Because the film is made by a straight, white, liberal man who is, moreover, the "pet" director of many *Voice* editors and critics, and *they* didn't want to be the ones to blow the whistle. Many of them were so blinded by his fabulous hipness that the movie's considerable flaws eluded them. And besides, they figured, even if there was any dissent, it might never reach the media.

But—boy, oh, boy—it did.

Several weeks before the movie's opening, GLAAD/LA planted a story in the *Los Angeles Times* in which they condemned the film's depiction of a queer serial killer as antigay. *OutWeek* picked up the story. Within days, the controversy was burning up the wire services.

That same week, Jodie Foster was outed by *Star*, which quoted my own references to her lesbianism in my criticism of the film's homophobia. By the time the movie opened, mainstream dailies across the country had dutifully attended to this debacle. "Gay Groups Decry Killer's Portrayal," blared the headline in *USA Today*, next to a rave review of the film. "Boycott Urged on Film; Stereotyping Is Alleged," reported the *Miami Herald* (I, by the by, never urged a boycott—that was GLAAD's doing).

The gay press nationwide also filed its opinions that week. "Can the filmmakers really have thought that it wouldn't matter that non-gay viewers could be trusted to see [the killer] as a sick person whose sexual orientation has no bearing on his illness?" mused Steve Warren in Miami's *Weekly News*. "Aside from the killer queer, which rankles my PC side, this is an exciting film with a particularly satisfying, unexpected ending."

Sally Irwin of the *Seattle Gay News* was more to the point: "It's an intelligent, even brilliant, genre-topper that thrills to gender violations just as shitty, openly bigoted movies do."

And Warren Sonbert at San Francisco's *Bay Area Reporter* wrote . . . that he "would have to admit that this is an excellent, if morally reprehensible, film." [His review] was placed above a sidebar story headlined "The Psycho Gay Killer Hall of Fame" and alongside a commentary piece that pointed out all of the film's anti-queer fare.

And where was the *Voice*? Well, nowhere really. I mean, by this time the established gay media watchdog group, GLAAD, had condemned the film, and the mainstream media was vigorously covering the exploding controversy. The gay press was calling it what it was— an entertaining thriller, deeply flawed with homo problems—and the issue was even addressed by film reviewers like Jan Stuart in *Newsday* and, amazingly, David Denby in *New York*.

But all the *Voice* had to offer by the time the film opened, in the midst of this raging media debate, was a review by J. Hoberman, which mentioned an "offensive" portrayal in the film, and an interview with director Jonathan Demme, in which Amy Taubin gratuitously inquired after the possibly homophobic character and accepted with dispatch his immediate denial. To add further conflict-of-interest embarrassment, two *Voice* critics had by this time done puff pieces on the film for other publications. Gary Indiana had interviewed Jonathan Demme for *Interview*, more or less glossing over the homophobia, and C.Carr had completely ignored the issue in her *Mirabella* interview with Jodie Foster.

The *Voice* found itself in a similar situation when it was pushing the rap group Public Enemy last year. With all their good intentions of backing a Black group, they overlooked certain problems and HYPED, HYPED, HYPED. Soon enough, charges of anti-Semitism and misogyny were being hurled at the rappers. And the *Voice*, once again, found itself caught with its pants down for not having addressed these issues earlier. Along the same lines, the *Voice* has built up director David Lynch (including a ridiculous puff piece on Laura Dern and *Wild at Heart*), whose work many perceive as misogynistic and who, [on the evidence of] his scripts, also clearly has a problem with homosexuals (although we've yet to see this addressed in the *Voice*).

But back to slaughtering *Lambs*. The *Voice*, which prides itself on being representative of so many different groups, should have been *leading* the debate. Why did we not see a discussion in the *Voice* until several weeks after almost every mainstream paper in America addressed the issue?

Asleep at the wheel, film editor Lisa Kennedy, in a transparent attempt at damage control, had quickly put together a panel of writers to discuss the film's problems. She simply had no choice: The controversy was being aired everywhere else. (She must have been pissed off, too: As this whole thing was coming to a head, she was trying to get out of town—off to the Berlin Film Festival.)

Originally, Kennedy had asked *OutWeek*'s arts editor Sarah Pettit to participate, but, perhaps eager to get out of town, Kennedy never followed through. Larry Kramer, one of nine writers who did give a short analysis of the movie and its sexuality problems, urged Kennedy to have me participate in the forum, especially if people would be refuting my criticism. After all, *OutWeek* speaks to tens of thousands of gay people; the *Voice* has hundreds of thousands of readers, most of whom are straight. It would be unfair if I were lynched for the sheer entertainment of all the breeders (which I was), without at least letting them read my opinion. But that is exactly what Kennedy decided to do.

Of the nine writers, all but three—whether they loved or hated the movie—pointed out that it was homophobic. And those three were the only *Voice* staffers on the panel. Two of them used the wonderful art of deflection and chose not to address the issue (Gary Indiana spent all his time raving about the monster Signorile, and Amy Taubin went off on some other tangent.) Cindy Carr, however, whirled herself into a dervish of denial and spun out all sorts of excuses about how the killer wasn't really gay. And Kennedy would later pull herself down deeper on this one, coming up with an even more ridiculous rationalization than Carr's for why the killer and one of his male victims weren't lovers.

(And yet, in a rigorous interview with David Ehrenstein in the *Advocate*, Jonathan Demme admits that the killer and the transvestite he killed were indeed lovers. But I suppose that Carr and Kennedy know better than the director himself.)

Of course, at this point, the story is all about protecting egos and shoring up the *Voice*'s rep. It's also about nailing Signorile, *OutWeek* and those darned activists. We'd crossed a line of some sort, finally calling *them* on something—especially Indiana and Carr, whose opportunism, revealed in their puffy interviews with the director and the star, I'd attacked. And suddenly they all began coughing up lots of phlegm and bile that they'd apparently been gagging on for the past two years.

After Indiana's original rampage, there would be weeks of further attacks. Lisa Kennedy wrote that my position as a "spokesperson" is "self-appointed," as if *she* got *elected* senior editor—or maybe the Fairy Queen appointed her. Guy Trebay attacked me for outing Jodie Foster when he outed her himself, coyly referring to her as "well, let's call her a famous young actress who's much in the news." (Who were you talking about, Guy, Shelley Winters?)

And Trebay gave a lot of shit to the activists who have been busy pasting up posters downtown of Merv Griffin and Jodie Foster, labeled "Absolutely Queer." How schizoid. He recently championed Queer Nation, in a *Voice* cover story, for the group's visibility actions, including, among other things, their outing people on street posters and at events—and he eagerly used the names of both k. d. lang and Greg Louganis as examples.

And just last week, C.Carr belched up the most reactionary, reductive, regressive anti-outing piece I've so far seen—even among the right-wingers who attacked us last year. Word has it that the *Voice* fact checkers themselves were hooting with laughter as they perused her copy.

Cindy, there are are actually some rather progressive anti-outing arguments going around—even among my colleagues Sarah Pettit and Andrew Miller here at *OutWeek*—but your piece is really inane. You sound like some sort of Bible thumper: "Outing must stop!" Oh, please. Where the hell have you been for the past couple of years? Nodding out in a sooty corner of some dark performance space on the Lower East Side?

You whine on: "We have lost thousands to an epidemic which is far from over. We live in a world of Helmses and Dannemeyers. We are officially illegal in many states. We can't marry. We can't join the military. And we're out picketing David Geffen? How can we go on trivializing our oppression this way?"

As if *your* column has covered the front line of activist politics. We all know about oppression, Cindy. Read our magazine some time. You, Cindy Carr, haven't written shit, sitting in your comfy hole at the *Voice* and spouting that ivory-tower drivel. It's actually wonderful to see you getting angry, riled up and excited about *something*. Now if we could only direct you toward the proper monsters, perhaps you could do some good.

Thankfully, no one has ever waited around for the *Voice*'s permission on a call to arms over the issues that are killing us—from homo-phobia in the movies to AIDS. And after this whole debacle, which writers there seem obsessed with covering up, twisting themselves into queerly shaped pretzels, it's not likely that many people ever will.

Clean up your act. Or shut up already.

VI. The Outing of the Pentagon

The Outer Limits
Richard Goldstein
(*Village Voice*, July 30, 1991)

The story begins, like so many at the *Village Voice*, with an outcry from the staff. The subject this time was a piece asserting that a top Pentagon official is gay. The author, Michelangelo Signorile, had planned to publish it in *OutWeek*, the gay/lesbian journal where he held forth as gossip-terrorist and editor at large. But the magazine folded before Signorile could strike. He offered the piece to the *Voice*, we bit, and then, as word spread internally, the staff erupted. We decided to hold an open meeting, if only to avert the post-publication revolt that occurred at the *New York Times*—as it should have—when a select group of editors made the ethically untenable decision to publish the name of the plaintiff in the Kennedy rape case.

In our case, a cross-section of writers and editors—male and female, gay and straight—agreed that it would be inappropriate to "out" this Pentagon official. I argued otherwise. The military, which actively discriminates against homosexuals, has no qualms about persecuting gay soldiers (including those who would rather keep their sexual identity private). It uses rumors and intimidation to stage purges (especially of women who seem too assertive to their superiors). The target of Signorile's piece, a close associate of the secretary of defense, symbolizes the hypocrisy of an institution that applies one standard to recruits and another to a man close to the seat of power. I was unable to convince my colleagues that all this added up to a case for outing. Some doubted that Signorile's target is a player in military policy; others worried that we hadn't proved he is gay. I could accept these caveats—journalistic standards are hard to set, especially in regard to outing, which is terra incognita. But I was left with an ominous sense that, for many in the meeting, there are no grounds for disclosing someone's homosexuality without consent.

No doubt this revulsion at the very concept of outing is a backlash against the indiscriminate way it's being practiced. Gender-based experiences of sexuality may make men and women see the ethics of this enterprise differently—and outing is primarily a male adventure. But to insist that it is never appropriate reflects a moralism that seems every bit as rigid as the anarchic adventurism of Outpost, those anonymous gay activists who pepper the streets (especially around media headquarters) with broadsides announcing that this or that celebrity is "absolutely queer."

What's needed now is an ideology of outing that takes into account concerns about privacy—and personal freedom—which are central to the gay movement, while preserving the political potential of this act. When, if ever, is outing progressive? The question is far from settled—in my own mind, at the *Voice*, in the gay and lesbian community, and in journalism. To arrive at a consensus, it's necessary to examine the impact of outing, and to confront its manipulation by the media.

Indeed, the meaning of outing has been shaped not by activists but by supermarket tabs and chat shows, whose preoccupation with the phenomenon hardly stems from a commitment to gay liberation. An actress branded as a dyke by Outpost becomes a "man hater" in the tabs, enabling reader and publisher alike to savor sexual secrets without seeming to approve. And there's the rub. What ideology is being served when a celebrity's sexuality is used to reinforce the presumption that lesbians hate men?

Then there's the matter of "selective outing." The activists believe any celeb who sings in the choir is fair game. But consider this confession by a programmer who recently interviewed me as a voiceover for shots of Outpost's oeuvre. His superiors were apparently willing to broadcast the names and faces on the posters—but not all of them. Seems one of Outpost's targets owns the station, so his face wouldn't be shown, and another celeb whose talk show is about to air on the same station would also be exempt. That's an ethic every bit as hypocritical as the Pentagon's.

Is it the activists' fault that the media distort their intentions? Absolutely. You don't fuck with a lion unless you know how to stroke its mane. But not even a master of media manipulation could control the connotations of outing, as long as its targets are honchos of the entertainment world. Trafficking in the sex lives of celebrities has never been a noble line of work. And the witch-hunts that periodically sweep through Hollywood (whether they concern drugs or deviant sex) stem from precisely the same rationale as outing. Celebrities must be held to a "higher standard" of personal conduct because they set an example for the young. In reality, of course, it's not the safety of children but the ritual of celebrity sacrifice that animates the gossip blitz. Outing can only be assimilated by the star-making machinery as an extension of the process of fixing sin to the successful, and there is certainly nothing liberating about that.

There's a more fundamental problem with outing celebrities. It doesn't make anyone free—not even the proverbial lonely gay teenager in Nebraska who's supposed to be bolstered by the knowledge that Bill and Ted's excellent adventure was actually a romp in the rump. Just what does it mean to have your hero dragged kicking and screaming out of the closet? If you're lucky, the target of an outing campaign will graciously deny the accusation while insisting she has nothing against gay people; if you're very lucky, he'll own up to being bisexual (meaning, in most cases, he once subscribed to *Playboy*). To date, I can't think of a single outed celebrity who went on to strike a blow for candor and liberation. That only happens when someone *comes out*, without a nasty shove from the *Star*.

As for the contention that outing celebrities catalyzes the gay movement's growth because it demonstrates the ubiquity of queers, I suspect it only reinforces the conviction that Hollywood is a nest of pervs, and that movie stars are different from the rest of us. Yet, it's precisely on one's home turf that the real battle for sexual freedom must be fought. To imagine that gay teens can overcome their panic and pain by focusing on fantasy figures rather than by forging bonds among their peers is to indulge in a particularly American illusion. Call it liberation by Geraldo.

But what if the ethic of outing changed? What if we outed people who contribute to homophobia by their actions rather than their status? What if celebrities were, for the most part, exempt and only public figures were targeted? By which I mean people who actually oppress homosexuals, by making anti-gay policy or executing it (say, by running an aversion therapy program or conducting job interviews in a way that weeds out queers). And what if we encouraged discussion of a hero's sexuality only after his or her death? That lonely queer teen would get nurturance enough from the obituary pages, and legitimate interests in documenting the lives of historic figures would be served. The tabs, on the other hand, would be all but foiled.

Not all closeted public figures ought to be exposed—a tactic that clearly plays into the hands of the right—just queers who cause gay suffering or justify it. Outing people according to their actions would go a long way toward dispelling the comparison with revealing the names of rape victims. A woman who is raped hasn't done anything to justify the stigma that could follow the disclosure of her identity; a homophobe has.

Would I have outed Roy Cohn, who was not above gay-baiting his enemies, or Terry Dolan, who raised funds for homophobic pols? You betcha. What about a Supreme Court justice who rules that states may lock up queers without violating the prohibition on cruel and unusual punishment, while enjoying cozy nights by the fire with his male lover? Yes, I would out him—for hypocrisy in the service of homophobia. By the same token, I'd print it if I could prove that a Grand Dragon of the Ku Klux Klan has a black grandmother. Privacy is moot when personal and political hypocrisy merge.

By this reasoning, the *Voice* effectively outed Father Bruce Ritter. The head of Covenant House was apparently having sex with young men in his care—even as he was condemning homosexuality as a member of the Meese commission on pornography. This decision was not so different from another we'd made some years earlier, to reveal that Meir Kahane once had a relationship with a Christian woman who committed suicide when it ended. The information offered an insight into Kahane's political development, and was therefore newsworthy. So was the revelation, printed by the *Times* more than 20 years ago, that New York State's top Nazi was a Jew. (The individual killed himself after the story appeared.)

Public figures who seek political influence are and should be subject to a higher standard of personal scrutiny—as libel law recognizes. Outing is most defensible when it meets this standard. And the activists are right to insist that homosexuality be openly discussed when it helps to explain a public figure's political development—especially since the closet is a pathological state that often leads to self-protective homophobia.

I'll abide by the consensus we arrived at by not mentioning the name of the official in Signorile's piece. But I'm glad to report that another publication, the *Advocate*, is considering full disclosure. I believe any gay person who plays a prominent role in the military—especially within the Pentagon—is guilty of political hypocrisy. Some of my colleagues disagree, and others are convinced that outing can never be an instrument of liberation politics. The debate we waged seems essential to the tricky task of deciding when—and whether—to publish information about someone's private life. In this case, I'll take my chances with liberation by Geraldo.

Editorial

Richard Rouilard
(*Advocate*, August 27, 1991)

Outing is a weapon of last resort.

In *Hardwick v. Bowers*, a 1986 Georgia sodomy case, the Supreme Court stated that gays and lesbians have no private lives, that our bedrooms may be invaded at random. The states, under their Tenth Amendment powers, may treat us like criminals if they choose to— and 25 states and the District of Columbia do. We are not humans worthy of basic constitutional protections.

We are beaten and murdered in unprecedented numbers, and our cities' police departments, in almost all cases, ignore the hate-crime aspects of these assaults. Judges mete out soft sentences, with the victim becoming the criminal.

Employment and insurance discrimination against gays and lesbians is rampant. Gay teens commit suicide at three times the rate of their straight counterparts, according to a report squelched by the Department of Health and Human Services. Gay artists are being dumped from the National Endowment for the Arts. And the armed forces are booting us out, ruining lives, at the rate of nearly 1,000 per year.

As we have come out and asked for basic protections afforded every other being in this country, we've witnessed a tremendous backlash. Senator Jesse Helms and Representative William Dannemeyer, conservative fundamentalists, and even White House chief of staff John Sununu have shown through their actions that they're out for blood. Ours.

The right-wing organizations attacking us have many homosexuals in their ranks. We have long known this. Previously, we never outed those who acquiesced to anti-gay activities, understanding that all of us have to make some accommodations in a principally heterosexual world and that some progress could, albeit slowly, be made by closeted homosexuals in high places. Of course, this rule of accommodation does not apply to the likes of J. Edgar Hoover, Roy Cohn, or Terry Dolan, for they directly involved themselves in anti-gay activities. They are our Frankenstein's monsters, reviled and pitied.

But what of those who acquiesce in very high positions, who are able to affect policy changes, and who do nothing? Can we afford to suffer these Uncle Toms in this increasingly violent climate?

In almost all cases, yes. They are our people, whether we like it or not, whether they like it or not. But no longer can we abide *every* omission to act. We cannot support the acquiescence of Pete Williams, the assistant secretary of defense for public affairs, to the policies of the most homophobic department of the U.S. government. Too many gays and lesbians have been harmed too egregiously. We commit ourselves to this singular instance of outing in the name of the 12,966 lesbian and gay soldiers who have been outed by the military since 1982.

The gratuitous outing of movie stars and politicians is not at issue here. We do not support outing based on rumor and innuendo. The journalistic standards of the *Advocate* preclude us, and, in most cases, the nexus of omission to act (acquiescence) and the ability to act would be insufficient to proceed anyway.

Deciding to out Pete Williams did not require us to search our souls very long. We had heard for some time that he is a closeted homosexual. Now, with Michelangelo Signorile's article, we know. We have been reporting military horror story after horror story since the beginning of this newsmagazine. Williams clearly is intimately involved in policy-making on the highest levels. His silent complicity in this noxious conspiracy against gay and lesbian soldiers implicitly allows his superiors to continue the blanket exclusion, the hateful investigations, the dishonorable discharges, the ruination of lives. What about the murders and suicides? Or don't you read the nation's newspapers, Mr. Press Secretary? Try the article in the *Los Angeles Times* on July 9, 1991, headlined "Base Killings Linked to Homosexual Relationship."

Pete Williams is not the innocent victim of rabid gay activists. We're talking about a man who knowingly assists in the promotion of policies designed to thoroughly undermine the community in which, part time, he lives. All reports confirm that Williams has never once interceded on behalf of gay and lesbian soldiers. He remains silent. We choose not to be, and we have that right. We censure.

It is time that we refute the double standards of the Department of Defense. Representative Barney Frank admits that if Williams's superiors don't know that he is homosexual, then "our FBI wouldn't be all that it's cracked up to be." They know. He knows they know. Homosexuals like Williams are common in antigay conservative circles. They are the welcome mats of the Republican party.

Homosexual homophobes deserve our scorn, our censure, and eventually our pity and help. They are twisted human beings, tortured souls acting out what society has taught them. And in some cases, they become so indifferent to the plight of the gay and lesbian community, they chose their careers at *any* cost to the community in which they live.

Pete Williams is just such an unfortunate being. There is no question that he is a very nice homosexual gentleman. Charming, in fact. Welcome mats are made that way. Signorile's carefully sourced article in this issue makes the case of Williams's sexual orientation and his other charms quite clear. The few gay men (no lesbians) who have spoken to us in his defense consistently assert just what a nice guy Pete is. When asked how such a nice man can participate in military gay bashing that has led to suicide, these people refuse to make the connection between Williams and these pogroms. Williams keeps his job because he allows his superiors to avoid the connection.

A veil of silence had descended upon this story. The article was originally slated to run in the now-defunct lesbian and gay newsmagazine *OutWeek*. The national media were well aware of its imminent arrival. Signorile received calls from columnists, editors, and news producers. But no news organization (assuming that the tabloid the *Globe* does not quite fit that category) would pick up the story and really run with it, printing Williams' name. Except for the *Village Voice*, only a few editors took up the question in news meetings, and almost all decided cursorily that outing in any context was reprehensible.

There is a national distaste for gay and lesbian rights. In newsrooms around the country, most editors will not equate the gay and lesbian struggle with that of blacks, Hispanics, or other minorities. The reason most editors will not participate in outing on any basis, we understand, is that labeling someone as homosexual is just too disgraceful a thing to do to anyone.

The media would silence our complaints against a member of our own community. No other minority in this country is treated in this fashion. Did the Congressional Black Caucus have the right to challenge the credentials of Supreme Court nominee Clarence Thomas? Will this outing, this censuring of Thomas's experience as an influential black official, have a detrimental effect on the confirmation hearings? Or on Thomas's career if he is not confirmed? Will the Democrats on the Senate Judiciary Committee ignore the justifiable outrage of the African-American community at a black man who thrives at the expense of his community?

Most gay and lesbian readers with whom we've spoken agree that we should proceed with this story. And so do our readers. In a November 1990 national readership survey (1,271 respondents) a majority of *Advocate* readers felt that outing was "sometimes a justifiable political action." Slightly more than 3 percent felt that outing was "always a justifiable political action." These gay leaders and our readers can carefully distinguish the Pete Williams case from others. The climate has changed. We cannot go back, and they will not let us go forward. Jesse Helms, Lou Sheldon, Dick Cheney and friends have upped the stakes. In many cases, we are fighting for our lives.

Should anyone think that homophobia in the Department of Defense is a matter of incidental concern, consider the headline on the cover of the *Advocate*. Since 1989, when Williams was appointed, 2,273 gay and lesbian soldiers have been discharged. The figure does not take into account those who have been court-martialed, nor those fortunate officers who've been able to cut a deal with their superiors.

The majority of these discharges involve routine third-degree harassing of the soldier, who is sometimes handcuffed and interrogated under bright lights. The officer in charge of the investigation threatens to reveal the soldier's homosexuality to friends, acquaintances, and family members. Many of these soldiers, young and vulnerable, have not yet begun to contemplate coming out. Investigating officers make wild assertions regarding the soldier's sexual activity (if there has been even that; a "propensity" toward homosexuality is sufficient for discharge) and, according to an April 1990 New York Times article, threaten to inform the soldier's hometown newspaper. When the soldier is a parent, investigators threaten loss of custody of the soldier's children.

And then, for the rest of these soldiers' lives, a paper trail exists that nearly every potential employer can decipher: The applicant was kicked out of the service because he or she is homosexual.

Today, former Army colonel Edward Modesto, dishonorably discharged, cannot get his oral surgeon's license because he was imprisoned in Leavenworth for being a gay soldier.

Lesbians are booted out at ten times the rate of gay men. Former Marine Corps corporal Barbara Baum's girlfriend was allegedly threatened with loss of custody of her child. Baum was sentenced to one year in the brig.

An estimated 700 gay and lesbian soldiers who fought in the Gulf war are about to be discharged from the service. The Wall Street Journal reported in January and again in July that their superiors had full knowledge of their homosexuality prior to their fighting in the Persian Gulf. The military's message is clear: It's OK for gays and lesbians to risk their lives for our country, and it's OK for the Department of Defense to then ruin the lives of these Desert Storm troopers.

There have been suicides, and there have been murders in relation to these discharges. The list of horror stories is endless. How many millions of dollars were wasted pursuing these discharges and courts-martial and maintaining gay prisoners? It is estimated that the discharge of Army reserve drill sergeant Miriam Ben-Shalom cost as much as $3 million.

The defense department does not know how much all this cost. They know that 12,966 gay and lesbian soldiers were discharged since 1982. And that's all they want to know.

But what did Pete Williams know? Is it possible, as one acquaintance of his maintains, that he knew nothing? How, we have to ask, could Dick Cheney say in a USA Today article that there is "no question in my mind that we've got a large number of gays in military service" and his homosexual press secretary not also know that is the case? According to congressional staffers, Williams is a policymaker. "He's in on many key decisions," one states. "He decides how things are going to play, and certainly he's involved in hushing things up."

Pete Williams knows that the military's blanket exclusion of gays and lesbians is wrong. And that his silent complicity encourages the continuation of this vile and despotic activity. The U.S. military is awash in lies and hypocrisy. Williams is the proof that we are not perverts, liable to be blackmailed at every turn, incapable of containing our sexual urges when necessary—all the stereotypical bullshit that is used to justify this purge of good soldiers. For much less than the very same activities Williams has been involved in, many of these soldiers have had their lives ruined.

We do not want to ruin Pete Williams's life. We are asking Pete Williams to confirm what is true: that he has security clearance on the highest level; that he is an excellent and effective spokesman; that he has the confidence of the President, the secretary of defense, and his co-workers; and that his sexuality has not interfered with his position.

Except when he hides it.

Editorial

Richard Rouilard

(*Advocate*, October 8, 1991)

Outing is nasty stuff. In spite of the number of letters we received in favor of the outing of Assistant Secretary of Defense Pete Williams, the offices of the *Advocate* suffer a lingering odor. The smell of guilt cannot be swept away with a dose of Carpet Fresh. Outing Williams hurt him, we imagine, and it also hurt the community, we know. The ferocity of some of the how-dare-you letters was painful for us. The panoramic anger expressed by some letter writers was probably frightening for them. We received death threats by mail and by telephone, reminders that there are many souls in our community lost in the netherworld of panic. Outing wasn't really the issue for these people.

The community, according to an *Advocate* survey taken last fall, is divided 55 percent for to 45 percent against outing. The statistics bear out in the proportion of positive to negative letters we received. Nonetheless, a small majority's opinion is not a persuasive ground swell for a fall gala of outings. We have been oppressed by an allegedly healthy majority for too long and outing is too complex an issue to pursue on the basis of a statistic.

One of the *Advocate* editors was completely turned around by the outing. He felt it was a violation of our fundament—privacy. He nonetheless participated in the mainstream media's interviews with *Advocate* editors. Listening to the tone of the interviewers, he was slapped right across the face by homophobia. An Epiphany.

Anger often replaces guilt. This editor is no longer our advocatus diaboli on outing. He is too angry about the distinction that is made catholically for heterosexuals, that of the readily acceptable public sphere versus the more questionable-to-report-on private sphere— George Bush's wedding band versus Gary Hart's bedroom. In all cases, it seems homosexuals, even those in the public eye, are relegated to the questionable-to-report-on even when their gross hypocrisy is apparent.

Had the mainstream media been following the appalling developments in the U.S. military, the *Advocate* would not have had to take the dramatic step of outing the assistant secretary of defense to get their attention. Considering the state of affairs—the imminent discharge of as many as 2,000 Desert Storm troops—we felt that briefly interrupting the career of one hypocritical homophobe (who happens to be gay) was, if not entirely justifiable, certainly not indefensible.

Editors and reporters, including a few gay ones, raced to the high moral ground, refusing to name The Name on the basis of invasion of privacy. Nonetheless, they were all just dying for one of the big papers to do it. The *Detroit News* apparently wasn't quite big enough. The ensuing who's-gonna-do-it-first? game regarding naming the alleged Kennedy rape victim had a certain sophomoric quality that was endearing. Having not named The Name then, these reporters went to bed unencumbered by bad thoughts—guilt. Guilt required, at least, a subconscious acknowledgment of failure. These reporters do not have enough knowledge, subconscious or otherwise, about their own internalized homophobia to feel guilty. That is why God made the alternative press.

The *Los Angeles Times* does not feel guilty. They didn't name any names. Not that alleged Kennedy rape victim. Not that Pentagon spokesperson. But they raced to publish a story about a major sports figure whose son had recently died. They noted the major sports figure's reddened eyes, his stiff upper lip, his resolve to get back in the game. Oy. The *Times* failed to note that the son died of AIDS, that he was a truly fine and flaming queer, and that the gay community in Los

Angeles is up in arms about the family's covering up the nature of the son's death.

Should the *Times* have outed the son posthumously? The medical reports maintain (and therefore, properly, the *Times* obituary stated) that the son died of pneumonia and dehydration. No newspaper (not even the *Advocate*) can go much further in this case without time-consuming investigative reports. But should the *Times* have participated in hiding the fact that the son was a—oh, yich, a homosexual?

If you can't name The Name, then don't play the closet game. Boldly ignoring someone's homosexuality is the purview of Hollywood PR flacks and society columnists, not responsible editors. To not out someone, in this case, is a great injustice, but journalistic standards preclude any responsible news organ from doing it. The solution is, Don't promote the closet. Watch those double standards.

The closet in the '90s is too complex a historical phenomenon to be dismissed perfunctorily by the moralists and activists du jour. Clearly, it shouldn't be supported and co-opted, but neither should it be invaded or evaded without some inspection of the homophobic undercurrent that insinuates itself in all Americans' consciousness, gay or straight. So sit back, think about hurting someone, helping thousands, and feel that guilt. Another closet door will certainly be pried open soon enough. More than likely not by the *Advocate*. But that is why God made Queer Nation.

References

Aaron, Charles. 1992. "Rockbeat: DeFaced." *Village Voice*, June 6, 83.

Adam, Barry. 1978. *The Survival of Domination: Inferiorization and Everyday Life*. New York: Elsevier.

Advocate. 1992. "Not Even Worth an Outing." June 16, 11.

Allen, Charlotte Low. 1990. "Gays Playing the Name Game." *Insight*, September 17, 8–17.

Altman, Dennis. 1971. *Homosexual: Oppression and Liberation*. New York: Avon.

Anderson, Jack. 1970. "Vice President's Son, Viet Vet, Breaks with Wife; Agnew, Deeply Pained, Had Boasted of His Family; Son with Beauty Salon Operator; Moving to Garage." Bell-McClure Syndicate Column, released September 8.

—— and Dale Van Atta. 1991a. "Gay Group Tries to 'Out' Pentagon Spokesman." United Feature Syndicate, released August 2.

—— and Dale Van Atta. 1991b. Letter to the Editor. *Time*, September 9, 9.

Anderson, Porter. 1992. "Teasers and Tormentors." *Village Voice*, June 16, 94.

Appleyard, Brian. 1990. "Closet Gays Fear Terrorism by a Militant Tendency." *Sunday Times* (London), May 6.

Arendt, Hannah. 1968. *Men in Dark Times*. New York: Harcourt Brace & World.

——. 1973. *The Origins of Totalitarianism*. New York: Harcourt Brace Jovanovich.

Atkins, Robert. 1992. "Scene & Heard." *Village Voice*, June 9, 97.

Bailey, Michael, and Richard Pillard. 1991. "A Genetic Study of Male Sexual Orientation." *Archives of General Psychiatry*, December, 1089–96.

Barnicle, Mike. 1990. "The Nonsense of 'Outing'." *Boston Globe*, May 10, 35.

Barron, James. 1979. "Warren and Brandeis, The Right to Privacy: Demystifying a Landmark Citation." *Suffolk University Law Review* XIII, 875–922.

Bartlett, Neil. 1988. *Who Was That Man? A Present for Mr. Oscar Wilde*. London: Serpent's Tail.

Bauers, Sandy. 1991. "Today's Storybook Families." *Philadelphia Inquirer*, March 10, 1L.

Bauman, Robert. 1987. *The Gentleman from Maryland: The Conscience of a Gay Conservative*. New York: Arbor House.

Baxter, Sarah. 1991. "Out Loud: Gays and Lesbians Are in Fighting Mood." *New Statesman and Society*, August 9, 8.

Beery, Steve. 1990. "Liz Smith Mon Amour." *OutWeek*, May 16, 44–46.

Bennetts, Leslie. 1983. "How Stars of *La Cage* Grew into Their Roles." *New York Times*, August 24, C15.

Berger, Maurice. 1992. "Too Shocking to Show?" *Art in America*, July, 37–39.

Berke, Richard. 1990. "House Ready to Take Up Arts Fight." *New York Times*, October 10, B4.

Berube, Allan. 1990. *Coming Out under Fire: Lesbian and Gay Americans and the Military During World War Two*. New York: Free Press.

Blauner, Robert. 1972. *Racial Oppression in America*. New York: Harper & Row.

Boswell, John. 1992. "Concepts, Experience, and Sexuality." In *Forms of Desire*, edited by E. Stein, 133–73. New York: Routledge.

Bowles, Jennifer. 1992. "Anthony Perkins; Starred in 'Psycho.' " *Philadelphia Inquirer*, September 13, 31.

Branch, Taylor. 1982. "Closets of Power." *Harper's Magazine*, October, 35–50.

Brand, Adolph. 1991. "Political Criminals: A Word about the Röhm Case" (1931). In *Homosexuality and Male Bonding in Pre-Nazi Germany*, edited by Harry Oosterhuis, 235–40. New York: Haworth.

Brigham, Roger. 1992. "The Importance of Being Earvin." *Advocate*, April 21, 34–39.

Broder, Michael. 1992. "The Posthumous AIDS Outing of Robert Reed." *QW*, May 31, 18.

Broderick, Frank. 1992. "Tid Bits: k. d. lang Comes Out." *Au Courant* (Philadelphia), June 15, 5.

Broeske, Pat, and John Wilson. 1990. "Out-and-Out Fear in Hollywood." *San Francisco Chronicle*, Datebook, August 5.

Bronski, Michael. 1983. "Probing the Personal?" *Gay Community News*, April 23, 12.

——. 1984. *Culture Clash: The Making of Gay Sensibility*. Boston: South End Press.

——. 1990. "Outing: The Power of the Closet." *Gay Community News*, June 3.

——. 1991. "Lamb to the Slaughter." *Z Magazine*, May, 80–84.

——. 1992. "Homos vs. Hollywood." *NYQ*, March 29, 26–31.

Brown, Howard. 1976. *Familiar Faces, Hidden Lives*. New York: Harcourt Brace.

Brownworth, Victoria. 1990. "Campus Queer Query." *OutWeek*, May 16, 48–49.

Bruni, Frank. 1991a. "Gay Troops Face Unfriendly Fire." *Detroit Free Press*, August 12, 1A.

——. 1991b. "Airman's Openness Led to Official Grilling." *Detroit Free Press*, August 12, 4A.

Buchanan, Patrick. 1989. "How Can We Clean Up Our Art Act?" *Washington Post*, June 19.

——. 1992. "Buchanan to Cuomo: This Is What 'Cultural War' Means." *Philadelphia Inquirer*, September 12, A7.

Bull, Chris. 1990. "Boston Activist 'Outs' a Politician but Ends Up Doubting Himself." *Advocate*, July 17, 13.

——. 1991. "In Minneapolis, Outing of Rabbi Spurs Hot Debate." *Advocate*, February 12, 23.

——. 1992. "The Outing of a Family-Values Congressman." *Advocate*, September 22, 38–45.

Bullough, Vern. 1979. *Homosexuality: A History*. New York: New American Library.

Bush, Larry. 1982. "Naming Gay Names." *Village Voice*, April 27, 22–25.

——. 1983. "Gerry Studds–I." *Advocate*, September 15, 15.

Byron, Stuart. 1972. "The Closet Syndrome." In *Out of the Closets: Voices of Gay Liberation*, edted by Karla Jay and Allen Young. New York: Douglas.

——. 1990. "Naming Names." *Advocate*, April 24, 37.

Cain, Roy. 1991. "Disclosure and Secrecy among Gay Men in the United States and Canada: A Shift in Views." *Journal of the History of Sexuality* 2, no. 1, 25–45.

Campbell, Tim. 1991a. "Response from a 'Pathological Liar.' " *La Crosse Tribune*, July 26, A4.

——. 1991b. "Gunderson Outing Rocks Wisconsin." *GLC Voice* (Minneapolis), August 5.

Canby, Vincent. 1992. "Time Was Dietrich's Most Ardent Lover." *New York Times*, May 17, H22.

Carlson, Ben. 1991. "Historic Smooch on *LA Law*." *Bay Area Reporter*, February 14, 26.

Carmody, Deirdre. 1991. "Debate Is Intense on Naming Accuser." *New York Times*, April 18, A22.

Carr, C. 1991. "Why Outing Must Stop." *Village Voice*, March 19, 37.

———. 1992a. "Here Comes the New Boss, Worse Than the Old Boss." *Village Voice*, March 3, 28–29.

———. 1992b. "The Decency Czarina." *Village Voice*, June 9, 41.

Castro, Peter. 1991. "Chatter." *People*, September 23, 126.

Chauncey, George, and Lisa Kennedy. 1987. "Time on Two Crosses: An Interview with Bayard Rustin." *Village Voice*, June 30, 27–29.

Chunovic, Louis. 1992. "Gay in LA." *Pulse!*, May, 91–94.

Cipriano, Ralph. 1991. "The Rev. David M. McGowan, 40, Ex-host of Catholic TV Program." *Philadelphia Inquirer*, May 18, 9B.

Clark, Keith. 1992. "Breaking Barriers in the Mainstream Press." *QW*, June 21, 16.

Clum, John. 1992. *Acting Gay: Male Homosexuality in Modern Drama*. New York: Columbia University Press.

Cockburn, Alexander. 1991. "Beat the Devil: The Old In/Out." *Nation*, August 26, 220–21.

Cohen, Richard. 1992. "Schlafly's Silence." *Washington Post*, September 24, A29.

Conason, Joe. 1992. "George Bush's Adultery Thing." *Spy*, July/August, 29–38.

Connant, Jennet. 1991. "Doesn't David Geffen Know the 80s Are Over?" *GQ*, March.

Cook, Blanche Wiesen. 1992. *Eleanor Roosevelt*. Vol. 1, *1884–1933*. New York: Viking.

Cory, Donald Webster (pseudonym of Edward Sagarin). 1951. *The Homosexual in America: A Subjective Approach*. New York: Greenberg.

———. 1956. *Homosexuality: A Cross-Cultural Approach*. New York: Julian.

———. 1964. *The Lesbian in America*. New York: Citadel.

———. 1965. "Introduction" to Albert Ellis, *Homosexuality: Its Causes and Cure*. New York: Lyle Stuart.

——— and John LeRoy. 1963. *The Homosexual and His Society: A View from Within*. New York: Citadel.

Coward, Cheryl. 1992. "Radice Draws Fire Over Rejected NEA Grants." *Advocate*, December 29, 21.

Decter, Midge. 1980. "The Boys on the Beach." *Commentary*, September, 35–48.

D'Emilio, John. 1983. *Sexual Politics, Sexual Communities*. Chicago: University of Chicago Press.

———. 1987. "Homosexual Professors Owe It to Their Students to 'Come Out.' " *Chronicle of Higher Education*, October 28, A52.

——— and Estelle Freedman. 1988. *Intimate Matters: A History of Sexuality in America*. New York: Harper & Row.

DeStefano, George. 1986. "The *New York Times* vs. Gay America." *Advocate*, December 9.

Deutscher, Isaac. 1968. *The Non-Jewish Jew and Other Essays*. New York: Oxford University Press.

Dowd, Maureen. 1986. "Razor-edged Race for Maryland Seat: Chavez's 'Tough' Strategy Hits at Mikulski's View of Men." *New York Times*, October 20.

———. 1991. "All That Glitters Is Not Real, Book on Nancy Reagan Says." *New York Times*, April 7, A1.

Drury, Alan. 1961. *Advise and Consent*. Garden City, N.Y.: Doubleday.

Duberman, Martin. 1973. "Coming Out." Reprinted in *About Time: Exploring the Gay Past*. New York: Gay Presses of New York, 1986.

———. 1974. "The Course of the Gay Movement." Reprinted in *About Time: Exploring the Gay Past*. New York: Gay Presses of New York, 1986.

———. 1986. *About Time: Exploring the Gay Past*. New York: Gay Presses of New York.

———. 1991. *Cures: A Gay Man's Odyssey*. New York: Dutton.

Dubin, Murray. 1985. "In Hollywood, Gays Remain in the Closet." *Philadelphia Inquirer*, August 11, 1A.

Dwyer, Sandy. 1991. "Wachs Confronted as Closeted Gay." *Vanguard News and Views*, April 19, 1.

Dyer, Richard. 1977. "Stereotyping." In *Gays and Film*, edited by Richard Dyer. London: British Film Institute.

———. 1979. *Stars*. London: British Film Institute.

———. 1986. *Heavenly Bodies: Film Stars and Society*. New York: St. Martin's.

———. 1990. *Now You See It: Studies on Lesbian and Gay Film*. New York: Routledge.

———. 1992. "*A Star Is Born* and the Construction of Authenticity." In *Stardom: Industry of Desire*, edited by Christine Gledhill, 132–40. London: Routledge.

Ehrenstein, David. 1992. "Talking Pictures." *Advocate*, May 5, 72.

Enrico, Dottie. 1991. "The Media Fallout from 'Lesbian Kiss.' " *San Francisco Chronicle*, March 5, E1.

Epstein, Steven. 1992 (original 1987). "Gay Politics, Ethnic Identity: The Limits of Social Constructionism." In *Forms of Desire*, edited by E. Stein, 239–94. New York: Routledge.

Escoffier, Jeffrey. 1985. "Sexual Revolution and the Politics of Gay Identity." *Socialist Review*, September, 119–53.

——— and Gene Rocchio. 1991. "AIDS Activism: Where We Stand." *Out/Look*, Winter, 87–88.

Fabrikant, Geraldine. 1989. "Ads Reportedly Lost Because of Gay Scene." *New York Times*, November 14, D21.

Firestone, David. 1991. "Columnist Stokes Gay-Naming Debate." *New York Newsday*, August 9, 17.

Fleck, Tim. 1991. "*Houston Post* Squelches Columnist's Coming Out." *Advocate*, August 27, 54–55.

Foucault, Michel. 1978. *The History of Sexuality*. Vol. 1, *An Introduction*. New York: Random House.

Freedman, Peter. 1992. "The Canadian Conspiracy." *Globe and Mail* (Toronto), August 8, D5.

French, Sean. 1989. "Diary." *The New Statesman and Society*, January 27, 9.

Friedrich, Otto. 1986. *City of Nets: A Portrait of Hollywood in the 1940s*. London: Headline.

Friendly, Fred. 1990. "Gays, Privacy and a Free Press." *Washington Post*, April 8, B7.

Fuss, Diana. 1989. *Essentially Speaking: Feminism, Nature and Difference*. New York: Routledge.

Gable, Donna. 1992. " 'Life' Story Looks at Roots of Homophobia." *USA Today*, June 2, 3D.

Gailey, Phil. 1982a. "Homosexual Takes Leave of a Job and of an Agony." *New York Times*, March 31, A24.

———. 1982b. "A Personal Issue for 'Nick-Pack' Head." *New York Times*, August 17.

Gallagher, John. 1991a. "Hollywood Watchers: Griffin Suit Exposes Industry's Intolerance." *Advocate*, May 21, 14.

———. 1991b. "Actor's Libel Lawsuit Leaves Media Asking How to Cover Outing." *Advocate*, August 13, 21.

———. 1991c. "Hypothalamus Study and Coverage of It Attract Many Barbs." *Advocate*, October 8, 14–15.

Gant, Cathy. 1991. "Kirkpatrick: Hinshaw Had Sex with Son." *Greensboro News & Record*, October 25, A1.

Garment, Suzanne. 1991. *Scandal: The Culture of Mistrust in American Politics*. New York: Times Books.

Gelman, David. 1990. " 'Outing': An Unexpected Assault on Sexual Privacy." *Newsweek*, April 30, 66.

Gerard, Jasper, and Tim Rayment. 1991. "Gays Threaten to 'Out' MPs in Poster Campaign." *Sunday Times* (London), July 28, 1.

Gessen, Masha, and David McGowan. 1992. "Raiders of the Gay Gene." *Advocate*, March 24, 60–62.

Ghiglione, Loren, Reid MacCluggage, Leroy Aarons, and Lee Stinnett. 1990. *Alternatives: Gays and Lesbians in the Newsroom*. Washington, D.C.: American Society of Newspaper Editors.

Gibbs, Nancy. 1991. "Marching Out of the Closet." *Time*, August 19, 14–16.

Gibson, P. 1989. "Gay Male and Lesbian Youth Suicide." *Report of the Secretary's Task Force on Youth Suicide*. Vol. 1: *Overview and Recommendations*. Washington, D.C.: U.S. Department of Health and Human Services: 110–42.

Giteck, Lenny. 1987. "The Traitors among Us: Horror Tales in D.C." *Advocate*, September 29, 6.

Gledhill, Christine, ed. 1991. *Stardom: Industry of Desire*. London: Routledge.

Goff, Michael. 1991. "Gaydar." *OutWeek*, February 20, 49.

Goffman, Erving. 1959. *The Presentation of Self in Everyday Life*. New York: Anchor.

Goldstein, Richard. 1990. "The Art of Outing: When Is It Right to Name Gay Names?" *Village Voice*, May 1, 33–37.

———. 1991. "The Outer Limits." *Village Voice*, July 30, 40.

Gordon, George. 1991. "This Fascist Gay Army Doomed to Failure." *Daily Mail* (London), July 30.

Grahn, Judy. 1984. *Another Mother Tongue: Gay Words, Gay Worlds*. Boston: Beacon.

Gray, Natasha. 1991. "Outing's German Roots." *NYQ*, November 3, 48–49.

Gross, Jane. 1992a. "Does She Speak for Today's Women?" *New York Times Magazine*, March 1.

———. 1992b. "Gay Journalists Gather to Complain and to Celebrate Progress at Work." *New York Times*, June 29, B6.

Gross, Larry. 1989. "Out of the Mainstream: Sexual Minorities and the Mass Media." In *Remote Control: Television, Audiences and Cultural Power*, edited by Ellen Seiter et al. London: Routledge.

———. 1991. "The Contested Closet: The Politics and Ethics of Outing." *Critical Studies in Mass Communication* 8, no. 3, 352–88.

———. 1993. "What Is Wrong with This Picture?: Lesbian Women and Gay Men on Television." In *Queer Words, Queer Images*, edited by J. Ringer. New York: New York University Press.

Grzesiak, Rich. 1983. "Truth and Consequences." *New York Native*, June 6–19, 30.

Gup, Ted. 1988. "Identifying Homosexuals: What Are the Rules?" *Washington Journalism Review*, October, 30–33.

Guthmann, Edward. 1990. "Whoopi Hits Gold Again." *San Francisco Chronicle*, November 18, Datebook: 21–24.

Hachem, Samir. 1987. "Inside the Tinseled Closet." *Advocate*, March 17, 48.

Hadleigh, Boze. 1991. *The Vinyl Closet: Gays in the Music World*. San Diego: Los Hombres.

Hall, Carla. 1992. "Jerry Brown's Silent Partner." *Washington Post*, April 27, D1, 4.

Halperin, David. 1990. *One Hundred Years of Homosexuality*. New York: Routledge.

Hardie, Chris. 1991. "Gay Rights Protester Arrested; Flier Targets Gunderson." *La Crosse Tribune*, July 5, A12.

Harding, Rick. 1989. "Legacy of a Double Life." *Advocate*, September 26, 12–13.

Harper, Phillip Brian. 1991. "Eloquence and Epitaph: Black Nationalism and the Homophobic Impulse in Responses to the Death of Max Robinson." *Social Text* 28, 68–86.

Harris, David. 1982. *Dreams Die Hard: Three Men's Journey Through the Sixties*. New York: St. Martin's.

Harwood, Michael. 1991. Letter to the Editor. *Village Voice*, April 23, 5.

Harwood, Richard. 1991a. " 'Untouchably Touchy.' " *Washington Post*, July 28, C6.

———. 1991b. "Sex and Sinners." *Washington Post*, August 18, C6.

Hayes, William. 1990. "To Be Young and Gay and Living in the 90s." *Mother Jones*. July/August.

Henry, William III. 1990. "Forcing Gays Out of the Closet." *Time*, January 29, 67.

———. 1991. "To 'Out' or Not to 'Out.' " *Time*, August 19, 17.

Hentoff, Nat. 1991. "Armageddon in Adrian, Michigan." *Village Voice*, March 5, 20.

Herzer, Manfred. 1990. "Kertbeny, Karoly Maria." In *Encyclopedia of Homosexuality*, edited by Wayne Dynes. New York: Garland.

Hitchens, Christopher. 1987. "It Dare Not Speak Its Name: Fear and Self-loathing on the Gay Right." *Harper's Magazine*, August, 70–72.

Hodges, Andrew, and David Hutter. 1974. *With Downcast Gays: Aspects of Homosexual Self Oppression*. Toronto: Pink Triangle.

Honan, William. 1992a. "Arts Chief Vetoes 2 Approved Grants." *New York Times*, May 13, C13, 14.

———. 1992b. "Judge Overrules Decency Statute for Arts Grants." *New York Times*, June 10, A1, C17.

Hunter, Nan. 1991. "Sexual Dissent and the Family." *Nation*, October 7, 406–11.

Indiana, Gary. 1991. "Movies: Heavy Estrogen." *Interview*. January.

Jacobs, Andrew. 1992a. "Q In." *QW*, May 31, 23.

———. 1992b. "Q In." *QW*, June 21, 21.

Jay, Karla, and Allen Young, eds. 1972. *Out of the Closets: Voices of Gay Liberation*. New York: Douglas.

Jetter, Alexis. 1986. "AIDS and the Obits." *Columbia Journalism Review*, July/August, 14–16.

Johnson, Dirk. 1990. "Privacy vs. the Pursuit of Gay Rights." *New York Times*, March 27, A21.

Johnson, Peter. 1992. "Inside TV." *USA Today*, June 11.

Jones, Alex. 1992a. "Report of Ashe's Illness Raises an Old Issue for Editors." *New York Times*, April 10, A25.

———. 1992b. "News Media Torn Two Ways in Debate on Privacy." *New York Times*, April 30, B11.

Jones, Lisa. 1991. "Passages." *Village Voice*, February 19, 72.

Kaiser, Charles. 1992a. "The Gay Marine." *Details*, January, 74–77.

———. 1992b. "Who Killed *OutWeek?*" *NYQ*, March 1, 26–33.

Kasindorf, Jeanie. 1990. "Mr. Out: A Gay Journalist's Campaign to Expose Famous Homosexuals Prompts Charges of McCarthyism." *New York*, May 14, 84–94.

Katz, Jonathan Ned. 1976. *Gay American History*. New York: Crowell.

———. 1983. *Gay/Lesbian Almanac*. New York: Harper.

Kauffmann, Stanley. 1966. "Homosexual Drama and Its Disguises." *New York Times*,

January 23, 2:1. (Reprinted in S. Kauffmann. 1976. *Persons of the Drama*, 291–94. New York: Harper & Row.)

Kinsey, Alfred, W. B. Pomeroy, and C. E. Martin. 1948. *Sexual Behavior in the Human Male*. Philadelphia: Saunders.

Kinsey, Alfred, W. B. Pomeroy, C. E. Martin, and P. Gebhard. 1953. *Sexual Behavior in the Human Female*. Philadelphia: Saunders.

Klaidman, Stephen, and Tom Beauchamp. 1987. *The Virtuous Journalist*. New York: Oxford University Press.

Kolata, Gina. 1989. "Lesbian Partners Find the Means to Be Parents." *New York Times*, January 30.

Kopkind, Andrew. 1991. "Naming Names." *Z Magazine*, July/August, 58–59.

Kraemer, David. 1991. "Q & A: The Osseo Republican Discussed Gay Rights, 'Outing' and His Reaction to Queer Nation." *La Crosse Tribune*, July 21.

Kramer, Larry. 1991. Letter to the Editor. *Village Voice*, August 20, 5.

Krebs, Albin. 1986. "Roy Cohn: Aide to McCarthy and Fiery Lawyer Dies at 59." *New York Times*, August 3.

Krier, Beth Ann. 1990. "Whose Sex Secret Is It? Do We Have a Right to Know a Public Figure's Sexual Orientation?" *Los Angeles Times*, March 22, E1.

Lacayo, Richard. 1991. "Tarting Up the Gray Lady of 43rd Street." *Time*, May 6, 44–45.

Larriera, Alicia. 1991. "Vicious Gay Campaign against Franca Arena." *Sydney Morning Herald*, August 9, 1.

Larson, Leslie. 1991. "Foster Freeze." Letter to the Editor. *Village Voice*, April 2, 5.

LaValley, Al. 1985. "The Great Escape." *American Film*, April.

Lazar, Jerry. 1990. "Hollywood Witch-hunt." *US*, August 6, 38–43.

Lazere, Arthur. 1987. "Gays and Lesbians in Academia: Laud Humphrey's Ironic Position." *Washington Blade*, May 16.

Ledbetter, James. 1991. "Media Blitz: A Long Hot Summer Outing." *Village Voice*, August 13, 8.

———. 1992. "Media Blitz: *Post* Styles of Courage." *Village Voice*, June 23, 9.

Lee, John Alan. 1977. "Going Public: A Study in the Sociology of Gay Liberation." *Journal of Homosexuality* 3, no. 1, 49–78.

Lemon, Brendan. 1992. "Virgin Territory: Music's Purest Vocalist Opens Up." *Advocate*, June 16, 34–46.

———. 1992. "David Geffen: Man of the Year." *Advocate*, December 29, 35–40.

LeVay, Simon. 1991. "A Difference in Hypothalamic Structure Between Heterosexual and Homosexual Men." *Science*, August 30, 1034–37.

Lew, Julie. 1991. "Why the Movies are Ignoring AIDS." *New York Times*, August 18, H18.

Lewin, Rebecca. 1990. "A Few Minutes with Fractious Fran." *Advocate*, July 3, 63.

Lewis, Claude. 1992. "Ashe's Star Quality Extended Far Beyond the Tennis Courts." *Philadelphia Inquirer*, April 15, A19.

Leznoff, Maurice, and William Westley. 1956. "The Homosexual Community." *Social Problems*, 3, no. 4, 257–63.

Lichtenstein, Bill. 1992. "The Secret Battle for the NEA." *Village Voice*, March 10, 35–37.

Loder, Kurt. 1991. Letter to the Editor. *Village Voice*, May 21, 5.

Longcope, Kay. 1990. "Gays Divided on Tactic of Forcing Others out of the Closet." *Boston Globe*, May 3, 1.

McConnell, Vicki. 1992. "Changing Channels." *Advocate*, January 14, 70–72.

McFarlane, Roger. 1991. Letter to the Editor. *Village Voice*, August 20, 5.

McHugh, Clare. 1990. "Gossip Heats Up." *Mirabella*, November, 100–101.

McWilliams, Michael. 1991. "Will Magazine's 'Outing' of Gulf War Spokesman Change Pentagon Policy Toward Gays?" *Detroit News*, August 3, C1, 12.

Mallinger, Scott. 1990. "Come Out, Come Out, Whoever You Are: The Politics of Outing." *Au Courant* (Philadelphia), May 14.

Manchester, William. 1968. *The Arms of Krupp*. Boston: Little, Brown.

Margolick, David. 1990. "Ascetic at Home but Vigorous on Bench." *New York Times*, July 25, A1, 12.

Marotta, Toby. 1981. *The Politics of Homosexuality*. Boston: Houghton Mifflin.

Marvin, Carolyn. 1988. *When Old Technologies Were New*. New York: Oxford University Press.

Maslin, Janet. 1991. "Filming Cannibalism with Restraint." *New York Times*, February 19, B1, 3.

Mass, Lawrence. 1990. "Sexual Categories, Sexual Universals: A Conversation with John Boswell." In *Homosexuality as Behavior and as Identity: Dialogues of the Sexual Revolution*, vol. 2. New York: Harrington Park.

Massa, Robert. 1991. "The HIV Closet." *Village Voice*, August 27, 18.

Massing, Michael. 1980. "The Invisible Cubans." *Columbia Journalism Review*, September/October, 49–51.

Matza, Michael. 1990. "Out/Rage." *Philadelphia Inquirer*, June 28, E1.

Maupin, Armistead. 1981. "Juned In and Gayed Out." *New York Times*, June 27.

Merton, Niles. 1992. "Homosexuality, Honesty, and Hypocrisy." *Advocate*, September 22, 6.

Metroline (Hartford). 1991. Editorial. April 19, 4.

Milavsky, Ron. 1988. "AIDS and the media." Paper presented at the annual meeting of the American Psychological Association, Atlanta, August 15.

Miller, Merle. 1971. "What It Means to Be a Homosexual." *New York Times Magazine*, January 17.

Mills, Kim. 1990. "Gays Crying 'Gay.' " *Washington Journalism Review*, October, 23–25.

Minkowitz, Donna. 1991a. "Bella She Ain't." *Village Voice*, August 13, 11.

———. 1991b. "Reply." *Village Voice*, August 20, 5.

———. 1991c. "Patricia Ireland Takes the Reins." *Advocate*, December 17, 38–44.

———. 1992. "The NEA Hurricane." *Advocate*, June 14, 44–45.

Mohr, Richard. 1992. *Gay Ideas: Outing and Other Controversies*. Boston: Beacon.

Monroe, Bill. 1991. "The Press Respected Privacy—Twice." *Washington Journalism Review*, October, 6.

Moor, Paul. 1990. "Remembering Lennie: Parting Notes on a Friend Who Never Quite Came Out." *Advocate*, November 20, 66–67.

———. 1991. "Fanfare for an Uncommon Man: The Real Score on Composer Aaron Copland." *Advocate*, January 15, 54–55.

Murphy, Ryan, and Bunny Mars. 1991. "Another Dialogue Begins." *Advocate*, October 22, 44.

Musto, Michael. 1991a. "Reply" (to several letters). *Village Voice*, April 23, 5.

———. 1991b. "Reply" (to letter from Jim Fouratt). *Village Voice*, May 14, 5.

———. 1991c. "Reply" (to letter from Kurt Loder). *Village Voice*, May 21, 5.

———. 1991d. "La Dolce Musto." *Village Voice*, July 30, 39.

Myrdal, Gunnar. 1964. *An American Dilemma*. New York: McGraw-Hill.

Nardi, Peter. 1990. "AIDS and Obituaries: The Perpetuation of Stigma in the Press." In *Culture and AIDS*, edited by Douglas Feldman, 159–68. New York: Praeger.

National Gay and Lesbian Task Force. 1992. "NGLTF Meets With NEA Chair." Press release, May 22.

Newton, Esther. 1979. *Mother Camp*. Chicago: University of Chicago Press.

Nobile, Philip. 1992. "Bush's Convention Speechwriter Is Gay." *QW*, August 30, 6.

Nochlin, Linda, and Harris Sutherland. 1976. *Women Artists: 1550–1950*. New York: Knopf.

Ocamb, Karen. 1991a. "Gay Video Magazine Premieres." *Bay Area Reporter*, February 14, 14.

———. 1991b. "Attorney Outs L.A. Councilman." *Bay Area Reporter*, April 4, 13.

———. 1991c. "Tommy Lasorda Jr.: The AIDS Coverup." *Bay Area Reporter*, June 27, 13.

O'Dair, Barbara. 1992. "News and Notes." *Entertainment Weekly*, June 19, 6–7.

O'Neill, Cliff. 1991a. "Cousin Lourdes Is Getting Married." *OutWeek*, February 20, 28.

———. 1991b. "Washington *Times* Prints Name of Congressman." *Philadelphia Gay News*, June 19–25, 6.

———. 1991c. "Inside a Witch-hunt." *Advocate*, August 27, 42.

———. 1992. "$27 Million Wasted in Military's Gay Witch Hunt." *Philadelphia Gay News*, June 26, 1.

Oosterhuis, Harry. 1991. "Male Bonding and Homosexuality in German Nationalism." In *Homosexuality and Male Bonding in Pre-Nazi Germany*, edited by Harry Oosterhuis, 241–64. New York: Haworth.

Ota, Alan. 1990. "Outing: Controversial Tactic to Expose Alleged Closet Homosexuals Just One Example of New Militancy Splitting AIDS Lobby." *Sunday Oregonian*, June 24, M1, 4.

Page, Clarence. 1990. "Should the Closet Be Forced Open?" *Chicago Tribune*, May 6, Perspective: 3.

Painton, Priscilla. 1992. "After Willie Horton, Are Gays Next?" *Time*, August 3, 42.

Palomo, Juan. 1992. "Re-Hire Palomo!" *Out/Look*, Summer, 22–23.

Parris, Matthew. 1991. "Whose Secret Is It, Anyway?" *New York Times*, August 13, A17.

Pela, Robert. 1991. "Dick Sargent, Openly Gay Mortal." *Advocate*, December 3, 85.

Penn, Faye. 1992a. "The Right Wing Press: Latest Frontier for Gay Rights Efforts?" *QW*, August 9.

———. 1992b. "Hush, Hush in the Bush." *QW*, October 4, 10.

Perry, James. 1989. "Washington's *Times* and *Post* Do Battle in Scandal Involving 'Call Boys' Fraud and Social Climbing." *Wall Street Journal*, July 28, A12.

Peyser, Joan. 1987. *Bernstein: A Biography*. New York: Random House.

Phelan, Shane. 1989. *Identity Politics: Lesbian Feminism and the Limits of Community*. Philadelphia: Temple University Press.

Phillips, Leslie. 1991. "3 in Democratic Field Play the Field." *USA Today*, September 18, 2A.

Phillips, Marshall Alan. 1991. "Hypocritical Rule of Invisibility Reigns." *Los Angeles Times*, August 7, 7.

Pierson, Randall. 1982. "Uptight on Gay News." *Columbia Journalism Review*, March/April, 25–33.

Plummer, Ken. 1981. "Going Gay: Identities, Life Cycles and Lifestyles in the Gay Male World." In *The Theory and Practice of Homosexuality*, edited by John Hart and Diane Richardson, 93–110. London: Routledge and Kegan Paul.

Randolph, Eleanor. 1990. "The Media, at Odds Over 'Outing' of Gays: Deciding Whether to Publish Names of Alleged Homosexuals." *Washington Post*, July 13, C1, 4.

Renton, Alex. 1991. "Press Loses Out as Homosexuals Remain in the Closet." *Independent* (London), August 1, 1.

Rich, Adrienne. 1980. "Compulsory Heterosexuality and Lesbian Existence." In *Women:*

Sex and Sexuality, edited by Catherine Stimpson and Ethel Person. Chicago: University of Chicago Press.

Rich, B. Ruby. 1991a. "Writers on the *Lamb*." *Village Voice*, March 5, 59.

——. 1991b. Letter to the Editor. *Village Voice*, April 23, 5.

——. 1992. "Undertone: B. Ruby Rich on Standing by Your Girl." *Art Forum*, Summer, 18–19.

Richardson, Valerie. 1989. "Gay Activists Drag 'Hypocrites' out of the Closet." *Washington Times*, September 20, A5.

Rockwell, John. 1990. "Why Aaron Copland and American Music Are Synonymous." *New York Times*, December 4, B1.

Roscoe, Will. 1988. "Making History: The Challenge of Gay and Lesbian Studies." *Journal of Homosexuality*. 15, no. 3/4, 1–40.

Rosenfield, Paul. 1991. "David Is Goliath." *Vanity Fair*, March.

Roshan, Maer. 1992. "Anne Radice and the Politics of Appeasement." *QW*, June 7, 22–25.

—— and Sean Hilditch. 1992. "Phyllis Schlafly's 'Deep Dark Secret.' " *QW*, September 6, 22–23.

Ross, Chuck. 1989. "Gay Stays on *thirtysomething*." *San Francisco Chronicle*, November 18.

Rotello, Gabriel. 1990. "Tactical Considerations." *OutWeek*, May 16, 52–53.

——. 1991a. "Why I Oppose Outing." *OutWeek*, May 29.

——. 1991b. Letter to the Editor. *Village Voice*, August 27, 5.

——. 1992. "Bi Any Means Necessary." *Village Voice*, June 30, 37–38.

Rothstein, M. 1990. "The Prince of Producers." *San Francisco Chronicle*, December 23, 37–38.

Rouilard, Richard. 1991a. Editorial: "We Commit Ourselves to This Singular Instance of Outing in the Name of the 12,966 Soldiers Who Have Been Outed by the Military Since 1982." *Advocate*, August 27, 6–7.

——. 1991b. Letter to the Editor. *Time*, September 9, 9.

——. 1991c. Editorial: "If You Can't Name the Name, Don't Play the Closet Game." *Advocate*, October 8, 7.

Royko, Mike. 1990. "Antsy Closet Crowd Should Think Twice." *Chicago Tribune*, April 2, 3.

Rubin, Gayle. 1984. "Thinking Sex." In *Pleasure and Danger*, edited by Carole Vance. Boston: Routledge and Kegan Paul.

Russo, Vito. 1987. *The Celluloid Closet: Homosexuality in the Movies*. New York: Harper & Row (revised edition).

——. 1990. Letter to the Editor. *Village Voice*, April 24.

Ryan, James. 1991. "Brad Davis Blasts AIDS-phobia in Hollywood." *Advocate*, October 22, 45.

—— and G. L. Whitington. 1991. "Homophobia in Hollywood." *Advocate*, March 26, 32–41.

Sabato, Larry. 1991. *Feeding Frenzy: How Attack Journalism Has Transformed American Politics*. New York: Free Press.

Sadownick, Doug. 1990. "The NEA's Latest Bout of Homophobia." *Advocate*, August 14, 50–53.

——. 1991. "Storming the Celluloid Closet: Activists Take Aim at Hollywood." *Village Voice*, July 2, 31–32.

——. 1992. "Gay in Hollywood." *US*, April, 61–67.

Sagarin, Edward. 1973. "The Good Guys, the Bad Guys, and the Gay Guys." *Contemporary Sociology* 2, no. 1, 3–13.

Salisbury, Stephen. 1992a. "Stricter Policy at NEA." *Philadelphia Inquirer*, May 6, A1.

———. 1992b. "NEA Grant Rejections Bring Protests." *Philadelphia Inquirer*, May 16, A1, 7.

San Francisco Chronicle. 1990. Editorial: "Gays and Privacy." March 13.

Schatz, Benjamin. 1991. "Should We Rethink the Right to Privacy?" *Advocate*, February 26, 90.

Schmalz, Jeffrey. 1992. "Gay Rights and AIDS Emerging As a Divisive Issue in Campaign." *New York Times*, August 20, A1, 21.

Schneider, William, and I. A. Lewis. 1984. "The Straight Story on Gay Rights." *Public Opinion* 7, March, 16–20, 59–60.

Schulman, Sarah. 1990. Letter to the Editor. *Village Voice*, April 24.

Sciolino, Elaine. 1991. "Voice of the Pentagon Delivers Press Curbs with a Deftness Honed on TV." *New York Times*, February 8, A6.

Sedgwick, Eve. 1990. *The Epistemology of the Closet*. Berkeley: University of California Press.

———. 1991. "How to Bring Your Kids Up Gay." *Social Text*, no. 29, 18–27.

Seib, Charles. 1977. "How the Papers Covered the Cinema Follies Fire." *Washington Post*, October 30, C7.

Shewey, Don. 1991. "The Saint, the Slut, the Sensation . . . Madonna." *Advocate*, May 7, 42–51.

Shilts, Randy. 1982. *The Mayor of Castro Street: The Life and Times of Harvey Milk*. New York: St. Martin's.

———. 1987. *And the Band Played On*. New York: St. Martin's.

———. 1990a. "Is 'Outing' Gays Ethical?" *New York Times*, April 12, A19.

———. 1990b. "Naming Names." *GQ*, August.

———. 1991. "The Nasty Business of Outing." *Los Angeles Times*, August 7, 7.

Sidebottom, Jean. 1991. "About This Survey and Other Revealing Facts." *Sappho's Isle*, October, 4.

Signorile, Michelangelo. 1990a. "The Other Side of Malcolm." *OutWeek*, March 18, 40–45.

———. 1990b. "Gaystyles of the Rich and Famous: How I Brought Out Malcome Forbes—and the Media Flinched." *Village Voice*, April 3, 23–24.

———. 1990c. "Gossip Watch." *OutWeek*, April 18, 55.

———. 1990d. "Gossip Watch." *OutWeek*, June 27, 101.

———. 1990e. "Gossip Watch." *OutWeek*, July 18, 45.

———. 1990f. "Gossip Watch." *OutWeek*, August 22, 51.

———. 1990g. "Gossip Watch." *OutWeek*, September 26, 45.

———. 1990h. "Gossip Watch." *OutWeek*, October 3, 47.

———. 1990i. "Gossip Watch." *OutWeek*, December 26, 45.

———. 1991a. "Gossip Watch." *OutWeek*, February 20, 48.

———. 1991b. "Gossip Watch." *OutWeek*, February 27, 44.

———. 1991c. "Gossip Watch." *OutWeek*, March 13, 48.

———. 1991d. Letter to the Editor: "Protecting the Pentagon?" *Village Voice*, July 23, 5.

———. 1991e. "The Outing of Assistant Secretary of Defense Pete Williams." *Advocate*, August 27, 34–44.

———. 1992a. "Absolutely Queer." *Advocate*, May 5, 31.

———. 1992b. "Out at the *New York Times*, Part 1. *Advocate*, May 5, 34–42.

———. 1992c. "Out at the *New York Times*, Part 2. *Advocate*, May 19, 38–42.

——1992d. "Absolutely Queer." *Advocate*, June 30, 17.

Simpson, Glenn, and Craig Winneker. 1990. "Press Gallery: What to Do When Members Are Cited as Homosexuals?" *Roll Call*, June 4, 14.

Smilgis, Martha, and Linda Williams. 1991. "A Screen Gem Turns Director." *Time*, October 14, 68–72.

Smith, Robert Ellis. 1980. *Privacy: How to Protect What's Left of It*. New York: Anchor.

Sontag, Deborah. 1992. "Hillary Clinton: Speaking about Rumors." *New York Times*, April 5, 14.

Spacks, Patricia. 1985. *Gossip*. New York: Knopf.

Spelman, Elizabeth. 1988. *The Inessential Woman: Problems of Exclusion in Feminist Thought*. Boston: Beacon.

Spivak, Gayatri. 1988. "Can the Subaltern Speak?" In *Marxism and the Interpretation of Culture*, edited by C. Nelson and L. Grossberg, 271–313. Urbana: University of Illinois Press.

Spoto, Donald. 1992a. *Laurence Olivier*. New York: HarperCollins.

——. 1992b. *Blue Angel: The Life of Marlene Dietrich*. New York: Doubleday.

Stanley, Alessandra. 1991. " 'Gay' Fades as Militants Pick 'Queer.' " *New York Times*, April 6.

Stapleton, John, and Phillip McCarthy. 1991. "Gay Guerrillas Come Out to Prey." *Sydney Morning Herald*, August 9, 36.

Steakley, James. 1975. *The Homosexual Emancipation Movement in Germany*. New York: Arno.

——. 1989. "Iconography of a Scandal: Political Cartoons and the Eulenburg Affair in Wilhelmin Germany." In *Hidden from History: Reclaiming the Gay and Lesbian Past*, edited by M. Duberman, M. Vicinus, and G. Chauncey, 233–63. New York: NAL Books.

Steele, Bruce. 1991. "The Needless Fear of Playing Queer." *OutWeek*, May 1.

Steele, Thomas. 1983. "The Keys to Horowitz: An Interview with Glenn Plaskin." *Christopher Street*, no. 71, 37–41.

Stein, Edward. 1992. "Conclusion: The essentials of constructionism and the construction of essentialism." In *Forms of Desire: Sexual Orientation and the Social Constructionism Controversy*, edited by E. Stein, 325–54. New York: Routledge.

Stein, Edward, ed. 1992. *Forms of Desire: Sexual Orientation and the Social Constructionism Controversy*. New York: Routledge.

Stevens, Robin. 1992. "Dykes' Night Out at the Oscars." *Out/Look*, Summer, 31–34.

Stokes, Geoffrey. 1988. "Press Clips." *Village Voice*, November 27, 8.

Stuart, Otis. 1991. "Fierstein Carries the Torch." *OutWeek*, March 13, 54–56, 65.

——. 1992. "The World's Most Famous Gay Actor." *QW*, June 21, 31–34.

Summerskill, Ben. 1991. "Forced Out." *Face*, August, 70–75.

Suro, Roberto. 1991. "Writer Ousted after Saying He's Homosexual." *New York Times*, August 31, A9.

Taubin, Amy. 1991. "Demme's Monde." *Village Voice*, February 19, 64, 76–77.

Thoburn, Jonathon. 1992. "Radice Alleged Lesbian." *Christian American*, July/August, 17.

Trebay, Guy. 1990. "In Your Face!" *Village Voice*, August 14, 34–49.

——. 1991. "Show and Tell." *Village Voice*, March 12, 16.

Trebbe, Ann. 1992. "Gay Activists Plan to Upstage Oscars." *USA Today*, March 13, 2D.

Tucker, Scott. 1982. "Our Right to the World." *The Body Politic*, July/August.

Tuller, David. 1990. "Uproar over Gays Booting Others Out of the Closet." *San Francisco Chronicle*, March 12, A9.

Vance, Carole. 1989. "The War on Culture." *Art in America*, September, 39–45.

Van Dyne, Larry. 1980. "Is DC Becoming the Gay Capital of America?" *Washingtonian*, September, 96–101, 133.

Van Gelder, Leslie. 1990. "Straight or Gay, Stick to the Facts." *Columbia Journalism Review*, November/December, 52–53.

Van Meter, Jonathan. 1991. "Child of the Movies." *New York Times Magazine*, January 6, 16–19, 50–55.

Voboril, Mary. 1991. "New President of NOW Making Her Own Statement." *Philadelphia Inquirer*, December 15, 20A.

Walker, Nancy. 1983. "Yanking Them Out." *Gay Community News*, May 14, 5.

Wallace, Mike, and Harry Morgan. 1967. "CBS Reports: The Homosexuals." March 7.

Wallis, Brian. 1992. "New NEA Chief Makes Her Mark." *Art in America*, July, 27–28.

Walters, Jim. 1991. "Dack Rambo's New Role, as HIV-Positive Activist." *Philadelphia Inquirer*. December 2, 4C.

Warren, Samuel, and Louis Brandeis. 1890. "The Right to Privacy." *Harvard Law Review* 4.

Warren, Steve. 1989. "Telling 'Tales' about Celebrity Closets." *Au Courant* (Philadelphia), October 23, 12.

Wayne, George. 1992. "Sandra Takes the Plunge." *QW*, July 5, 45–48.

Weeks, Jeffrey. 1977. *Coming Out: Homosexual Politics in Britain, from the Nineteenth Century to the Present*. London: Quartet.

———. 1981. *Sex, Politics and Society*. London: Longman.

Weinraub, Bernard. 1992. "Diller Intrigues Hollywood by Giving Up a Power Post." *New York Times*, February 27, 1, 16.

Weir, John. 1992. "Gay-Bashing, Villainy and the Oscars." *New York Times*, March 29, H17, 22.

Weisel, Al. 1992. "Heavy Denial." *QW*, May 17, 36.

Weiser, Benjamin. 1989. "Gay Activists Divided on Whether to 'Bring Out' Politicians." *Washington Post*, September 19, A4.

Weiss, Andrea. 1991. " 'A Queer Feeling When I Look at You': Hollywood Stars and Lesbian Spectatorship in the 1930s." In *Stardom: Industry of Desire*, edited by Christine Gledhill, 283–99. London: Routledge.

Welch, Paul. 1964. "Homosexuality in America." *Life*, June 26, 66–80.

Wilkie, Curtis. 1984. "Too Hot to Handle: The Mississippi Story Editors Wouldn't Touch." *Washington Journalism Review*, March, 38–39, 58.

Williams, Marjorie. 1991. "Is It Any of Your Business?" *Washington Monthly*, September, 39–44.

Winans, Christopher. 1990. *Malcolm Forbes: The Man Who Had Everything*. New York: St. Martin's.

Wockner, Rex. 1990. "In Support of Outing." *Philadelphia Gay News*, June 29, 7.

———. 1991. "German Gays Win Battle for Lower Age-of-Consent." *Bay Area Reporter*, February 14, 2.

Wolfenden Report: Report of the Committee on Homosexual Offences and Prostitution. 1964. New York: Lancer.

Wolff, Janet. 1988. "The Culture of Separate Spheres." In *The Culture of Capital: Art, Power and the 19th Century Middle Class*, edited by Janet Wolff and John Seed. Manchester: Manchester University Press.

Woods, James. 1992. *The Corporate Closet: Managing Gay Identity on the Job*. Unpublished Ph.D. dissertation, University of Pennsylvania.

Yang, Jacob. 1991. "Judge Denies Thompson Guardianship." *Gay Community News*, May 5, 1.

Yarbrough, Jeff. 1991. "A New Hollywood?" *Advocate*, October 22, 36–45.

——. 1992. "Vanity Fairies." *Advocate*, March 10, 30–37.

Young, Perry Deane. 1982. *God's Bullies: Power Politics and Religious Tyranny*. New York: Holt, Rinehart & Winston.

Zeh, John. 1991. "Gay Art Foe Congress Member Outed on TV." *Au Courant* (Philadelphia), November 18, 16.

Zonana, Victor. 1992. "Kramer vs. the World, Part 2." *Advocate*, December 15, 42–48.

Index

Larry Gross is professor of communications in the Annenberg School for Communication, University of Pennsylvania. He is editor of *Studying Visual Communication*, coeditor of *Image Ethics*, associate editor of *The International Encyclopedia of Communications*, and coeditor of Columbia University Press's *Between Men/Between Women: Lesbian and Gay Studies Book Series*. He is cochair of the Philadelphia Lesbian and Gay Task Force and cochair of the Task Force on Lesbian and Gay Concerns of the International Communication Association.